Frick*

Frick*

Baseball's Third Commissioner

JOHN P. CARVALHO

McFarland & Company, Inc., Publishers
Jefferson, North Carolina

LIBRARY OF CONGRESS CATALOGUING-IN-PUBLICATION DATA

Names: Carvalho, John, author.
Title: Frick* : baseball's third commissioner / John P. Carvalho.
Description: Jefferson, North Carolina : McFarland & Company, Inc., Publishers, 2016. | Includes bibliographical references and index.
Identifiers: LCCN 2016046068 | ISBN 9780786495320 (softcover : acid free paper) ∞
Subjects: LCSH: Frick, Ford C. | Baseball commissioners—United States—Biography. | Baseball—United States—History.
Classification: LCC GV865.F68 C37 2016 | DDC 796.357092 [B] —dc23
LC record available at https://lccn.loc.gov/2016046068

BRITISH LIBRARY CATALOGUING DATA ARE AVAILABLE

ISBN (print) 978-0-7864-9532-0
ISBN (ebook) 978-1-4766-2663-5

© 2016 John P. Carvalho. All rights reserved

No part of this book may be reproduced or transmitted in any form or by any means, electronic or mechanical, including photocopying or recording, or by any information storage and retrieval system, without permission in writing from the publisher.

Front cover: Ford Frick in the office as president of the National League (National Baseball Hall of Fame Library, Cooperstown, New York)

Printed in the United States of America

*McFarland & Company, Inc., Publishers
Box 611, Jefferson, North Carolina 28640
www.mcfarlandpub.com*

To Mom and Dad
I wish you could have read this

Contents

Introduction 1

1. The Maris Decision 11
2. Early Years 25
3. The Babe Ruth Problem 38
4. A New NL President 56
5. Fame and Fighting 74
6. The War 86
7. A New Commissioner 100
8. Integration 118
9. Chandler Out, Frick In 137
10. Reconstruction 150
11. Old Problems, New Problems 166
12. To the West Coast 183
13. Game Two Begins 197
14. The Third League 213
15. Expansion 230

Contents

16. Exit Strategy   248

17. Extra Innings   263

Chapter Notes   273

Bibliography   308

Index   313

Introduction

It is both an expectation and a liability that the commissioner of baseball be a devoted fan. The expectation part is obvious; the liability, not so much. Consider, however, the baggage that comes from a lifelong devotion to the game—a burden carried by Ford Frick, his two predecessors, and most of his eight successors. (Frick's immediate successor, William Eckert, curiously admitted that he had not attended a game in ten years.) The young boy's fascination with baseball might not serve him well when he assumes leadership of the national pastime decades later.

Such zeal toward the game is no surprise. No sport occupies such a mythic place within American culture as baseball. Football and basketball might have closed the gap in the twenty-first century, taken the lead to some, but for the Gilded Age America of Ford Frick, baseball was a national ritual whose heroes represented a working-class rugged individualism and the American dream. Thus, by the mid-twentieth century, the baseball commissioner, more than an innovative CEO of a successful sports business operation, functioned more like a self-appointed protector of the faith.

The complaint against Frick, as with every commissioner, was his conservative approach to the game, which his critics claimed impeded progress on and off the field. This should not surprise any baseball fan today. They, like modern-day sports writers, see most commissioners as obstacles to progress. Witness the frustration with Bud Selig over his reluctance to expand instant replay. In the same way, Frick no doubt saw his mission as preserving the best of the baseball of his youth. To jettison the baggage of a lifelong fan would betray his lifelong love.

Thus, as commissioner, Frick seemed trapped out of time, even more so as his tenure progressed. He was a newspaper man in a television era. He was an East Coast man in a West Coast era. He was an owners man in a players era. He was a train man in a jet airliner era. He was an eight-team league man in an expansion era. He was a 154-game man in a 162-game era. He was a Babe Ruth man in a Roger Maris era.

But Frick's closet hides another skeleton that would affect his decisions as commissioner. He started out as a journalist, a Jazz Age sports writer who even did some early radio work before moving into baseball administration. He matured, not in the front office, but in the press box. And not just any press box: He was a recognized member of the freewheeling New York City sports writing fraternity that brought juicy copy to a hungry audience during the Jazz Age. The impressions that would inform Frick's future judgment happened early in his career as much as in his childhood. The result was the same.

There seems to be a danger in allowing journalists to be in charge of anything (even their own publications). Consider that the only newspaper publisher to serve as president was that MVP of ethics, Warren Harding, who for good measure was also part-owner of a minor league baseball team. It's probably safer to leave the journalists on the sidelines, reporting and criticizing, than to put them in a position to actually do something like oversee the national pastime.

Columnist Red Smith, when asked if a different fellow journalist would make a good commissioner, doubted that the team owners would pay a journalist to tell them how to do things, when they did that daily in the sports pages, without the owners paying them. *New York Journal-American* columnist Frank Graham noted, "They wound up with one, however," when they selected Frick.[1]

Frick would argue, perhaps in defense of his administrative talents, that he never was much of a journalist. But he sells himself short. And the 1920s journalistic culture would affect anyone, even the minor character Frick claimed to be. Coming out of the horror of a savage war, society was looking for a release—emotionally, morally, and culturally. They found it in relaxed sexual mores, in a flow of alcohol that Prohibition could not stem, in films and vaudeville, and in sports. It was the era of Babe Ruth, Jack Dempsey, Red Grange, Bobby Jones, and Bill Tilden. It was also the era of Grantland Rice, Damon Runyon, Ring Lardner, W. O. McGeehan, and, yes, Ford Frick.

True, his writing did not create the legacy of the preceding names; people don't approach Frick's work with the same reverence as Rice or Runyon. His greater potential fame as a sportscaster and radio host, as is so often the case, evaporated into the air along with his words. Unlike Graham McNamee, no recordings that feature Frick's voice survived the early 1930s. Still, the Golden Age of sports journalism would influence his actions as commissioner, and in particular his relationship with the media. Sadly for him, the cronyism he enjoyed with his contemporaries diminished as he approached retirement, and after.

Earlier in his career, he could have assumed the cooperation of his friends in the press box. Well liked, he could count on them to float proposals, fortify him against undue criticism, and even promote his candidacy to be commissioner of baseball—twice. But the new generation of sports journalists, combining the skepticism that would fuel the press of the 1960s and 1970s with a commitment to a more literary writing form, was neither appreciative nor cooperative, nor at times even kind to him.

But they were closer in spirit, as legendary New York sports columnist Jimmy Cannon claimed. "There is some of Frick in the modern literature of baseball, although the kid reporters would resent the assumption," he wrote in 1970. "Their response to the Mets might have been turned out in the seasons when Frick was riding on the trains with the Yankees."[2]

Carrying the heavy dual baggage of a lifelong fan and an early-career journalist, Frick assumed the office of baseball commissioner in 1951 at the age of 56, after 17 years as National League president. He would remain in the position for 14 years, as the sport faced the rise of television, West Coast relocation, league expansion, the diffusion of racial integration, the seeds of a labor movement, and, yes, Roger Maris's home run record. As this book will demonstrate, his previous experience within baseball's organizational culture could hardly create an aggressive visionary, a counterpart to the NFL's Pete Rozelle, similarly determined to carry his sport to a new age.

Frick definitely had his moments. When as young as Rozelle, he championed interleague play decades before it became a reality[3]—though in the 1930s, without the power of television and the help of computers, scheduling issues overwhelmed the concept. He also claimed to have developed a more progressive approach to owner-player labor relations.[4] Beyond that, however, his approach seemed to be that baseball would do fine as long as the social and cultural forces surrounding it would just lighten up and let events take their course.

Still, the purpose of this book is not to subject Frick's tenure as commissioner to another damning critique, or even to present an alternative. Instead, this book will strive to present a comprehensive picture of the man who found himself in the middle of baseball history for more than four decades—even if he seemed an enthusiastic spectator more than an active participant.

Given his leadership style and the owners' straitjacket, Frick being "on the field" during most of baseball's history does not mean he was a sparkplug energizing all of the big plays. But like any player on the roster, regardless of skill, he had a front-row seat to most of baseball's biggest moments over the period, with some influence. In that role, he became something of a Zelig—an otherwise low-key character who found himself sharing the stage with icons—Ruth, Jackie Robinson, Ted Williams, and every U.S. president from FDR to LBJ. While the magnitude of the changes might have overwhelmed anyone in his position, he survived and even left an impression on the game.

It will be a long and lively trip that will take Frick from an Indiana childhood and college education to Colorado, where he taught English, wrote for daily newspapers, and even played a little semipro baseball. His coverage of the 1921 Pueblo flood will gain the attention of Hearst newspaper publisher Arthur Brisbane.

Brought to New York by Brisbane, Frick will find his place within the city's journalism fraternity. In particular, Frick will ingratiate himself to the city's, and era's, dominant sports icon, becoming one of Ruth's ghostwriters and strongest promoters, both in print and on the radio. As the decade progresses and radio emerges as the hot new medium, Frick becomes one of the first sports talk radio personalities.

Such promotional capabilities are not lost on baseball's leadership, as they tag Frick to serve as public relations director for the National League (putting him a safe distance, a league away, from Ruth). Within nine months, following the unexpected retirement of the league president for health reasons, Frick is promoted. In that position, Frick will spearhead the establishment of the Baseball Hall of Fame in 1939 and be one of baseball's most ardent supporters during World War II.

Frick will be a leading candidate to replace Judge Kenesaw Mountain Landis as baseball commissioner in 1944, but team owners pass over him in favor of A. B. "Happy" Chandler, a U.S. senator from Kentucky. Three years later, his most important actions as National League president revolve around the integration of baseball. Even as Chandler seems to steal the spotlight, Frick as league president makes his impact by supporting Robinson, even staring down a threatened player strike by the St. Louis Cardinals.

But Chandler's time in the spotlight ends four years later, as owners tire of what they perceive as high-handedness and autonomy—a mortal sin to the alpha males who ruled baseball teams. They depose him and replace him with Frick. Baseball fans—and even some candid owners—blast the decision as a move by Type A owners to replace a strong leader

Introduction 5

with a more pliant figurehead groomed from within (sound familiar, NFL fans?).

Baseball is about to enter its most turbulent time, a decade marked by the emergence of television and the sudden wanderlust of baseball franchises, particularly to the untapped West Coast. The process of integration continues, with all of the attendant effects—not the least of which is spring training issues in Florida, a former Confederate state with pockets of backward thinking. A more activist commissioner might have grasped the opportunity to speed important change. But that is not Frick's style. His actions, or lack thereof, frustrate those who see lost opportunities.

When he does step forward, in 1961, to defend Ruth's home run record, it becomes an infamous gaffe. By setting himself as a Tory within a revolutionary age, Frick accelerates the media relations decline that marks the close of his second term as commissioner. It no doubt stings that what he sees as an effort to promote fairness and preserve the purity of the game is interpreted as protecting an old friend and demeaning an active player. His final years should be filled with tributes and reflections appropriate to an individual who served baseball faithfully for so long. Instead, until his retirement in 1965 at age 71, with increasing frequency he is cruelly derided as a useless relic by the new journalists who had replaced Frick's friends, a lacking counterpart to the NFL's Pete Rozelle.

Once the required five years pass, Frick is deservedly elected to the Baseball Hall of Fame in 1970. The Hall of Fame also creates the Ford C. Frick Award in 1978—the year he died—which annually recognizes a baseball broadcaster who has made significant contributions to the game. It is a fitting tribute to the radio pioneer who ended up as one of baseball's most important leaders for 31 years.

As we reflect on Frick's career, one observation is unavoidable: The job did not change him, for better or worse. He did not morph into an authoritative general, astounding and disturbing those who knew him previously. He remained the same unrepentant baseball fan, enthralled as much by the small-town Little League field as by the lights of a packed stadium. In one 1932 radio editorial, talking about heroes, he said, "[A]ll of us, mature and gray and harassed, are only boys grown older," and his actions often reflected a boyish wonder with baseball and its icons.[5] He was baseball's most fervent evangelist, even writing an article for a music teachers' magazine that emphasized the rhythm and grace of the pickoff and the double play[6]—anything to draw more fans to his beloved game.

Columnist Dick Young captured the relationship on the back cover of Frick's memoirs: "The revealing inside stuff is here, but more is the romance, the burning love affair between him and his inanimate lady, from that first kiss, the day outside the ball park gate, when the little kid, openmouthed, carried the big leaguer's spikes inside, through the day the kid became Commissioner of Baseball." (Young remains a curious choice to endorse the book, since it was he, and not Frick, who mentioned the asterisk at the raucous press conference where Frick announced his ruling on Maris's home run record. Chalk that up to Frick's forgiving nature and noteworthy appreciation of the role of the media.)

Young does pinpoint the center of the strike zone in describing Frick's relationship with baseball. It was more than fandom; it was romance. With romance comes a degree of delusion, which is acceptable when taken as a sign of affection rather than an abdication of rational judgment. Keep that in mind as you read Frick's tribute to baseball from a 1950 commencement address at Concordia College (in his adopted hometown of Bronxville, New York). Later in his speech he will venerate baseball for exhibiting constitutionally guaranteed freedoms of assembly, speech, religion, and opportunity. But earlier, he waxed poetic on the pastime itself:

> For baseball is an integral part of our American life. It has grown up with the country. In time of war and in time of peace, in times of prosperity and times of depression it has offered our people a bit of surcease from worry, an opportunity to relax and forget their troubles. And more important it has, through the years, been a simple living example of democracy at work. It is as American as the cornfields of Indiana or the pine woods of Maine; as traditional as Independence Hall, and as virile and cosmopolitan as the teeming city streets of New York or San Francisco.

In introducing you to this book and its treatment of Frick's career, I should point out one mitigating and frustrating factor: Frick did not leave official archives. The Baseball Hall of Fame provided about 250 pages' worth of clippings and memos. But there was little of the correspondence that provides an inside look at the character of a historic person and the background to game-changing moments.

For historical information, I have relied heavily on the *New York Times* and *The Sporting News*. The *Times* has made itself useful throughout the years through its easy availability to researchers—first on microfilm and now on the Internet. It also covered Frick extensively during his years as National League president and commissioner, because in the former position he resisted joining Landis in Chicago, and in the latter he moved the commissioner's office to New York City.

The Sporting News provided much more than the extensive coverage of baseball that marked it as the "paper of record" for the game—particularly in its earlier years, before it diversified to covering other sports.

Almost from its beginning, and certainly during Frick's career in baseball, it enjoyed such a close relationship with the pastime's leadership that it almost seems like an archive of organized baseball in itself. It is also of no small convenience that the *Sporting News* used baseball beat writers for much of its coverage; many of these were Frick's colleagues during his sports writing days, and their friendship continued after he left the profession. One name in particular, Dan Daniel of the *New York Telegram*, became something of a chronicler of Frick's career over the decades—the person as well as the events.

To try to reconstruct what would be in archives, I worked with surviving family members in Indiana, where Frick was born, where I was able to interview his niece, Mary Jane Lepird. I also met with his two grandchildren: Kelly Richards, in Atlanta, and Ford C. Frick, in Denver. Grandson Ford had only a few boxes, but they were filled with amazing, helpful artifacts. Some fueled the narrative; others simply warmed a fellow baseball fan. Richards was able to provide interesting letters, photos and stories, as did the Fricks in Indiana. But none of them knew what had happened to his official papers—the letters, memos, agendas, and personal notes that shed light on the stories and decisions that received the most publicity.

On a visit with the Indiana family, I came across a random slip of paper in a folder that said, "J. P. Morgan Museum (New York?) Frick Collection." I thought I had found the "Holy Grail" of my search. But it was a blind alley. The Morgan does have a Frick collection. However, it was donated by Henry Frick, whose H. C. Frick & Company merged with Andrew Carnegie's steel firm to create the predecessor to U.S. Steel. No connection to Ford.

There is a rumor that Frick was so stung by the media treatment he suffered at the end of his career and during his retirement, that he did not leave archives. One Indiana sports journalist speculated that he had destroyed his papers. But such a response would be inconsistent with the cooperative, humble character he forged over his career and the grace he displayed toward even the most hostile sports journalist. Perhaps he considered his memoirs to be sufficient to the task of archives.

Another, more sinister theory is offered by baseball historian (and former rap musician with the group 3rd Bass) Peter J. Nash. On his website, haulsofshame.com, and in an upcoming book with a similar title, Nash alleges that Frick's papers, like many baseball artifacts within the Baseball Hall of Fame and other repositories, have been stolen and sold on the black market, eventually finding their way to sports memorabilia auctions and online auction sites. Grandson Ford C. Frick voiced the same suspicions. While that might not explain the overall dearth of archival sources (which have not turned up via that route in subsequent years), it definitely makes a tough job even more difficult.

It is more likely to speculate that the man saw his archives stored in the changes that happened during his 30-plus years in baseball administration. The insistence by others that he organize an intimidating pile of papers might have come off as so much unnecessary concern to him. What happened from there is anybody's guess.

Instead, we have a legacy reflected in a sport's developments and in newspaper and magazine articles, and in memoirs that are consistently positive and uncritical. Frick did not leave baseball fans with much of an inside story through his papers. But even the existing record provides insight into the man whom baseball led through four decades.

The task of putting together such a biography requires a degree of help and support that must be mentioned within the resulting book.

Auburn University—particularly the College of Liberal Arts and the School of Communication and Journalism—has provided support in the form of two research leaves devoted to this project. Acknowledging the lonely ordeal of authors who must wedge out time within busy lives to complete such projects, I feel truly privileged (even as I type these specific words) to have the opportunity to work full-time on this project for two separate semesters, without classroom responsibilities.

The Society for American Baseball Research inspires in so many ways. Its access to the *Sporting News* archives is one of many membership benefits—join today! But its members also provide a community that reminds its members that our projects are not foolish obsessions, but a cooperative effort to piece together a comprehensive understanding of an important cultural force in America.

A succession of research assistants have combed books, websites, microfilms, and Lord knows what else at my direction. Even when not fascinated by the content, they have remained diligent to the task and very helpful. Thank you, Loren Hawkins, Lindsey Icenogle Lyells, Molly Malone Cowles, Carrie Reif, Nicholas Kirby, Jon-Marc Larson, Calli Robinson, Candace Aikens, Matt Stilwell, and Jade Reynolds. Yes, the book took that long.

The Ralph Brown Draughon Library at Auburn University boasts a helpful staff, none more so to me than Barbara Bishop, reference librarian, and Pam Whaley, who directs document delivery. Both constantly amazed me with their abilities to find books and articles that I assumed were no longer available.

Introduction 9

Most important, I thank my partner, David Self. He never asked if I was finished with that book yet. He did more than observe. On our visit to the Baseball Hall of Fame, David noticed what thousands of visitors and baseball history nuts had missed: that the plaque describing the Frick Award erroneously listed his tenure as 1941–1965. His pointing it out to Hall of Fame personnel remains one of my proudest moments.

I promise a lively read, given the characters and dramas that surrounded Frick during his career. As the English poet George Herbert said, "Living well is the best revenge." Frick's life well lived will provide much worth discussing. But as with any historical biography, the main point will be that a decision made about a home run record in 1961—far from being an isolated point in time—was surrounded by four decades of work, relationships, and a lot of strong, if conflicting, influences.

1

The Maris Decision

By mid–July of 1961, Babe Ruth's 34-season-old home run record was in danger. The American League had just increased its season to 162 games, the result of adding franchises in Los Angeles and Minneapolis (though technically the Senators moved to Minnesota and the league replaced them with a new Senators franchise). The expansion itself had also made the talent pool shallower, putting players on the field, especially pitchers on the mound, who could not have made it the season before. Already, it looked like players would take advantage of the increased opportunities. Roger Maris of the New York Yankees had hit 35 home runs with the season barely half over. His teammate, Mickey Mantle, was close behind with 31 homers. The Babe's record, which seemed untouchable for so long, now looked vulnerable.

An article in the *New York Times Magazine* mused on the potential cultural impact:

> Over the years, the nimbus of sanctity that gathered about Babe Ruth's head has become all but inviolable. His record of sixty home runs in 1927 had an enduring impact on the psyche of the American people. It has become a symbol of constancy in a capricious world. It is a last link with a carefree and romantic past when man could flex his muscles without destroying civilizations.[1]

The emerging crisis of a lost "symbol of constancy" was apparent to Ford Frick. He had expressed protectiveness toward Ruth's record in the past. In 1958, when the Dodgers announced plans to play in Los Angeles's minor-league Wrigley Field—an acknowledged home run haven—while their new stadium at Chavez Ravine was under construction, Frick groused, "I don't want to see Babe Ruth's home-run record beaten by playing in ... some small cow pasture."[2] While Dodgers owner Walter O'Malley was stung by Frick's comments, they no doubt moved his team to change their plans and temporarily play in the Los Angeles Coliseum.

Even moving games to the Los Angeles Coliseum did not quiet the critics, because that field had a 250-foot left-field fence, the shortest permitted by major league rules. Frick was not the only one concerned. The Associated Press surveyed almost 200 sports writers, of whom 60 percent said that any home run record set—whether Babe Ruth's or Hack Wilson's National League record—should be disallowed or, yes, footnoted. Frick, ironically, did not criticize the Coliseum fence, comparing it to the short left and right field porches at the Polo Grounds.[3]

When the American League announced its plans to expand in 1961 with a 162-game schedule, Frick confronted the possible effect on baseball records, including Ruth's.

> My opinion on that is almost a conviction. I don't think the Babe's record is vulnerable. I intend to ask the rules committee to study this problem and try to soften the impact wherever necessary. My own idea is that some records might deserve to be listed in two categories—the one made during a 154-game schedule and the one made during a 162-game schedule.[4]

By 1961, the home run barrage by Mantle, Maris, and all major league power hitters was apparent. Some even blamed the baseball, forcing Spalding to defend its manufacturing consistency for the previous 25 years. Frick grumbled that the homer itself was losing its appeal. "In the old days, everyone would be on his feet when a homer was hit," he said. "Today, unless a homer's been hit by a player challenging Ruth's record, the fans just sit on their hands."[5]

Frick would turn to his allies in the press box for help. According to Dan Daniel of the *Sporting News*, his friend for almost 40 years, Frick planned to call a meeting with the Records Committee of the Baseball Writers' Association of America to discuss what to do.[6] Frick also alluded to such a consultation in late June, following the mid-season owners meeting where the main topic of conversation was a free-agent draft to curb bonus spending.[7] No records of such a meeting with the Records Committee have survived, and subsequent complaints by baseball writers indicate that the meeting might have been strictly advisory. Finally, whether by joint deliberation or unilateral fiat, Frick was ready to announce his decision.

On July 17, 1961, Frick held a press conference to announce a ruling that many had wondered about, but none had asked for. Although he did not mention Maris or Mantle specifically, he did state, "Any player who may hit more than sixty home runs during his club's first 154 games would be recognized as having established the new record."[8] He mentioned no other record specifically—only the home run rule.

As often happens in administrative gaffes, his announcement did not stop there. Frick added, "if the player does not hit more than sixty until after his club has played 154 games, there would have to be some distinctive mark in the record books to show that Babe Ruth's record was set under a 154-game schedule and the total of more than sixty was completed while a 162-game schedule was in effect."[9] Although Frick did not specify which distinctive mark would be used, critics refer to this as Frick proposing to add an asterisk to Maris's record.

In his memoirs, Frick claimed that he made his ruling in response to constant questions from sports writers,[10] although subsequent debate would center on whether it was his place to answer the questions himself, without formal advisement. In any case, a commissioner whose policy had been to avoid intervention at all costs—who did not consider his own involvement the most crucial and publicized component of a controversy—did something completely out of character. He intervened. One baseball historian who has chronicled commissioners' actions called it the first time a commissioner had made a ruling about a player's on-the-field accomplishment—quite a change from the limited authority Frick, unlike his predecessors, had claimed.[11]

But be clear: Frick did not specifically rule that an "asterisk" be placed next to Maris's record. Frick blamed columnist Dick Young of the *New York Daily News* for that term. He claimed in his memoirs that during the raucous press conference announcing his decision, Young quipped, "Maybe you should use an asterisk on the new record," and that the concept survived and thrived.[12]

The response over the years might give the impression that Frick's announcement was met with the near-unanimous outrage that has dogged it and its source for more than 50 years. To be fair to the commissioner, however, much of the initial response was as positive as in 1958—even from some who would later be his most virulent critics.

New York sportswriter Joe King, writing in the *Sporting News*, the "Bible of Baseball," praised Frick's decision in the weekly's next issue. "Because it is obviously unfair to subject 154-game records to feats achieved in the expanded 162-game schedule ... Frick did the game a distinct service on July 17 when he announced that all shots at Ruth's mark would be judged on the 154-game basis."[13]

Arthur Daley, long-time *New York Times* columnist, also agreed with Frick. He quoted Frick's frequent analogy—"You can't set a 100-meter record in a 100-yard race"—and added, "The conviction here is that Frick is absolutely correct.... [I]f that sixty-first comes during the extra eight games everyone is going to find that it's a rather sticky wicket, one that will make everyone angry and please no one."[14]

A subsequent poll by the *Sporting News* of 55 baseball writers showed support for Frick's decision by a two-to-one margin. Shirley Povich, legendary columnist for the *Washington Post,* responded, "The slugger who equaled or surpassed Ruth's record with the help of a 162-game schedule should not be allowed to inherit Ruth's crown.... At best it would be artificial or synthetic."[15]

Even Young, originator of the asterisk concept, was a supporter (though his support was based on a prediction that never came to pass): "I believe, as he, that we are in a transitory stage, and that eventually, perhaps in five more years, further expansion will produce 24 teams and a return to the 154-game sked. Therefore, all records should be preserved on the 154-game basis—with a special section for those interim years of 162."

But not all writers agreed. Those who opposed cited more complex arguments than the numbers argument offered by Frick and his supporters. Francis Stann of the *Washington Star* added, "Commissioner Frick is a nice man but he is going to make blithering idiots of us all if records are going to be departmented." Jimmy Powers, Young's co-worker at the *Daily News*, said, "I feel that the 154-game restriction is ridiculous. There have been so many changes through the years, playing habits, the physical layout of the parks, encroachments on space in so many ways that the record book would be full of asterisks if we tried to reduce everything to a certain era and freeze it."[16]

Complex as Powers' argument was, it omitted another significant factor. Subsequent critics have noted that Ruth and his generation benefited from a substantial "asterisk" of their own: a racially segregated baseball system that probably padded the statistics of Ruth, Ty Cobb, Christy Mathewson, and other standouts of their era.[17] It is, of course, not only a factor that was too risky to be discussed within the baseball culture of 1961, but also a subtle, crafty argument that, while not offered during the home run race, certainly adds another important, though redundant, nail in the asterisk's coffin.

One of the quickest, but best written, early critiques came from Walter Bingham of *Sports Illustrated,* who called Frick's action "a foolish, pathetic little statement, foolish because it makes so little sense, pathetic because it will be ignored." Bingham offered the hypothetical of Maris hitting his 61st home run in 154 games, but Mantle surpassing him in the eight games that followed. Mantle would earn the home run championship but not the record; Maris would earn the home run record but not the season championship. Bingham concluded,

1. The Maris Decision

> What Ruth was to baseball in his generation no man can ever hope to duplicate. He needs no legislation to be remembered and honored, and this is the most unfortunate and unforgiveable aspect of Ford Frick's decision. Frick's attempt to protect the record, undoubtedly well-intentioned, is an insult to the man who set it.[18]

A poll of players at the All-Star Game produced the same two-to-one support that the writers poll did. Of 17 surveyed, 12 supported Frick's decision, while five opposed it. Even Mantle himself said, "I think it's right.... If I should break it in the one hundred and fifty-fifth game, I wouldn't want the record." Stan Musial, one of baseball's "elder statesman" of the period, added, "Eight additional games can make a big difference in the records, not only in hitting home runs but also in pitching."

Maris, however, disagreed. "I think the commissioner shouldn't have made any 154-game ruling when he did. But if Mick breaks it, I hope he does it in 154. The same goes for me." Al Kaline of the Detroit Tigers added, "Whoever hits 61 home runs is entitled to the record, no matter how many games it takes. The owners and leagues made out the schedules and told us how many games we would have to play. So if a record is broken in the official number of games scheduled, it should be a record."[19]

Even Yankees manager Ralph Houk had his share of fun. "If after 154 games we're still on top, I certainly will wire the commissioner that that's the pennant so far as I'm concerned," he said.[20]

Even though the initial response was more favorable than unfavorable, both supporters and opponents agreed with Maris that Frick's timing was terrible. Hy Hurwitz of the *Boston Globe* said, "I don't think a rule should have been made in midseason, when it seemed possible that Babe Ruth's record might be broken. I do believe that a rule should have been made or specifications spelled out, covering rules under the 154-game schedule and the 162-game schedule."[21] Eddie Mathews of the Milwaukee Braves agreed: "The regulations should have been put in before the season started and not when a couple of guys get within reach of it."[22] *The Sporting News* concurred in an editorial ("any such action should have taken place before the season opened") and called on the National League, which would not adopt a 162-game season until the next year, to be more proactive.[23]

Later in the season, New York fans weighed in—it was their Babe and their record, after all—in a casual *Times* poll. Fan opinion also split in favor of Frick's decision. One fan suggested, "Maybe the United States Golf Association will change its rule too. Then duffers like me can turn in cards for ten holes and get credit for an 18-hole round." A taxi driver was not impressed with Maris anyway: "Another thing, suppose Maris ate twenty hot dogs and drank ten bottles of beer before a game? He wouldn't get the ball out of the infield. Ruth did." One long-time fan who claimed to be there when Ruth hit his 60th said, "Maris has got to do it in 154. Even then I won't like it."

Maris still found fan support. One bartender pointed out, "Do the Yanks have to win the pennant in 154 games? No." A cab driver added, "I'd like to see the record broken in any number of games." A maintenance worker wisely predicted, "If Maris breaks the record in 162 games, the people will accept it as a record."[24]

Ruth's family offered their opinions. His wife, Claire, said, "The Babe loved that record. He wanted to be known as the king of home runs forever." His stepdaughter, Mrs. Julia Stevens, expressed a similar sentiment, though she added, "I know that if Maris does break it, Daddy won't be jealous. He was too much of a sports fan."[25]

Sadly, it was not a good-natured debate of the good old days vs. today, and the media were partly to blame. Perhaps if it were Mantle alone chasing the record, his pursuit would have generated the same festive coverage that Mark McGwire and Sammy Sosa would enjoy 47 years later. Add in Maris and the New York media were far from friendly—in contrast with their treatment of Ruth. In some ways, it presaged the social media age: all of the obsessive attention without the immediate technology. Fans were conditioned to wait for each morning's and afternoon's sports section to be overwhelmed by the flood of information, analysis and personal comments. And those sports writers, most in cities with at least two competing newspapers, were obsessed with providing it.

For Bob Fishel, who was Yankees public relations director at the time and later was American League executive vice president, it was the first time that the sports media had tracked a record pursuit so closely, with day-by-day updates. Team personnel, in later similar efforts, learned from Fishel's self-admitted mistakes and held daily press conferences outside of the clubhouse. One reason was that they helped to shield the teammates of the player—whether Pete Rose chasing Joe DiMaggio's consecutive games hitting streak in 1978 and Cobb's career hits mark in 1985, George Brett's 1980 pursuit of a .400 batting average, or Nolan Ryan and Steve Carlton's duel for Walter Johnson's career strikeout mark in 1982–1983—from the insanity creeping into the clubhouse and affecting the entire team.[26]

Fishel long regretted not providing the same service to Maris. He could have used it. Mantle, a career Yankee, was used to the media attention and got along with the writers. Maris, however, who had been traded to the Yankees before the 1960 season, was a quiet North Dakota native who struggled with adapting to the Big Apple baseball and media culture. The home run record chase only intensified the divide between media expectations and Maris reality.[27] As author David Halberstam pointed out,

> Unfortunately, his assault upon Ruth's record was probably the first great sustained sports story in the age of modern media. At first print reporters seized on it, which soon whetted the appetite for television coverage, and as television coverage followed the chase with an ever more watchful eye that inspired even greater print coverage.... Millions of Americans wanted to know what Roger Maris was really like, and they wanted to know every day for more than two months.[28]

Frick's announcement seemed to increase—or at least parallel—the media frenzy. It did not sabotage Maris's quest, but it did make it more difficult by making his life more miserable. In retrospect, under that level of daily pressure, that Maris could play at all, much less break a home run record, seems superhuman. Although Frick was not criticized for his contribution to the pressure on Maris at the time, it provided more ammunition for those who would chime in later. Some, however, saw the situation as far more sinister. Harvey Rosenfeld's biography, *Roger Maris*, A Title to Fame*, framed it as baseball's entrenched establishment of old men conspiring with cooperative baseball writers to doom Maris's efforts through constant pressure and sports page harassment.[29]

To Bill Veeck, baseball's ultimate showman, Frick's worst sin was that he denied the Yankees a slam-dunk promotional opportunity. The team's last five games, when Maris was making his last push to tie and break the record, were at home, promising capacity crowds to cheer him on. Instead, the Yankees, with a stadium capacity of 67,000, averaged just over 18,000. Why? "What he did, in one brilliant stroke, was to build the interest up to that 154th game and throw the final 8 games out in the wash with the baby," Veeck complained. "It was blow-proof and they still blew it!"[30]

Frick's frequent defender Daniel, who at this point wrote for the *New York World-Telegram and Sun*, thought the commissioner should not have been involved in the decision at all. He noted that when a situation on a player record arose in 1956 (concerning Stan Musial and the National League consecutive games record), league president Warren Giles deferred to the baseball writers for a ruling. Daniel repeated his contention that the Records Committee of the Baseball Writers' Association of America should rule on the matter.[31]

The BBWAA, at its World Series meeting, would in fact pass a resolution calling on the records committee to protest Frick's decision on the grounds that he had usurped its authority to determine and confirm such standards. Reports indicated that Leonard Koppett of the *New York Post* and Joe Reichler of the Associated Press (one of Maris's strongest critics) were the primary sponsors and supporters of the resolution.[32] According to Jack O'Connell, long-time secretary/treasurer of the BBWAA, no minutes survive from that meeting.[33] While Frick expressed a willingness to meet with the committee, he was firm: "I have made my ruling and it stands. The record for home runs in 154 stands to the credit of G.H. Ruth, Yankees, at 60. The record for home runs in 162 games stands to the credit of Roger Maris, Yankees, at 61."

According to later reports, the BBWAA did authorize Daniel to set up a meeting at the December meetings with Frick to discuss who had authority over baseball records. When the big moment arrived, however, Daniel had trouble finding volunteers. It finally came down to a subcommittee of two—himself and Reichler. "I'll be glad to meet with them and I'll even buy their lunch, but they're mistaken if they think they're going to win in the Maris matter," Frick said. "The broad policy of records falls within the province of baseball."[34]

He also affirmed his authority to become involved in the determination of records if they reflected on baseball policy, adding, "I have received a tremendous number of letters from fans on my stand, and 99 percent have backed me up."[35]

Before the season ended, however, high-level criticism within baseball emerged from American League President Joe Cronin. As Frick and his league presidents refined their plans for the 1961 World Series, Cronin tossed barbs at Frick's ruling. "I certainly respect the commissioner's feelings about the matter, but so far as I am concerned, it will be a new official record if either or both do it in 162 games." Frick would not join the battle, instead agreeing with Cronin that a record would be set, but emphasizing that it would be one of two records.[36] Cronin did gain a measure of satisfaction. When the American League sent out its release about records set within the preceding season, Maris' home run mark was noted without qualification,[37] and Cronin personally congratulated Maris on the milestone.[38]

When Maris finally broke the record on the last day of the season, the debilitating controversy had robbed the moment of its celebration. "There was a strange feeling in the ball park all day," said Clete Boyer. "There was surprising quiet until Roger hit it and even more quiet afterward. The ruling by Commissioner Frick ... took so much joy away from the feat.... It just gave us all, especially Roger, some feeling of emptiness about the final homer."[39]

The *Sporting News* editors seemed to echo Frick's relief.

1. The Maris Decision

> In the final analysis, maybe the home-run derby in the American League worked out just right.... Babe Ruth is still the king. In 154 games, he still has hit more home runs than any other man in the game.... As it stands now, Ruth still is Number One. But Roger Maris is Number Two, only one away from the mighty Babe. It is an equitable finish, one that should be satisfying to almost everyone who followed Maris' valiant effort.[40]

For years, the *Book of Baseball Records* identified the home run record: "Most Home Runs, season, 61-Roger E. Maris, A.L., N.Y., 1961 (162-game season); 60-George H. Ruth, A.L., N.Y., 1927 (154-game season)." Eventually, public opinion would turn, the earlier support would be conveniently forgotten, and Frick's decision would evolve into a blooper that would dog him the rest of his tenure as commissioner and mar his legacy.

Daniel reported a discussion with Frick in January 1962, when the commissioner admitted that focusing all record talk on Ruth was a mistake: "I should have made no mention of Ruth, and announced that all baseball records made inside 154 games would stand unless beaten in 154 games, and that all baseball records made in 162 games would be so listed." He also invited the BBWAA to continue its oversight of baseball records, within his stated policy.[41]

Frick stubbornly continued to defend his decision for years. At first, he found the asterisk comments annoying—particularly the implication that he was minimizing Maris's accomplishment. In the heat of the home run race, Frick seemed annoyed by the asterisk craze. "As for that star or asterisk business, I don't know how that cropped up or was attributed to me, because I never said it," he complained. "I certainly never meant to belittle Maris' feat should he wind up with more than sixty. Both names will appear in the book as having set records, but under different conditions."[42]

Later, like a wise public relations practitioner, he good-naturedly adopted the asterisk into the title of his memoirs. In those memoirs, Frick maintained, "I still think it was the right decision."[43] For all of his initial intensity in defending his decision, however, Frick was unusually reticent about the issue in his memoirs, beyond the details quoted (title notwithstanding). The chapter titled "Records, Asterisks, and People" contains precious little about the actual decision. Instead, Frick compared earlier players to modern players and discusses other records that might never be broken. Of the ten records listed, four have since been broken—Walter Johnson's career strikeouts mark, by Nolan Ryan; Lou Gehrig's consecutive games record, by Cal Ripken, Jr.; Ty Cobb's lifetime hits record, by Pete Rose; and Babe Ruth's career bases on balls standard, by Barry Bonds.

The media's subsequent response, however, was to subject Frick's decision to columns blasting it. Many saw it as Frick defending the legacy of Ruth, his old friend. Frick's affection for Ruth was apparent. One of his favorite anecdotes involved his visiting Ruth's bedside the night before his death.[44] And his ghostwriting for Ruth (which will be detailed in Chapter 3) was well known.

As the creator of the asterisk, Dick Young, pointed out, Frick at least should have been credited with the foresight of facing the issue at mid-season, which might not have been as proactive as handling it before, but was better than waiting until after. From his perspective, the later ridicule emptied onto Frick was conveniently self-serving. "[Sportswriters] attached no particular importance to the ruling at the time," he wrote. "Then, gradually, as Maris closed in on the record, they opened fire on Frick."[45]

Koppett claimed that Frick's actions diminished the record itself. When Harmon Killebrew of the Minnesota Twins challenged the record in 1964, it barely moved the needle "and re-emphasizes the futility of Frick's backward-looking intervention."[46] Koppett later wrote that he considered Frick's actions "a remarkably foolish thing." In his opinion, the decision was motivated by Frick's realization that "Ruth's persona and records represented the essence of 'baseball as we know it' that was dissolving before his eyes, with his participation."[47]

An exchange at an awards banquet in January 1962 did not stem the surge of bad publicity. First Frick, in awarding Maris the Van Heusen Outstanding Achievement Award before a distinguished audience, said, "Roger and I argued last season about 162 games and 154 games. However, under great stress and under great strain he came along and broke a record." Frick later explained that he actually meant to say, "Roger did not break an old record; he set a new record."

Maris fumbled his speech as well. "I have just learned that Mr. Frick and I have something in common." Maris meant to say, "He doesn't like to make a speech, either." Instead, he said, "He doesn't know how to make a speech, either." Although he apologized for the misstatement, he remained firm in his opposition to Frick's ruling. "Through most of last season I said and repeated, 'a season is a season,' and I still think so. But Mr. Frick is the commissioner and he makes the rules."[48]

As time passed, players like Mantle, who originally deferred to their commissioner, were more critical. In his memoirs, Mantle wrote, "I thought it was a ridiculous ruling. It made no sense at all." Mantle pointed out that Sandy Koufax broke Christy Mathewson's National League strike-out record that same year in the team's 151st game with no such marking (though that detail likely was supplied by co-author Herb Cluck instead of Mantle).[49]

In a ten-year *New York Times* retrospective, Maris alternated between apathy and defiance. "I don't think about that much anymore," he told Marty Ralbovsky. But when he did, the indignation was apparent. "Do you know any other records that have been broken since the 162-game schedule that have an asterisk? I don't." For good measure, Maris added the calculation that, using the last 154 games of the season, he would have passed Ruth easily: "I didn't hit my first homer until the 11th game that year."[50]

Some critics carelessly perpetuated the myth that Frick had ordered the hated asterisk. In his obituary of Maris, *New York Times* columnist George Vecsey specifically noted that "Ford Frick, the presiding keeper of baseball tradition, affixed the infamous asterisk to Maris in the home-run season of 1961." In the same column, he alleged that Frick "slapped the asterisk on [Maris], allowing some fans, some reporters and some traditionalists to think somewhat less of an excellent young player."[51]

Ken Rosenthal of *The Sporting News* would rank Frick's home run decision No. 15 among baseball's most shameful acts. He quoted Maris as saying (in 1980), "They acted as though I was doing something wrong, poisoning the record books or something."[52]

Frick and Maris would have another encounter during the 1963 season, but in that instance, Frick came to Maris's defense. In a May game at Minnesota, Maris was booed after he did not run out a grounder to first base. The throw skipped off the first baseman's glove, but he was able to retrieve the ball and tag Maris out. As Maris walked back to the dugout, the fans started yelling. After he got into the dugout, he replied with an obscene gesture that the cameras caught.[53]

Frick did not excuse Maris's behavior. He did not talk to Maris directly or punish him, but he did tell the Yankees to take "whatever steps it feels are necessary to see that such actions do not happen again."[54] But Frick went a step further, ordering broadcasters not to follow players into the dugout. "It's all right to follow a player in after a home run, but they move around in there, change shirts and such, and it isn't for the cameras."[55]

One of Frick's most frequent critics, *Milwaukee Journal* sports editor Oliver E. Kuechle, could not believe that Frick was holding everyone accountable but Maris. "Perhaps the television viewers should have turned off their sets on the day Maris made his gesture," Kuechle wrote. "Or perhaps those people in the park who saw it in person should have stayed home."[56]

Frick's minimizing of Maris's record had an expiration date. On September 4, 1991, Commissioner Fay Vincent convened a meeting of the major leagues' Committee for Statistical Accuracy. The committee had been formed by A. Bartlett Giamatti during his brief tenure and comprised three baseball officials, a statistician, two reporters and two professors. They adopted Vincent's recommendation that the parenthetical notations be removed and Maris recognized as having set the home run record.[57]

Baseball's paper of record, *The Sporting News*, remained defiant, even in recognition of Vincent's efforts. "If baseball wants to give official word that Maris is the all-time record holder for home runs, that's great. Maris should be recognized as such. But we'll keep Ruth on the books, parenthetical qualifiers and all."[58]

For the record, and steroid allegations notwithstanding, it should be noted that when McGwire set his home run record at 70 in 1998, he broke Ruth's record in the Cardinals' 144th game and Maris's record in the 145th game. His Mantle, Sosa, broke both in the Cubs' 150th game on his way to 66 home runs. Barry Bonds hit both his 61st and 62nd home runs off Scott Elarton of the Colorado Rockies in the Giants' 144th game. He then broke McGwire's record in the 160th game before finishing with 73.

Pop culture's most effective takedown, of course, was the 2001 Emmy-nominated HBO movie *61**, directed by Billy Crystal. By focusing on the personal struggles Mantle and Maris faced as teammates—and their bond amidst the surge—the film humanized both. In Maris's case, given his shunning of the limelight and complicated relationship with the media, it generated empathy and goodwill among baseball fans. The film had its inaccuracies—not the least of which was its insistence that Frick had specifically prescribed the asterisk. As a dramatic convention, it was as effective as the spinning newspapers Crystal incorporated. As historical fact, it cemented an unfair verdict against Frick that did not need further hardening.

Frick appears in only four scenes, but his dour countenance seems to darken the background. Frick is played by Donald Moffatt, a British actor who also played LBJ in *The Right Stuff*. His face seems pre-pickled to accommodate the curmudgeonly fuddy-duddy the film tried to provide.

As the film opens, Frick and Babe Ruth's widow, Claire, are at the Yankees' 1961 Opening Day, where Claire presents the 1960 Most Valuable Player Award to Maris. Frick speaks admirably about Claire's late husband, foreshadowing the conflict between Frick and Maris over Ruth's record.

Because of the film's focus on Maris and Mantle, Frick does not appear again until about 40 minutes later, when he meets with three journalists to decide what to do, as both Yankees sluggers threaten Ruth's record—the meeting with baseball writers that might or might not have occurred. The journalists are Milt Kahn (Richard Masur), based on veteran Milton Gross of the *New York Post*; Artie Green (Peter Jacobson), based on Leonard Shecter, a younger writer for the *Post*; and Sam Simon (Seymour Cassel), who represents Young, the originator of the asterisk concept.

The debate is spirited and by no means unanimous, with Kahn/Gross supporting Maris, Simon/Young agreeing with Frick, and Green/Shecter playing the hostile punk (much to the disgust of those who knew Shecter). True to history, the Simon/Young character even suggests that Frick use an asterisk to set Maris's record apart, as Young had done 40 years earlier.

Soon after, the film shows Frick, in his office, announcing that Maris would have to surpass Ruth's record in 154 games. Moffatt delivers the announcement with an angry, harsh tone. Frick sounds bitter—quite out of character for him.

In Frick's final scene, he is shown watching the 154th game on television. The setting is accurate: The game took place in Baltimore, not New York. In the seventh inning, Maris hit a long fly ball that looked like it might clear the fence. The film shows Frick following the ball's flight, angrily mouthing an obscenity, and changing to relief after the ball is caught near the fence.

The steroids controversy that began to rage at about the same time as the film's release provides a telling context to the Frick-Maris controversy. The debate over records by Bonds and McGwire centers on unfair, unnatural advantages that they utilized to break home run records. From that perspective, Maris's "advantage" was one not of his own doing, nor one that was not available to all players then or since then, nor one that broke any existing rules. Maris played within the rules and broke the record.

So who was the better home-run hitter for one season—Ruth in 1927 or Maris in 1961? That question has been debated, though never answered. Ruth was part of a lightning-in-a-bottle season, with the New York Yankees at the top of their game. And his glowing personality certainly cast him in a more favorable light with the media than Maris's Midwestern reticence. Ruth owned New York City like Maris never could, and that swayed the debate. Maris was no single-season spectacle; he had won the league's Most Valuable Player the year before, after all. But his own magic season of 1961 would be harder to replicate as injuries dogged his career.

In either case, the pro-active, well-intentioned efforts of a baseball commissioner—recognizing an accomplishment while trying to set it within a larger context—overshadowed both the debate and its implications. And it cast Frick in the spotlight, unfairly, as a holdover from a bygone age. Who did he think he was to make such a ruling?

What brought him to center stage in a Big Apple sports circus actually began almost 70 years earlier, in an Indiana farm community.

2

Early Years

Christian Frick, Ford's grandfather, was born in Erlensbach, Switzerland, in 1819. His father, also named Christian, had moved north from the town of Diemtigen with his wife, Katharina. Their only recorded births were to sons, Christian and John. One family account indicates that they were twins; another says that they were born a year apart. Like their parents, the brothers would soon be on the move from the small, wine-growing community.

At some point around or before 1850, following the death of their parents, the brothers emigrated to the United States—a journey that would take six weeks. They settled side-by-side homesteads along the Elkhart River in northeast Indiana's Noble County, where many Frick family members still live today. On September 16, 1852, Christian Frick married Emily Dukes, who was 13 years younger. They would have ten children, rearing them in a log cabin. The oldest, Jacob Frick, born August 4, 1853, would be the father of Ford Frick. Christian Frick died in 1880, three years after the birth of his tenth child, and was buried in the Cosperville Cemetery.

A Frick family history describes Jacob as an "ardent reader and learner." He did not attend college, but that did not deter him from building and then staffing one of the first schoolhouses in Noble County. Some of his students were older than himself.

Jacob Frick married Emma Prickett on February 10, 1875. According to family histories, Prickett's father was an itinerant Baptist preacher who shared her later husband's name of Jacob. Jacob Prickett's courtship of Emma's mother, Barbara Gray, did not meet with the approval of her parents, who were prosperous members of Wolf Lake, Indiana, society and probably had loftier goals for their daughter than being a preacher's wife. Jacob Prickett moved his family to a church in Lafayette. But Barbara Gray Prickett died when Emma was ten, and so Emma was sent to be raised in her uncle's home in Noble County, where she would meet and marry Jacob. She would see her father when he came to the area to preach.

The marriage of Jacob and Emma Frick would last for 57 years, until she died in 1932. Jacob died in 1947, at the age of 94, as his son was nearing the end of his tenure as National League president.

Before their only son was born, they had three daughters. One, Barbara, died in infancy. Sophronia, also known as Frona, was born in 1878, and Gertrude was born in 1881. Thirteen years later, Ford was born. His middle name was not Christian, but Christopher—suggesting that his grandfather might have changed his own name from the Germanic "Christian" to the more American "Christopher."

Ford Frick was born on his family's farm near Wawaka on December 12, 1894. Another sister, Clara, joined the family in 1900. All of these towns that figured in Frick's family—Wawaka, Brimfield, and Cosperville—represent small, unincorporated hamlets that dot the farmland surrounding the larger towns of Ligonier, Albion, and Kendallville. The smaller towns are mainly signs—some do not even require reduced speeds as motorists drive through—on and even a ways off highways like U.S. 6 and State Highway 9.

In an interview when he was named National League president, Frick said, "I was born of poor parents, but they felt that they could not give me the best advantages at Wawaka, so they moved to Brimfield, Indiana. I was five years old at the time."[1] According to his obituary, Jacob, also known as Jack, left farming and schoolteaching to become postmaster in Brimfield for many years. He also started work as a foreman of a "section gang" when the New York Central Railroad came through town, and even ran a small general store. He settled his family in a house at the corner of Summit and Main in Brimfield, according to Mary Jane Lepird, Ford's niece and, until 2014, his oldest surviving relative.[2] The Brimfield School was two blocks away. North of a creek that ran alongside the school was a baseball field. After Jack Frick retired from the post office, he moved the family to Kendallville, then to a 12-acre farm near Ligonier.

It is no surprise that Frick described his Indiana childhood in idyllic terms: "We had the whole world to ourselves. We had the woods to play in and the rivers and the lakes to swim in. We skated in the winter and played baseball in the summer. We made our own recreation, and I think that's really good. We never thought of ourselves as underprivileged."[3]

According to a speech given when Frick was named "Hoosier of the Year" in 1952, Frick was known for being an energetic child—so much so that his mother would tie him to a pear tree with a long rope, so that she

On one of his frequent side trips to Indiana, Frick visited with (from left) his younger sister, Clara (Frick) Couts; his older sister, Gertrude "Gertie" (Frick) Zimmerman, and his father, Jacob (right) (courtesy Carol Madden Werker).

could complete her chores.[4] It was a favorite disciplinary strategy. One of Mary Jane's earliest memories is of her grandmother also tying Mary Jane's energetic younger sister, Ethel, to a tree on the farm property. After a sympathetic Mary Jane freed Ethel, Emma tied them both to the same tree.[5]

Frick's memoirs do not mention his father, but in his chapter in Jerome Holtzman's book, *No Cheering in the Press Box*, he describes him as "stern but very generous and honest," and his mother as "saintly." He also remembered them as working hard on the farm—though the description also fits Jacob's time in Brimfield working several jobs.[6] No doubt Jacob approved of his son's workaholic reputation that would distinguish him among his Jazz Age journalism colleagues.

A proud Ford Frick was able to take his father to see the Yankees play an exhibition game in 1933, in Fort Wayne, Indiana. Jacob had been introduced to all the players before the game, and Babe Ruth approached Jacob's seat in the ninth inning with the score tied, 7–7. Ruth noted that his ghostwriter's father looked tired and hungry, so he promised to hit a home run to end the game, which he did. When Ford Frick saw his father after the game, Jacob was not entirely impressed. "It was swell, but there is something screwy about baseball when a man can call his shots like that. Why don't they have him hit one every game, so all the fans could see it?" he asked his son.[7]

Ford distinguished himself academically at the Brimfield school; he completed the eighth grade two years early, at age 11. A family history claims that Frick's first job was selling newspapers in Brimfield, though he also earned extra money weeding onions and working alongside his father on the railroad. But baseball always came first. "I never really cared much for anything but baseball," he said in 1934, reflecting on his youth. "I never played anything else nor was much interested in it, to tell you the truth."[8]

Soon after moving on from the Brimfield school, he had his "first date" with baseball, to extend Dick Young's metaphor on the book cover of Frick's memoirs. As he recalled in his memoirs, the Chicago Cubs visited Kendallville in the summer of 1907 to play an exhibition. Johnny Kling, a catcher for the Cubs, offered the wide-eyed youngster the chance to carry his shoes to the ballpark, which allowed Frick to sit near the players' bench during the game. "For the rest of the summer, I lived in a dreamworld. I was the hero of the village, the envy of every kid in the community, the hometown boy who, for a few minutes, hobnobbed with greatness."[9]

The family history notes that Ford and Clara had to walk from Brimfield to Rome City—around five miles—to attend a consolidated high school. The family did own a horse, but it was so uncooperative that it was easier for Clara to walk alongside. They would meet up with friends along the way, and by the time they arrived at school, the group would number as many as 15. During bad weather, Ford and Clara would stay with friends in Rome City. Ford graduated from Rome City High School early, at age 15, with nine other classmates, though he was edged in the race to be valedictorian.

He did not enroll immediately in a four-year college, but instead, at the recommendation of his principal, he took classes in stenography and typing at the International Business College in Fort Wayne, to prepare for a newspaper career. "I was a hell of a typist," he later told Holtzman. "Maybe I wasn't a good writer, but I could type.... I could turn out a hell of a lot of copy."[10] He also got his first experience in newspaper work, as an office boy and police reporter for the *Fort Wayne Gazette*, earning $3.50 a week.

After a year, Frick enrolled at DePauw University, where he pledged Phi Kappa Psi and played for the baseball team, earning a letter. He also ran the quarter mile for the track team.[11] He was a proud DePauw alum: "Listen, feller, in those days DePauw used to raise hell with Purdue in football. DePauw was—and is—a noble college." For all the institutional opportunities available to someone of his professional status, Frick would also send his son, Frederick, to DePauw.[12] He also served as a member of the DePauw Board of Trustees.

Speaking at his fraternity's centennial, Frick listed memories of his DePauw days:

> Meetings of the ungodly at Charley Bells for a quick Coke and a hot ham sandwich during Chapel period while the saintly were enjoying prayers at Chapel. Fred Crawford's all night beanery; and the clatter of inter-urban trains down Seminary Street. Clandestine dances at Calumet Hall. Vestal's Livery Stable where phaetons were available for a Sunday drive if you were lucky enough to have a date and $3 in cash. The College associations. Eight o'clock classes; and the East College Bell calling us to Chapel or to a football celebration.[13]

He worked his way through school, firing the furnace and waiting tables at his fraternity house.[14] But he also picked up early experience as a sports writer. As he told Holtzman, "One of the things I did was correspondence sports stuff for the Indianapolis and Terre Haute papers. Occasionally I did special assignments for the Chicago *Tribune*, like when we had our traditional football game with Wabash College, or when the Notre Dame baseball team came to town."[15] By his graduation in 1915, however, none of those newspapers would hire him full-time, so he headed westward, to Walsenburg, Colorado, south of Pueblo.

So why Walsenburg, which seems a random choice? Actually, the city superintendent of Walsenburg schools, S. M. Andrews, had been principal of the Brimfield town school and had roomed with the Frick family when Ford was in third grade. There is no information as to whether Frick and Andrews maintained a regular correspondence over the years, or whether Frick thought to contact Andrews after he graduated. In either case, years later, when Frick was looking for a teaching position, Andrews was able to help.[16]

Frick pointed out that his first job was not teaching, but playing first base for the Cubanolas, a semi-pro baseball team sponsored by the Colorado Fuel and Iron Company the summer after he graduated from DePauw.[17] It was as close as he would get to his dream of following his childhood idols into the major leagues. "I was a first baseman but couldn't throw," he told Holtzman. "I had to wind up to throw to third."[18] He claimed more success at the plate. "I could hit sometimes," he told the *New York Times* in 1934. "Yes, sir, I could hit that old apple pretty well at times."[19]

Frick played his only season of pro ball under the pseudonym of Chris Ford, according to a 1935 *Baseball Magazine* profile. Other players on the team included Thad Holt, later director of Alabama's Relief Administration during the Depression and a Birmingham broadcast executive, and E. W. Hughes, who started a successful investment firm in Colorado Springs and remained wealthy even after the stock market crash.[20]

Once the season and summer ended, he began teaching English and coaching at Huerfano County High School. His sister, Clara Couts, said that he wore glasses so he would look older to his students.[21] Andrews claimed that Frick taught the first high school journalism classes offered in Colorado. He also worked as a clerk for a coalmine.[22]

The move to Walsenburg brought another perk. As a newly arrived high school teacher, Frick needed housing, so Andrews returned the favor and let him rent a room. The family next door included a daughter, Eleanor Cowling, who was a senior at the high school. On September 18, 1916, she became Frick's wife. The wedding took place in the family home.[23]

Eleanor Frick would remain a complicated but mostly unexamined part of Frick's life. His Indiana relatives express some resentment toward her, feeling that she kept her husband from his farm-boy roots except when absolutely necessary—a speech or award in the state. Her grandson, Ford Frick II, noted with some amusement her upward revisionism of her own background; her family did own a small store in Walsenburg, but it was not as large or successful as she sometimes related. Where her husband's career was concerned, it is acknowledged that she probably encouraged him toward the advancements that moved him past the writing he enjoyed so much, but it would be unfair to exaggerate either her role or her character. Still, without her influence, he might not have ended up in the commissioner's office.

Eleanor was still alive when her granddaughter, Kelly (Frick) Richards, had a daughter in 1984. Kelly had given her daughter the middle name Kennesaw, because she and her husband had climbed Mount Kennesaw outside of Atlanta right before she learned she was pregnant. They also decided to call their daughter by her middle name instead of her first name, Katherine, because of the excess of "Katherines" and "Katies" at the time. Great-grandmother Eleanor hated the idea as much as she hated Judge Kenesaw Mountain Landis, one of her husband's predecessors as commissioner. "How could you name a beautiful baby Kennesaw?" she asked. "I'm going to call her Katie."

2. Early Years

Ford brought Eleanor to Colorado Springs, where he was a teacher "in the commercial department" at Colorado Springs High School. Another new faculty member that year, Dr. Lloyd Shaw, recalled that the school was so crowded, only half of the student body could be jammed into the auditorium for an assembly at one time. The other half would be entrusted to Shaw and Frick, in the equally crowded school library. "(We) told them stories and jokes and made brilliant extemporaneous speeches and did anything we could think of to keep them happy till classes were resumed again," Shaw recalled.[24]

He also picked up a gig teaching business English at Colorado College, a private liberal arts college in town. It was during this time that their son and only child, Frederick Cowling Frick, was born, on November 5, 1917. But Frick had given up teaching to be sports editor of the *Colorado Springs Gazette*.[25] (He had abandoned his baseball career after two summers.)

Charles Dudley, long-time city reporter and columnist for both the *Gazette* and the *Telegraph*, recalled one occasion where Frick riled a local high school football team by calling them poor losers. "The crowd of high school students that collected in front of the *Gazette* building was formidable, and when the boys started climbing the stairs to the editorial rooms on the third floor, the building shook." Frick gained control of the situation, Dudley recalled. "Standing on a desk, he addressed the throng with a Mark Anthony [sic] style that Shakespeare would have approved. Imprecations subsided, and before long the room was ringing with cheers."[26]

Like many men of his time, Frick stepped away from his newspaper job in 1918 to help with the World War I effort. He worked with the War Department's rehabilitation division, helping wounded soldiers in a four-state district (Colorado, Utah, Wyoming, and New Mexico) with their rehabilitation, training, and eventual job placement.

After about a year of that, Frick was ready to return to newspaper work, so he worked briefly for the *Rocky Mountain News* in Denver before returning to Colorado Springs. He wanted to work for the *Telegraph*, but the only position available was editorial writer, for which Frick would be paid by the column inch, so of course he wrote long editorials. He picked up whatever other assignments he could, whether sports, police beat—even interviewing distinguished visitors to Colorado Springs hotels. Those interviews often appeared in the "Here and There and Everywhere" column he wrote for the Sunday *Telegraph*, a collection of anecdotes and commentary, starting with a poem.

He returned to the Colorado College faculty; he was listed as an instructor of journalism in the 1919 edition of the college yearbook, the *Nugget*.

He also opened an advertising agency that apparently occupied at least as much of his time as the newspaper writing did, and probably more.[27] The agency provided much-needed additional income to the young family and prepared Frick for his post-journalism career as baseball's most literate promoter.

Perhaps Frick was seeking a full-time return to newspaper work. Maybe he was seeking a ticket out of Colorado. He never hinted at what his long-term career plans were. But a sudden, persistent, and ultimately disastrous thunderstorm in June 1921 would earn him a full-time newspaper gig at a large newspaper far away from Colorado.

According to the many analyses of the Pueblo flood, the disaster had its origins in the foothills north of the town on Thursday, June 2, 1921. Between 3 and 4 p.m., the rain started falling heavily along Eight Mile, Rush, and Rock Creeks. The lack of vegetation in the region meant that the runoff was both quick and complete. The first two creeks fed into the Arkansas River; Rock Creek caused Fountain Creek to swell. It was unfortunate timing that both flood surges reached Pueblo at the same time, intensifying a dangerous situation into overwhelming tragedy.[28]

The first surge hit overnight, at about 3 a.m. on Friday, June 3. The danger emerged from far enough upstream that messages could be dispatched downriver, warning residents of the danger from the surging wall of water. As the sun rose, however, rather than head for higher ground, hundreds of residents rushed for the levees to watch. Because of the sporadic intensity of thunderstorms, the residents were impressed by how the waters would rise and subside.

This time would be different, however. The waters did not subside, but kept rising. As a result, some of the levees gave way, and many who did not drown in the initial collapse were doomed, as the water cut them off from the escape route to higher land. Others who did not join the rush to the levees but remained in their homes, refusing to evacuate (mainly foreign-born railroad workers), faced a similar fate.[29] Although the official fatality count was 150, estimates placed the loss of life at more than 1,500.[30]

The river would rise and subside to and from flood stage over the next two days, hampering rescue and recovery efforts. In fact, two days after the initial devastating flood, on June 5, the Schaeffer Dam on Beaver Creek failed, 11 miles upstream from its junction with the Arkansas. The reservoir emptied into the creek in 30 minutes, and about five hours later, the wall of water had traveled the 33 miles to Pueblo, adding to the destruction.[31]

The floodwaters downtown were not the only challenge as Friday's horror continued. Burning piles from a lumberyard blaze were carried downstream, setting off fires that were impossible to fight. Floating houses, boxcars, and wagons were also carried downstream, causing additional damage.[32]

Frick was one of the first reporters to witness the devastation. He flew over the town in a plane piloted by Charles Mays. As the newspaper itself reported, the plane left Colorado Springs at 11 a.m. Friday—"the first outside conveyance to reach the city since the flood"—in still threatening weather, before returning northward. The newspaper noted "the glowering sky and rain which fell heavily, making the flight doubly perilous." The newspaper pointed out that it was "able to give to the outside world the first authentic news of this disaster."[33]

The ambition of the strategy was apparent: Hours after the flood first hit, with flood waters still overwhelming the Pueblo downtown, in unstable and stormy air, Frick flew over it and recorded his impressions. Some later accounts claimed that Frick also photographed the flood. These are uncertain (the report does not mention a photographer as a third passenger, and Frick mainly describes his own reporting), but that does not diminish Frick's individual enterprise. As a result of his daring—keep in mind that air travel was less than 20 years old—the *Evening Telegraph* was able to provide its readers with a vivid description of the scene, along with photographs.

The plane dared not land; the local landing strip was under three feet of water. Reporters from the Associated Press and Denver newspapers had also flown down to cover the devastation. However, they made the mistake of landing in Pueblo and were not able to take off for the return trip.[34] Their mistake would provide Frick with an even greater audience for his reporting.

Flying at an altitude between 1,000 and 1,500 feet, Frick and Mayse made several passes over the city. The photographs that were taken of the destruction—whether by Frick or someone else—did not appear in the June 4 edition of the *Telegraph*. The newspaper did print on page 3 a ground-level photo of a house that appeared to have tipped into a hole created by the floodwaters, but it was not credited to a photographer or agency.

In place of the photographs, Frick was able to provide the *Telegraph's* readers with vivid description and commentary. That he was able to turn around the assignment, after returning to Colorado Springs at 2 p.m., is a testament to Frick's ability to write (and type) quickly. His front-page article combined description, commentary, and even preliminary damage reporting.

In reporting damage, Frick said they were able to count 17 bridges washed away. He also reported that the flood's destruction moved northward and eastward from the downtown area, with an estimated 25 blocks under water. But the Minnequa area, to the south of Pueblo, was not affected. An industrial plant along the highlands south of the city was still operating.[35]

Frick's description allowed the images, not overwrought prose, to provide the drama. He described "the seething mass of waters as they worm their way thru stone walls, tearing away heavy foundations, sweeping bridges from their path—taking their toll of human lives.... Box cars, swept from the tracks, are scattered about the streets, houses, floated from their foundations, are piled together in the greatest confusion."[36] Even in the midst of such grand destruction, he showed the ability to capture the poignant small moment:

> Yet it is the little things which impress themselves. Sweeping over the city we saw scores of buildings absolutely torn to pieces by the powers of the flood—yet the greatest impression made on both the pilot and observers—when they saw a horse alone on a little knoll from which the waters had receded—head down and dejected, apparently deserted to its death by the owners who had been forced to flee before the advancing waters.[37]

Frick was careful to give the physical details of the damage: "[I]t was easy to see that the water had reached the second story of many of the buildings." He also reported that most of the fires caused by the floating piles of timber had been extinguished ("one cheering note"). Flying over the city in the midst of two days of rushing water, he wrote, "Although the storm ceased last night, the waters have not yet begun to recede, the floods from the northwestern highlands keeping the water coming faster than it can be drained away."[38]

The *Telegraph* did run its first photos on June 6, 1921—two days after Frick's account. The newspaper ran one photo on the top of the front page and devoted Page 3 to six photos. Although the subhead credited "Chas. Mays" for piloting the airplane, it also credited the photos to "H. L. Standley," who is not mentioned in the June 4 article describing the flight. It is possible that Frick was never assigned to take any photographs, but instead to provide an eyewitness description of the destruction, and that Standley flew the next day with Mays and snapped the photographs. It is a plausible explanation, because Frick at no point in any record discussed an interest or experience in photography.

An article on Page 6, extolling the newspaper's leading role in reporting the disaster, said that "a reporter for The Telegraph was sent by plane to get a general view of the city,"[39] but did not identify the reporter as Frick. Two photographs were also reprinted in the June 10 edition of the *El Paso County Democrat*, a weekly newspaper in Colorado Springs.[40] But after his initial reporting, Frick was not mentioned in the *Evening Telegraph*, nor did he generate any bylined articles.

Was there resentment that Frick, not a full-time news staff member, had taken hold of such a great story? Was he taken off the story after the brave flight? It didn't matter. Because Frick and the *Telegraph* had the first accounts of the flood, while the Associated Press and Denver *Post* photographers were still grounded, the description and photos were a regional and national hit. The *Telegraph* even used the content as leverage to get the *Post* to allow it to run "The Gumps," Sidney Smith's popular comic strip of the time.[41]

After the flood, Frick returned to the task of sports writing. Among the clips he saved from that period was a report of a February 1922 basketball game in which Colorado College defeated Wyoming, 43–16. He had already adopted the breezy style of a 1920s sports writer, even before moving to New York. Attributing the win to Colorado's best player, he wrote, "Bob Allen, erstwhile Wheatridge star, was the leading lady in last night's performance. But Bob had durn good support, and while the boys didn't display a lot in the way of basketball, they did get a lot of good exercise. Which is something—and certainly not to be sneezed at."[42]

Apparently Frick was a big fan of the new sport and tried to convince his friend, city side reporter Charles Dudley, to check it out. In a column noting Frick's appointment as commissioner, Dudley recalled, Frick—with the same fervor he would later apply in promoting baseball—"tried to persuade me that if I ever saw a basketball game, I would become an ardent fan." So Dudley accompanied Frick to a Colorado College game; "In the heat of the battle, I fell asleep, leaning against a brick wall in the back row."[43]

He also put his writing skills to other uses. Frick penned a satire titled "Much Ado About Nothing" for the El Paso Club's annual dinner in February 1922. The El Paso Club is a private social club founded in 1877 and a favorite of the newly minted millionaires during the region's boom time in the 1890s. It still exists today as a private organization, and its building is a Colorado Springs landmark. Only the evening's program from 1922 in a scrapbook survives, but it shows inclusion among the Colorado Springs fashionable elite for the Fricks, which was certainly important for Eleanor.

Somehow, Frick's work—and certainly the daring, vivid flood reporting—caught the attention of Arthur Brisbane, managing editor for William

Randolph Hearst's *New York American* newspaper. Several accounts exist of how this happened. Frick recalled that it involved a veteran printer in Colorado Springs: "That old printer knew Arthur Brisbane and he kind of liked my stuff out there. He sent some of it on to Brisbane in New York, and Brisbane wired me the offer of a job. Well, after I'd been convinced that I wasn't being kidded, I headed for New York."[44] Most accounts claim the printer had retired to Colorado Springs from New York and was living in a printers union retirement home.

Sporting News columnist Fred Lieb told a similar story, but credited the retired printer-Brisbane contact to Hyde S. Rogers. "This young man should be in your organization," Rogers reportedly told Brisbane. According to Lieb, "Brisbane, as anxious to bring up new talent as Connie Mack or Branch Rickey, wired Frick: 'Can you come to New York and see me?'"[45]

Within his grandfather's memorabilia, Frick's grandson, Ford II, has a typewritten letter to Frick that confirms this narrative. It is certainly from Hyde Rogers and is dated October 17, 1922. It starts, "I read your story on the Short Line sale last night, and liked it immensely. It was almost literature and certainly drew pictures that were quite real. That is high art in newspapering, I think."

Rogers then expresses concern for Frick: "Do you know that I am worrying about you. I don't want you to write yourself out or get into hack work for small pay. You belong in a larger field. I have seen a lot of the boys come up, and I think I know."

Rogers goes on to list some of the journalists he worked with: Gene Field, managing editor of the *Denver Tribune* from 1881–1883 and noted satirist; Arthur Chapman, whose books and poems detailed Colorado's beauty as much as its history; Bide Dudley, who started with the *Denver Post* and later wrote a syndicated theater column in New York City; and even Damon Runyon ("when he was young and a bad actor").

Then he reaches the real business of his letter. "Now, I want you to pick me out some specimens of your best stuff, including this article last evening and send [them] to me.... I'll send that to Arthur Brisbane, from who I have had letters but never met.... You certainly are as good as Gene Fowler, and they say he is the best find that Hearst has made in a long time." The letter is simply signed, "Rog," implying that Frick and Rogers had met or corresponded.

Other less reliable or accurate accounts differed. According to N. D. Holman, a Colorado Springs expatriate who had moved to St. Petersburg, Florida, Frick caught his own break. In 1964 he recalled Frick as "a bright young fellow on the local newspaper who used to dig up the darndest angles to all stories. He would call me in, give me photo assignments and then send me to get pictures for the proposed articles." Holman claimed that Brisbane vacationed in Colorado Springs. "After reading this young man's stuff for a couple of days, Brisbane went to interview him and finally wound up taking him off the little paper and back to New York."[46] Frank Graham, New York sports columnist, reported that Frick actually interviewed Brisbane for a feature article, and that was how he came to his attention.[47]

After Rogers sent his work to New York, Frick recalled seeing a telegram in his typewriter when he arrived at the office. "Would you be interested in coming to New York at my expense to discuss working for us? [Signed] Arthur Brisbane." Like any skeptical journalist, Frick tried to figure out who among his co-workers had come up with that prank. Much like any intense young professional would respond to a practical joke, he crumpled the note and tossed it in the wastebasket. His managing editor suggested that he check with the nearby Western Union office, which confirmed the telegram's origin. Frick made the trip, his first to New York, but couldn't stay long—among the jobs Frick juggled was refereeing, and it was football season, so he had to return quickly. Ultimately, Brisbane invited him to work for the *American*.[48] Given the October 1922 date on the letter and that Frick began work for Hearst in January 1923, circumstances must have moved quickly.

Regardless of the details, the narrative was clear. The Indiana farm boy had gone to Colorado to discern his career path. That path would bring him to New York City and his own place among the Jazz Age's sports and journalism icons.

3

The Babe Ruth Problem

It's a familiar scenario. A section editor is down one beat writer, so the editor often ends up carrying two loads while waiting for the front office to make the hire. Such was the lot of Wilton S. "Bill" Farnsworth, sports editor of the *New York American*. The sports pages of the *American* in late 1922 included articles by Farnsworth reporting on the New York Giants baseball team. It seems no big deal until you realize that Farnsworth was filing the articles while running a sports department under the watchful eyes of William Randolph Hearst and his managing editor, Arthur Brisbane. But help was coming from Colorado, as Ford Frick was making the move to New York City, under Brisbane's guidance, to start work in January 1923.

Brisbane and Farnsworth made sure that New York City made a strong first impression on the Midwestern boy and his wife. As Frick recalled in his memoirs, his first night in the city "was highlighted by an introduction to Jimmy Durante and Eddie Jackson at Jimmy Kelly's place in the Village, and … a backstage visit to the 'Follies,' as the wide-eyed guest of Bill Shrode," Ziegfeld's stage manager.[1] It was not the last time he would be starstruck.

Frick's small-town roots remained, however. In fact, as his former *Journal-American* colleague Frank Graham recalled, Frick did not enjoy New York City and spoke often of returning to Colorado Springs. "I'm a small town guy," he would say. "This place is too big and too noisy and too hurried to suit me."[2]

He would settle his family not in Manhattan, but in the Westchester County community of Bronxville. Just north of New York City, Westchester County was among the first suburban areas developed and has long remained one of the most affluent locales in the state and nation. Bronxville, a mere 15 miles from Manhattan, is one of the state's richest communities. Frick would live there until his death almost 60 years later.

3. The Babe Ruth Problem

He and his wife did move once, in the late 1930s, but remained within the city limits.³

At his new job back in the city, the impression left by the journalists he met was just as daunting as that first night on the town. At the *American*, where he began his 13 years of covering baseball, he met Damon Runyon (whom he considered a guide and mentor). The affinity between the two is not surprising. Runyon, like Frick, had come to New York from Colorado—Pueblo, in Runyon's case. Frick's reporting on his hometown's flood no doubt impressed Runyon as well.

As Frick recalled, "Bill (Farnsworth) thought it would be a good idea to have Damon Runyon take me around. Damon was a Colorado boy."⁴ Through Runyon, Frick was introduced to Grantland Rice, the preeminent sports columnist of his generation. That same day, he met Heywood Broun, W. O. McGeehan and Ring Lardner at the Yankees' office, and John Kieran and Fred Lieb at the Giants' office.⁵

The meetings might have taken place at a delicatessen next to the Yankees' office that the writers frequented, where Frick recalls, "The first time I was there ... Ring Lardner came in. Granny Rice was there. Heywood Broun and John Kieran. Bugs Baer. Sid Mercer. Frankie Graham. And of course, Damon Runyon. Damn, you could go on and on. Good Lord, I was goggle-eyed and scared to death."⁶ All of these names represent a "Murderers' Row" of sports journalism—who created some of the most memorable sports reporting and writing ever and influenced both the sports and journalism cultures.

But the New York sports writing community comprised more than big names. It also included workaday professionals like Dan Daniel of the *Telegram* and Bill Slocum of the *Tribune*. Frick fell in with this group—hard-working journalists who rode the trains and chased scoops at spring training, all in the quest to deliver the latest dope, if not the most flowery writing, to crazed baseball fans. From a celebrity perspective, they might have seemed the supporting players to the ring Lardners and Runyons, who enjoyed a more leisurely life and work schedule. But to their editors and publishers, Frick and company were mining circulation gold.

Frick might not have shared the same reputation for wordsmithing that his more famous colleagues did, but his ability to work hard and fast became legendary. As one colleague from the period noted, "My opinion is that the secret of his success is a mind that works with lightning precision. On sports assignments he invariably would be packing up his portable typewriter while the rest of us were struggling to get into the second paragraph."⁷

Graham recalled Frick as "a fine reporter with a brisk writing style." As he put it, "His mind agile and his fingers nimble, he could whip out a story in a handful of minutes immediately following the conclusion of a major event, working so fast it took a high speed telegrapher at his elbow to keep up with him."

In the baseball press boxes, the tall, slender Indiana newbie immediately established his lifelong reputation for being friendly and approachable. As Lieb recalled, "He wasn't exactly garrulous, but he liked to talk, and fellow baseball writers called him 'the barber.' He always has liked people, felt the good ones far outnumbered the bad ones, and that if you give a person a fair shake, you are likely to get a fair shake in return."[8]

His nickname among the sportswriters, given to him by Dan Parker of the *Mirror*, was "Cuthbert," reflecting a devotion to his work that was almost saintly.[9] Parker even gave that as Frick's name to the officials managing the Yankees press box at spring training in St. Petersburg in 1925 so that when Frick arrived, he saw a spot reserved for "F. Cuthbert Frick."[10]

Graham also provided one of the few descriptions of Frick's style. "He never wrote a poor story and, very often, his was the best story in town. His approach, in writing about the athletes, was a friendly one but, on occasion, he could rear back and hit one of them over the head with a few hundred well chosen words."[11]

For an idea of Frick's approach to sports writing, fast-forward almost 20 years, to a speech Frick made to minor-league baseball writers on December 3, 1941. His style reflected the "Gee Whiz!" tone of Rice more than the "Aw Nuts" cynicism of McGeehan and Lardner. He even harkened back to his early meetings with Runyon and Rice and relayed their professional counsel: "Write your story, remembering that you are the eyes and ears of the kids who think the game is great and the men playing it are honest. Remember that ridicule, for the sake of a funny line, or comedy at the expense of someone's pride, never paid dividends."

In remarks as serious and sober as the deteriorating global politics in 1941, he pointed to young readers as the focus. "Youngsters are looking for someone to adopt as an idol," he said. "Such youths pay more attention to what you write than anybody else. As a result, you must realize your responsibility."

In discussing the sports craze that had survived the Jazz Age and endured through the Depression, Frick made the leap from sports to politics. He claimed that sports had fueled his country's democratic spirit, given their attraction to competitors from every economic background.

He also attributed America's political stability during the Depression to sports' cathartic ability to help citizens "let off steam."[12]

In his memoirs, Frick was as romantic toward sports journalists as he was toward baseball. "No other group of men, through the years, has contributed more to baseball and American sports," he wrote. "Yet no group has received less public recognition for the job they have done or the contribution they have made."[13]

Whether cynical or optimistic, these sportswriters found a hungry audience nationwide. Coming out of World War I, American society was eager to cast off the burden of war and embrace pleasure. They found stimulation on several fronts, of course: relaxed sexual mores, alcohol (despite Prohibition), silent movies, and, of course, jazz music. Sports capitalized on the decade's spirit as well, and the sportswriters' prose fanned the flame.

But the New York sports writing scene was also an ethical problem child when Frick arrived. The angst was not limited to New York City; publishers nationwide were struggling with how to address the exploding interest in sports while maintaining their newspapers' journalistic integrity. A lively sports section, with lots of pages crowding out serious news, was considered crucial to healthy circulation. "There is no single classification of news that sells more papers than sports," said W. P. Beazell, managing editor of the *New York World*, in 1929.[14]

The struggle has been a familiar one and has colored sports journalism even today. Sports writers are expected to reflect the professional ethic of objectivity, but between the close relationships they enjoyed with the players (more of a factor in the 1920s), and the realization that their audience comprised fans of the team, it has been difficult to maintain. In today's sports, while the advent of free agency has eroded player loyalty and made them franchises unto themselves, the pressure to reflect partisan fan sentiment remains, particularly in the college ranks. The multiplication of media outlets on the Internet doesn't help. The 1920s provided the first fruits of an ethical struggle that survived changes in medium.

The sports journalists producing 1920s copy seemed to play by their own rules—standards that originated in sports' yellow journalism roots. (It was a favorite strategy of not only Hearst and William Pulitzer, but almost every New York newspaper publisher.) Sports writers were notorious for accepting money from promoters and, in return, producing high-octane hype promoting those events. The low salaries and recognition (bylines were a recent innovation) provided a reason, though not necessarily an excuse, for such actions. Plus, sports journalists seemed to enjoy an autonomy that other journalists could only envy. The sports section often went directly from the sports desk to the composing room, bypassing the scrutiny of the copy desk and managing editor.[15]

So deep was the concern that twice during the decade, in 1923 and 1927, the American Society of Newspaper Editors appointed committees to study how to keep sports from overwhelming newspapers, in terms of both space and ethics. The committee recommendations addressed such issues as pay and ethical training, but avoided undermining the profit machine that sports represented. The relationship between newspaper publishers and sports had been that way since the Penny Press days of the nineteenth century. The publishers loved the profits generated by sports, but felt compelled to distance themselves through well-timed condescending expressions of disdain for America's sports mania.

Perhaps the most troubling ethical struggle involved the widespread practice of ghostwriting. Within the sports coverage that attracted readers, the most popular features were columns "written" by sports superstars. A few athletes, like tennis champion Bill Tilden, wrote their own stuff. Most athletes, however, did not. The newspaper or syndicate would match the athlete with the journalist, and print whatever was turned in. Some athletes did not even bother to read what went out under their names. The name, more than the writing, sold papers anyway.

According to Frick himself, he began to provide the same service for Babe Ruth soon after he moved with Brisbane from the morning *American* to Hearst's other New York property, the *Evening Journal*, in 1924. In his own memoirs, reluctant to add fuel to the Maris asterisk fire, Frick only briefly mentioned his ghostwriting for Ruth, and then simply to set up an anecdote: "Some days later, when I was doing a bit of 'ghosting,' I had occasion to bring up the subject with Babe."[16] ("The subject" was whether Ruth had pointed to center field before hitting his home run off Charlie Root in the 1932 World Series. The outcome of the anecdote was equally noncommittal.)

Frick also referred to his ghostwriting casually in a first-person *Sporting News* article on his greatest baseball thrill. "I was a busy guy in the Yankee-Pirates World Series of 1927; in addition to writing my usual stuff for the New York Journal, I also was ghosting for Babe Ruth, Miller Huggins and Lou Gehrig. Hug and Babe were regular assignments, but they tossed in Gehrig in that Series for good measure."[17]

Besides serving as Huggins' ghostwriter, Frick enjoyed a close relationship with the Yankees' manager. According to Lieb, they were also golf buddies, with a furious rivalry both during spring training and in New York, "each crowing to roof-tops if he achieved victory."[18] For someone as private as Huggins, it might have seemed a risk to have a member of the media for a golf partner. But given the compliant nature of Frick and many of his colleagues, and his expressed interest in the success of Ruth and the Yankees, it was a pleasant arrangement, beyond the intramural trash talking.

During his career as a sportswriter, Frick was a frequent ghostwriter for Babe Ruth. That led to conflict-of-interest charges that he was trying to protect Ruth's home run record in 1961 (courtesy Ford Frick II).

In going over to the *Journal*, Frick replaced Warren Brown, the Chicago sports journalism icon, who was actually well-traveled preceding the 50-plus years he spent in Chicago, mostly at newspapers owned by Hearst. One of his stops landed him at Hearst's *New York Journal*, starting in late 1922. About a year later, his services were needed at Hearst's *Herald-Examiner* in Chicago, so he departed.[19] There was no tragedy, no mistake, no being run out of town—just a chance to head to what would become his home. In Chicago, as sports editor of the *Herald-Examiner* for the next 40 years, he was known for dubbing Red Grange "the Galloping Ghost" and for his friendship with Knute Rockne. Brown had dinner with Rockne the night before his plane crash and later wrote his biography.

On the day of Frick's move from the *American* to the *Journal*, he was writing about a Giants rainout when an office boy summoned him to Brisbane's office. The managing editor informed him of the switch and sent him to Atlantic City to write about Luis Firpo's preparations for his fight with Jack Dempsey. Frick recalled the exchange with his boss:

> I started to walk away and he said, "Where are you going?"
> "I'm going back to the *American* to finish my story."
> "To hell with the *American*. You're working on the *Journal*."
> I never did go back. As far as I'm concerned that rainy day story, on the Giants, is still in the typewriter.[20]

Frick's new typewriter would soon be churning out copy under his own byline and under Ruth's, thanks to Christy Walsh. After his arrival in 1919, Ruth had established himself as a sports phenomenon in New York City, but he had not learned to take advantage of his own celebrity, whether in the newspaper pages or in his own bank account. Enter Walsh, a sports cartoonist turned agent. Walsh had gotten into syndicating ghost-written columns by celebrities in 1919, when World War I hero Eddie Rickenbacker accepted his offer to "write" about the Indy 500. Walsh marketed the idea to newspapers and wired the results; Rickenbacker read over his draft and made a lot of corrections. The experience convinced Walsh that his smartest strategy would be managing such projects rather than writing them.[21]

In 1921, Walsh succeeded in getting Ruth to sign on as a syndication client. He showed an agent's chutzpah in getting Ruth's attention—volunteering to deliver beer to Ruth's apartment when the delivery boy failed to show. But as their professional relationship developed, he became a valued adviser, convincing Ruth to control his spending and invest during his prime earning years, so that even as his salary decreased during the Depression, Ruth never lacked money.

3. *The Babe Ruth Problem*

Walsh's stable of sports personalities was impressive. Besides Ruth, Gehrig, and Huggins, it included virtually every well-known baseball player of the 1920s, like Walter Johnson, Rogers Hornsby and even Ty Cobb; and other pennant-winning managers, including Donie Bush of the Pittsburgh Pirates.

Walsh even developed successful business relationships outside of baseball. Like any proud Irish sports fan of the 1920s, he was a Notre Dame fan, which in his case led to close ties with Rockne. When Rockne died in the 1931 plane crash, he was flying to Los Angeles to sign a $50,000 movie contract that Walsh had arranged.[22]

The two main sports writers hired to help Ruth were Frick and Slocum. Under Walsh's strategy, Ruth earned $5,000-$7,000 annually from newspapers syndicating his articles.[23] (By comparison, Tilden earned about $25,000 annually from his writing in the mid–1920s, though he was both more committed and equipped for the task.) Walsh himself estimated that he paid Frick $10,000 during his working relationship with Ruth.[24]

Slocum, however, was Ruth's favorite. "Bill writes more like I do than anyone I know," Babe was quoted as saying[25] (which no doubt earned Slocum some ribbing from his colleagues). Slocum was a sports writer and editor for Hearst in New York City until 1937, when he moved into a public relations position with General Mills. There he helped the cereal maker, which had already started its tradition of featuring athletes on Wheaties cereal boxes, continue to enhance its profile in the sports world.[26] His son, Frank, worked for Frick for almost his entire term as baseball commissioner. The New York chapter of the Baseball Writers' Association of America established the Bill Slocum Award in 1930 to recognize long and meritorious service to baseball. Ruth received the award in 1931, Frick in 1949.

Slocum's and Frick's long and meritorious service to Ruth was no secret either. Thus it was no huge scoop when Frick candidly told sports writer Jerome Holtzman, in a book that came out soon after Frick's memoirs:

> I was Babe Ruth's ghostwriter from 1924 until I stopped working [1934]. I think we wrote a schedule of three stories a week. I know we did more than one. Lots of times I would talk to him, but there were times when I'd pick up a story and didn't talk to him. But I lived with the old guy, really. Babe was always around and I was traveling with the ball club, and so there was no excuse not to contact him. I always believed he felt that these stories were important. But he never showed much.[27]

Frick was correct. Sadly, for all of his devoted attention and hard work for Ruth, Frick was not as appreciated by Ruth as Slocum was. An anecdote from Lieb also confirmed Frick's observation about Ruth's level of appreciation. He recalled a train trip, at least three years after Frick started ghostwriting for Ruth, when Ruth called out to him, "What's the name of that guy that writes for me? It rhymes with 'quick,' 'thick,' 'Dick.'" After Lieb reminded him, Ruth said, "That's it. I should have remembered it."[28]

Walsh was equally unappreciative of Frick. In a self-published retrospective of his ghostwriting industry, he omitted Frick from his list of his ten best ghost writers.[29] But Frick loyally soldiered on, helping Ruth earn thousands of dollars every year. Thanks to Walsh's management and his writers' work, Ruth "covered" every World Series from 1921 to 1936.[30]

Frick did much to extend the legend of Ruth and his fellow "Murderers' Row." As the 1927 World Series opened, Frick described a pre–Series workout where the Pirates, having finished their batting practice, stuck around to watch Ruth and the Yankees. The display of home run power left the Pirates stunned and was so intimidating that they ended up losing the Series in four straight games, the first National League team thusly swept.

At the Pirates' next World Series appearance—33 years later and against the Yankees again, Pie Traynor, third baseman for the 1927 team, said, "It's high time that story was debunked. It's just not true." He claimed the Pirates went immediately to a team meeting after batting practice. Frick replied, "Of course it happened. I remember as if it happened yesterday." He doubted such a ploy would be effective in 1960. "As a baseball writer in 1927, I thought it meant something. In 1960, as the commissioner, I cannot subscribe to such a theory."[31]

That close relationship with Ruth had its advantages for Frick as well, saving him from embarrassment at 1930 spring training. Ruth was suffering through an unpleasant contract negotiation with the Yankees that year. Frick and Daniel convinced him that it would be in his best interest to sign his new contract. Ruth initially agreed, but as usual changed his mind and told Frick, so he held off on running a story that would be disproven the next day. Daniel, however, didn't know, and his story hit the *New York Telegram*. He employed a different strategy to save his scoop. In a panic, Daniel convinced Ruth that it would be wise to accept the Yankees' offer, particularly given the rough economic times—a unique (and unethical) way to avoid looking foolish.[32]

Frick's relationship with Ruth also gave him stories that might not have made his column, but were great to share off the page. He recalled one formal dinner where Ruth, picking at an asparagus salad with the correct fork, finally pushed it away. In response to the host's concern that Ruth didn't like the food, Ruth replied, elegantly and courteously, "Oh, it's not that. It's just that asparagus makes my urine smell."[33]

Writing for a disinterested athlete could be challenging. In 1927, as Ruth was chasing his own home run record, Frick was ghostwriting his daily columns about it. Frick was forced to miss an opening game on a road trip. "Here's what I'd like you to do, Babe," Frick recalled telling him. "As soon as the game is over, write out all the details and telegraph them to me at the office. Then I'll dress it up and stretch it out." The wire came with this information: "Hit another. Babe."[34]

On another occasion, according to columnist Bob Wolf of the *Milwaukee Journal*, it almost caused a different set of problems. Frick predicted on Ruth's behalf that the Philadelphia Athletics would win the 1929 World Series. The problem was that Ruth actually favored the Chicago Cubs. To Frick's relief, and Ruth's unearned credit, the Athletics won the Series.[35]

Such situations—the ghostwriters pushing out copy without talking to the "author"—occurred frequently, with Walsh's endorsement. To him, it was much worse (and less profitable) to disappoint a newspaper sports editor who was expecting an article, not to mention the sports-crazed readers/fans who loved to see such expert pieces. As for the deception involved, Walsh waved it away: "No one has been deceived, no harm has been done, the dear public gets its accustomed article and the boss is none the wiser but nevertheless, that is ghostwriting. Such fraternal cooperation among newspaper men is not often required but it does happen."[36]

A good example of a column Ruth "wrote" with Frick's involvement was a March 1933 preview that speculated on the prospects for the Philadelphia A's outfield that season. The level of reporting alone seems beyond Ruth's practical capabilities, and the article reflects the clichés that marked Jazz Age sports writing: ("it will cut quite a figure"; "report now has it that the new group will sparkle also"). But it would require an extreme suspension of disbelief to imagine that Ruth would take the time during spring training to review the previous season, get information on the upcoming season, and organize his analysis into a coherent article.[37]

But sometimes, a column could not be written without Ruth's input, and the result was pretty good. That same month in 1933, the *Journal* published Ruth writing candidly about signing his contract for that year after a brief holdout. Ruth even mentioned specific contract numbers. He ultimately accepted the Yankees' offer of $52,000, a cut of $23,000 from the previous year. The column definitely provided readers with inside insights that they could not get anywhere else—Ruth's claim that the holdout was not prearranged, the parade of intermediate contract offers, and his insistence that retirement was never an option.[38] This, however, was the exception to the typical article.

Frick was also acknowledged as the ghostwriter of *Babe Ruth's Own Book of Baseball*, in the introduction to a later edition of the book. Ruth supplied the anecdotes; Frick supplied the writing. Thus, the book reads more like it was written by an over-the-top Jazz Age sportswriter than an athlete. But Frick is not listed anywhere in the book as the co-author. As Holtzman, who wrote the introduction, noted, "No coauthor is listed, only a notation: 'By arrangement with Christy Walsh.' Walsh, who had been a sportswriter, was among the pioneer player-agents and employed a stable of ghostwriters." Frick did not deny his involvement and even presented his personal copy of the book, the first one off the press, to the Baseball Hall of Fame library in 1968. It was signed by Ruth, Huggins, and Yankees owner Jacob Ruppert.[39]

To Holtzman, that was sufficient evidence that Walsh retained Frick's services to ghostwrite the book for Ruth. Holtzman even speculated that Frick had to do most of the writing himself, given Ruth's other demands. Holtzman pointed out one section of the book in which the language is undeniably Frick's, where "Ruth" responds to those who would dismiss major league baseball players as nothing more than ditch diggers who happened onto a more profitable pursuit: "You know, if Galli-Curci couldn't sing she might be doing hard tasks in her native land; if Booth Tarkington couldn't write books, he might be an Indiana farmer or if Arthur Brisbane couldn't write editorials he might be a subway guard." The sentence reflects Frick's love of opera, his Indiana roots, and a desire to tweak his boss more than anything related to Ruth.[40]

As author Louis Rubin pointed out, Ruth would have been lost without Frick's help.

> For from all accounts Ruth had little gift for recall and none whatever for reflection. He lived almost totally in the present, was largely unconcerned for anything but his own personal doings, took almost no interest in the lives and activities of his teammates except as affecting him, and was without awareness of or curiosity about the complexities of personality. The retelling of amusing anecdotes, the accumulation of colorful diamond lore—such was not his forte. For the most part he couldn't even remember the names of most of those who played with and against him; habitually he addressed each and all as "kid."[41]

Beyond his ghostwriting for Ruth, however, Frick served as a promoter for the Babe, whether in his *New York Journal* columns or in other publications. In 1931, Richfield Oil Company, which sponsored Frick's program on WOR radio, published a small paperback of sports records, written by Frick. Among the many sports listed in the book, three pages were devoted to baseball. Frick devoted one of the three pages to Ruth exclusively, including mention of his pitching talents ("one of the greatest left-handers of all time") and worshipful exclamations like "Quite a boy, that Ruth—quite a boy!"[42]

It is not surprising that decades later, Frick would devote an entire chapter in his memoirs to Ruth. Such was the man-crush that in the chapter, Frick credited Ruth for the restoration of baseball's popularity in the public eye following the Black Sox scandal of 1919, though he also cites the hiring of federal judge Kenesaw Mountain Landis as the first baseball commissioner. Landis might have banned the offending players, set high standards for ethical behavior and basically enabled baseball to evolve into a major cultural force. But to Frick, Ruth's home runs—no accompanying mention of the end of the so-called "deadball era"—brought the fans back. Whether such hyperbolic praise was wise in his memoirs, given the Maris controversy, is another question.

Such Ruth-loving language was a reflection of his newspaper days. For his column on the inaugural All-Star Game in 1933, it is telling that Frick did not travel to Chicago to cover the game, but listened to it on the radio. After pedestrian game analysis ("Great pitching, great hitting, great fielding"), he launched into praise for Ruth: "What a man is Babe Ruth! What a man! There'll never be another like him." Ironically, the column never mentioned that Ruth hit a home run, an All-Star Game first and a feat that supported the hype. Instead he concluded, "Aside from Ruth there was no hero—or perhaps I should say heroes of a lesser stature."[43]

In discussing Ruth's often controversial public actions, Frick said, "Ruth recognized the difference between right and wrong. What he did not recognize, or could not accept, was the right of society to tell him what he should do, or not do."[44] Such words don't sound like the "hot takes" about athletes today, but the sports media world of the 1920s was quite different. Sports writers of the 1920s showed much more deference toward their male subjects and would conspire in the hiding of bad behavior off the field. A superstar's antics today would fuel a journalistic competition by sportswriters armed with blogs, Twitter, and Instagram. Back then, journalists competed for the superstars' favor, and their confidentiality was one strategy.

Sports writers might have overlooked the Babe's "peccadilloes" (Frick's term) during his career, but Frick was more candid, though still forgiving, in his memoirs years later. "Every day was a new challenge, every night a promise of a new adventure. Yet, somehow, there never seemed to be anything vicious or sordid," he wrote.⁴⁵ Such a statement would be horrifying today, particularly to women. To him, however, Ruth's conquests were as much a part of his legend as the stories of charity toward kids, and only slightly more worrisome.

Writing for Ruth and traveling with the Yankees had other benefits for a beat writer. Yankees traveling secretary Mark Roth often helped sports writers with travel arrangements (another ethical quagmire)—even providing Frick with a train ticket from Chicago to Greencastle, Indiana, for his 15-year class reunion at DePauw University in 1930. On the trip, Frick noticed a level of service and deference that he was not accustomed to. It was only after he arrived in Greencastle that he realized why. Roth had put Tony Lazzeri's name on the envelope, so everyone from the conductor to the porter thought they were helping the Yankees second baseman.⁴⁶

The benefits extended to Frick's family. His grandson, Ford Frick II, said his father, Frederick, would leave school for weeks at a time to travel with his parents to Florida for spring training, in both Frick's journalism and his baseball administration days. During one such trip, Lou Gehrig taught him to roller skate. Kelly Frick Richards said her father recalled that Gehrig, being both childless and of a less raucous character, was sympathetic to Frederick's plight, being away from his friends at home, and enjoyed spending time with him more than the usual spring training shenanigans.⁴⁷

Of course, Ford Frick was about more than Babe Ruth. In both Colorado and New York, he applied his speedy writing to a variety of topics, trying to find the niche that would take him to the next level. The clips he saved of those writings often eliminate the folio, so it's difficult to tell where he wrote them, even in context. He penned humorous observations from an individual, Cale Pottle, modeled after Finley Peter Dunne's popular "Mr. Dooley" character of the turn of the twentieth century. Like Dooley, Pottle provided homespun takes, phrased in a vernacular that is hard to identify in Pottle's case. "Guys that is ambitious to do things, and really feel th' need for workn' ought to know better than to get elected to office anyhow," he said of a Congressman.

He also flexed his fiction muscles in writing a couple of magazine articles that reflected the same approach popularized by Runyon and Lardner. He created a fictional baseball player undone by love, Lefty "Mail Order" Morse, for a short story in *Liberty* magazine.⁴⁸ He also wrote a lively short story of a jockey facing a decision of whether to throw a horse race for *Red Blooded Stories*, a classic example of cheaply priced pulp fiction (the non–Tarantino kind) that later changed its named to *Tales of Daring and Danger.*[49]

The former English teacher even had a love for writing poetry that cannot be dismissed as an attempt to imitate Rice. His papers included a collection of poems, "Land O' Dreams." He wrote free verse poems for the *Journal* under the heading, "Baseball Anthology." His poem about Landis concludes, "I have to smile/At the serious fans who greet me/As the saviour of baseball./For after all/The real saviour is not I/But the dirty-faced kids/Playing on corner-lots/Or choosing sides/In a cow pasture./And so I go my way/And laugh up my sleeve/And thank God/For a sense of humor."[50]

It was particularly gratifying for Frick when, at a Dodger Stadium party given by baseball writers to honor him upon his retirement, Bob Addie of the *Washington Post* recited a poem that Frick complimented. Addie told Frick, "You should like it. I lived in New York as a boy and memorized the poem. It was one you wrote long ago."[51]

He also tried to keep his writing muscles flexed early in his time as National League president, though he wrote mostly about baseball. Besides his annual pre-season previews for the Associated Press, he wrote about umpires for the *Saturday Evening Post,*[52] previewed the 1935 season for *Liberty* magazine,[53] and encouraged young boys to play and follow baseball in *All-America Sports Magazine,*[54] a popular pulp youth periodical of the 1930s.

As the 1920s closed, Frick diversified in medium if not topic. Hearst purchased a radio station, WINS, for his Independent News Service and had one of his writers broadcast a daily sports wrap-up. In July 1930, Frick was a last-minute substitute for the regular announcer. As Frick tells the story, "I was sitting around the office one morning and the managing editor came in to find a substitute for the regular news broadcaster, who was sick. He saw me and pointed a finger, saying, 'You're it.'"[55] Frick did the broadcast, then immediately left on a road trip with the Yankees.

According to the *Brooklyn Eagle,* "On his return to New York, he found gentlemen knocking each other out of the way to hand him radio contracts. It seemed that he had a clear, distinctive voice and he knew his sports."[56] Only two months later, NBC was pairing Frick with Graham McNamee, radio's first great sports broadcaster, to announce the World Series on its nationwide hookup.[57] Eventually, Frick would also provide a daily 15-minute evening sports wrap-up to radio station WOR, a more successful station that granted him a wider audience.

Broadcasting for WOR, Frick was also part of the first regular-season baseball game broadcast in New York. The administrators for the city's three major league teams were slower to embrace the new medium than their peers. Like Landis, they feared that radio broadcasts would discourage fans from attending games. As a result, even though the World Series was annually broadcast, it was not until 1931 that the first regular-season game involving a New York team was broadcast on radio. Ironically, it was for the Brooklyn Dodgers, not Frick's beloved Yankees. He was one of four radio station broadcasters covering the game. ("Exclusive rights" was a later concept.) He also called a crucial season-ending series against the Cardinals, by which point the teams were convinced of the wisdom of broadcasting not only the World Series, but also important games, though it took years for them to allow all games to be broadcast.[58]

When Frick and McNamee called the 1931 World Series, he recalled years later, the facilities presented a challenge. The broadcasters sat in the press box with the newspaper folks, which risked a "Hello, dear!" shout-out into a microphone or a hat thief who knew he could not be pursued. The engineers sat one row in front.[59]

Among Frick's radio fans was the noted entertainer George M. Cohan, an ardent baseball fan who even wrote columns for the *Chicago Tribune* during the 1924 World Series.[60] "Baseball on the air I can enjoy if the announcer is good because I can dramatize the game in my mind.... I think Ford Frick does a splendid job. In fact, the majority of announcers are very good; they have no easy job to put over a prepared script and still imbue it with their own personalities."[61]

His schedule over those four years was brutal. He wrote and read a news broadcast at noon and a sports news broadcast at 6 p.m., then did a sports show at 7 p.m.[62] He did not speak off the top of his head, but worked from a script that he prepared. In between, he wrote his *Journal* column. Add to that the occasional game broadcasting for WOR, and it's clear that while broadcasting provided Frick with a nice second income, he definitely earned it.

One of Frick's radio commentary scripts, from 1932, gives his philosophy of sports and its heroes, and his words reflect his philosophy of life in general. He wrote:

> This is an age of cynicism. We have too many detectives and far too few philosophers—too many Pharisees and too few good Samaritans.
> I believe in sports heroes. I believe there is a real place for such heroes in the lives of all of us.
> I believe in the fundamental honesty of sport.... Perhaps I'm wrong, but to me the harping critic who cannot see beyond the feet of clay to glory in the sparkle of an occasional halo ... is the poorest sportsman of all.[63]

His sentimentality apparently won over even the hardened inmates of Sing Sing Prison, in Ossining, New York. He visited the prison in October 1933 and talked about his impressions of the men there on the radio. A letter from Warden Lewis Lawes, one of the few Frick kept, said, "They appreciate the kind interest you have taken in them and in telling the world that they are at least human regardless of their failures."[64] A second letter from the warden, in December, accompanied the gift of a football from a game in which the Sing Sing prisoners played a semi-pro team from New York, the Kingston Yellow Jackets. "We sincerely appreciate your sympathetic understanding of the benefits of football to the men confined here and the 'boys' want you to have the ball as an expression of their gratitude," he wrote.[65]

The *Journal* capitalized on Frick's radio popularity. Not only was his daily newspaper column titled "Ford Frick's Broadcast," but the column mug shot also showed him behind a microphone. Frick was not a big fan of his own writing, particularly his column later in his newspaper days. In his memoirs, he wrote of them, "[It] was a lousy column because I didn't get around too much. It was a very demanding schedule."[66] His appraisal, sadly, is accurate, and the writing meshes well with the reporting. Each column started with the same phrase, "Howdy, folks!" and ended with "Adios," probably adapted from his broadcast. In between, Frick used the same clichés that pervaded journalism in that era. As he implied, fans gained little new inside information.

For his part Frick, in his own memoirs, discussed the advent of radio in great detail, but he did not mention his own experience. The omission is a shame, because Frick was one of radio's most popular personalities in the medium's early days. Such were Frick's radio talents that he even served as emcee for famed conductor

Toward the end of his sports journalism career, Frick became a popular sports radio personality in New York City (courtesy Ford Frick II).

Andre Kostelanetz's radio program, which was broadcast on CBS and sponsored by Chesterfield cigarettes. The program was one of the first to bring classical music to the masses over the radio. Frick admitted, "I know nothing about music. I can't even keep time." But for the program's first year, as announcer, he earned $100 per program, until he became president of the National League.[67]

The gig did create in Frick a lifelong love of opera. He and his wife, along with four neighbors, owned a box at the Metropolitan Opera House. "I like opera from the standpoint of a student," he said years later. "I read up on it. There is always a libretto in our box." Frick reported that when they did their opera nights, "we go in class—white tie and tails."[68]

One benefit of his radio work is that it gave him a much higher profile in New York City than his work as a journalist provided. Thus, broadcasting, more than print, set him on the path to baseball administration and made him a more attractive candidate—particularly with his voice—for a career that would involve broadcasting appearances as well as print coverage.

That career began with a brief tenure in public relations. By 1934, the Great Depression had forced baseball owners to take steps in addressing the new economic realities. Previously, the game's very existence—with its dramatic narratives and characters—was enough to pack in the fans, particularly during the 1920s. But then came the effects of the Depression: high unemployment and a shrinking economy. The disastrous conditions forced greater competition for Americans' dollars, and even baseball owners realized they needed to invest in promotion to keep the sport from being displaced in the public consciousness, particularly as other sports (pro football, for example) emerged to provide competition.

The effort had started in 1922. Responding to the sports mania of the Jazz Age, the National League had established a "Service Bureau" to handle the increasing flood of media requests. Media representatives like John Spink of *The Sporting News* had lobbied that the newly created office of baseball commissioner handle press relations, but it was left to the leagues to develop their own strategies.[69] Cullen Cain, a baseball writer for the *Philadelphia Public Ledger*, convinced National League President John Heydler to set up a public relations effort, and Cain would direct the Service Bureau for 11 years before returning to newspaper work. As the economic crisis deepened, the Service Bureau served an important function. It expanded its mission from media relations to public relations and became as important a strategy to baseball as public relations had become to industry.

3. The Babe Ruth Problem

In February of 1934, Frick was summoned by future Hall of Fame manager John McGraw (part-owner of the New York Giants) to the National League meeting at the Waldorf Astoria in New York City. Cain had announced his departure, and Frick was offered $10,000 a year to replace him as head of the National League's Service Bureau. As part of his deal, he could maintain his radio work.

Why Frick? Frick had covered the National League Giants and Dodgers during his years with the *American* and *Journal*, so he had the baseball knowledge and newspaper background. Frick himself speculated that McGraw was behind the offer. The previous year, Frick had encouraged fans to write the Giants and thank them for allowing the games to be broadcast. It must have gotten enough of a response to impress McGraw, who had also recommended Frick as a broadcaster for Giants games.[70] Perhaps Frick had tired of the newspaper grind or had lost the drive to write the output expected. The concession to continue his lucrative broadcasting career was an attractive perk. So Frick accepted the offer.

Joe Vila of *The Sporting News* praised the selection in his column. "'Ford ... is well qualified for the post by reason of his background, his energy and his personality. The league long has needed somebody who could match the efforts of Henry Edwards on behalf of the American League and in Frick it has got him."[71] *The Sporting News* article that announced the appointment was more roast than reporting, claiming that Frick "according to local tradition, 'began to talk at the age of three weeks and three days.' ... In fact, as he grew up, Frick talked more and more and now there is no way of stopping him."[72]

By the time Frick took office, the Service Bureau had grown into a media relations machine, sending information to newspapers and dramatizations to radio stations. His combination of baseball knowledge, newspaper experience, and promotional abilities made him the best candidate to continue, and even expand, the work.

In his brief tenure as director of the National League Service Bureau, Frick was also credited with producing the first *Green Book*, which still is published online today. The book is a favorite of sabermetricians, providing career stats, rosters, and records. (The American League counterpart is called the *Red Book*.)[73]

He would not be in the position for even a year, but not because of poor job performance. In fact, by moving from journalism to organized baseball, Frick was preparing himself for the opportunity to make an even sharper move upward, into the top echelon of baseball administration, before he reached his 40th birthday.

4.

A New NL President

John Arnold Heydler had already forged his place in baseball history. He is credited with creating the earned run average statistic in 1912, while secretary of the National League. Years before, while a junior clerk on an errand for the Government Printing Office, Heydler supposedly recited "Casey at the Bat" to a private party hosted by President Grover Cleveland, and ended up with a congratulatory note to prove it.[1]

By 1934, Heydler, 65, had been National League president for a total of eighteen years. From the GPO, where he was a linotype operator, Heydler had originally gone to work for the National League in 1895 to set up the official statistical averages.[2] A difficult situation—the suicide of predecessor Harry Pulliam in 1909—had elevated him to the interim presidency. In 1918, Heydler was promoted to the position permanently, having served as secretary-treasurer for 11 years. In the interim, former National League umpire Thomas J. Lynch and former Pennsylvania Governor John K. Tener had served terms at the head of the league.

Heydler, however, would face his own struggle, with health issues that forced him to announce his retirement on November 2, 1934, to take effect at the baseball winter meetings on December 11. The announcement shocked league owners, who asked Heydler if he would accept an indefinite leave of absence instead, of sufficient length to regain his health. But he resisted the offer; it was reported that Heydler was in tears as he begged the owners to accept his resignation.[3] League owners, in appreciation, created for Heydler the honorary lifetime title of National League chairman of the board (which he would hold until his death in 1956, 22 years later).

So speculation turned to possible successors. Names tossed around included Judge Emil Fuchs, president of the Boston Braves, which was a surprising rumor, given the chronic financial problems of his mismanaged franchise. Perhaps his colleagues thought the Boston team, and thus the league, would be safer with him in the league office. Other reported candidates were James J. Tierney, secretary of the New York Yankees; Judge William G. Branham, president of the National Association of Professional Baseball Clubs (which supervised the minor leagues); and Branch Rickey, vice president of the St. Louis Cardinals.

The name that emerged as the favorite, however, with Heydler's endorsement, was Ford Frick. After only nine months in the league office as head of the Service Bureau, Frick was promoted to one of the top positions in organized baseball. The vote was unanimous; no other candidates were considered.[4] Frick would be the ninth president since the league's establishment in 1876—and at age 39, its second youngest president ever. The owners also created a separate position of secretary-treasurer (Heydler had occupied all three titles) and named Harvey Traband, Heydler's personal secretary, to the job. *The Sporting News*, in fact, speculated that Heydler, recognizing his looming health issues, might have been grooming both candidates for the position by naming Frick to the public relations post and turning over many of his duties to Traband even before his formal appointment.[5]

If sportswriters were hoping for the intrigue and drama that often accompanies such shifts in power, they would be disappointed. According to columnist John Kieran of the *Times*, the decision was made so quickly that by the time sports writers were let in, the owners were clearing out. "It was explained that Mr. Crosley [owner of the Cincinnati Reds] who has his own private fleet of airplanes, was flying back to Cincinnati and had left in a hurry. Apparently he flew right out the window."[6]

While it might seem unusual, and even a little dangerous, to put a sportswriter in charge of anything, it was not a first. As a 1948 *Sporting News* article pointed out, Ban Johnson, who served as president of the American League from 1901–1926, began as a baseball writer for the *Cincinnati Gazette*; his successor, Ernest Barnard, was sports editor of the *Columbus Dispatch*. The article noted other former sportswriters and editors sprinkled throughout major and minor league baseball administration.[7]

Frick gladly accepted the new position, even if he actually had to take a pay cut. He had continued his broadcasting commitments, even doing a daily sports wrap-up, while directing the league's public relations efforts: The *New York Times* daily radio program guide through the first nine months of 1934 shows him doing his 15-minute sports broadcast at 7 p.m.—a quarter-hour after the program, "Babe Ruth's Club." Frick actually did his 7 p.m. broadcast from his National League office.[8]

But when he ascended to the National League presidency, he agreed to step back from all other distractions. He told a *Sporting News* interviewer that he would have to give up three commercial contracts—with

Dodge Motor Company, the Mennen Company, and Liggett & Myers Tobacco Company—because of his new job.[9] As a result, his salary as president, estimated at somewhere between $18,000 and $25,000, was less than he had been making.[10]

Though losing income, Frick gained in other areas. As his friend Dan Daniel pointed out, "For one thing, Ford will now be able to have his dinner at home, in the family circle at Bronxville, N.Y. Because of his radio work, he hasn't had a dinner with his family more than once a week in the last three years."[11] So regular did Frick's routine become that one office mate said he was knew when it was 4:35 p.m., because at that precise moment Frick would head out the door to catch the 5:06 train from Grand Central Station.[12]

Daniel would play a key role in Frick's career. They were close friends within the New York sports writing fraternity, and when Frick moved into the National League presidency, Daniel became his most trusted media contact. When a decision needed explaining, or a proposal needed floating, Frick would turn to Daniel and get a report that was accurate and fair, though often positive and supportive.

Daniel had the sports writing career Frick might have had if the National League had not enticed him away, and he might even have envied Daniel for his longevity. The dean of American baseball writers of his time, he started covering New York baseball in 1910 and did not stop until the 1960s, mainly for the *New York World Telegram* and *World Telegram-Sun*. He also was a correspondent for *The Sporting News* and estimated that between his daily newspaper articles and columns and his three *Sporting News* articles, he wrote 5,000 words a week for several years.[13] As a result, during Frick's terms as league president and MLB commissioner, many felt that Daniel, not Frick, was the voice of baseball.[14]

Frick also found time for charitable

Frick had not yet reached his 40th birthday when he was named president of the National League, the start of a 31-year career in baseball leadership (National Baseball Hall of Fame Library, Cooperstown, New York).

work in Bronxville. Annually, he served as master of ceremonies for a "Night of Sports" event that raised money for such charities as the Bronxville League for Service, the Boy Scouts and the Girl Scouts. In 1935, World War I aviation ace Eddie Rickenbacker was among the celebrities appearing, film comedian Joe E. Brown among the performers, with baseball players Dizzy and Daffy Dean along for entertainment as well. In 1936, Bob Hope served as a co-emcee.[15]

Frick's position at the NL Service Bureau was filled by Dr. William E. Brandt, a practicing osteopathic physician who wrote for several New York newspapers before replacing Frick. He remained in the position for ten years before resigning to pursue a radio career. He later stepped aside from sports and returned to his original vocation, as president of the Philadelphia College of Osteopathy from 1953 through 1958.

Having just ascended into his new job, and less than a year away from the press box, Frick insisted that he would "remain one of the boys" and not distance himself from his newspaper cronies. He frequently wrote preseason columns (emphasis on diplomacy) for the Associated Press and newspapers.[16] Frick's favorite venue for watching games, particularly in New York City, was not a field box but the press box, where his presence was duly reported. Unlike the front office folks and even the players, who were more careful in their relations with the beat writers, Frick considered those friendships important enough to maintain, even if he could not deepen them. In fact, while waiting to hear whether he would be named league president, Frick waited outside the owners' meeting with the sportswriters, talking baseball.[17]

Frick would employ several strategies to stay in good with sports writers. Annually during spring training, he would host a dinner for club officials and media members—an on-the-record event that included no speeches, only food and networking. The event was men only, however. The wives held a separate event at another restaurant. There is no record of Frick's wife, Eleanor, hosting the event, though she annually joined him in Florida. The 1949 event was hosted by the wife of Gabe Paul, then assistant general manager for the Reds.[18]

Thus, it is not surprising that Frick's friends in the sports media praised the decision. Daniel predicted a strong, authoritative leadership style—although his forecast concerning owner relations would not be proven over time: "Frick is an ambitious, able man and the National League is going to see things done—unless the owners step on his toes. And if this happens, Ford is the sort of young man who, after handling the job for a year, might reach for his hat and tell the owners to get somebody else to run their old league."[19] *The Sporting News*' editorial on the selection was more measured, saying Frick "possesses the poise, education, training and public-consciousness to fit him eminently for the task ahead of him."[20]

The honeymoon continued at a dinner in Frick's honor held by the BBWAA. The dinner featured Commissioner Kenesaw Mountain Landis teaching Frick the basics of "addressing newspaper men" and Brooklyn manager Casey Stengel offering to let Frick know who the bad umpires were. "Or perhaps it would be better to name the good ones," Stengel quipped. "That wouldn't take so long."[21] Stengel offered to help Frick recruit new umpires and announced that he had six good prospects in mind. Five were Stengel's cousins and the sixth was his uncle.[22]

Frick's background in sports writing and radio would help him deal with Heydler's well-intentioned but poorly designed efforts to maintain fan interest during the Depression. Going into the 1933 season, Heydler had released a statement to NL players, exhorting them to a level of aggressive, competitive play that would keep the fans coming back, despite "stringent money conditions." He required "action and hustle," even during blowouts, as well as enthusiasm, cheerfulness, and alert engagement in the game. Heydler also banned interaction between opponents, whether on the field or in the clubhouse before or after the game. Of course, he knew better than to extend the ban to off-the-field socializing.[23]

An earlier strategy did not work out as well. Heydler actually banned player-fan contact in 1931, after seeing a photo of Gabby Hartnett of the Chicago Cubs signing an autograph for Al Capone's son. Yes, Dad was in the photo, along with his menacing security entourage. Still, Heydler's reactive rule caused outrage. John Kieran complained that the rule alienated both younger and older fans and claimed that one player was even fined $10 for greeting a family member who had traveled a great distance to see him. Heydler was forced to rescind it within a few months.[24]

Frick, by contrast, had an intuition for public relations that marked his early years in the position. To him, promotion of any kind was legitimate if it could make more people aware of the game, potentially creating more fans (though he insisted that any promotion not distract from the game itself). Having moved so quickly from a public relations position to the league presidency, he maintained his interest in seeing baseball promoted on the sports pages he had written for.

Frick also expanded the league's public relations efforts, insisting that individual teams adopt the service bureau concept and set up "Information Departments" of their own. His objective was to supply local sports journalists with baseball-friendly items and keep smaller rural newspapers stocked with stories that would heighten reader interest in radio broadcasts.[25] Earlier, such efforts would be centralized through the league office. But Frick was savvy enough to realize that the effort was best assigned to the local teams.

The emphasis on public relations was derided by cynics of the era as "ballyhoo" (Jazz Age for "hype"). One writer absolved Frick of the excesses committed by other promoters, even while acknowledging his efforts to improve league promotional strategies: "Mr. Frick is not in sympathy with out-and-out circus methods; he believes that honest baseball will do the trick." Written by Gerald Holland, who later helped to start *Sports Illustrated*, the article criticized the over-the-top marketing techniques prevalent in the minor leagues—including an appearance by exotic fan dancer Sally Rand.[26]

One of Frick's ideas was a National League 60th anniversary celebration for 1936, even though the league had ignored its golden anniversary ten years before. The celebration included eight "birthday parties" at league games, starting with the two surviving original franchises, the Chicago Cubs and the Boston Braves. The *New York Times* reported, "The leading feature of the celebration will be the reconstruction of a typical baseball scene of the '70s, with costumes, playing rules and background details to fit the picture,"[27] though it stopped short of the throwback uniforms so popular today. At the Boston event, Frick and the players rode to the park in open carriages, much as they did in 1876. The guest of honor was George Wright, 89, who played shortstop for Boston's National Association team in 1871 and the 1876 Boston team in the NL.[28]

As Frick moved past the pageantry and took on the responsibilities of his position, he had a competent tutor in Landis. In Frick's memoirs, he strived to give a balanced picture of his boss. "He was intolerant of opposition, suspicious of reform and reformers, and skeptical of compromise," Frick said of the commissioner, whom he would butt heads with over the next ten years. "Yet with it all, he was a kindly man, with a sense of sympathy and compassion that bubbled to the surface at the most unexpected times and places."[29]

Early on, Landis had advised Frick, "Never go looking for trouble. Let 'em come to you. And don't start bothering me with your own league problems. They're your babies. I've got problems of my own."[30] And Frick had his problems. In 1934, it was agreed that while the National League might have been the "senior circuit," it had been surpassed in prestige and financial stability by the American League. The struggles of the Boston Braves, guided from crisis to crisis by Judge Fuchs, reflected the malaise that Frick would have to address. The franchises in Philadelphia and Pittsburgh also required administrative intervention.[31] His acknowledged success in turning around these franchises enhanced his reputation and certainly did not hurt his later candidacy as commissioner.

The problems in Boston, however, would provide Frick's biggest immediate challenge, and it had less to do with baseball and more with dog racing. By 1934, the Braves' situation was desperate, but Fuchs apparently had a plan to solve those problems. Even before Frick was at his desk on the nineteenth floor of the Rockefeller Center Building, it was reported on December 7 that the Braves would seek a license to run dog races at Braves Field. Frick's response was quick and uncompromising: "Baseball cannot mix with dog races and open betting and I am sure that it will never have to stand for that mixture."[32]

Fuchs announced the specifics in January 1935. He would surrender the Braves' long-term lease—to which Fuchs was behind in payments by a reported $11,000[33]—to the Boston Kennel Club, which would stage dog races at Braves Field. The field was owned by the estate of James E. Gaffney, whose construction company built the park during Gaffney's brief tenure (December 1911 through January 1916) as Braves owner.[34] Fuchs' lease ran until 1946, but he was willing to sell the lease to the kennel club.

On January 12, the Boston Kennel Club, Inc., applied for a license to operate a dog track and install the facilities needed for pari-mutuel betting in Braves Park. Frick, reached by phone in Atlantic City, where he was meeting with American League President Will Harridge, responded emphatically: "There will be no dog racing in any of our parks so long as baseball is played there."[35]

But Fuchs saw a loophole and proposed that the Braves lease Fenway Park from the Red Sox for their home games.[36] Thus, he could get around Frick's ban (the Braves would not be *playing* where the dogs were racing, technically) and still draw the income from the dog racing operation. The only catch was that no one besides Fuchs and the Kennel Club supported the idea. Red Sox owner Tom Yawkey was on vacation at his hunting lodge when the plan was announced, but he returned quickly and declared his refusal to approve the lease arrangement, because of the implied endorsement of gambling.[37] If Fuchs thought he could appeal to the commissioner, Landis was just as opposed.[38]

The crisis gave Frick his first opportunity to show decisiveness in dealing with such problems, and he took advantage of it. The "series of yelps which at the moment seems to have tossed the National League into another panic," as John Drebinger described it, forced Frick to call a special meeting of league owners on Friday, January 14. Some claimed the future of the Boston franchise was at stake if the team lacked a place to play.[39]

4. A New NL President 63

The meeting convened at 10 a.m. but did not adjourn until almost midnight. The dog-racing question was answered quickly; the owners unanimously opposed it, including Fuchs. The Braves' financial issues, however, proved more complex. The meeting minutes reflect a clogged process, with Fuchs and minority owner Charles Adams engaged in futile exchange about the Braves' current financial situation. Most of Fuchs' contribution consisted of an impassioned, often irrational defense of his financial decisions to his fellow team owners.[40] After the meeting, Frick declined further comment, deferring to official actions expected at the next league meeting on February 5, although Fuchs hinted that his team would indeed play at Braves Park the coming season.

Although Frick downplayed early rumors that the league would assume the lease from the Braves,[41] that is exactly what was decided in February. The National League signed an 11-year lease with the Gaffney Foundation, and then turned the lease over to the Braves to operate. Fuchs claimed that the arrangement provided the team with the financial breathing space it needed to continue to operate in Boston, at Braves Field, for the coming season.[42]

But Frick and Fuchs had another strategy to turn the Braves' fortunes around. It involved a reunion of sorts for the league president, Boston,

William Harridge, American League president from 1931 to 1959, was Frick's counterpart during his NL presidency, and they met frequently, as in this 1937 meeting to discuss the All-Star Game (Library of Congress).

and Babe Ruth. Although Ruth had expressed a reluctance to return to baseball after the 1934 season, and Yankees owner Colonel Jacob Ruppert was unwilling to send him to another team, Fuchs' Braves signed the aging Ruth to a $25,000 contract for the 1935 season. Frick predicted that Ruth's presence would add 500,000 to overall National League attendance, with the Braves benefiting the most. Frick the promoter also planned receptions at each city for Ruth's first visits. "If it's any inspiration to the Babe to know that he is still the idol of baseball followers he ought to make something of a comeback," Frick raved.[43]

The relationship showed promise. At the 1935 spring training opener, Ruth and the Braves defeated his old team, 3–2, before a crowd of almost 5,000.[44] Ultimately the team won 40 fewer games, and Ruth left the Braves after only three months.[45] Appraising the situation as a league president rather than a ghostwriter, Frick adopted a sympathetic but more objective tone toward his friend. "I would like to see the Babe get a break, but I do not know of any further opportunity for him now," he said. "He failed to take advantage of the chance given him in Boston. If any other club in our league is considering making him an offer, I am not aware of it."[46] As a parting gesture, Frick granted Ruth a lifetime pass to NL baseball games, which Ruth accepted as a "touch of sentiment and appreciation that will never be forgotten."[47] Sadly, no such courtesy was granted by the American League. Outside of "Babe Ruth Day" festivities, if Ruth wanted to watch his Yankees play, he had to buy a ticket.[48]

Three years after the Braves fiasco, Ruth would make his final return to baseball in 1938, signing a $15,000 contract to coach first base for the Brooklyn Dodgers. Many felt that Frick was behind the signing, in part because of his relationship with Ruth and in part because he was instrumental in the Dodgers' hiring of Larry MacPhail. "There's nobody more popular than the Babe in Brooklyn," Frick said, "and don't forget that he knows plenty of baseball. He's a valuable asset for the Dodgers."[49] But he was strictly window dressing: Ruth did not even relay signals to base runners, and despite his own delusions to the contrary, was never considered as a managerial candidate.[50]

Fuchs did not last any longer than Ruth did in Boston. By the end of June, it was apparent that—advantageous lease notwithstanding—the Braves were still in serious financial trouble, and a sale of the team was the only solution. A suitable buyer did not emerge, however, so Fuchs was forced to resign as president in August and turn his ownership stake over to Adams, who would run the club until it could be sold. Adams named long-time manager Bill McKechnie as interim club president.[51]

4. A New NL President

By the end of the 1935 season, however, no viable buyer emerged. Eventually, the situation got so desperate that in November the league had to take over team operations and assume its debts. That arrangement, Frick believed, would allow the greatest likelihood of an uncomplicated purchase—even if it raised the possibility of the previous owners losing their investments.[52]

The club owners' decision soon attracted a bid from Baltimore, which was eager to grab the Braves' franchise and bring it to Charm City. Harry Goldman, an insurance executive there, announced an effort, with the mayor's support, to return major league baseball to the city.[53] (The team had been awarded an American League franchise in 1901, but the franchise had transferred to New York and changed its name to the Yankees.)

The Baltimore bid was unsuccessful, however, as the league owners accepted a bid from Bob Quinn, business manager of the Dodgers and a previous Red Sox owner. Quinn's bid was financed by Adams, who had no interest in baseball beyond its investment potential and would allow Quinn to operate the team. That was fine with Frick; Adams' ties with horse racing, as owner of the Suffolk Downs racetrack, were troubling.[54] The franchise celebrated the new ownership and break from its old problems by changing its name from the Braves to the Bees.[55]

The gambling connection would plague the Bees ownership situation until the team was sold again in 1941. Landis had been prodding Adams for years, telling him that he would eventually have to sell either the Bees or his racetrack interests. (Given the headaches of owning a baseball team, the former was always the more comforting option for Adams.[56]) Even that year, a deal for singer Bing Crosby to become a part-owner was quashed by Landis because of Crosby's ownership interests in race horses and race tracks. Frick indicated that the National League would have turned down the deal had Landis not done so.[57] The Bees were ultimately sold to a syndicate of Boston business leaders in 1941 and eventually changed the team name back to the Braves.[58]

Another strategy to improve team finances was night baseball. At the 1934 winter meetings where Frick was confirmed, National League owners agreed to permit clubs to schedule games at night. The minor leagues had been playing at night since 1931, when a young, ambitious American Association general manager named Larry MacPhail drew 21,000 fans to watch his Columbus Red Birds defeat the St. Paul Saints on the evening of June 17.[59] But the major league owners had consistently voted against the innovation. New York Giants owner Charles A. Stoneham was a vocal opponent. Night baseball was not without its supporters, however; team owners in smaller markets, represented by Powel Crosley of the Reds—who had hired MacPhail as general manager—argued that it was crucial to their success, particularly on poorly attended weekdays.

At the December 1934 meetings, MacPhail presented a spirited promotion of night baseball, noting that in 1932 Columbus had set a minor-league season attendance record, and with a team that finished 10 1/2 games out of first. "Opponents of night baseball in any form have argued that playing under the lights is detrimental to the players," MacPhail said. "It very doubtful if it is any more of a detriment to the player ... than it is to play under a sun of 110 degrees." In the discussion that day, Frick established his leadership style, offering no opinions of his own while explaining the differences between a resolution that would allow clubs to experiment with night baseball and an amendment to the by-laws that would have made the innovation something permanent.[60]

The owners yielded (Stoneham actually abstained) in allowing each team a maximum of seven night games, but stipulated that no team would be forced to play at night and that visiting teams could veto a night game.[61] The American League, however, was consistent in its opposition to night baseball. The St. Louis Browns would be given the option of playing night games in 1937 but would not exercise it.[62] The AL would not play its first night game until 1939.

On Thursday, May 23, 1935, Frick and Harridge arrived in Cincinnati for the inauguration of night baseball. Frick had supported the idea, though not 100 percent. In one pre-season column, he expressed interest in the upcoming experiment, despite the reluctance of some owners. He devoted more space to defending those owners than he did to the teams that would be playing at night. "It should be made clear that the league owners were unanimous in deciding to try the experiment," he wrote. "Three clubs, New York, Brooklyn and Pittsburgh, expressed themselves as unwilling this year to play night games, but they are entirely agreeable to having others try out the idea."[63]

The first night game was a sellout far in advance, which was rare for the Reds, particularly on a weekday. Rain actually postponed the milestone until the next night, but Frick and every other ticket holder returned for Friday night lights. The event was marked by fireworks and by President Franklin Roosevelt turning the lights on from the White House by telegraph key. Landis did not make the trip, so Frick threw out the first ball. The Reds beat the Phillies, 2–1, and most there declared the experiment a success. "It was swell," Frick said. "One game, of course, is no criterion, but the players were not handicapped in any way that I could see and I believe we will have more of it in 1936." Consensus was that the lights did not affect the hitting or fielding. No errors were recorded, but two dropped fly balls to the outfield were apparently scored as hits.[64]

Despite the success of the Cincinnati experiment, other teams were slow to follow the trend, even with Frick's endorsement. The second team to institute night baseball, the Brooklyn Dodgers, would not do so until 1938. The force behind the innovation was again MacPhail, who had left the Reds at the end of the 1936 season. After a brief stint in the banking business, MacPhail was hired by the Dodgers, with Frick's support, to resuscitate the dormant franchise. Night baseball was, of course, his go-to strategy, despite the protests of the other New York franchises, which claimed an informal agreement banning the practice.[65]

From there, it spread much more quickly. In 1939, Philadelphia's Shibe Park (which hosted both the A's and the Phillies), Cleveland's Municipal Stadium, and Chicago's Comiskey Park installed lights. In 1940, St. Louis's Sportsman's Park scheduled night games for the Browns and the Cardinals, as did Pittsburgh's Forbes Field. By 1941, the Washington Senators were also playing at night.[66] Even the stodgy New York Giants instituted night games at the Polo Grounds in 1940.[67] World War II would expand and then stall—through temporary "dim-out" orders—the spread of night baseball. After that, the New York Yankees (with MacPhail as president) added lights in 1946, followed by the Boston Braves (1946), Boston Red Sox (1947), and Detroit Tigers (1948). The Chicago Cubs would not make it 100 percent for another 40 years after Detroit.[68]

League presidents had disciplinary responsibilities as well, and Frick's first test came less than a month after the 1935 season opener: a brawl involving the Cubs and Pirates. Pirates second baseman Harry "Cookie" Lavagetto felt that Chicago shortstop Bill Jurges had spiked him while sliding into second, and a fight ensued. Cubs pitcher Guy Bush "was aching for a fight and found it," according to one newspaper account. In announcing penalties, Frick singled out Jurges and Bush, but excused Lavagetto, who was pronounced as merely acting in his own defense.

As Kieran interpreted the actions, "Frick came into office as president of the National League with a newspaperman's point of view and appreciates the fact that a little scrapping now and then helps, rather than hurts, the game, and apparently he acted with that in mind."[69] Frick's doctrine was, "he won't stand for strangers coming in and getting into the quarrel," Kieran noted. "That's why Guy Bush was fined.... It wasn't his fight at all. He butted in."[70]

Not only did Frick tolerate a degree of in-game skirmishing, but he continued Heydler's edict against players fraternizing on the field, adding a $10 fine and penalties against the manager for permitting it. The rule could, however, be waived by the umpires for specific cases—pregame photo shoots, for example.

Baseball writers had fun prodding Frick about fines for both fighting and fraternizing. In explaining the latter, he said that casual greetings were allowed, "but we won't have any more of those social sessions around the batting cage." These "sewing circles," as Frick called them, are common today. But to him, they cooled the competitive fires, and that would ultimately disappoint fans.[71]

Did it stop there? In a 1937 feature on umpires, Kieran noted that more players were fighting in the National League than the American and wondered if Frick had been "egging on the players in his league to stir the pot." He repeated, "It makes stories, and as an ex-newspaper man, Mr. Frick could appreciate that too." Frick admitted that, as Kieran paraphrased, "He was in favor of high salaries for skilled athletes, but he didn't want them acting with the staid dignity of business men."[72]

Frick could influence such on-field behaviors because in those days, league presidents had charge over the umpires. In 1949, he issued his Ten Commandments for umpires. Though issued fifteen years in, the directives reflect Frick's attitude toward life as much as toward the men he employed to enforce the rules:

1. Keep your eye on the ball.
2. Keep all personalities out of your work. Forget and forgive. It's the first rule of the book.
3. Avoid sarcasm. Don't insist on the last word.
4. Never charge a player and, above all, no finger pointing and yelling.
5. Hear only the things you should hear—be deaf to others.
6. Keep your temper. A decision made in anger is never sound.
7. Watch your language.
8. Take pride in your work at all times. Remember respect for an umpire is created off the field as well as on.
9. Review your work. You will find, if you are honest, that 99 percent of the trouble is traceable to loafing.
10. No matter what your opinion of another umpire, never make an adverse comment regarding him. To do so is despicable and ungentlemanly.[73]

Frick's early years as league president brought several issues involving umpires, who enjoyed his strong support. He even allowed them to remove their coats if the weather was too hot. But Frick followed a strict principle: the home team, not the umpires, would be responsible for fan behavior. He enforced that by fining two umpires—"Beans" Reardon and "Ziggy" Sears—who confronted irate fans in Cincinnati on July 17 for throwing bottles onto the field to protest a call by Sears. According to one report, "Reardon, it seemed, attempted to quiet the spectators by a personal speech, but did not succeed." His undisclosed fine reminded all umpires to leave crowd policing to the home club, for their own safety. Umpires reserved the prerogative to forfeit a game in extreme cases, but could not address the behavior until then.[74]

An umpire also added drama to Frick's first World Series as league president. During Game Three of the 1935 Series, umpire George Moriarty—after ejecting manager Charlie Grimm and two players—scorched the Chicago dugout with an impressive display of profanity. His boss, however, was seated behind the dugout and caught the entire performance. Frick volunteered to testify before Landis. "Moriarty used blasphemous language in talking to the Cubs bench," he said. "Undoubtedly there were a lot of hot words on both sides. In at least one instance I overheard the word 'meathead' directed at Moriarty." Landis would later fine Moriarty, Grimm, and three Cubs players, deducting the fines from their World Series checks.[75]

As the next season began, Frick found himself facing a holdout from one of his best umpires. Dolly Stark announced that he would seek other work if he did not get a raise. Stark had earned a reputation for being one of the game's most popular (by fans) and respected (by players and managers) umpires, albeit with a mercurial nature that carried him in and out of the league before this holdout. Frick had even honored him with a "day" on August 24, 1935, at the Polo Grounds, presenting him with a car. Frick expressed frustration with Stark ("We thought we had given him a substantial increase over this year"), but signed two replacement umpires just in case. Hoping that Stark would reconsider, the league owners voted him a one-year leave of absence, with Frick acknowledging that Stark could return at any time. He spent the season broadcasting games in Philadelphia, but returned to umpiring in 1937.[76]

The umpires also supported Frick in his efforts to improve the game. By the 1942 season, Frick (and no doubt his umpires) had tired of the manager squabbles and interminable mound conferences that slowed play. So he forbade rushing the field to protest calls on pitches and limited conferences to the manager, the pitcher, and two players. Base coaches were also banned from crossing the chalk lines to protest calls. "Play will be lively, and time—an important factor in these war days—will be saved for the fans," he predicted.[77]

The umpires, under Frick's orders, enforced the policy early and often once the season began, despite the players' and managers' protests. Five managers were ejected for advancing toward home plate to argue a pitch call. Frick was adamant. "Fans come to the park to see ball games, not to sit in on stupid, time-killing arguments at the plate," he said, adding, "I can't recall a single case in which an umpire ever changed his decision on a ball or a strike." He also stressed that batters and catchers still were allowed to register disagreement without penalty.[78]

As the 1936 season began, Commissioner Landis's misgivings about radio re-emerged. He had reluctantly allowed broadcasting of major league games, despite unfounded fears of its effect on attendance. As with night baseball, the team owners were slow to adopt the new technology. By 1930, radio fees represented only 0.3 percent of total revenues. By 1935, owner William Wrigley was allowing all of the Cubs' games to be broadcast, the first to do so.[79] Minor league team owners were complaining that major league broadcasts in small towns were keeping the fans away, so Landis declared a moratorium on additional broadcasting agreements, causing some to predict limitations for the 1937 season. For a radio veteran like Frick, such a Luddite edict had to be troubling.[80]

But no such edicts or limits were forthcoming. At the National League meetings in December, the team owners agreed to continue under the current system, with each team setting its own policy.[81] The opposing owners eventually came around; the gush of new money was the most convincing argument. As late as 1938, the three New York teams operated under an agreement that they would not broadcast their games. But in December, MacPhail broke the agreement, announcing that the Dodgers had signed a contract to broadcast their games for the 1939 season. It was characteristic of the same aggressiveness that had brought night baseball to Cincinnati and then New York, but officials from the other two New York teams were outraged and threatened to bring the matter up at the upcoming league meetings. Frick, however, declared it a matter for individual clubs to determine and declined to intervene.[82] By the next week, the Giants announced that they would begin broadcasting their games as well.[83]

By 1939, every team was broadcasting at least some of its games, and radio's share increased to 7.3 percent of major league baseball's revenues.[84] The minor league owners would be pacified by an increase in major league support for the minors through the development of a more formal farm system, though many small towns lost their teams to the advent of first radio and then television.

Once the 1937 season started, Frick and his umpires faced a storm after league managers demanded that they enforce the balk rule, which had been in the rulebook but rarely acknowledged in games. Frick instructed his umpires to require pitchers to come to a stop while pitching from the stretch position and dispatched his supervisor of umpires, Ernest Quigley, to team clubhouses to explain the balk rule. But when umpire George Barr called a balk on St. Louis pitcher Dizzy Dean—after two warnings—it precipitated an on-field brawl that resulted in $50 fines to Dean and Giants pitcher Jim Ripple.[85]

It would not be the last time that Barr ended up in a balk brawl. Six years later, Barr called a balk on Dodgers relief pitcher Johnny Allen. With the score tied, no outs and the tie-breaking runner on third, Barr's balk sent the pressured Allen over the top. He charged Barr and threw a punch at the umpire, sparking a fracas that took the umpires ten minutes to calm. Frick fined Allen $200 and suspended him for 30 days—the stiffest penalty he handed out for such on-field actions.[86]

Dean was as annoyed by Frick's ruling as by Barr's enforcement of the balk rule. Supposedly, he was already angry at Frick for telling *The Sporting News* that Dean's wife had a "dominating personality." Patricia Dean called her husband, who was traveling with his team to New York, and said, "The first thing I want you to do when you get to New York is to go to Ford Frick's office and punch him on the nose. If you don't, you're yellow"[87] (no dominating personality there). Dean declined, but the cut was deep.

After the balk brawl, Dizzy was in full tantrum. On May 23 he offered $1,000 to any sports writer who would print what he really felt about Frick. (No one claimed the money.) Then, speaking at a father-son sports dinner at the First Presbyterian Church of Belleville, Illinois, on May 25, Dean reportedly called Frick and Barr "the two greatest crooks in baseball."

On June 2, the angry National League president suspended Dean until he apologized, in writing. When Frick announced the suspension to reporters gathered in his office, a copy of the May 26 *Belleville Daily Advocate* was displayed prominently on his desk, the story circled with a red crayon. "It's got down to a question of whether Dean is bigger than the National League, and I don't think he is," Frick said. Interviewed in the clubhouse, Dean denied making the statement, claiming he merely called Barr's balk "the unfairest decision I ever saw." He refused to apologize, "because I ain't got nothing to apologize for."[88]

A conference at Frick's office at 11 a.m. the next day with Dean and St. Louis manager Frankie Frisch resolved nothing. A mob of reporters and photographers—which seemed to erupt each time a conferee came out to get a cup of water—reported several bellows of "I ain't signin' nothin'" from within Frick's office. Allowing the mob into his office to announce the meeting a failure and Dean still on indefinite suspension, Frick reluctantly allowed the media to see the letter of apology. In signing it, Dean would have denied making the statements, but he also, no doubt to his galling, acknowledged not only being repeatedly informed on the increased enforcement of the balk rule but also that the call was "a matter of umpire's judgment" that Dean disagreed with.

In Frick's office, Dean's expression "was that of a slightly bewildered and even a trifle frightened youth." Leaving the meeting, Dean made no statement but was overheard discussing an appeal to Landis. But that night in his hotel room, he was more combative, vowing, "I'll sue Ford Frick and the National League if I'm deprived of making a living, which is pitching for the St. Louis Cardinals."[89] He claimed he would rather jump out the 20th floor hotel room window where he was being interviewed than apologize, and threatened to spend the summer on a Florida sabbatical. That alarmed the Cardinals' front office, because St. Louis was contending for the pennant.

The Belleville sports writer involved, Murray Parres, stuck by his story. "I made notes on his talk just as I would have on any other assignment." He quoted Dean as calling Frick "our great little president—but a pain in the neck to me." Parres also revealed that for all the trouble he caused, Dean was not the main speaker at the event (Francis Laux, St. Louis radio announcer, was) and was not on the program, but merely showed up and was asked to say a few words.[90]

By Friday, June 4, Frick's suspension was threatening to cause the Cardinals some real damage: Dean was scheduled to pitch the next day. Dean requested a meeting with Frick to present a telegram from nine Belleville Presbyterians, which supported his explanation. Frick revised the statement, but Dean still refused to sign. A more forceful leader might have sent Dean home until he was literally ready to "play ball." Instead, in a scene from a Ben Hecht movie, Frick turned to his friends in the press box for a solution. He had Dean answer questions in the presence of the sports writers and photographers, then had the journalists—not Dean—sign a statement that they had witnessed his testimony. Based on that, Frick accepted Dean's statement, lifted the suspension, and pronounced the incident "closed."[91]

4. A New NL President

In the view of economist and baseball writer Andrew Zimbalist, Frick gave in to a strong-minded, popular player, an action that "suggests the hand of a weak leader" and presaged the accommodating style he would show as baseball commissioner.[92] To Kieran, who attended the meeting, "The Dean influence was so all-pervading in the atmosphere that Mr. Frick had neatly worked himself into a jam."[93]

A decade later, Frick had come to see things more or less as Kieran had. "I acted before I had all the facts," he confessed. "I should have armed myself with all the data before leaping to a decision. It was the biggest error of my regime. It taught me a valuable lesson." The interview was actually about Sam Breadon, whom Frick credited for not making the situation worse with angry public complaints (the MacPhail method). "Now, some other club owner would have hollered plenty and with just cause. But Sam took it—well, he took it like Sam Breadon."[94]

Frick's run-ins with Dean's manager, Frisch, were just as memorable. Frisch was a frequent target of Frick's suspensions and fines, usually for umpire abuse. On one occasion, Frisch enclosed his gas bill and electric bill with his fine check. The attached note read, "Since you've got all my money, you might as well pay my bills."[95]

On another occasion, Frisch was fined $75 by Frick, so for revenge, he called Frick collect to discuss it. He kept his league president on the line as long as possible while he objected and appealed and talked about a few other unrelated concerns, until Frick finally caught on. Frisch recalled, "Suddenly, Frick yelled: 'Hey, Frisch, I just remembered I am paying for this conversation. The heck with you, Frank,' and he hung up on me."[96]

In his memoirs, Frick also remembered an occasion when Frisch came through on behalf of the league and one of its umpires, Charlie Moran. A specific team that had a long-term feud with Moran filed charges and demanded a hearing after a game in which several players were ejected. Frisch attended the hearing and defended Moran, even though he considered him an average umpire. "This thing has been framed," he said. "You guys are out to get Charley and you're making a big issue out of nothing. You're trying to ruin a guy's life because you're sore at him. You're wrong and you're imagining a lot of things that are not true. That's all I've got to say. Good day." Frisch left the meeting, and the team dropped the charges later that day.[97]

5

Fame and Fighting

Next to integration, the best-known achievement of Ford Frick's tenure as National League president was the establishment of a Hall of Fame at the National Baseball Museum in Cooperstown, New York. The idea emerged after a blue-ribbon panel was commissioned in 1905 to determine who invented baseball. A mining engineer from Denver, Abner Graves, claimed that Abner Doubleday had adapted a game called "Town Ball" and laid out a field with new rules in their hometown of Cooperstown in 1839. The commission accepted Graves' version over the claims of veteran journalist Henry Chadwick (considered "The Father of Baseball") that baseball was based on the British game of rounders. The commission's motivation seems more a nationalistic obsession to guarantee the perception of baseball as a truly American game than to build a reliable narrative of its development, but the theory stuck long enough to ensure the establishment of baseball's shrine in the small New York town.

When an old baseball was found among Graves' possessions after he died in 1932, philanthropist Stephen Clark purchased it with the idea of establishing a baseball museum in Cooperstown.[1] Today, of course, the Doubleday theory is taken for legend, not historical fact, but it does not diminish the appropriateness of Cooperstown as the Hall of Fame site—especially for a sport as steeped in historical legend as baseball.

Frick's predecessor, John Heydler, had supported efforts by Clark and one of his foundation staff members, Alexander Cleland, to build the museum, and Frick pledged his office's continued support to Cleland soon after becoming league president. Granted, the citizens of Cooperstown had worked hard, led by Cleland, to develop Doubleday Field and the concept of the baseball museum. But it is accurate to say that Frick, with his public relations instincts, was the league official most suited to the project and the one who would lend it the strongest support, thus enabling its success.[2]

5. Fame and Fighting

Later implications that Frick had stolen credit for the project from Cleland both ignore Frick's actual contributions and subvert his words in which he stressed his idea for the Hall of Fame, not for the entire project. While Cleland and Clark are credited with the idea of the Cooperstown shrine to the game's history, it was Frick who suggested a Hall of Fame, the first devoted to a specific pursuit, in the museum.[3]

According to Frick, a timely visit to NYU provided the inspiration: "By happy chance I had visited the National Hall of Fame at New York University a few days before Cleland's visit. I was much impressed, and had a notion that a Baseball Hall of Fame would be great for the game. Cleland's visit afforded opportunity to try the idea out."[4] Frick also supported the museum concept, donating the only existing National League championship cup, from 1889, to the collection, along with other subsequent donations from the league's teams.[5]

At the August 1935 meeting in Frick's office, where the Hall was announced, selection was assigned to the Baseball Writers' Association of America. The inaugural induction class would ideally comprise ten players—five from the nineteenth century and five from the twentieth century.[6] The BBWAA's involvement has always caused controversy—whether in 2013, when the writers passed over eligible nominees tainted by baseball's steroid scandal (Barry Bonds, Mark McGwire, Sammy Sosa), leaving the Hall with no living inductees, or in 2014, when ESPN broadcaster Dan LeBetard allowed the controversial Deadspin website to fill out his ballot, resulting in disproportionate outrage. Such critics can blame Frick for the system that baseball writers have so jealously guarded. He credited Alan Gould of the Associated Press with the idea, but Frick endorsed the writers' central role in the process over a "cumbersome fan vote."[7]

In December, the BBWAA was ready to announce the first list of candidates and the voting system. It included 33 players from the modern era and 26 from pre–1900. The writers would choose ten from the modern list, and a committee would choose five from the earlier list. Fan outcry over their lack of involvement, which had been hinted at earlier, prompted Frick to consider a new vote. Ultimately, the Hall's inaugural class of electees—Ty Cobb, Walter Johnson, Christy Mathewson, Babe Ruth, and Honus Wagner—met with overwhelming approval, while the pre–1900 issue was left unresolved until the next year.[8] The selection process did cause criticism and controversy between 1936 and 1939, but it also provided valuable free publicity as a demonstration of fan passion and focused fans' attention on the museum and Hall of Fame leading up to the opening.

By mid–1939, the community of Cooperstown had followed through on its commitment to build a suitable home for the baseball museum. For Frick, the process challenged both his public relations and his interpersonal skills. He served as the middleman between Landis, who did not want to move too quickly on publicizing the official opening of the museum, and the people of Cooperstown, who were growing tired of waiting for the official announcement that would put their small village on the map.[9]

On June 12, it officially opened. All the living inductees of the Hall of Fame attended, and Cooperstown boys recreated the game of town ball as Doubleday "invented" it. U.S. Army soldiers, in New York Knickerbocker uniforms, reenacted a game from the 1850s, when Doubleday's original rules were supposedly still in effect.

Landis, at the insistence of the Centennial Commission, had retained the services of renowned Depression-era publicist Steve Hannagan to promote both the museum and the baseball centennial. As part of the media relations strategy, Hannagan's firm developed speech templates that could be used at centennial ceremonies nationwide. Landis was impressed not only by the success of Hannagan's strategy, but also by his refund of $35,000 from the original $100,000 budgeted.[10]

The Cooperstown myth also was blessed with U.S. government approval, as the Post Office issued a stamp honoring the 100th anniversary of baseball. Sixty-five million three-cent stamps depicted an early game at Doubleday Field, and sales at the Cooperstown Post Office were part of the opening events, with Landis solemnly bestowing three pennies at the window to buy the first one.[11] (Envelopes bearing stamps cancelled in Cooperstown that first day are valued by collectors, fetching as much as $50.)

For all of his work in helping the Hall of Fame become a reality, Frick's role was reduced to helping to cut the ceremonial ribbon to open the museum—an honor he shared with Will Harridge. He was fortunate, however, compared to Clark and Cleland, whose contribution was ignored in most newspaper reports.[12]

Frick remained involved in the Hall of Fame its first couple of years, mainly as a member of the "Centennial Commission" committee that voted on pre–1900 players. After the original Old-Timers committee was not able to agree on five players for the inaugural class, Frick and five other of baseball's top men (Landis, Harridge, Heydler, Branham, and George Trautman, president of the minor league American Association) formed and appointed themselves onto a committee to fix the situation. In 1937 and 1938, they selected three former players: George Wright, Connie Mack, and John McGraw—though Mack and McGraw were probably selected for their records as managers. They added four non-players—the two original league presidents, Morgan Bulkeley and Ban Johnson, Alexander Cartwright, and Henry Chadwick. Chadwick was a sports writer who is credited with helping to develop much of baseball's original analytic structure, including the box score.[13]

Landis, Frick, and Harridge also appointed themselves as the first members of another Committee on Old-Timers in 1939. In that capacity, they picked six more pre-1900 players: Cap Anson, Buck Ewing, Charles "Old Hoss" Radbourn, Charles Comiskey, Albert Spalding, and Candy Cummings (supposed inventor of the curveball). Their work done, they turned the duties over to a four-member Old-Timers Committee: two team presidents, a manager, and a baseball journalist. Frick would not participate in Hall of Fame selection again until after he retired as commissioner and served on the Veterans Committee for four years (1966–1969).[14]

Still, Frick continued to demonstrate support and interest toward the Hall of Fame. In 1944, Landis (finally) appointed a committee to oversee the Hall and serve as its Old-Timers Committee. Although Frick was not appointed to the committee, he worked closely with the committee members in developing standards for both the Hall's selection methods and its overall administration. Although the Hall had been in operation for nine years, it had no formal by-laws.

Hall of Fame treasurer Paul Kerr met with Frick, soon after Landis appointed the new committee, to get his advice. Frick reiterated most of Landis's priorities, though he particularly stressed the need to formalize (and thus protect) the baseball writers' monopoly over the selection process for recent players. Frick also suggested that a separate process be established to recognize non-players who "had made such outstanding contributions to baseball that the Hall of Fame should not be closed to them."[15]

The committee adopted the by-laws establishing the authority of baseball writers over the selection process at its first meeting on December 10. Frick's suggestion for including non-players in the Hall was discussed, but no action was taken. The two sports writers on the Old-Timers Committee, Sid Mercer of the *New York Journal-American* (Frick's old paper) and Melville Webb of the *Boston Globe*, favored limiting the Hall to players only. The committee deferred on further action until its next meeting.[16]

The debate between whether players only or non-players also should be inducted to the Baseball Hall of Fame has generated much debate—

both in terms of the policy and the selections that have resulted, particularly by the various versions of the Veterans Committee. Even as commissioner, and even with his role in the Hall of Fame's establishment, Frick maintained a hands-off policy, allowing the various committee members and the Hall of Fame board to debate the issues, along with the public.

Frick supervised other public relations strategies, including the establishment of the National League Film Bureau in 1938. The bureau produced several films, starting with "Baseball, the National Game," which Frick commissioned as part of baseball's centennial. The short films were written and directed by Ethan Allen, a former major league outfielder. They ran about 30 minutes and were marketed more to colleges and local sports clubs as a way of promoting baseball. According to league financial information, the league spent almost $38,000 to fund the films in 1940, and $20,000 on all other public relations efforts.[17]

The second film in the series, "Play Ball, America," provided instruction, while the next two, "Winning Baseball" and "Safe at Home," featured a personal look at players and amusing plays (the first blooper reels?). They were repackaged as newsreel shorts by Pathe News. In the early 1940s, Allen and the bureau produced a two-reel film, "Baseball: Techniques and Tactics," which was used to spread the sport to Central and South America, through the addition of Spanish and Portuguese soundtracks. The distribution strategy succeeded at first but had to be curtailed as World War II–related material needs limited the number of available prints.

The film strategy would be revived in 1946 as part of organized baseball's postwar promotional strategy, still under Frick's leadership. The league announced that a library of films on fundamentals of play would be produced, featuring popular players as instructors and sponsored by Spalding.[18]

The strategy was adapted to television by the mid–1950s. Frick endorsed the production of "This Is Baseball," a 15-minute program produced by Emerson Yorke. The films showed baseball stars such as Stan Musial, Yogi Berra, and Pee Wee Reese, both at home and on the field.[19]

Any good feelings generated by such strategies could be easily wiped out, as demonstrated by an inter-borough feud between the Giants and the Dodgers. It started on July 2, 1939, when Giants first baseman Zeke Bondura, incensed that Dodgers player-manager Leo Durocher had stepped on his foot running out a grounder, chased him into right field, where their brawl—celebrated by thrown bottles—lasted longer than the average fight before the umpires could break it up.

5. Fame and Fighting

Dodgers president Larry MacPhail claimed that Durocher was defending himself and should not have been ejected. But after Durocher was also fined, MacPhail (as was his custom) went further, complaining to the National League Board of Directors, which would meet at the All-Star Game the following week, that the Giants and manager Bill Terry were intimidating National League umpires and that Frick had done nothing to stop it.[20]

When the teams moved their rivalry to Brooklyn for the next series, 25 plainclothes police were dispersed among the crowd.[21] But no further trouble occurred, on or off the field, except for MacPhail's constant yelling in the press box, where Frick also sat. Frick chose not to reply, and MacPhail retreated after a five-run Giants rally.[22] Perhaps Frick's reticence resulted from an awareness of MacPhail's well-known drinking problem, which fueled his extended commentary. MacPhail's drinking, with the accompanying unpredictable behavior, was common knowledge in baseball circles. One sportswriter called him "a great promoter and an impossible man: loud, belligerent, unsteady, alcoholic. With no drinks he was brilliant. With one he was a genius. With two he was insane. And rarely did he stop at one."[23]

At its meeting the following Monday, the board did not address MacPhail's accusations, even though he had filed a brief outlining his contentions before leaving the meeting, and unanimously upheld Frick's decisions (though Frick did imply that he had discussed the matter with Terry privately).[24]

Within the next week, Frick faced another player fight, this one involving one of his umpires. Giants shortstop Billy Jurges and umpire George Magerkurth exchanged punches after a Cincinnati home run that Giants players insisted was foul. Frick fined both Jurges and Magerkurth $150 and suspended both for ten days. Sports writers criticized the quick decision, which was announced without a hearing, and disputed Frick's claim that the umpire threw the first punch.[25] An editorial in *The Sporting News* supported the ruling, however, noting, "Magerkurth had ample means to punish Jurges without resorting to violence. Respect of players and fans is not earned in that way."[26]

The incidents caused Frick to reconsider his lax policy on player fights. His earlier approach of allowing players some latitude to work out their differences had created more lively games, but now the frequent fisticuffs were becoming too much of a distraction. Heading into the 1940 season, Frick instructed his umpires to clamp down more firmly on player misbehavior and eject offenders more quickly.[27]

The 1939–1940 off-season allowed Frick to indulge a new passion: curling. Frick played "lead-off man" (though he also did some sweeping) for a St. Andrews rink curling team, the Callipygians, which won its share of matches in regional and national competitions.[28] The St. Andrews Club was one of the oldest and most successful in the country, and with Frick's help, its bonspielers even made the semifinals of the national "junior" tournament that year.[29] The team might have gone further if not for an illness on Frick's part that also caused him to cancel a speech to the Connecticut Sports Hall of Fame induction dinner on the way back.[30] For several years, Frick would compete with the St. Andrews team, and his exploits were noted in news briefs.[31]

In a 1944 interview, Frick said he gained interest in the sport after accompanying a friend to a "bonspiel." "Funny thing is that you usually can do fairly well the first few times you try and you think you've got the game licked." It provided a break from the headaches of professional sports. "What appeals to me most about it is that there are no amateur-professional distinctions in the sport. Instructors receive no pay, expenses are not given." He added without irony, "And no bets are made."

Frick even donned his black curling tam—complete with pompom, flowing ribbons, and club pins from defeated opponents, for a photo feature in January 1946. He demonstrated both his putting down and sweeping techniques, both of which were praised by his fellow club members. They did point out, however, that with only eight years of curling experience, he had yet to ascend to the position of team captain.[32]

For the 1939–1940 offseason, the curling, in fact, gave Frick a respite from the turmoil Landis had created. After the 1939 season, the commissioner proposed extensive changes in the agreement between the major and the minor leagues, which was set to expire at the end of 1941. In particular Landis, unlike most major league owners, did not like the close working relationship between major league and minor league teams, particularly as it related to player movement, which was marked by frequent duplicity to the players' disadvantage. He might be remembered for his draconian punishment of the players involved in the Black Sox scandal, but for the rest of his tenure as commissioner, Landis developed a reputation as supporting player interest over the owners.

Landis, wanting to protect the players, had proposed sweeping changes—for example, that players become free agents after three years in the minor leagues. The owners protested, as did the minor league team owners. Some felt that Landis was also setting the agenda for his successor's job description, which the contract also covered. No one knew if

5. Fame and Fighting

Landis would retire when his current contract expired, leaving his successor to function under the new agreement, and the commissioner was giving no clues as to his plans. The major and minor leagues had planned their first joint meeting in 16 years, ostensibly to close the celebration of baseball's centennial. But with Landis's proposals, the meetings provided more turmoil than pomp.[33]

The commissioner quickly eased his opposition on major league ownership of minor league teams, which also lowered the temperature at the convention.[34] The debate was energized, however, when the minor league teams passed a series of amendments to the major-minor agreement designed to limit Landis's authority to approve or deny player movements and, as he had done in many cases, declare players free agents.[35] Frick's National League owners unanimously sided with the minor league team owners. The American League owners, however, voted down the amendments, in a move designed to limit the success of the New York Yankees (who did not vote)—meaning that National League teams apparently were supporting the Yankees' efforts to continue dominating their American League rivals. With the rival leagues deadlocked, Landis cast the deciding vote, defeating the amendment and angering the National League owners.[36]

The only result was that each league appointed a four-member committee to draft proposals for the revised major-minor agreement, and to come together to present their proposals and compromise from there. What is telling about Frick's approach is that the American League proposed and passed the idea at the December meeting. Acting more cautiously, the National League owners, under Frick's recommendation, did not propose or pass the idea until their February meeting. According to *The Sporting News*, Frick "withheld action at the time because of the unsettled conditions at the joint meeting in Cincinnati, desiring more time to consider the situation." It is equally telling that the process left out Landis's involvement, though his influence would be assumed.[37]

At their pre-season meeting in February, the National League owners approved the committee idea and urged the minor league association to do the same.[38] Only a few days later, in a specially called meeting, Landis yielded on the three-year rule and the minor leagues ended the major league club agreements that worked against the players. The compromises reduced the angst between the commissioner and the leagues, allowing negotiations for a broader inter-league agreement to resume.[39]

Before the meeting, however, Frick had apparently written a letter to Landis outlining the National League's objections to the commissioner's original plan. He would not comment on the letter's specifics, though he did tell *The Sporting News* he "called a spade a spade." One American League owner worried that Frick was unnecessarily prodding Landis, who did not like being pushed. It could be interpreted as a shrewd move on Frick's part—opposing a commissioner whose tenure would be ending soon, while also promoting the interest of the National League and its owners.[40] Despite the constant drama, the new agreement would not take long to conclude.

By the 1940 season, Frick, like fans, was growing more concerned with the issue of player safety. Until then, players batted wearing only their cloth caps. After Joe Medwick of the Brooklyn Dodgers was knocked out by a pitch from Bob Bowman of the St. Louis Cardinals, Frick and MacPhail suggested that players test various forms of protective headwear. Similar tests in the minor leagues resulted in players discarding the helmets. They considered the helmets "sissy" (though, as one journalist pointed out, no one made the same accusations against catchers and umpires of the era). As John Kieran put it, "[T]he hitters seem to feel that the chance of being seriously injured by a pitched ball is about as slim as the chance of being struck by lightning, and they probably will be against any protective headpiece until ordinary citizens go about wearing lightning rods." Players suggested instead that the National League strengthen its beanball rule, modeling it after the stricter American League rule.[41]

In early July, Frick announced that he would propose the mandating of batting helmets when he met with league owners at the All-Star Game. "I know of no other way to prevent head injuries," Frick said. "I do not think it would help much to suggest to the players that they wear them. There is a certain prejudice against such protection by the players, who think it would make them appear effeminate."[42] The owners did decide at that meeting to allow the helmets, but made them optional for teams and players.[43]

MacPhail, Frick's frequent nemesis but an ally on this issue, would experiment with helmets in spring training the next season.[44] The head protectors that MacPhail ordered the Dodgers and their farm system players to use actually covered only part of the head and slipped inside of a specially designed cap.[45] Medwick himself began using a helmet in 1941, with no negative effects on his hitting.[46]

By the 1942 season, Frick decided to address the beanball issue, in the name of player safety. The American League for years had authorized umpires to eject pitchers they felt were throwing at batters, but the National League had no such policy. Minor beanball wars had erupted periodically,

5. Fame and Fighting

with no league action, beyond Frick's earlier promotion of batting helmets. Frick was forced to create the policy after an August 8 game between the Dodgers and the Braves in which pitchers Whit Wyatt (Brooklyn) and Manuel Salvo (Boston) engaged in a beanball duel with no intervention or warning by the umpires. "[The] National League has officially persisted in its refusal to recognize that such a thing as a bean-ball exists," one writer complained. Frick's new policy, however, included a $200 fine for the manager of the offending pitcher's team, to be determined based on umpire reports.[47]

MacPhail was not pleased with the new policy and claimed (as usual) that it was yet another rule aimed at his team. "Do you think that anybody except yourselves, the officials of the Brooklyn club and the Brooklyn fans are pulling for you to win the pennant?" he asked his players. "Do you think Frick is pulling for you? No!" He demanded that Frick convene a hearing, with sports writers present, to air his grievances, but Frick declined, declaring the new rule permanent and MacPhail's hearing unnecessary.[48]

MacPhail might have been wrong to oppose a beanball rule, but he had a point. His Dodgers were the "bad boys" of their era and probably the most hated team in baseball. But that could be traced to an antagonistic manager (Durocher) and a confrontational general manager more than the players themselves. (It should be noted that, for all of the supposed ill will between the two, MacPhail would be one of Frick's strongest supporters in 1945, when baseball owners were deliberating the selection of a new commissioner.)

Frick gained a reprieve at the 1942 season's end, when MacPhail re-enlisted in the Army, working for the undersecretary of war, Robert Patterson, with the rank of lieutenant colonel. He was replaced in Brooklyn by the general manager of the St. Louis Cardinals, Branch Rickey, who would eventually present Frick with another, more daunting and consequential challenge—the integration of major league baseball.

A year later, Frick would extend the ban to "body balls" as well, deeming them as potentially dangerous as beanballs. Frick fined Les Webber of the Dodgers $100 for throwing at Stan Musial. One reason for the perceived offense was that catcher Mickey Owen had told Webber to put Musial on base. But rather than throw pitches far outside, Webber threw them right at Musial's body. Based on the umpires' account, Frick fined Webber, though he did not fine Durocher the $200 stipulated earlier, since it was Webber's decision to throw at Musial.

"I'm getting sick and tired of hearing pitchers say they've got to throw at batters to protect their bread and butter," Frick said. "The batter is up there earning his bread and butter too." Durocher, despite Frick's charity, threatened to appeal the fine, though Rickey was a stated opponent of beanballs and body balls.[49]

A May 1941 protest by (again) MacPhail and the Dodgers allowed Frick to establish his doctrine for what constituted a forfeitable offense. MacPhail claimed that the Cubs had added a player from a trade without releasing one to bring the roster back to 25. The added player, Charles Gilbert, had stopped in Philadelphia on his way to join the Cubs, for treatment of an injury, but that did not placate Dodgers brass. Technically, he was on their list as soon as the trade occurred, so manager Durocher protested two losses to the Cubs.[50]

Frick acknowledged the Cubs' error, but he also contended that their actions had no practical impact on the games' outcome. As a result, he fined the team $500 but refused to forfeit the games. In announcing the fine, Frick stated a preference for protests that involved actions on the field rather than administrative technicalities. "Frick pointed to a sane way of handling infractions of player limits, ... and it should serve as a future for all league prexies—thus providing for playing the game as it should be PLAYED," *The Sporting News* wrote in support (emphasis theirs).[51]

Such a policy was certainly farsighted on Frick's part; a league president in the 1940s faced far more game protests than they do today, if newspaper reports are any indication. Yes, managers would protest interpretations of the rules by umpires. But just as often, they would also protest judgment calls—foul/fair balls, tags. In those cases, Frick almost always sided with his umpires. In a television age, the ubiquity of video evidence and replays might delay games, but they also render most protests meaningless, to the relief of league presidents and commissioners.

Baseball's most threatening hazard, however, was the war that had erupted in Europe. In his pre-season article leading up to the 1940 season, Frick acknowledged that World War II was occupying the news and everyone's thoughts. He couldn't resist the chance to make the clumsy-but-sincere point, "[Our] young men and boys are mobilizing with bats and gloves and baseballs instead of guns, gas masks and tanks.... The only masks they need are for the catcher and umpire."[52] But early on, Frick was developing what would be his narrative throughout the war—that baseball represented what was best about America and in that function, it served as a national inspiration.

A decade later, in the middle of the Korean War, Frick offered a similar sentiment, during a speech in Columbus, Ohio, in December 1951. "If Germany had had baseball, World War II would have been prevented, and if

5. Fame and Fighting

Russia had a sports program like the Americans' with a chance to let off steam, there would be no danger of Communism," he claimed. Baseball provided the additional benefit of teaching its younger players the virtues of democracy, assuring that baseball would "remain a proud part of our ideal way of life."[53]

By the end of the season, however, even Frick could not deny that the war in Europe was casting its shadow on his country and his pastime. The 1940 institution of a peacetime draft only drew the war closer. "We are fully awake to the national and international situation as it pertains to baseball. However, we are going along as before," he said. "Some of our young men will be conscripted, and if a greater emergency arises, we will meet any demands made upon us." But he did not fear a stoppage of the game: "Even in war-torn Europe, sports have continued and I feel that our government will want us to continue baseball."[54]

At the annual league meetings in December, the owners decided to create a special "national defense service list" for drafted players, whose contracts would remain with their original teams during their service. The meeting was also significant because the issues regarding major and minor league team relationships that had caused so much hostility between the National League and Landis had fizzled, and the new agreement, as discussed and negotiated by the appointed committee, was adopted.[55]

In the speech that provided Frick's editorial philosophy as outlined in Chapter 4, the league president also acknowledged the challenges posed by World War II, only days before his own country would be drawn in. "Certainly the Army draft will catch up with us," he told a group of baseball writers. "We may be playing with willow baseballs before we get through. All forms of athletic competition will be affected."[56] His predictions would soon be tested, as would his and baseball's ability to deal with them.

6

The War

Immediately following the attack on Pearl Harbor, organized baseball pledged its cooperation with the government for whichever direction the season would take—whether cancelled or not. Both leagues were planning to meet in Chicago on December 9 (the meetings had been moved from New York because Landis and Harridge were battling health problems that precluded travel), but any substantive action would be premature.

Instead, both leagues agreed to raise funds to provide baseball equipment to the United States military. The owners pledged $25,000 toward the effort, with $20,000 to be repaid by the proceeds of the 1942 All-Star Game.[1] By the first of the year, 1,500 kits—including 18,000 baseballs and 4,500 bats—were on their way. The effort was directed by Washington Senators owner Clark Griffith, who had led a similar drive during World War I, with Frick assisting. The goal was for $100,000 worth of baseball equipment to be donated and distributed.[2]

Frick was an enthusiastic supporter of the war effort, beyond the equipment drive. Instead of visiting baseball camps during spring training, he toured Armed Forces training posts and delivered lectures. His frequent meetings with War Department officials had so impressed them that they set up the tour. The lectures were not about baseball, but about the recruits' mission and its importance. Heading into the 1942 season, he confessed that the only baseball he had seen was a workout in Fort Benning, Georgia.[3]

For Frick, the sacrifice was as personal as it was for other wartime parents. His own son, Frederick, had begun his post-graduate studies at Cambridge University (Trinity College) after completing his undergraduate degree at DePauw, where he had roomed with future baseball executive Buzzie Bavasi. Even as an international student, Frederick had been pressed into the war effort during his time at Cambridge, serving two years with the Office of the Coordinator of Information in London. When

6. The War

OCI transitioned to become the U.S. Office of War Information, he made the switch too, serving in North Africa before enlisting in the Army Air Force in February of 1944.

After the war ended, Frederick earned a Ph.D. in psychology from Columbia University and taught at Harvard for three years. He moved

Frick with his son, Frederick (right), served in the Armed Forces during World War II. He later worked for a military intelligence research firm in Boston (courtesy Ford Frick II).

down to Washington, District of Columbia, for three years as chief of a Pentagon-affiliated communication research facility. He and his family returned to Boston, where he began to work at MIT's Lincoln Laboratory, which had been established in the early 1950s to spearhead air missile defense research, though its mission expanded as security needs became more complex.[4]

The position required high security clearance—so high, as Frederick's daughter (and Ford's granddaughter) Kelly Richards recalled, he was not allowed to visit her in Poland when she was an English teacher at the American School of Warsaw from 1973 to 1975. Frederick Frick lived in Lexington, Massachusetts, with his wife, Jere, until he died in 1992 after a five-year battle with progressive supranuclear palsy.[5]

On January 14, 1942, Landis wrote to President Roosevelt to ask whether the upcoming season should be canceled. Roosevelt responded with what would become known as the "green light letter." Termed a "personal and not an official point of view," Roosevelt wrote, "I honestly feel that it would be best for the country to keep baseball going." He acknowledged that, with so many top players serving in the Armed Forces, "the actual quality to the teams is lowered," but still considered the pastime a useful distraction for the hard-working folks back home. "Incidentally," he added, "I hope that night games can be extended because it gives an opportunity to the day shift to see a game occasionally."[6] Landis even allowed *The Sporting News* to run a photo of the actual letter, which is now displayed in the Baseball Hall of Fame, on the front page.

While the survival of the game itself was definitely a relief, the president's incidental comments were also an endorsement to owners and league officials (particularly Frick) who had supported night baseball. Even obstructive owners like Horace Stoneham of the Giants recognized that to stonewall the expansion of night baseball would seem treasonous.[7]

Frick met with league owners privately on January 17 to discuss the letter. Going into the meeting, Frick had wired Roosevelt, pledging the National League's "complete cooperation and assistance in this time of national crisis." He concluded, "We are yours to command."[8] At first he denied to sports writers that the owners' meeting had taken place, but yielded, admitting its existence as a conference. He said the owners had discussed night baseball leading into their regularly called February 2 meeting, but that they also discussed the status of 1942 player contracts, which had been delayed pending action on the season.[9]

Frick reported that the owners had suspended the seven-game limit for night games that had been adopted earlier. He mentioned a possible increase to 14 night contests a year, but reaffirmed that no specific limit was approved. "We still do not believe it is a good thing to play more than seven night games, but since Mr. Roosevelt wants more, we will go along with that request," he said. He couldn't miss an opportunity to nudge the rival league, however, adding, "We are opposed to unlimited night competition, which they say may be requested by the American League."[10]

At the "secret" January meeting, the financial problems of the Philadelphia Phillies were also discussed, although briefly. Ownership problems had also emerged in Philadelphia, where poor team performance (a 43–111 record) in 1941 had resulted in poor attendance and financial losses. A syndicate headed by Jack Kelly, Sr., father of Grace Kelly, announced an offer to buy the team. But team owner and president Gerry Nugent rejected it—flush with new cash, it was noted, after a late-season visit by the league-leading Dodgers added $60,000 to the team's bank account. Frick, as was his custom, declined involvement: "I've seen Kelly's offer, but it's not within my jurisdiction to say whether Nugent should accept it or not."[11] Kelly subsequently announced that the bid, reported to be $500,000, would be withdrawn.[12]

Nugent surprised his fellow owners in January by claiming that his finances were strong enough that league help was not needed, though he acknowledged that he might need help later. The concern was that the Phillies would have to sell some top players to survive, but when Nugent announced that was not necessary, Frick reported that the other owners cheered. He added, "The league will take no action until Nugent makes a plea for help."[13]

By the end of the 1941 season, however, there was no reason to cheer; the Phillies were in their customary state of financial crisis after another disastrous season, and Nugent was in plea mode. He begged permission from the league—which held a loan to the team—to sell some of his young prospects to raise money. In a November emergency meeting, the league board of directors denied that, along with his request for another loan. Further action was delayed until the December meetings. Nugent claimed that he was ready to sell the team at a fair price, but that Kelly's bid was in fact much less than the reported $500,000, and amounted to a gift.[14]

In the midst of Nugent's issues, Frick supposedly made a statement to a Philadelphia reporter that he would never live down, thanks to columnist Red Smith. "Disregard any reports you hear that might involve moving the franchise," he told reporters, "because baseball franchises do not move." That would go down in false sports prophecies history as one of the most inaccurate.[15]

At the business meeting the next day, the National League owners agreed to double the night game limit to 14, but at the American League meeting, Griffith demanded the option of as many as 28 night games, stalling the negotiations. He argued that two-team cities like St. Louis and Philadelphia could have that many night games, so he should have the same option.[16] The next day, Landis got Griffith to agree to a compromise of 21. Landis noted that to reach the quota of 28 night games, the Senators would have to schedule all night games for some series—standard practice for early-week series today, but too novel for baseball in 1942. Yankees President Ed Barrow promised that his team would play its share of night games on the road, but that the Yankees would not schedule any night games at home.[17]

Griffith would not back down. At the midseason owners' meeting before the All-Star Game, he requested that his Senators be allowed to play all of their games at night, except for Sundays and holidays, but the owners voted it down in a tight vote, with Landis casting the deciding vote. (Apparently night baseball did wonders for the Senators' bottom line.) However, the owners and Landis did allow him to move the games to a 7 p.m. twilight start as a compromise.[18]

To support the war effort, the leagues decided on having two All-Star Games, both at night. The first game would take place at New York's Polo Grounds on July 6. The following night, in Cleveland, an All-Star team would play a team of players who had enlisted in the Armed Forces. All gate receipts for both games would be given to charities—the first $100,000 going to the Baseball Equipment Fund and the remainder divided between the Navy Relief Society and Army Emergency Relief.[19]

But whether the New York All-Star Game—or any games in the city, for that matter—could take place at night suddenly became a topic for debate. One obvious question was whether "dim-out" policies instituted early in the war applied to baseball. New York Police Commissioner Lewis Valentine speculated as much once the season began, after receiving the "dim-out" order from the Department of the Army that was directed at coastal cities.[20] The decision is famous for dimming the lights of Broadway during the war. But would that order apply to the night baseball that had just been expanded? Valentine said yes, but then backed away the next day, wondering if the lights could be pointed down toward the field without beaming up into the sky.[21]

For Frick and the other baseball officials, the indecision created scheduling hell, so they decided to wait until getting a final decision, all the while pledging their support to whatever the government came up with. The answer came on May 18: Valentine announced that night baseball would indeed be banned throughout the war in New York City. Twilight games were permitted, but games could last only an hour past sundown, blending with the "ambient light."[22]

The New York dim-out order did affect the July 6 All-Star Game at the Polo Grounds, which had been scheduled as a night game. Moving it to a daytime start would have prevented Cubs and Cardinals players from getting there in time by train; they were playing a doubleheader in St. Louis the Sunday before. So the game was moved to a 6:30 p.m. twilight start.[23]

The order would not affect teams further inland, of course—a relief to owners in smaller markets, who were relying on night baseball to increase attendance. "There is a big difference between New York and Pittsburgh," Pirates president William E. Benswanger told the *Post-Gazette*. "We are close to 400 miles inland and I don't believe the dim-out regulations will hit us or any other city not on the coastline."[24]

By the 1944 season, the dim-out restrictions for Eastern seaboard metropolitan areas had been eased, and night baseball could resume in New York City, as long as Mayor Fiorello LaGuardia approved. He did, of course, and the Dodgers and Giants announced schedules of 14 night games—the agreed-on National League maximum. With their return, the National League would increase from 60 to 91 night games in 1944. The Yankees would continue their policy of day games only.[25]

The National League continued its night game expansion after the war. In 1949, league owners voted to do away with the 12:50 a.m. curfew (unless local laws dictated otherwise) and to allow lights to be turned on if an afternoon game lasted into evening. Frick strongly advocated those changes, and others, to promote attendance, which had leveled off after a postwar surge.[26]

Throughout the 1942 season, all of the major league teams had scheduled exhibitions on off days to raise money for the equipment drive and Army and Navy relief funds. Frick made a point of attending the National League games, praising local efforts and publicizing the gate receipts. The August 3 exhibition fund raiser between the Dodgers and the Giants devolved into a twilight fiasco, however, as the umpires ended up calling the game in the ninth inning, squelching a Giants rally and preserving the Dodgers' 7–4 victory. A solemn post-game ceremony—in which a spotlight illuminated the American flag and "The Star-Spangled Banner" was played—was marred by fans booing. The experience led Stoneham to declare that he would end twilight games at the Polo Grounds until after the war. Lost in the baseball wrangling was the $80,000 the game raised for the Army relief efforts.[27]

During the war, baseball also had to deal with limitations on travel. Following the 1942 season, both leagues worked on plans to cut the number of long road trips from four to three—saving as much as 40,000 travel miles. Some advocated shortening the 154-game season, but baseball leaders, including Frick, believed that was not necessary, particularly with the new travel plan.[28]

A report in the *New York Herald Tribune*, which claimed that officials were considering combining the two leagues into one, with eastern and western divisions, was dismissed as "silly." Sam Breadon, Cardinals president, said, "If transportation difficulties required such drastic restrictions the authorities would close baseball."[29]

Such drastic measures were back on the table by the December 1942 owners meeting, however. On November 30, Joseph B. Eastman sent letters to Landis, Harridge, and Frick urging more draconian travel restrictions beyond what was proposed. Eastman acknowledged the decrease in road trips from four to three, but also asked the teams to consider extending away series as a means of eliminating duplicate travel.

In perhaps the most disruptive suggestion, Eastman also suggested that the league consider moving 1943 spring training closer to their home cities: "Subject to suitable weather conditions, the selection of a training site as near as possible to the permanent headquarters of the team would save transportation." Eastman's letter concluded with an ominous prediction: "I am basing my suggestions on conditions as we see them at present. Improvement and easing of the situation is not likely to occur.... [A]ccordingly, this letter can not be taken as a guarantee of the future."[30]

The Eastman letter officially "arrived" too late for the leagues to take much official action at the December meeting. Everyone professed solidarity with the government's strategy, as evidence by the reduction in road trips already planned. Team owners also discussed ways to limit spring training travel, such as scheduling exhibition games on a more direct route.

On December 14, Griffith met with Eastman to get some guidance on what the government was expecting from baseball leaders. Eastman told Griffith that, with Florida, Texas, and California offering benefits as a winter training site for the armed forces, it might make sense for major league teams to yield that territory and move north with their training camps.[31] As the month progressed, more team officials announced plans to abandon Southern climates altogether and do spring training closer to (a much colder) home. By the end of the year, every team except Cincinnati had moved its spring training base northward. The Reds were waiting for additional guidance from Frick.³²

Finally, Landis himself met with Eastman on December 30, and then with owners in Chicago on January 5 to discuss what they talked about. The changes were drastic. Landis announced that spring training would take place north of the Potomac River and east of the Mississippi (though the St. Louis teams got a break on the latter requirement)—what sports writers would dub the "Landis-Eastman Line." The major leagues also agreed to delay Opening Day until April 21 and open camp on April 1, to allow the weather to catch up. Landis left it to Frick and Harridge to work out the schedule arrangements.³³

Frick and Harridge presented their revised schedules in late January. Besides the longer road trips, the schedule featured intersectional games on Independence Day and Memorial Day, as well as season's end. Although neither league had geographic divisions, both leagues had been scheduling holiday and season-ending games within unofficial geographic divisions, to allow the players less travel. To reduce travel expenses—which they did, saving an estimated 5,000,000 passenger miles—that tradition could not be guaranteed.³⁴

The World Series would face a similar travel reduction. After the Cardinals and Yankees clinched as league champions, Landis, Harridge, and Frick reduced travel by announcing that the first three games would take place in New York and the final four in St. Louis, cutting one train trip. Players supported the Series opening in New York because the three guaranteed games in the larger stadium fattened their bonus pool.³⁵

Between the 1942 and 1943 seasons, Frick and Harridge announced that their teams would be using new wartime baseballs with a different rubber compound; the war effort required the rubber used previously. Frick spent part of the 1943 schedule meeting administering the exchange of old baseballs for new baseballs among the various teams. Barely a month before spring training, however, Frick had no samples on hand. He could only tell the owners, "The baseballs will be changed."³⁶

As the season began, Frick had to face some angry owners, who claimed that the new wartime baseballs in play were dead. Eleven of the first 29 games were shutouts, and batters seemed baffled. At first, company officials at Spalding, which had switched to balata, a South American gum, attributed the weak offensive output to cold, wet weather. Cincinnati Reds general manager Warren Giles groused that the new balls were filled with "ground baloney" instead of balata. "Asking big leaguers to play with the sort of a ball with which we are opening the season would be like asking our soldiers, sailors and marines to win the war with blanks instead of real ammunition," he said. The *New York Daily News* sports staff took some of the new balls to Cooper Union Institute of Technology. Scientists there deemed the ball 25.9 percent less resilient than the 1942 model. The new baseball was dubbed "the fake ball," the "no-ball," the "stone ball," and even "Hitler's ball."[37]

On April 23, following a phone conference with Frick, Spalding admitted that the ball was the problem; the wartime rubber cement had "proven of an inferior quality." Spalding Vice President Lou Coleman promised that a newer rubber cement compound being tested was of a higher quality and that livelier baseballs would be shipped in two weeks. Frick authorized teams to use 1942 baseballs until then, though many teams had already disposed of them. The American League at first continued using the new ball, with Harridge allowing ten extra minutes of batting practice. It also adopted the new ball once it became available.[38]

Some criticized Frick for creating a situation where the two leagues would be using different balls, if only for a couple of weeks. But Frick said he was looking out for the fans:

> There is nothing in the book that requires the two major leagues to use the same ball. We simply got together and agreed to use a ball that met certain specifications. Baseball faces a tough enough year as it is, without continuing play with a dead ball and thus alienating the spectators. You can imagine the fans' reaction to going to a game and watching well-hit balls plop feebly into fielders' hands.[39]

The Philadelphia Phillies' weak finances produced a similar effect. Going into the 1943 season, it became apparent that Nugent had not turned around the team's finances. On February 9, when the NL owners usually discussed the schedule, they also decided that it was Nugent, not them, and it was time to move on. Attempting to stave off a league takeover, Nugent and his attorneys brought an offer from a group headed by Sayre Ramsdell, a former Philco executive who ran an advertising agency. The owners started sour on the proposal, particularly Cubs owner Phil Wrigley, who doubted Ramsdell's fiscal stability. "An advertising agency doesn't need any capital. They always do business on the advertisers' money," he said. "The only asset they have is an account. If the account takes another agency on, the agency, if it had only one account, folds up." The offer was rejected, on Wrigley's motion.[40]

Frick then presented the framework of an offer he had received representing a group headed by William Cox, a local lumber magnate. The group included two uncles of future president George H.W. Bush: George Herbert Walker and Louis Walker, who like Cox were Yale graduates.[41]

Stoneham tried to warn them. "He tried to run professional football here in the Stadium, and he left things in a pretty tough shape," Stoneham said. "I mean, he ran out on everyone, including the players."[42] The league owners authorized Frick to purchase all of the Phils' stock, including Nugent's share. As part of the purchase, the National League assumed the Phils' debt of more than $200,000—$136,000 of which was owed to the League, with the plan of selling the team to Cox's group (though they went unidentified in the league's post-meeting statement).[43]

Many in the Philadelphia media were indignant at the league's action. Columnist Ed Pollock of the *Philadelphia Evening Bulletin* described it as "what amounts to a dignified bum rush" on Nugent; "the Phils were sold out from under President Gerry Nugent today," Red Smith wrote in the *Record*.[44] It took a few days more than Frick had hoped, but on February 20, he announced that the league had sold the Phils to Cox's syndicate. The price was estimated at $230,000, less than the offer Nugent had rejected the year before as a "gift price." The identities of Cox's syndicate members were not disclosed, but Jack Kelly was not one of them.[45]

Cox turned out to be a suitable replacement for MacPhail as a thorn in Frick's side. He quickly became a source of protests and appeals. The St. Louis Cardinals' ground crew moved too slowly in covering the field for a rain delay with their team at bat, and Cox protested.[46] Frick called for the game to be completed, and Cox demanded a forfeit instead.[47] Then Frick upheld a Giants protest that Phils player Babe Dahlgren should have been called out for stepping into a pitch (the umpire had turned his head to respond to a coach's complaining and missed the play, calling it a no-pitch), instead of being allowed to continue batting and hitting a three-run double, breaking a 1–1 extra-inning tie. Following that decision, Cox made his appeal to the media rather than to the commissioner. "We have no confidence that the rule book is the backbone of baseball law," he said. "It is merely a vehicle to be interpreted at the whim of the president of the National League."[48]

Cox also appealed to the National League owners, who upheld Frick's decision. After the meeting, Cox semi-apologized. "I have heard that some considered this to have been a personal attack upon the integrity of President Frick. I wish to correct any such impression as being erroneous and never so intended by me." He restated his disagreement with Frick's decision, but added, "If my desire to fight as hard for the boys on my team as they have fought for Philadelphia on the field has led me into a statement susceptible of interpretation as a personal attack on Mr. Frick's integrity, I regret it and apologize for it."[49]

Soon Cox's status soured, and deeply—not from injudicious comments, but gambling. By August, Landis was asking him to respond to rumors that he had bet on games. Landis's main witness, as it turned out, was Bucky Harris, whom Cox had deposed as Phillies manager in midseason. At first, Cox denied the reports, saying "an associate in his lumber business" had placed such bets until Cox told him to stop. After the season ended, however, Cox admitted to Landis that he had bet on the Phillies as many as 20 times from the beginning of the season until May, when he realized such betting was against the rules. Landis scheduled a hearing for December 4, 1943.

Before the hearing could take place, Cox resigned as team president and announced his intentions to sell the team. Frick was no doubt stung that his handpicked Phillies owner should self-destruct so promptly and impressively, but he deferred to the commissioner for further action. Cox assumed his resignation would spare him a public grilling by the commissioner, but he was wrong. Landis responded with a blistering letter that concluded by permanently banning Cox from baseball.[50] Cox added a sad sign-off with an appearance on WOR radio (Frick's old station) in which he characterized his bets as evidence of his support for his team and gave a dramatic farewell to baseball.[51]

Frick then supervised the sale of the Phillies for the second time in a year. This time around, it was bought by Robert Carpenter, Sr., who had married Margaretta Lametta DuPont in 1911 and joined the family company, DuPont Chemical. He had helped guide the company beyond its roots as an explosives manufacturer to the conglomerate it is today. Carpenter installed his 28-year-old son, Robert Jr., as team president, making him the youngest in major league history.[52] Frick was as enthusiastic about the Carpenters as he had been about Cox nine months earlier: "I consider the National League mighty lucky to have a man of Mr. Carpenter's caliber now one of us," he said. "I am certain both he and his son will do a fine job with the Phillies."[53] The second time was luckier for Frick and the Phillies. The Carpenters would own the team until 1981.

Cox added a surreal epilogue to his Phillies ownership when he changed his mind and demanded that Landis hold the hearing, as scheduled. Landis concurred, and even opened the hearing to sports writers. Cox claimed at the hearing that his confession was part of a ruse to expose a disloyal employee, and three witnesses supported his alibi. They were contradicted not only by Harris, but also by Nathan Alexander, Cox's longtime friend and personal assistant, who claimed that he had called on Cox to resign at a team directors meeting in October. Ultimately, Landis cited

Cox's radio broadcast confession as the most damning evidence and upheld the lifetime baseball ban. Frick did not participate in the hearing.[54] Cox would be the last person banished from baseball for gambling until Commissioner A. Bartlett Giamatti conferred the penalty on Pete Rose in 1989.

The 1943 post-season was supposed to be a much more positive time for major league baseball. By late August, Landis, along with Frick and Harridge, was ready to announce plans for a post-season Armed Forces tour by two teams of major leaguers. Details—where the players would visit, who would be on the team—were sparse. But the plan was known to have the approval of the two commanding officers, General Dwight Eisenhower in Europe and General Douglas MacArthur in the Pacific— both rabid baseball fans.[55] Within two weeks, Frick announced that 124 National League players had volunteered for the tour.[56]

The two teams were assembled, with Frankie Frisch of the Pirates and Joe Cronin of the Red Sox as managers. Sadly, the tour was indefinitely postponed by the War Department on October 2. Major General A.D. Surles wrote Landis, "Increased activities in the Pacific have created greater demands upon transportation than was anticipated." The USO was able to put together a six-week tour, with four players and a manager visiting Alaska and the Aleutian Islands. At a press luncheon hastily put together by Frick following their return, Stan Musial and Danny Litwhiler of the Cardinals, Hank Borowy of the Yankees, Dixie Walker of the Dodgers and Frisch reported that the soldiers were as hungry for baseball talk as they were for photos of Betty Grable.[57]

By the approach of the 1944 season, the tides of war were beginning to swing in favor of the Allied Forces, and the human demands had increased. Baseball owners began to worry whether they would have enough players available to field teams. Breadon said that so many of his Cardinals players had been drafted since the 1943 season, he did not know if he could put together the minimum roster of 19. Frick replied, "Of course our 1944 season isn't going to be easy. But I still feel that as long as we have nine men to a team we should play ball."[58]

Branch Rickey backed up his league president. "We would not need more than seventeen men, and there is no chance that we will quit," he said, adding, "It is bad taste for any club owner to imply that we will not be able to continue because of a lowered standard of players and a manpower stringency."

Quickly, Breadon cried misquote. "Rather, say I misunderstood the man's questions, or he failed to understand my real feelings on the matter," he said. "I answered some questions, admitted there were dark clouds in the picture, but certainly did not wish to convey the impression we did not expect to go on in 1944."[59]

As the teams prepared to open their training camps, Frick reported that every team had at least 28 players on its roster. The armed forces were not accepting as many men over 30 as had been anticipated, and these and other players who were being returned promised potentially larger reserve lists.[60]

As the 1944 season began and the war dragged on, Frick intensified his mission as baseball's defender of the faith. To him, the continuation of baseball was a matter of morale overseas, citing "the thousands of men far from home, in camps and on the seas—eager to find out the score, to know who pitched … details that bring them a touch of America as they knew it before war entered their lives." The fiery preaching continued at a late-April talk to the New York Advertising Club. After citing donations of almost $1 million to war-related charities and the donation of 647,000 pints of blood, Frick concluded: "The real example of genuine democracy is on the playing fields of America. It is the one place American youth meets on common ground and the real lesson of democracy can best be preached."[61]

When league owners met for the 1944 All-Star Game in Pittsburgh, two items were on the agenda. First, the owners approved unlimited night baseball on weekdays, though not unanimously and only for the 1944 season. The two leagues also debated whether to extend the contract of its 77-year-old commissioner beyond 1946. Off the record, several team owners expressed a desire for Landis to quit and accept his pension. One owner, looking ahead to postwar baseball, said the game needed an energetic promoter, not "a cop to tell us whom we can send to Squeedunk and whom we have been covering up. Those details have become ridiculous in the face of vaster, more vital issues." Landis's health was also a concern. It was reported that during the meeting he "visibly showed the effects of the intense heat."[62]

The commissioner's apparent poor health, as well as the upcoming end to both his contract and the war, set off speculation concerning his successor. Many owners and journalists agreed that baseball was far past the "Black Sox" scandal that brought about Landis's hiring, and needed a promoter more than a police officer. As they looked for a strong public voice and enthusiastic promoter, names that popped up included former New York mayor Jimmy Walker and a former journalist and enthusiastic baseball promoter, National League president Ford Frick.

6. The War

The talk about Landis's potential successor intensified heading into the World Series, after it was announced that the commissioner would not be able to attend, because of illness.[63] He remained in the hospital October and November (not voting in a national election for the first time in 57 years), so a committee met, with Frick and Harridge as members, in Chicago on November 16 to determine what to recommend at the December league meetings.

The committee concluded that any such decisions should be left to Landis himself. Not only did they avoid asking Landis to resign, as some had rumored, but they also recommended that he be granted another seven-year contract, assuring him of the office of commissioner until he was 83. Landis was reportedly cheered by the news, while his secretary, Leslie O'Connor, said, "That ought to kill all the silly rumors going around the country."[64]

7

A New Commissioner

Barely more than a week after being recommended for another term, Landis passed away. O'Connor, in tears, read a brief statement: "Judge Kenesaw Mountain Landis died at 5:35 with his family at his bedside. In compliance with his wishes no funeral services will be held. Also in accord with his desires cremation will take place privately and friends have been asked not to send flowers."

Frick called Landis's passing "a terrific loss to baseball. He contributed more to the game than any other man. I feel a deep personal loss, for through our years of close association I developed for him an intense personal affection."[1] Landis had been born the year after the Civil War ended, and died less than a year before World War II ended.

Before the earlier meeting, some had speculated that a three-man advisory board—comprising Frick, Harridge and O'Connor—would be commissioned to run baseball until a new commissioner could be appointed. After Landis's death, the advisory board idea was revived, though most observers assumed that O'Connor would decline.

Attention thus turned to the December major league meetings, which had moved back to New York City after several meetings in Chicago (out of deference to Landis's health problems). Some speculated that Frick would be elected commissioner there, to fill the void quickly.[2] Instead, separate resolutions in both league meetings endorsed the formation of the advisory council, with O'Connor accepting membership, though strictly as a temporary measure until a new commissioner could be appointed.[3] The owners also approved a ten-member committee, five from each league, to initiate a search for a new commissioner.[4]

Thus the owners left convinced that there was no hurry in finding a new commissioner, with Frick, Harridge and O'Connor in charge. It soon became clear, however, that baseball would need a strong voice to address emerging threats to the game. On New Year's Day, War Mobilization

Director James F. Byrnes suggested revised guidelines for 4-Fs, who made up the majority of major league baseball players, to direct them toward war-related industries or even appropriate military service.[5] The new guidelines threatened not only major league rosters, but also the season itself. Given this threat, respected voices began to call for the prompt selection of a new commissioner. "Baseball is going on," a *Sporting News* editorial proclaimed. "But baseball would be in a much happier position if it knew that in the office of the high commissioner another Landis sat, ready to fire if firing became necessary."

So sports journalists sustained a favored narrative that at the February meeting, the owners committee would present a new agreement defining the commissioner's duties and then quickly elect a new commissioner to guide the sport through this crisis. Within this scenario, John Drebinger of the *New York Times* claimed that Frick was the favorite, for several reasons: his years of experience as National League president, his balanced vocal support of the war effort and the survival of baseball, and the expressed lack of interest in the position by his American League counterpart, Harridge.[6]

The Sporting News blazed a similar sentiment in its lead headline on January 18: "Ford Frick Reported Choice for Landis Post." The article was written by Frick's good friend Dan Daniel. Daniel based his prediction on statements by Ed Barrow, Yankees owner, who declared his opposition to bringing in another outsider (like Landis). He named several insiders, Frick included, whom he considered equal to the task. Daniel surmised, without even an anonymous source, that Barrow supported Frick for the job and had done some telephone campaigning on his behalf, "because, almost overnight, talk of an outsider was hushed, and Frick began to stand out, even in the American League."[7]

What was generating the pro–Frick buzz? Was it his friends in the press box? It is likely that team owners, particularly in the National League, were open to Frick's promotion to the top position, especially after his good work in stabilizing the National League franchises. However, Daniel's article inflated Barrow's comments beyond his expressed support for Frick. Rather than intention or cooperation, however, it was probably the result of sports journalists letting their excitement over a former colleague's possible great fortune get the better of everyone, combined with their obsession with trying to appear ahead of the curve on important developments—even if those predictions turn out to be completely wrong.

The Sporting News, noting that Frick was "one of the outstanding prospects for the post of baseball commissioner," had Ward Morehouse, drama critic of the *New York Sun*, "review" Frick's career as a sports journalist and baseball administrator. The review provided details on Frick's past and current life more than a critique of his job "performance." "Always a leader type, Ford Frick has developed as an executive with the passing years," Morehouse wrote. "Any doubts that may have existed as to his lack of forcefulness and decision when he took office have completely disappeared. He has been a great promoter for his league and has proven himself, it is now freely admitted, an excellent president."

That definitely sounds like some intense campaigning, but the article finished with a diplomatic statement from Frick, who acknowledged the attention but refused to discuss it: "He will tell you, as he has told me, that, at 50, he is quite content with the job he has had for ten years, and is looking forward to four more years in his present office, the presidency of the National League."[8]

The Sporting News' readers would only have to read the facing page to see that Frick's candidacy was already in trouble. President Roosevelt had tempered Byrnes' general warnings with specific comments that seemed to protect baseball for at least the 1945 season, thus slowing the rush to appoint a new commissioner as soon as possible. A letter by Reds President Warren Giles suggested a delay in appointing a commissioner until after the war, and many club owners expressed support for the idea.[9]

As the meetings approached, however, news emerged that perhaps the 1945 season would in fact be in jeopardy, and the information came from Frick himself. After meeting with Selective Service leadership, Frick would not give details but intimated that based on the information he would bring to the owners' meeting, both leagues would have to judge whether baseball could continue in 1945. The announcement set off grave speculation on the immediate future of the game.[10]

Frick's trip also set off criticism from O'Connor, Landis's former secretary. Landis had instituted an unwritten policy that baseball officials should not travel to Washington on their own initiative, but should come when called, and O'Connor criticized Frick for violating that policy, noting that Frick represented neither baseball nor its three-man advisory council. Harridge joined in the disapproval.

Frick asserted that he had traveled to Washington as National League president, seeking guidance that would help him and his league plan ahead. Daniel supported his friend's decision: "Horse racing hung around waiting to be asked to Washington, and got the axe. Baseball is not equally vulnerable. But, why sit around waiting? The time for such tactics is gone. The situation is serious."[11] Other National League owners, like Sam Breadon, also came to Frick's defense.[12] To many, like *Times* columnist Arthur Daley, the back-and-forth demonstrated the unworkability of the advisory council concept and pointed to baseball's need for a strong single voice.[13]

Was Frick inserting a touch of urgency into the upcoming owners' meeting to promote his own candidacy for baseball commissioner? Probably not. Clark Griffith, owner of the Senators and well connected among Beltway politicians, had accompanied Frick on his visit, and he did not criticize Frick's actions.[14] The next day, however, Griffith gave his own opinion of the sentiment in Washington, and while he professed some uncertainty, he also predicted the season would be preserved.[15]

The same issue of *The Sporting News* that included Daniel's defense of Frick's trip also had a news item that would ultimately prove foreboding for Frick's chances at assuming baseball's top position: A front-page article noted the announcement by U.S. Senator Albert "Happy" Chandler of Kentucky that he would oppose "work or fight" legislation rumored to be in the works, to protect baseball. The article concluded, "Senator Chandler frequently has been mentioned as a prospect for the post of commissioner left vacant by the death of Judge Landis. He is said to be the choice of a leading club owner in the National League and two in the American."[16]

To some sports writers, however, the baseball owners were not willing to wait. The *Times'* Drebinger insisted that the owners were prepared to extend their meeting to discuss and vote for a new commissioner, with Frick as the leading candidate. The main task would be to approve a new working agreement for the new commissioner, whoever he might be.[17] Drebinger's prediction was bolstered by Larry MacPhail, who had returned from his World War II service as a part-owner of the Yankees. To MacPhail, the only debate was whether the owners would prefer an internal candidate like Frick or a candidate outside organized baseball. If they chose to look within, MacPhail said, his candidate was Frick, despite their earlier conflicts.[18]

But both Drebinger and MacPhail were wrong. The owners approved the new major league agreement, but the election of a new commissioner had not been placed on the agenda, and only a unanimous vote would allow its discussion. Enough owners opposed Frick to prevent that. It was acknowledged to be a severe blow to Frick's chances.[19]

Coming out of the meeting, the pro–Frick forces—among both the owners and the journalists—believed that his candidacy was not dead. A confidential poll of league owners showed that Frick had 11 of the 12 votes needed to be named commissioner.[20] Other leading candidates were FBI Director J. Edgar Hoover and former Postmaster General James A. Farley, both of whom fit the preference of someone outside of baseball but well-connected in Washington.[21]

A four-owner committee—Sam Breadon (Cardinals) and Phil Wrigley (Cubs) of the National League and Donald Barnes (Browns) and Alva Bradley (Indians) of the American League—was appointed to sift through candidates and choose finalists for the other owners to consider. The committee choices did not enhance Frick's odds. Barnes and Bradley had stated their preference for a commissioner from outside baseball. Wrigley and Breadon had expressed a willingness to vote for Frick at the February meeting, but later backtracked, acknowledging an openness to outside candidates.[22]

As the new season approached, Frick's fortunes seemed to change week to week. His and Harridge's work had improved baseball's status to the point where the 1945 season seemed assured. Then, on March 13, at a press conference following a visit by Griffith, President Roosevelt declared baseball safe. Even with the various laws addressing 4-F status going through Congress, Roosevelt endorsed a continuation of baseball, assuring that the 1945 season would proceed.[23] Following Roosevelt's lead, the War Manpower Commission allowed players to leave their factory jobs until October. In the opinion of commission chief Paul V. McNutt, the players were performing as important a function on the playing field as they were in the factory. Frick applauded the decision, adding, "The use of these players should enable us to go through the coming season in good shape."[24]

The increasing good news actually decreased support for Frick's candidacy. His successful navigation of the wartime bureaucracy showed a statesmanship that his opponents claimed could be found only in an outside candidate. That same success, however, also worked against his candidacy by removing the urgency that would have helped it. Thus, in the midst of circumstances he could not control, Frick worked for the best interests of baseball, even if those efforts undermined his goal of becoming its commissioner.

The selection committee surprised everyone on March 31, announcing that they had completed their work and had arrived at a "recommendation." The committee had been criticized for its slow deliberations and for canceling one meeting because it had attracted excessive publicity. Thus, the announcement, like the secret meeting it followed, sidestepped the baseball writers' attention, increasing the speculation it unleashed.[25]

On April 9, O'Connor, as chair of the Advisory Council, called a meeting for April 24 in Cleveland, to discuss the committee's recommendations.[26] The committee members continued their discipline of silence, but the interim allowed greedy speculation on the leading candidates. The usual suspects (Frick, Hoover, Farley) continued, but as the meeting approached, Happy Chandler's name moved from the fringes toward the center as a leading candidate.[27]

In the interim, the tragic death of President Roosevelt on April 12, besides removing the nation's leader at a crucial point in the war and history, also deprived baseball of a trustworthy ally. As the meeting approached, pessimism ruled, with most assuming that the owners would defer on choosing a commissioner until after the war, when the pool of high-quality candidates supposedly would deepen. A *Sporting News* survey of sports writers and editors found deep support for the "do-nothing" option.[28]

A report emerged that Barrow had been offered the position as a temporary stopgap option, but had turned it down.[29] As the owners prepared for the meeting, the Associated Press proclaimed, "[T]oday they were still as far from one mind as last Nov. 25, when the death of Kenesaw Mountain Landis vacated the office for the first time since it was established twenty-four years ago."[30]

At the meeting in Cleveland, the owners agreed to reduce the number of candidates to five. The five "finalists" were Frick, Farley, and Chandler, along with Frank Lausche, governor of Ohio, and Robert Hannegan, former commissioner of the Internal Revenue Service and current chairman of the Democratic National Committee.

As the owners discussed the five finalists, a curious turn of events took place. Griffith, a strong supporter of Frick's who had lobbied federal government officials with him throughout the war, announced his opposition to Frick's candidacy. An astonished Branch Rickey (whose memorandum provided the most complete record of the meeting) realized at that moment that Frick's chances were dashed. Sadly, Frick was also in attendance at the meeting where his opportunity to become commissioner of the game he loved cruelly passed.

In a later interview responding to claims that he had engineered Chandler's ascension, Larry MacPhail said that he had voted for Frick on the first two ballots, as he had promised Barrow. MacPhail said he switched his vote to other candidates only when it became clear that Frick would not be selected.[31] A few years later, MacPhail actually blamed Warren Giles for Frick's defeat. He claimed that Giles undercut support for Frick by making a strong speech that expressed respect for his league president but declared the need for owners to bring in someone outside of baseball.[32]

The owners reduced the finalists to three—eliminating Frick and Farley and moving ahead with Chandler, Hannegan, and Lausche. They took a vote, and Chandler got eight of the 16 votes cast, with Hannegan getting five and Lausche three. Giles opposed Chandler, considering him something of a clown politician, with his showboat singing, often with his children. But the other owners overruled him and conducted another vote, this time with the top two candidates. Chandler barely gained the magic 12th vote; it was the final secret ballot read. Frick, ever the loyal soldier, dutifully drafted the press release announcing the appointment of Chandler to the position Frick had come so close to attaining. It reported that Chandler was elected unanimously on the first ballot.

The owners also tasked Frick with traveling to Washington to help Chandler prepare to assume his new duties.[33]

As something of a consolation prize, a *Sporting News* editorial praised Frick: "There is no doubt that if the two leagues had been able to get together on Ford Frick, he would have made a splendid commissioner. No man in baseball has done more for the game in this wartime period, with its myriad difficulties." At the same time, the editorial affirmed the wisdom of the decision to hire someone from outside baseball.[34]

Recalling his selection

In April 1945, the owners passed over Frick as baseball commissioner in favor of A. B. "Happy" Chandler, a U.S. senator from Kentucky (Harris and Ewing/Library of Congress).

in his memoirs, Chandler did not acknowledge how close Frick came to the job. In discussing controversies during his tenure, however, he betrayed suspicion toward Frick that was left over from the selection process. "The New York writers wanted the job to go to Frick," Chandler wrote. "He was an old sports writer—one of them. He was already climbing in baseball, having made it to president of the National League."[35] As Chandler's term proceeded, he would clash with Frick—and with virtually every baseball owner.

As the season heated up and World War II continued to wind down, Frick had no choice but to return to the background. For five head-spinning months, he had helped to guide baseball and had been discussed as its next leader. But the stage now belonged to Chandler, and Frick once again was the commissioner's dutiful deputy as National League president. To those who complained about Frick's meek compliance when he later assumed the commissioner's office, his response to the owners' treatment during the 1945 search certainly set the stage.

The media tension Chandler cited was not evident at the beginning of his tenure. At a press conference on June 4, Chandler handled a two-hour barrage of questions so deftly that *The Sporting News* declared, "And when it was all over, the finicky specialists of the New York newspapers voted Chandler the right man for the job, and put their stamp of approval on the magnates' choice."[36]

His life having returned to the old normal, Frick faced the usual challenges. One of his more colorful umpires, George Magerkurth, faced charges in Cincinnati after punching a heckler after a game. That was bad enough, but the umpire had also punched the wrong fan, and his wrongly victimized victim, Thomas J. Longo, was a sports official himself, having refereed local boxing matches for 15 years. Although Magerkurth at first insisted that he had socked the right heckler ("I have pretty good eyes, even for an umpire," he told local reporters), he apologized to Longo and gave him a $100 check for medical expenses, so the charges were dropped. Just as noteworthy is Frick's response; no record exists of him suspending or disciplining Magerkurth. Frick must have been satisfied with how the umpire made the call in handling the incident.[37] It was later reported that baseball fans in Dayton, Longo's hometown, were taking up a collection to repay Magerkurth the $100 he had paid Longo.[38]

Frick's disciplining of his umpires could veer toward the comical. In one such situation in 1947, umpire "Beans" Reardon accepted an offer by Cardinals manager Frisch to borrow his car rather than pay cab fare, apparently clueless to the conflict of interest. It came to Frick's attention after

Reardon ejected Frisch the next day, which cost the manager a $50 fine. With the fine, Frisch sent Frick a note suggesting that he charge the fine to his umpire as a car rental fee. Frick forgave the fine, but reminded Reardon and his other umpires that it was a bad idea to borrow a car—particularly from a manager or player.[39]

On August 15 in the United States, Japan announced its surrender. For the entire nation, a long nightmare was over, and baseball was no different. Chandler proactively called an immediate meeting of baseball's leaders, including Frick, to enable the game to return to its pre-war state as quickly as possible. The most important decision arising from the "postwar planning committee" meeting was a promise to give returning veterans "every opportunity to re-establish themselves in the game, regardless of physical condition." The players would return to their former clubs at their full previous salary for 15 days, guaranteed. Players who could not return to old form would not be assigned to a lower league for 30 days, having been allowed to pass through the waiver process.[40]

Frick would do his part to apply the spirit of the policy in 1946, when he declared that Reds catcher Ray Mueller's 217 consecutive games played streak was still intact, because it had been disrupted by his military service. The streak would last only 17 games more.[41]

At Chandler's urging, the committee also decided to allocate $50,000 toward a promotional campaign aimed at youth, to assure baseball of its stature as the national pastime. The decision included no specifics, however, except to place the strategy under the commissioner's authority—separate from the major and minor leagues. The move ignored Frick's promotional background and experience, directing instead the appointment of a promotional director reporting to Chandler.[42]

Perhaps the first seeds of discord emerged when *The Sporting News* reported on Chandler's enthusiastic negotiations with the Navy to bring the World Series champions to the South Pacific, where they would play a team of Armed Forces all-stars. Only Frick seemed cool on the idea, wondering whether the commissioner had the authority to send such a team. "It is up to the men themselves," he said. "Just as soon as the final out is flashed in the World Series, the members of the two clubs are on their own. Baseball cannot tell them where to go after that."[43]

The situation became tenser as the commissioner and league presidents planned the 1945 World Series. Chandler reportedly rankled Frick and Harridge by suggesting that they increase the umpires' World Series pay from $2,500 to $4,000. The league presidents were offended on two counts: not only was the umpires' pay a league matter, but Chandler had proposed the raise with the umpires in the room, creating an awkward situation.[44]

From there, the story escalated, as several newspapers reported that the owners, dissatisfied even as Chandler's tenure had barely begun, had offered to buy out his seven-year, $50,000/year contract. At a hastily called meeting, the 13 of 16 owners present unanimously adopted a resolution that stated, "There is no basis of fact to the story." *The Sporting News* story ominously concluded, "[T]he trouble is not yet ended. In fact, more of it is reported to be on the way."[45]

Despite Frick's apparent lukewarm response to the South Pacific tour, the National League was able to pull together a team of 15 players for a South Pacific tour, sponsored by the USO along with the Army and Navy. No American League players signed up, though they were invited. Harridge repeated Frick's assertion that it was up to the players themselves to decide, and when they decided not to, Harridge did not exert the effort that Frick did.[46]

Heading into the December league meetings, the tension was still apparent. At its first meeting on December 4, the baseball promotional committee, which had been established at Chandler's urging, decided that the efforts should be directed by an independent foundation, not one working under the commissioner's office—certainly a rebuff directed at Chandler.[47] He responded by withholding his office's support for the new arrangement—not only because the idea was his originally, but also because he felt that the goal of the campaign would be jeopardized.[48] In a speech before the meetings, Chandler described the idea as "personally obnoxious to me and it will be fine with me if it does not pass." Chandler prevailed: the proposal for the independent foundation was withdrawn, with a revised proposal promised by the February meetings.[49]

The annual baseball writers' dinner held in conjunction with the February league meetings provided an awkward moment as the writers had their first shots at Chandler. In one of the skits that lampooned baseball executives, Louis Effrat of the *New York Times* portrayed Frick and satirized his loss of the commissioner's post to Chandler by singing, "I Wish I Could Be Happy."[50]

Coming out of the meetings, Frick and Chandler discovered an adversary whose intrusion would require them to set aside any lingering drama. Hopes of postwar tranquility were shattered when Mexican League baseball magnates Jorge and Bernardo Pasquel began conspicuously courting major league baseball players. It created what became known as the Baseball War of 1946.

Luis Olmo, a Brooklyn outfielder holding out for a better contract, told a reporter in early February that he was considering an offer from Bernardo Pasquel, who promised to beat the Dodgers' offer by 50 percent.[51] The Dodgers raised their offer from $10,000 to $12,000, but Olmo spurned it and signed a three-year contract with the Mexican League's Veracruz club. The contract was estimated as high as $40,000. Dan Gardella, a Giants prospect who had fallen out of favor with team management, announced that he had signed a five-year contract.[52] The game was on.

What caused the players to consider opportunities south of the border was baseball's reserve clause, which bound a player to one team throughout his career. To Frick and the other leaders of organized baseball, the reserve clause prevented chaos, and the majority of fans agreed. Public support was girded by traditional sentiment towards sports as innocent play that did not deserve high pay—nostalgia that would be severely challenged as television flooded the revenue stream. For the players with no other options, a well-funded opportunity, even in a foreign country, was at least a choice.

In his memoirs, Frick defended the reserve clause as something that preserved the competitive integrity of baseball.[53] "How can public confidence in player loyalty and will to win be maintained, if the player, while playing for one club, seeks a job with another club or is pressed with offers from several other clubs, against some of which he is playing?"[54] In fairness to his arguments, these comments were published years later, as the reserve clause was in the process of being set aside and before the emergence of free agency reset the relationship between individual and team success.

The American newspapers cast the Mexican baseball conflict in racist terms, with allusions to Pancho Villa and pesos and descriptions of departing players as "Mexican jumping beans." At the same time, they ignored the wartime raids of Latin American baseball leagues by major league owners seeking remedy to depleted talent resources in the United States. In those cases, complaints to Landis and Chandler were brushed off or responded to weakly, in the opinion of the international league officials.[55]

Such was baseball's alarm that Chandler held a meeting in Havana on March 9–10, originally scheduled to welcome a Havana team to the Florida-International League. Chandler used the occasion to state that any major league baseball player who jumped to the Mexican League would have until Opening Day to return or face a five-year banishment from the league. Harridge and Griffith accompanied Chandler on the trip. Though Frick was not there, Chandler stated, "Ford Frick, president of the National League, will approve of my action, I am sure."[56]

Throughout spring training, the specter of the Mexican League provided pre–Opening Day drama. St. Louis Browns infielder Vern Stephens signed with the Veracruz team but returned to the United States after only two games, declaring that he "didn't like Mexico and wasn't happy among all those Spanish-speaking people."[57] Dodgers catcher Mickey Owen waffled indecisively at the border, but ultimately decided to accept the Pasquels' offer and play for the Torreon club. He attributed the indecision to fan and media pressure.[58] Frick remained in the background during this phase of the conflict, deferring leadership to Chandler.

Organized baseball turned to the courts for relief, with the Yankees gaining a temporary injunction restraining the Pasquel brothers from signing any more of their players. Justice Julius Miller rejected the Pasquels' argument that baseball was an illegal monopoly.[59] The judge set a May 28 trial date for making the injunction permanent, but the trial was delayed until June.[60]

Throughout the controversy, sports writers framed the story as a Chandler-Pasquel conflict, leaving Frick in the background. Even a widely reported meeting between Chandler, Frick, and Harridge on June 3, formally to discuss the next month's All-Star Game, brought no new developments on the Mexican League, with Frick merely hinting that a change in the All-Star team selection had been discussed. Significantly, by this time, Chandler had begun to institute a policy of silence toward the baseball press, leaving Frick to supply his former colleagues with meager scraps of information.[61]

The conflict hit closer to home for Frick in June. As Chandler later described the exchange, Frick "called me in New York while I was attending a game at Ebbets Field. He asked me, 'Did you know Sam Breadon was in Mexico?' 'No,' I replied. 'Did you know about it?'" Frick told the commissioner he did not, either.[62] Breadon, owner of the Cardinals, claimed that he traveled south to meet with Pasquel on his own, without seeking Frick's or Chandler's approval, on a fact-finding mission—though Pasquel's league had signed away three of Breadon's players earlier that month.[63]

Breadon was contacted by Chandler in Mexico and summoned to Cincinnati to meet with him and Frick. When he could not report as quickly as they wished, Chandler fined him $5,000 and told him that he would not be able to participate in league meetings or business for 30 days. The owner suspension was later rescinded, thanks in part to the intervention of Red Sox owner Tom Yawkey, at a dinner before the All-Star Game meetings.[64] The fine was returned to Breadon on the advice of both Frick and National League attorney Lou Carroll, Chandler later said.[65]

Frick also faced a personal drama during the All-Star Game joint league meetings: His hotel room was robbed as he slept. The burglar stole his money ($85) but left the league souvenirs and mementoes Frick had brought to the game—"watches, tie clasps, plaques, and cigarette cases"—probably because they were inscribed with player names. "I'm darned glad I didn't wake up," Frick said afterward.[66]

With the end of the war, combat more physical than legal returned to the baseball field, and along with it Frick's role as disciplinarian. The main event of the 1946 season was a pregame batting practice brawl between the Dodgers and Cubs. Attempts by umpires and security to restore order were complicated by the crowd of players surrounding the fight. Frick ended up suspending four players and even a Chicago coach who reportedly shoved a police officer trying to reach the center of attention.[67]

Frick also had to address again the practice of throwing at opposing batters, particularly in the context of a fiery series between the Dodgers and Cardinals, with the victims being mostly Cardinals. Dodgers manager Leo Durocher claimed that Frick's crusade was focused mainly on his pitchers and that Cardinals manager Eddie Dyer had complained to Frick. Frick denied Durocher's claim and said his comments were directed across the league, though Durocher rejected both Frick's explanation and his directive.[68]

In a shocking development from the league meetings—and a response to the Mexican League intrusion—Chandler announced that the players themselves would be included in a committee deliberating a new major league player contract. The Mexican League, along with the seeds of a union movement (the American Baseball Guild, launched by Boston attorney Robert Murphy) had forced organized baseball to do more to recognize the rights of players, particularly if it wanted to avoid judicial scrutiny of the reserve clause.

Frick served on the committee drafting the new agreement; it included two owners and three players from each league. The players' demands included a $5,000 minimum salary, expense money for spring training, and moving expenses for traded players. The players also proposed a pension for all former major leaguers, to replace the benevolence fund avail-

7. A New Commissioner

able only to those who could demonstrate need. The players also demanded an end to the ten-day "notice of release" clause—which at the time was the only provision for a player about to be cut by his team and typified the excessive unbalance of power in owners' favor.[69]

As the committee met and a new draft agreement emerged, Chandler shrewdly moved to the background and allowed Frick to act as the media contact. Given his still-strong relationships with baseball journalists, particularly in New York City, Frick allowed organized baseball to gain a public relations advantage over those who sought to undercut it.

In particular, Frick gained positive coverage for his disputing of a claim by Murphy, the would-be union organizer, that 40 percent of the Boston Braves earned less than $5,000 a year. Frick pointed out that his number was around ten percent in the National League, with an average salary of $9,500. Murphy was forced to backtrack and correct that the 40 percent referred to the Braves who earned less than the new minimum of $7,500 that his organization was proposing.[70]

Frick claimed that most of the player demands were reflected in a new contract proposal he had developed in 1936 but had never submitted. "I drew up this entire reform plan as far back as 1936. I should have had the National League adopt it then. But again I plead the foe of progress, inertia," he said, dutifully quoted by Dan Daniel, whose name always seemed to be at the top of such pro–Frick articles. Frick said he "dragged it out" as the various forms of unrest swept over baseball. "The American League asked to see it. One thing led to another and we are going to get the reforms we should have instituted long ago."[71]

As the amicable player-owner negotiations moved toward a conclusion, Owen, one of the highest profile players to sign with the Mexican League, returned to the United States and applied for reinstatement. He sent his request to Frick, who forwarded it to Chandler, since the five-year suspension for Mexican League players was his decision.[72] Owen even traveled to Cincinnati to personally plead his case to the commissioner, but Chandler was out of town. His former fellow major leaguers blasted his return, with many claiming it was precipitated by the progress they had made in seeking a new contract. Chandler sided with the players, upholding Owen's suspension—which Frick called "a good ruling."[73]

The owners were interested in negotiating quickly, and not just because an improved player contract would undercut further Mexican League efforts to lure players during the coming off-season. The owners also faced a deadline on the labor front: The Pennsylvania Labor Relations Board had ordered that the Pittsburgh Pirates, who had pushed back a unionization effort in June, vote again on August 21. By that time, with the owners having indicated acceptance of most of the players' demands, the Pirates players voted 15–3 against guild representation.[74]

At a joint meeting of the owners in both leagues in Chicago, they approved the contract proposals on August 28. Included in the owners' decision was the establishment of a new executive council that would include not only the commissioner and the two league presidents, as before, but also two owners and two player representatives.[75] The player contract proposals emerged out of a more comprehensive document from the executive committee that addressed several issues facing baseball in the post-war era. The report's most controversial features—a discussion, and rejection, of integration—will be outlined in the next chapter.

The owners also approved an expansion of the baseball schedule from 154 games to 168 games, effective with the 1947 season. The expansion was proposed by the two league presidents, although some later indications laid the blame on Frick.[76] To some, the owners were forcing the players to play more games to pay for the concessions they had just won. One criticism that would later prove ironic was the effect the new schedule would have on baseball records. Frick and Harridge claimed that the 154-game schedule was "too loose," and that fitting in more games was a simple adjustment. Much of the criticism came from baseball journalists who could see the effects on their work schedules.[77]

The 168-game schedule's doom was sealed when the players themselves publicly criticized the idea. Their deepest frustration arose from the realization that the expanded schedule had not been a part of their negotiations on the new contract, but had been introduced later. As Fred "Dixie" Walker of the Dodgers, one of the player representatives, said, "To me, this 168-game schedule looks like this: The magnates vote the concessions, and then they say, 'Gee whiz, this is going to cost us something. How about sticking on more games and making the players pay?'"[78]

The new contract was officially accepted at the newly revised council's first meeting on September 16, with most of the player demands accepted. The minimum salary was "believed to be $5,000," according to the *New York Times*. The pension proposed by the players was initiated, with the players and owners matching a $250 annual contribution and the commissioner proposing $175,000 from World Series radio rights.

It was later revealed that one sticking point had emerged: a disagreement about what to do with the increasing money promised by the emergence of television. Although it was not part of the agreement, the players made it clear to the owners that they considered themselves just as entitled to the bonanza they accurately believed was coming. Frick also took occasion at the meeting to inform the players that the 168-game schedule would likely be abandoned by a vote at the December owners meeting.[79] That might have marked the first time that the players were able to change a league policy that worked against them—a subtle but significant shift in player-owner relations that would turn into a monstrous swing in the decades ahead.

In these negotiations, the radio money also proved to be a potential sticking point, because $115,000 of it would have gone to the players and $60,000 to league administration. Players on both World Series teams, the Cardinals and the Red Sox, generously agreed to the arrangement anyway (with the exception of five Red Sox reserves who feared that they would not qualify for the pension and preferred their money up front).[80]

The players did not demand any adjustment to the reserve clause as part of the 1946 negotiations. In an interview decades later, after the clause had been eliminated by court action, Marty Marion, who was a player representative for the St. Louis Cardinals, explained why. Before the flood of television money, he said, the players didn't feel that baseball could survive without the reserve clause. He also noted that baseball's tradition of strong owner control during that time intimidated players from demanding too much; the players knew they could easily be replaced, even more so now that the war had ended.[81]

At the December league meetings, the owners formalized the pension arrangement, with the $250/year team and player contributions. It was also decided that at age 45, any player with ten years of major league service could collect $100/month, adjusted proportionately for fewer seasons of play.[82]

With the conclusion of labor unrest, Frick knew, as did the owners, that the relative peace baseball enjoyed during the postwar boom would soon be disrupted once again. During the Mexican League invasion and guild intrusion, a Brooklyn Dodgers prospect had been putting in his time for the organization's Montreal farm team. Everyone in baseball's leadership understood what was about to happen and the upheaval that it would cause. That player, Jackie Robinson, would make his major league debut the next season—yet another revolutionary change to the idyllic game Ford Frick had tried to maintain.

8

Integration

If the actions of Ford Frick as he guided the National League through baseball's most important moment—integration—seemed complex and even contradictory at times, it's because race was a complicated issue in a different way back then. Frick would consider himself a racially progressive man with no hostility toward African Americans. Still, while a member of the New York chapter of the Baseball Writers' Association of America in the 1920s and 1930s, Frick was a regular in the blackface minstrel band that performed at the annual banquet. The format was familiar: Frick would play "Mr. Interlocutor," the straight man, and his fellow band members—Arthur Mann (who, ironically, wrote the book and screenplay for *The Jackie Robinson Story*), Tom Meany, Henry McLemore of United Press, and Roscoe McGowen of the *New York Times* were frequent sidekicks—would all take the role of "Mr. Bones," whose answers to the questions provided the humor.

The photos would not create the furor in 1947 that they would today, cannonaded across social media and decried on sports talk, all the while impugning Frick's moral standing to address racial issues. These were simply the cultural differences that would not leave Frick open to charges of racism, as judged in 1947. While Frick did step away from the minstrel band after being named National League president,[1] he did a return performance in the minstrel show to mark the baseball dinner's 25th anniversary in 1948—ironically, the first after integration.[2]

As conveyed by Chris Lamb's well-researched book, *Conspiracy of Silence: Sportswriters and the Long Campaign to Desegregate Baseball*, team owners and white sports journalists were reluctant to push for the integration of baseball. In fact, many press boxes were also segregated. Black and labor newspapers were more aggressive in the crusade. One leading journalist and crusader, Wendell Smith of the *Pittsburgh Courier*, a prominent character in the film *42*, interviewed Frick in February 1939.

Though Smith and other African American sportswriters would maintain pressure on Frick and baseball's other leaders for the next decade, in this article Smith seemed encouraged by the league president's apparent openness to black players in the major leagues. "Organized Baseball Willing to Accept Colored Players!" a front-page banner proclaimed.

Smith could not interview Frick in a major league press box, so they had to meet at Frick's hotel. Frick invited him to his "luxurious suite" and once there, presented a surprising openness to integration. "We have always been interested in Negro players," Frick said, "but have not used them because we feel that the general public has not been educated to the point where they will accept them on the same standard as they do the white player."

Frick acknowledged to Smith that there was no policy against African American baseball players, adding, "I think that in the near future people will be willing to accept the Negro ball player just as they have the Negro boxer and college athlete. Times are changing."

To illustrate his own openness, Frick pointed out that as a college basketball player at DePauw, he had an African American teammate ("Noble Sissle, who is now a great orchestra leader"). At a restaurant in Richmond, Indiana, the owner refused to serve him. "Angry, we all got up and walked out," Frick told Smith.

Frick closed the interview with an encouraging, but noncommittal statement: "I can not name any particular day or year, but assure you that when the people ask for the inclusion of your players we will use them. I do not think the time is far off and with constant crusading by the press of both races it is bound to come. However, you must keep fighting."[3]

Frick was repeating what he had said in earlier interviews, including one with Ted Benson of the radical labor newspaper *The Daily Worker*: that there was no stated major league policy against African Americans, that the decision lay with owners rather than league officials, and that opposition came from players and the public. Benson, however, was not as accommodating as Smith. He described Frick's statement as passing the buck and urged readers and fans to pressure him and all of baseball's leaders to integrate.[4]

Blind to its self-forgiving insincerity, Frick maintained that perception of his and others' inertia throughout his career and later life and even mentioned it in his memoirs, well into the civil rights era:

> What baseball operators had done, through the years, was bow abjectly to what they thought was overwhelming public opinion. They were afraid to make a move. They were afraid of upsetting the status quo, afraid of alienating the white clientele that

largely supported the professional game. Through the years that fear crystallized into accepted tradition—and traditions, at times, can be more stultifying than law or statute.[5]

But in 1939, Smith's patience had apparently run out as well. Stung perhaps by criticism of the accommodating tone of his earlier interview, Smith dismissed Frick's rationale. "Mr. Frick, however, couldn't explain satisfactorily how it is that these same Americans (who are not ready for baseball to integrate) will pay as much as $100 to see Joe Louis, a black man, knock a white man out in quicker time than you can say the white man's name," he wrote two weeks after his first interview. His piercing conclusion said, "They call organized baseball the national past time, the game of the American people. But they don't really believe that. How can they?"[6]

By this time, pressure was emerging from political sources as well. In May 1939, Charles Perry, a state senator from New York, introduced a resolution opposing discrimination against African American baseball players.[7] Apparently the resolution failed, because Perry, who represented Harlem, reintroduced it in January 1940. The resolution cited the "unwritten law of baseball" excluding black players and called it "ridiculous."[8] The resolution made its third appearance in February 1943.[9]

Some critics claim that Frick prevented baseball integration in 1943 by allowing the Phillies to be sold to an alternate buyer after Bill Veeck had revealed his plans to buy the team and sign Negro Leagues players. Veeck, gregarious owner of the St. Louis Browns and later the Chicago White Sox, claimed in his autobiography that Frick privately bragged about preventing him from "contaminating the league."[10] Numerous authorities, including Jules Tygiel, have disputed Veeck's account. It was also refuted in a 1998 article co-authored by sports author David Jordan; then-Society for American Baseball Research President Larry Gerlach, a history professor at the University of Utah; and John Rossi, a history professor at La Salle University.[11]

As Jordan, Gerlach, and Rossi point out, no reports from that period exist, whether in major newspapers or in the African American press, about Veeck's proposal. In fact, Veeck did drop in on Nugent after he put the team up for sale. Nugent said, "Veeck stopped in to see me on his way to the World Series and did not mention buying or even being interested in the club." Nugent added, "I saw a clipping from a Milwaukee newspaper which quoted Veeck as saying he had stopped in to see me because he had read that he was interested in buying my club—and he wanted to see what the fuss was all about."[12]

Frick himself made no mention of Veeck's accusations in his own memoirs, and did not attempt to refute them or defend himself when Veeck's book came out. While Veeck's anecdote has been repeated often, the authors claim that there are more credible examples of the opposition by organized baseball (and particularly Landis) to integration.[13]

After Frick's death, a story emerged that indicated race was not the only factor that could bar entry to the major leagues. Sports writer Bob Paul claimed that he tried to get Frick's backing for a Jewish business leader, Dr. Leon Levy, to buy the Phillies from Nugent. Frick said there was no rule against it, written or unwritten, so Paul offered to talk to Frick during a train trip to Chicago. According to Paul, Frick later told him, "I've thought over what you said, and I've come to the conclusion I cannot discuss anything about the sale of the Phillies. So don't bother meeting my train. Besides, I'll be very busy." The prospective owner realized what Frick was saying, and decided not to pursue the matter.[14] Author Bruce Kuklick was more explicit; he claimed Frick "made it clear he wanted neither Jews nor blacks in the majors," though such a view sounds extreme.[15]

In fact, the most effective opposition to integration came from Frick's boss. Landis was a powerful commissioner as the first in the position and had the support of most team owners in both his leadership and his bigotry. Leonard Koppett referred to Landis as "not only a bigot but also a hypocrite" who made it clear "that any club trying to hire [a black player] would have to deal with him." As David Pietrusza noted in his excellent biography of Landis, however, the picture is more complicated. As a judge and as a commissioner, Landis could be progressive in his treatment of African Americans. However, despite his authority to influence such a change, baseball would not integrate until after his death.[16]

Frick acknowledged as much in his own memoirs, with some of his strongest opinions. He noted a meeting in the mid–1930s, when two club owners invited a committee of prominent African Americans, headed by Paul Robeson, to discuss an end to the discrimination that kept non-white players out of major league baseball. Landis blocked such discussion, claiming not only that it contradicted public opinion, but also that it had not been added to the agenda properly.[17]

Baseball was integrated during Landis's tenure, however, in one sense: off-season barnstorming tours pitting African American superstar teams against idle major leaguers. One such tour took place in Southern California in 1935, far from Landis's scrutiny and in a favorable climate, by several definitions. Player-manager Willie Wells claimed Landis personally intervened to cancel the series, in which African American players toured against a ball club that included Lefty Grove and Dizzy Dean. Wells said his team had won 21 straight games before Landis put a stop to it.[18] A similar tour of California in 1943 was also nixed by Landis, according to Negro Leagues star Buck Leonard. By pretense more than sincere concern, Landis claimed to be skeptical of the ethical dealings by the promoters more than he was motivated by racial concerns.[19]

When forced into a public relations corner, Landis could sound judicious and equitable. "There is no rule, formal or informal, or any understanding—unwritten, subterranean or sub-anything—against the hiring of Negro players by the teams of Organized Baseball," said Landis in 1942, responding to a column in the *Daily Worker*.[20] But those who knew Landis recognized that when the theoretical became practical, the rules became informal, the noble became racist, and African American players were excluded.

Landis's opposition was evident at the December 1943 league meetings. In the midst of a meeting devoted to wartime preparations, a representative from the Congress of Industrial Organizations asked to be admitted, to present their case on discrimination against African American players. The request was met by an emphatic "no" from Landis, despite threats to take the case to the Fair Employment Practices Committee.[21]

The death of Landis in 1944, with U.S. Senator A. B. "Happy" Chandler of Kentucky replacing him the next year, sent mixed messages of hope to supporters of integration. While Chandler did represent a Southern state, he was neither as strident nor as racist as Landis. When Chandler attended a Washington Senators game the day after his appointment, a group of African American leaders approached him to discuss the issue. Chandler said, "I told them there was nothing I could do at this time, but that I would be glad to hear fully what they had to say later."[22]

But Branch Rickey could do something, and the general manager of the Brooklyn Dodgers began the process toward revolutionary change when he signed Negro Leagues star Jackie Robinson to a minor-league contract before the 1946 season. Frick's initial response to the Montreal Royals' October 1945 announcement that they had signed Robinson was evasive silence. He, Chandler, and Harridge were all officially "unavailable for comment."[23]

The situation alarmed not only major league baseball, but also the Negro Leagues, which asked Chandler for protection from such player raids. The new commissioner, with Frick and Harridge, deferred on the request, challenging them to "get their house in order, then come to baseball with a petition for recognition."[24]

The owners did call a meeting, in August 1946, to discuss integration, among other issues. The purpose of the meeting was to discuss a report, a strategic planning document, as Andrew Zimbalist describes it, developed by a committee that was chaired by Larry MacPhail and included Frick, Harridge, and three other owners: Yawkey, Breadon, and Wrigley. All copies of the report were supposed to be collected and destroyed, but Chandler saved his copy. It later emerged in 1951, as a Congressional committee was investigating baseball's status as a monopoly. The race-related content was ignored and the discussions of the reserve clause were highlighted, but the report remained available in Chandler's papers.[25] It is now available online, through the University of Kentucky library.[26]

By far the most controversial and pressing point of the report involved integration. The MacPhail report is certainly a product of its time. On the one hand, it states, "The thousands of Negro boys of ability who aspire to careers in professional baseball should have a better opportunity. Every American boy, without regard to his race or his color or his creed, should have a fair chance in baseball." But then the report highlights "the technique, the co-ordination, the competitive attitude, and the discipline" needed for a major league career as being available only through a minor league apprenticeship, as opposed to Negro Leagues experience, without discussing baseball's exclusionary policies that had eliminated the minor league option.

Frick and Chandler had conflicting accounts of the meeting. Frick claimed that MacPhail's report actually urged the owners to integrate baseball. According to Frick, the paragraph was deleted and the issue was tabled. He cited it as yet another example of baseball's inertia toward racial issues.[27] In his memoirs, Chandler recalled that a secret ballot was taken, and the vote was 15–1 against integrating baseball—a detail no other account includes—with Rickey casting the only "yes" vote. Chandler met with Rickey later, at his home in Kentucky, and pledged his support, despite the owners' opposition.[28]

It appears that both were adding a portion of revisionism—Frick to protect the image of baseball, its owners, and himself, and Chandler to enhance his own role in integrating baseball. In Frick's case, it might be understandable, given his role in writing the report, but that is no excuse. Looking back at a racial rationale that had been decimated by subsequent events and knowing that it was publicly accessible, Frick tried, and failed, to frame a flawed document in the best possible way.

Jerome Holtzman speculated that the vote actually took place subsequently, at a September 16 owners meeting.[29] A speech by Rickey at Ohio's historically black Wilberforce State University in 1948 both confirms and confuses Holtzman's dating. Rickey referenced such a "secret meeting" where a document criticizing his signing of Robinson was approved unanimously by the other owners. Frick was responsible for distributing a copy to each owner, and then collecting and destroying them all (or so they thought).[30] And Rickey was adamant about the previously unreported report and vote on integration: "Let them deny that they adopted such a report if they dare."[31]

After angry pushback from other owners, Rickey backtracked and acknowledged that other issues were discussed in the report, and that owners' approval of the report should not have been taken as opposition to integration. To confuse the matter even further, Rickey dated the meeting as being in September, though he also related its content closely to the August 1946 meeting where the MacPhail report was adopted.[32] It could be that MacPhail's thinly veiled swipes at Rickey's signing of Robinson so outraged him that it shaded his recall of the meeting and its outcome.

Frick did not confirm Rickey's account as given in the speech: "I remember the meeting and recall that we were dealing with changes in player contracts, but I don't remember anything about that Negro phase or phrase." He was relieved to be able to add, "However, as it was a confidential meeting, I'm afraid I must say I have no comment." Frick predicted no further action by owners in response to Rickey's speech: "After all, he's a free citizen."[33]

The media accounts of the 1946 meeting made no attempt to get beyond the company line and did not mention integration. *The Sporting News* report, written by Dan Daniel, framed the document as "a 90-page report on the demands of the players, which incidentally was later burned."[34] The Associated Press report also focused on the player contract negotiations. When Frick emerged from the raucous meeting where the draft of the report was edited, the *Times* reported that he smiled and repeatedly said, "Fine meeting"—an ironic appraisal.[35] The lack of digging recalls a criticism that would dog sports journalism into the modern era—that its practitioners lacked the background to recognize and investigate complex non-sports topics—whether they involved race, labor, economics, or almost anything else off the field. That would make them easy pickings for baseball officials seeking to keep certain difficult stories, like integration, off the sports page.

Other authors, such as Tygiel and Zimbalist, provide more skilled critiques of MacPhail's report—in particular, his race-baiting by planting the fear that African American baseball fans would scare away white fans and thus threaten the value of major league franchises. Tygiel also takes him to task for the out-of-context citation of a Sam Lacy column. Lacy was decrying how Negro Leagues baseball was not preparing players sufficiently for the major leagues; MacPhail turned that into agreement by African American opinion leaders that their own players were not talented enough to play at the top levels.[36]

A sympathetic biography of MacPhail claims that the Yankees' GM's report supported integration and even laid out an orderly process for bringing in African American players. The biography cites the report's system for paying bonuses to previously unsigned players as evidence of MacPhail's and the committee's intent.[37] But the logic behind the application is flawed. The report makes no mention of Negro Leagues players while discussing the bonus system, but does reference previous discussions on the topic between major and minor league club owners, independent of any discussions of integration. Neither does Frick cite that information in the MacPhail report as outlining a pathway to integration.

Even as the major leagues prepared for integration, the baseball writers showed that racism was an equal opportunity plague at their annual dinner in February 1947. Drawing on the Mexican League battles of the previous season, the writers' skits included characters wearing sombreros and Mexican blankets, with the Chandler character riding in on a burro.[38]

On April 15, Robinson made his debut at Ebbets Field. Judging from the matter-of-fact coverage, either the buildup had spent the energy, or the sports writers were determined to treat the event as normally as possible, or all involved agreed to minimize it. The *New York Times* gamer did not even mention Robinson's name, although columnist Arthur Daley did write about Robinson's performance on and off the field. "The muscular Negro minds his own business and shrewdly makes no effort to push himself," Daley wrote. "He speaks quietly and intelligently when spoken to and already has made a strong impression."[39]

Frick made no comment on the event, and neither was his presence at the game noted, though as league president, he did approve Robinson's contract with the Dodgers.[40] He and official baseball remained silent until a May uprising—the details of which might have been up for debate, but the results of which provided Frick with priceless publicity and goodwill.

On May 9, 1947, Stanley Woodward, sports editor of the *New York Herald Tribune,* reported that Frick and Breadon had just thwarted a National League players' strike in protest of Robinson being allowed to play. Woodward wrote that the strike, "instigated by a member of the Brooklyn Dodgers who has since recanted," was scheduled to take place on May 6, with the anticipation that it would spread throughout the entire league.

The highlight of the account was a dramatic speech that Frick delivered to the Cardinals. According to Woodward, he said,

> If you do this you will be suspended from the league. You will find that the friends you think you have in the press box will not support you, that you will be outcasts. I do not care if half the league strikes. Those who do it will encounter quick retribution. All will be suspended and I don't care if it wrecks the National League for five years. This is the United States of America and one citizen has as much right to play as another. The National League will go down the line with Robinson whatever the consequences. You will find if you go through with your attention that you have been guilty of complete madness.[41]

Years later, columnist Dick Young would quip, "Reading Ford Frick's words, I could hear the 'Battle Hymn of the Republic' playing in the background."[42]

Woodward's account might have won an award for "Best Sports Story of 1947," but it was minimized by Frick himself. In his memoirs, Frick acknowledged that a minor player uprising had occurred, but he dated it six weeks earlier, during spring training. Frick had indeed threatened to suspend the players, but not directly through such a stirring speech; he left the communicating to Breadon. The matter quickly blew over without incident, walkout included. Frick speculated that one of Woodward's sportswriter colleagues had heard the anecdote and passed it along without confirming the details.[43]

Frick was correct and might even have been aware of the specifics. According to Harold Rosenthal, former *Herald Tribune* baseball writer, the source for the story was a colleague on the paper, Rud Rennie, who was good friends with Dr. Robert Hyland, team physician for the Cardinals. Hyland had overheard the players debating the strike and had related the troubling development to his friend. Rennie put personal friendship above a tempting scoop and passed the story along to Woodward; Rennie knew that if he wrote it, Hyland would be implicated and run out of town.[44]

The next day, within a follow-up report, Woodward admitted that he had never interviewed Frick, because he knew he would deny the story. He also acknowledged that Breadon, not Frick, had spoken to the team, so perhaps the speech he had published the day before had an audience of one. Still, Woodward was so taken with Frick's sentiments that he ran the speech again, writing, "It obviously is the most noble statement ever made by a baseball man."[45]

Woodward also commended Frick for his candor in acknowledging the Cardinals' strike talk in responding to questions about the article. "The admission by Ford C. Frick, National League president, that the strike was contemplated was above and beyond the rabbitry generally adhered to by the tycoons of our National Game," he wrote. "Such frankness, when compared to the furtiveness of other baseball barons, makes Frick the Mister Baseball of our time, whoever gets the $50,000."[46]

A May 9 *New York Times* report on the matter included quotes from Frick that in many ways lined up with the explanation in his memoirs. The *Times* article, however, quoted Frick indirectly as saying Breadon "informed him that he understood there was a movement among the Cardinals to strike in protest during their just-concluded series with the Dodgers if Robinson was in the line-up." The writer might have applied Woodward's chronology to Frick's scenario, but the brief still confirmed player unrest and firm league response.[47]

In a more detailed article the next day, Frick claimed that "a mountain had been made out of a molehill anyway," and declined to speak further. He reiterated that Robinson "had the full backing of the National League and that any unwarranted persecution of him would result in severe disciplinary action against the offenders." Breadon and manager Eddie Dyer also denied the strike, though Breadon seemed to confirm that the situation had occurred during the Cardinals' recent road trip to New York, as opposed to spring training.[48]

The Sporting News quoted Frick as saying Breadon actually used the word "strike": "[T]he St. Louis club owner advised him that he understood there was a movement among the Redbirds to stage a protest strike during the Dodger series if Robinson was used in the Brooklyn lineup." A story right below quoted the Cardinals' owner as labeling the strike report "ridiculous." That article did note, "[Breadon] indicated he did talk to two of his players allegedly balking at playing against Robinson, but they no longer were objecting."[49]

Molehill or mountain, Frick had confirmed Woodward's story—perhaps not the details, which had to navigate a maze of denials and contradictions, but certainly its foundation. Woodward could glory in that later, in his memoirs: "[The] thing that pleased us was that we had an exclusive and that every paper in the country and half the magazines picked it up from us with full credit, in spite of the fact that our managing editor had refused to put it on page one."[50]

Arthur Daley praised Frick's decisiveness in his *Times* column: "He didn't shilly-shally or equivocate. He leaped in and grasped the bull by the horns." Daley also took the opportunity to express his support for integration: "Robinson will rise or fall, stick or drift back to the minors, solely on his ability as a ball player.... [He] hasn't been any ball of fire, but he deserves his chance. What's more, he's getting it." Reflecting the continuing media criticism surrounding Chandler, Daley added, "The pity of it is that all the club owners didn't elect Frick as commissioner when they had the chance."[51]

The Sporting News, however, continued its "lukewarm" view of integration. An editorial briefly mentioned the Cardinals' strike threat and slurs by Ben Chapman, manager of the Phillies, but chose also to reprint an editorial from five years earlier. The previous commentary had speculated on how integration would harm the Negro Leagues—which the paper had never covered anyway—and how fans might react if an African American pitcher threw a beanball. *The Sporting News* editors apparently saw no need to update their perspective, even in view of the new reality.[52]

Tygiel's judgment is that the truth of the St. Louis "strike" lies somewhere between Woodward's alarm of pending racial strife and the team's denials that anything had happened. Perhaps some veteran Cardinals players had chafed at Robinson playing, and might even have braggadociously thrown out the word "strike," but it never amounted to anything formal or threatening.[53]

What it did amount to, however, was a strong show of support toward Robinson from baseball leadership, and Frick was the voice of that support. This was not a story manufactured by Frick's friends in the press box to advance his interests. His response might not have been as powerful as depicted by Woodward. But it was strong enough to help turn the tide of public debate and let the baseball world know that Robinson, like integration, was here to stay.

One scholarly analysis of the commissioner's role as an organizational communicator claimed that it was Frick, not Chandler, who deserved credit for confronting the issue. Chandler, in their opinion, was "noncommittal, noncontroversial, and obtuse," which abdicated his role of communicating and explaining important trends and issues to fans. The article also noted that in dealing with the Cardinals' uprising, Frick never communicated directly with Chandler, thus lessening the commissioner's role even more.[54]

Frick was recognized for his actions. The NAACP immediately sent him a letter congratulating him: "Your statement has been applauded by all lovers of fair play and especially by Negro citizens and sports fans. The consensus of opinion is that it is the most pointed and unequivocal statement on fair play in sports as far as racial minority participation is concerned that has ever been made."[55] The release announcing the correspondence commended Woodward and Breadon as well.

8. Integration

The next year, Frick would be honored, along with Rickey and Robinson, by the Council Against Intolerance in America, which awarded them the Thomas Jefferson Prizes for the advancement of democracy. The three were named in a nationwide poll of 1,000 civic organization officials and 500 newspaper editors.[56] Frick was able to accept the award in person at the organization's April ceremony in New York, while baseball concerns, and perhaps humility, kept Rickey and Robinson away.[57]

Around the same time, it was also reported that Frick had ordered Chapman to tone down his language while "bench-jockeying." The Phillies manager, a Southerner, was said to be using racial epithets toward Robinson, and Frick believed he had gone too far. But Frick was not alone in dealing with this situation. Chapman also heard from Chandler and from his own front office, which was flooded with letters from fans disgusted by his behavior. In what read like a defense, *The Sporting News* protested, "It would be impossible to prove that Chapman was abusing Robinson the Negro rather than Robinson the Dodger."[58]

Frick was drawn back into the race debate after a 1952 Robinson television interview. On a Sunday WNBC radio/television show, "Youth Wants to Know," a young audience member asked Robinson if he thought the Yankees (the inquirer's favorite team) were prejudiced. Robinson gave a one-word answer, "yes," though he added that he was referring to the front office and not the players. He noted that the Yankees had no African American players on their roster and few in the farm system. The statement drew a swift denial from Yankees general manager George Weiss, but the episode provided the off-season drama that all media crave.[59]

Initially, Frick's response was to decline involvement, saying, "Baseball still has the right of free speech."[60] After returning from the baseball meetings, Frick did meet with Robinson and asked him to avoid the issue when possible. Robinson agreed, but added, "I also told him.... I would give the same answer if I were ever asked the same question again. I'm not looking for any arguments with anybody but I have to live honestly with myself."[61] Years later, announcing his retirement, Robinson recalled the episode. He said Frick told him, "When you think you are right, Jackie, swing a big bat, not a fungo stick. But make sure you are right."[62]

Frick summarized his philosophy of race in Robinson's 1964 book, *Baseball Has Done It.* The book includes extended quotes by several men involved in baseball's integration, particularly African American players who endured insults and racism to claim the right to play that was theirs. Robinson would often follow their comments with his own, but after a brief introduction, he presented only Frick's thoughts for the rest of the short chapter.

For his part, Frick was certainly consistent, reflecting the same philosophy in 1964 that he had for decades. That 1934-vintage philosophy would come off as disappointing in 1964: "Baseball's function is not to lead crusades, not to settle sociological problems, not to become involved in any sort of controversial racial or religious question."[63]

He rationalized the years it took baseball to integrate by blaming slavery and Jim Crow laws for slowing the development of African American players: "It was more than fifty years after the introduction of baseball before colored people in the United States had a chance to play it. Consequently, it was another fifty years before they, by natural process, arrived at the stage where they were important in the organized baseball period."[64] Such flawed logic ignores the role of athletic talent for any potential baseball player, regardless of race, who picks up the game quickly.

He also pointed out the way that baseball had encouraged integration in Southern towns by withholding minor league teams and claimed more of a role for the game in integrating Florida spring training hotels than actually existed. Still, Robinson was gracious to allow Frick an opportunity, to the extent that Frick did the same for him. Frick concluded, "There has been nothing in my life to which I can point with more pride than to the progress baseball has made in this field."[65]

Frick was also rewarded by the National League team owners. At the 1947 All-Star meetings, he was re-elected to another four-year term as president (the maximum extension allowed by league rules), and given a $10,000-a-year raise.[66] As a *Sporting News* editorial noted, the league was in much better shape than when Frick had taken over in 1934. Ownership issues in Philadelphia and Boston had been resolved. A smooth transition to new stable ownership in St. Louis had been finessed. The editorial credited Frick for the bottom-line "era of good feeling" among National League owners.[67]

Even Frick could not resist glorying in the good times. Going into the 1948 season, he noted the solid financial condition of all league clubs. He credited the improvement not only to stable ownership, but also to improved postwar attendance, which had approached 20,000,000 for the season. And he was quick to credit night baseball for the attendance jolt, noting how it had encouraged the surge in weekday attendance.[68]

As baseball transitioned into a new era, Frick and everyone had to confront the inevitable passing of the old era and its heroes—in particular, his friend Babe Ruth. With Ruth battling cancer, Chandler declared April

27 "Babe Ruth Day." More than 58,000 fans filled Yankee Stadium to honor Ruth, who was celebrated with gifts and speeches.[69] Even though he had been Ruth's ghostwriter for almost ten years, Frick spoke only as National League president, not as a close friend. Reading from the inscription of a book the league was presenting to Ruth, Frick said:

> To Babe Ruth. Whose batting average through the years is exceeded only by the size of his heart, and whose capacity to hit home runs is surpassed only by his capacity to make and hold friends among the people who know him. That you ruined our hopes in many a World Series and too often batted our brains out and made us like it, does not diminish our pride in your accomplishments.[70]

Although Ruth would make two more emotional appearances at Yankee Stadium, in September 1947 and finally in June 1948 for the 25th anniversary of Yankee Stadium,[71] the April ceremony marked the occasion where baseball officially recognized an icon, while confronting that he, like his time in baseball, would soon pass.

Ruth did not forget Frick or his kindness, however. Soon after the Yankees honored him, Ruth set up a foundation to help underprivileged youth. He asked Frick to serve on the board. While he did also add Chandler and Harridge to the board, no doubt Frick considered it a particular honor and pleasure to be so acknowledged by the Babe.[72]

By mid–August 1948, Babe Ruth's condition had deteriorated and he was near death. His condition was a matter of national concern; even President Truman inquired. One reported visitor was Frick. Ruth's close associate, Paul Carey, had called Frick and told him of Ruth's desire to see him. Frick navigated the "three-ring circus, with reporters and photographers waiting." Upon his entrance, the newspapers reported, Ruth greeted him: "Hello, Ford, how are you?"[73] In conversation with Ruth biographer Robert Creamer, Frick recalled, "When I came in he lifted his eyes toward me and raised his right arm a little, only about three or four inches off the bed, and then it fell back again. I went over to the bed and I said, 'Babe, Paul Carey said you wanted to see me.' And Ruth said, in that terrible voice, 'Ford, I always wanted to see you.'"[74] Frick recalled Ruth dying the next day, but the span in newspaper reports between his visit and Ruth's death was actually three days. Still, the invitation and recognition were a favored memory for Frick years after, though he did not mention it in his memoirs.

On August 16, 1948, Ruth died. In his official statement, Frick said, "Babe Ruth needed every inch of that big chest of his to protect the world's largest heart. I knew the Babe well when I traveled with the Yankees as a baseball writer, and I never saw a man with more heart—and you can interpret that as meaning both courage on the field and consideration for others."[75] In a nationwide radio tribute broadcast by the Mutual network, Frick added, "He did more for our game and while he was doing it, did more for the youngsters, did more for Americans and did more for America than a great many men who were certainly better educated, perhaps better known and came from higher positions."[76]

As franchise problems returned, Frick was forced to confront issues in St. Louis, related not so much to the Cardinals as to the baby brother Browns—and to the city's capacity to support two major league teams. Frick's suggestion was to move the Cardinals to Chicago and turn it into a two-NL team city. His preference was to establish a National League franchise in Detroit, but he doubted the Tigers would allow it.[77]

Cardinals owner Breadon disagreed, of course. But Frick stressed that it was merely a suggestion from a baseball fan more than a directive from a league president. As a *Sporting News* editorial pointed out, it was also an idea worth discussing, given the Browns' attendance woes.[78] Time would show that major league baseball was moving away from the era of two-team cities. Within the next seven years, three cities—Boston, Philadelphia, and St. Louis—would lose their second teams.

Frick also never lost his ability to gain good press. Though the Dodgers lost the 1947 World Series to the Yankees, Frick was unbowed. He predicted that the National League would win the next ten World Series, based on the success of their minor league clubs. "We have bigger, better men on our clubs—as shown by the records," he said. "Figures sometimes lie, but not in baseball."[79]

He continued the theme in a 1948 pre-season interview. "Our whole league, as a matter of fact, is getting the cream of the young talent," he said. In his opinion, the NL had overcome the effects of World War II. "By 1950, I think we will be back to our pre-war standard. Not just two or three clubs will be back, but all of them." He added, "I would be willing to bet, say, an ice cream soda that we beat the American League in six out of the next ten World Series."[80] In fact, the National League would win only three, and his remarks preceded the second year of a six-year American League winning streak, dominated by the Yankees.

The 1947 off-season brought loss for Frick, as his father, Jacob, died at the age of 94 on November 12. It can be inferred from the obituary that Jacob suffered from dementia as his death approached, and Frick's sister Clara Couts was taking care of him as he declined. Frick was able to travel to Indiana in time for his funeral. His father was buried in Rome City.[81]

At the 1947 December meeting, baseball had to deal with the emerging issue of television. Games had already been televised in seven cities, something predicted for every major league city by 1950. Frick, the old radio hand, was appointed to a "television committee" to study the issue. "Television within another few years is going to be a big problem for us," Frick said, noting that radio still outnumbered the new medium, 3.25 million to 90,000, in New York City. "Baseball already is studying what this increase will mean to its own business as well as to the commitment it now has with radio."[82]

Even with the "problems" cited, Frick embraced the new medium's potential. He began including an annual trip to California in his spring training travels, but he focused on television rather than major league expansion. On this first trip, he arranged for a television crew from Chicago to visit Hollywood to learn how to incorporate three cameras into a game broadcast. Under this new system, the announcer ("a seasoned baseball man") would also serve as one of the broadcast's directors, signaling the camera operators and crew as to the best shooting angles. Frick said the National League would spend as much as $50,000 on television development.[83]

Frick was ready to turn his attention back to on-field subjects as the 1948 season approached. Earlier, he had instructed his umpires to enforce rules concerning balks and beanballs. Frick added spitballs to the banned list in his instructions to umpires. His new rule interpretations were not limited to pitchers, however; Frick also outlawed the practice of batters and base coaches erasing chalk lines.[84]

By the middle of the 1948 season, it became obvious that baseball and television were not on the same channel. Already minor league officials were warning that television would destroy their attendance, particularly in light of networks' plans to provide coast-to-coast programming. The major leagues had a rule that teams—which at the time had set up their own broadcasting agreements—could not broadcast within 50 miles of another team. But the minor leagues had no such protection, and team officials were certain (and presciently so) that fans would prefer staying at home watching Ted Williams for free to heading to a minor league baseball park.[85]

Frick was perceived as leading baseball's fledgling forays into the new medium, and he promised a television task force report at the All-Star Game owners' meetings. The parallels with radio were striking. At the time, revenues from television were still low; some teams did not charge for television rights at all. But the potential for all numbers to skyrocket— audience, coverage, and revenues—threatened a level of upheaval unlike what radio had brought about.[86] Frick was the best man for the job, not only because of his radio experience, but also because he, unlike his colleagues in the 1930s, was ready to embrace a media innovation to baseball's advantage, and he was most likely to bring that mindset to the television drama.

Frick ended up in the middle of the biggest job change story of 1948: manager Leo Durocher's move from the Brooklyn Dodgers to the rival New York Giants. Giants owner Horace Stoneham had kept Frick informed of his interest in hiring Durocher, so Frick allowed Stoneham to use his office to meet with Branch Rickey. No doubt Stoneham was trying to avoid allegations of tampering by involving Frick, but the league president left as soon as Rickey arrived, leaving the two to their negotiations.[87] According to one account, Stoneham actually requested permission to talk to Burt Shotton, who had led the Dodgers to a World Series title subbing for the suspended Durocher. Rickey hesitated: "No, I may need him at any moment myself." A shocked Stoneham caught Rickey's drift and queried whether that meant Durocher was available. By the end of the meeting, Durocher was the new Giants manager, and Rickey was free of a chronic headache.[88]

During the 1948 off-season, Frick returned to his favorite non-baseball pastime, curling, though more as ceremonial spectator than participant. As president of the St. Andrews curling club, he hosted the powerful Royal Caledonian team from Scotland on its tour dominating U.S. teams.[89] Frick stayed active in the sport until 1957 when, 62 and suffering from bursitis, he decided to hang up his brooms and leave the stone chucking to the younger curlers.[90]

But he also found time to lead the fundraising drive for the New York Heart Association, a sign of his growing public persona. As usual, he went beyond the ceremonial in his role, getting New York Mayor Paul O'Dwyer to issue a proclamation urging public support for the fund drive, which would begin in February.[91]

Another 1948-49 off-season highlight for Frick was his selection by the New York baseball writers to receive the Bill Slocum Award, for outstanding service to baseball. The award, at the annual baseball writers' dinner, was accompanied by an ovation, as well as a roast by columnist "Bugs" Baer, who carried on an imaginary telephone conversation with one of Frick's former colleagues. "I never felt closer to the writers of New York than I do this minute," Frick said in accepting the award.[92] It was a particularly treasured honor for Frick, who considered Slocum a close friend and colleague.

At its December meetings, the owners had deferred on any actions related to television, awaiting the results of surveys being conducted by Frick. In a January interview, Frick expressed confusion at the preliminary numbers—indicative of public response to a new, revolutionary innovation. "In short, there isn't a man in the world who can give you a sound, factual answer to questions involving television insofar as it concerns baseball," he said. He recommended a policy "built on short commitments, and recognition of the fact that we have no definite basis on which to work."[93]

Respondents varied in their preference for baseball on television. The results reflected two separate trends: the emergence of other programming that displaced sports, and the poor quality of baseball broadcasts, which could be expected to improve. Frick also acknowledged that if baseball were kept off the air to protect live attendance, it would be replaced by other sports, thus missing a good public relations advantage.[94]

By June of 1949, the cases of players who had jumped to the Mexican League had taken a turn that could have threatened the sanctity of baseball's reserve clause. In February of that year, a New York appeals court had refused to dismiss the case of former Giants outfielder Danny Gardella, opening the door for a jury trial by a lower court.[95] The appeals court refused to reinstate the suspended players in June, but urged that the aforementioned jury trials begin soon, with baseball's antitrust exemption that protected the reserve clause specifically mentioned. That was all Chandler, an attorney, needed to hear, and he announced on June 5 that all players under the five-year 1946 ban would be welcomed back immediately. He also offered Gardella a generous settlement.[96]

Like his American League counterpart, Frick left the day-to-day legal skirmishing to the commissioner, though he was specifically named in the lawsuit. Frick, like all baseball leaders, realized the upheaval that would be caused by elimination of the reserve clause, and his comments reflected that fear. "We will carry it all the way to the Supreme Court," he said after the February ruling. "I'm not a lawyer, however, and can't say too much about these decisions."[97]

Frick did not discuss the particulars of the 1949 case in his memoirs except to say that Chandler "handled that situation promptly and firmly." His main complaint was that the implied success of the Gardella case sparked litigation fever. "But the fat was in the fire," he said. "Minor league owners and radio stations with any sort of grievance, real or imaginary, started legal action. At one time, baseball was faced with more than a dozen different antitrust cases, asking for a total of more than a million dollars in damages."[98]

Chandler did charge his league presidents with handling the formal reinstatement of players. Frick sent telegrams to his players: "By the commissioner's ruling you are reinstated to [name of team], provided you obtain clearance from the league in which you are now employed, showing that you are not violating any existing contracts by reporting."[99] Many of the players had left Mexico but had signed with other non–American leagues.

Frick was not afraid to take on his former sports writing colleagues when necessary, and by the 1949 season, the official scorekeeping performance of sports writers became an issue. (Major League Baseball would not hire official independent scorers until 1980.) It was bad enough that the writers were giving players hits that should have been errors and misinterpreting baseball rules. One scorer awarded a sacrifice on a fouled-off bunt that the catcher caught far beyond home plate, allowing the runner to advance. But the busy writers often would put off official game reports to the leagues, so long that it delayed official stats from being released.[100] *The Sporting News*, which prided itself on being the official record of baseball and provided complete statistics, ran the story on its front page.

Times columnist Daley, not surprisingly, defended his colleagues and their opportunity for extra income. In his opinion, scoring involved difficult calls no matter who was making them. Hiring official scorers "would be a costly method with few benefits." While acknowledging "comparatively few incompetents among the writers," Daley suggested Frick and Harridge could gain equal benefit by "clarifying existing rules and insisting on uniform interpretation."[101] A *Sporting News* editorial acknowledged the difficulties facing a sports writer who had to keep sending running updates to his newspaper while also keeping score. But the editorial also advocated keeping the responsibility in the press box, while urging the writers to do better.[102]

Frick's proposal no doubt caused some pushback from his former colleagues, so he floated a proposal that would limit the sports writers eligible for scorekeeping duties to the most competent. The players, of course, never did like the idea of sports writers calling hits and errors, and suggested the hiring of former major leaguers to create an official scorers staff.[103]

Always with an eye toward younger players, Frick provided umpires for the 1949 Little League World Series and even attended the final game on August 27. "It's a great thing," he said at the game. "I had never seen a game prior to this one, but it was much more than I ever expected to see. Those kids really play excellent ball for their age." He called on his radio experience, broadcasting play-by-play for two innings.[104] Convinced of its value as a promotion to younger players and fans, Frick would make the LLWS a frequent visit.

"Another season, another balk rule debate" marked 1950 spring training. National League umpires informed teams that a pitcher would have to come to a full stop for one second before pitching or throwing to a base, and the stop could come at any position.[105] Managers complained that the interpretation would make base stealing impossible, but Frick argued that it was an improvement over the previous rule, which required merely a hesitation. Pitchers in spring training games had a hard time adjusting to the new rule, with a record numbers of balks being called.[106] Frick required his umps to count an entire second after the pitcher stopped, while the American League umpires looked for only a clear stop by the pitcher.[107] The player representatives were expected to ask for a return to the old balk rule at the Executive Council meetings, but the controversy eventually passed.[108]

In 1951, even with baseball facing wild transitions, Frick remained consistent in his aggressive enforcement of balk rules. He announced that league umpires would continue the previous year's strict enforcement, despite complaints from pitchers and managers. Frick again instructed umpires to direct pitchers to come to a one-second stop with runners on based. One Giants rookie was called for balks on successive pitches in a spring game.[109]

More specific issues regarding television did press on Frick. When on-field microphones picked up the entire content of a Durocher rant, including obscenities, Frick blamed the broadcasters rather than Durocher. "So long as you have baseball, with its close decisions in the heat of battle, I guess you'll always have raw, bitter words of protest," he said. "Those microphones shouldn't be down in a position to pick up the arguments." He suggested closer vigilance by broadcast technicians.[110]

Later, as commissioner, Frick did take on a couple of broadcasting annoyances. In January 1953, his complaint resonates even with fans today: excessive commercial spots on both radio and television. "I have a recording of a game that ran one hour and 58 minutes," he recalled. (Fans today would envy such speed.) "Would you like to guess how many commercials, how many blurbs they jammed into this broadcast? A total of 106!" He feared that game listeners would end up thinking about promoted products more than the game itself.[111]

Later that year, he also complained about broadcasting dugout shots during games. Cameras caught Dodgers pitcher Russ Meyer, a noted young hothead, making an obscene gesture from the dugout after being tossed from a game. Most of his teammates did not see it, but thanks to television, thousands of viewers did, and many complained. "I have always felt that a fellow has certain private rights; that the dugout is more or less his home while he's at the ball park, and that the TV cameras have no business focusing on things that occur there," Frick said.[112]

Philadelphia Evening Bulletin columnist Ed Pollock was not impressed by Frick's take. "Commissioner Frick appears to place all the blame on television camera and attributes none to Meyer," he wrote. "These words reflect an oblique view of the incident. Meyer clearly was not looking for privacy when he went through his obscene gestures."[113]

As spring training began in 1950, an odd rumor concerning Frick popped up. An apparent bout with pneumonia sparked rumors that he, like Heydler 15 years before, was planning to retire from the league presidency, citing ill health, and return to Colorado, "taking over the operation of a newspaper in Colorado Springs." The report incorrectly said that he had been born and raised in Colorado (his wife had), but Frick swiftly denied the rumors anyway.[114]

By the end of the season, however, Frick was more in a mood to move on. Buzzie Bavasi, his son's lifelong friend, recalls how after the 1950 season, Frick contacted him. He had an opportunity to take over a community newspaper in Colorado, and it was tempting to return to his home state and his profession. He wanted Bavasi to join him, as business manager. Bavasi declined, enjoying his baseball career and fearing that working together would work against their friendship.[115] For Frick, family issues weighed in more heavily: His mother-in-law, Susan Cowing, was in her early 90s,[116] and that might have made it the right time to bring his wife, Eleanor, back home.

Frick decided against the Colorado move as well. He chose wisely. He would be receiving a much more attractive job offer within the next year.

9

Chandler Out, Frick In

In one sense, Commissioner Happy Chandler was on the chopping block almost from the day of his hiring. When he was named to the post, he asked for a cushion of 30 to 60 days to resign his U.S. Senate seat. But even after that he hedged, claiming his Kentucky constituency needed his continued service. One owner grumbled that if he and his colleagues had known that, they might not have selected Chandler in the first place.[1]

Chandler had his own doubts going in. He recalled a conversation with Indians owner Alva Bradley after an informal meeting in July 1945, before he officially moved into the commissioner's office. Bradley told him, "We all cheat, if we have to. This fellow cheats, that fellow cheats. I cheat, too." Chandler replied, "Well, Mr. Bradley, I wish I'd known that before I signed on for this because I didn't agree to leave the United States Senate to preside over a bunch of thieves."[2]

Chandler's difference in style from his predecessor also required an adjustment. While Landis was a gruff, behind-the-scenes attorney, Chandler was an out-front, boisterous politician, always ready to sing "My Old Kentucky Home."[3] The scene mortified some owners.

By June of 1950, the owners were expressing defiance toward Chandler that they never would have tried with Landis. Cardinals owner Fred Saigh had rescheduled a rainout with the Brooklyn Dodgers for the night of Sunday, July 16. The scheduling drew Chandler's immediate disapproval; he claimed that because it would conflict with Sunday night church services, it would offend baseball fans who were also church members. While Chandler acknowledged that authority on such scheduling matters belonged to Frick and not to him, he still made his opposition clear.[4]

An obstinate Saigh said he would ignore Chandler's statement and that the game would be played. This happened, even after Frick also ordered Saigh not to play the game on Sunday night. Frick claimed the Sunday game violated the night game rules adopted at the previous league meeting. Those rules banned night games on a travel date, unless the visiting team consented, and on Sunday. Saigh interpreted that to mean he could schedule on Sunday with consent; Frick said the consent applied only to "getaway" days.[5]

Branch Rickey, who had originally agreed to the Sunday night game and had denied Chandler's claim that he had sent a telegram withdrawing consent, then announced he was doing just that and had informed Frick of his opposition. When Saigh backed down and agreed to reschedule the game for the next day, he specifically stated that his decision was based "entirely" on Frick's ruling, which was supported by his league counsel, Louis Carroll.

As the *Times* article noted, "Saigh's statement taking issue with the reasons advanced by Chandler for cancellation of the game was highly unusual for a club owner. The commissioner has the powers of a czar over organized baseball. His word is usually regarded as law."[6] It might have been unusual, but it would become more frequent, and it would get worse.

By November, however, it appeared that circumstances had swung back in Chandler's favor. Frick and Harridge informed Chandler that owners had quickly and unanimously approved a second contract, anticipating his re-election. Chandler's contract called for 18-month notice if his contract was not going to be renewed. Reports indicated that Chandler would not only receive a positive evaluation, but that he would be given a contract for a second term.[7]

The warm feelings of November were a deceptive tactic by a group of seven team owners who had banded together to remove Chandler. So how did this happen? From the start, Chandler faced a challenge. Following Landis's tenure as commissioner, the owners had made several changes in the post's duties, as outlined in the Major League Agreement—something they never had the courage to do when Landis was alive. The new agreement limited the commissioner's ability to declare anything as detrimental to the game's interests and restored the owners' right to sue, something waived within the previous agreement.

Perhaps the most ominous change was that a commissioner's re-election would require a three-fourths vote rather than a simple majority. That stipulation would ultimately prove Chandler's undoing, but the three changes together would send a message to him and all future commissioners, Frick included: The owners were not looking for another Landis-style czar.[8]

But why the direct challenge to Chandler himself? No single factor emerges. At least five owners did hold grudges against him, and that provided enough opposition to the five votes needed to block his re-election. Saigh was already frustrated with Chandler over his criticism of the Sunday night rescheduled game. An attorney who was called in to consult on the Gardella case, he also was unimpressed with how Chandler had handled it.

Del Webb of the Yankees was angered by Chandler's investigation of his tax problems and his connection with Las Vegas gamblers.[9] Webb had made his fortune building Las Vegas hotels, with casinos attached, thus arousing suspicion.[10] In his memoirs, Chandler referred to Webb as "the most refreshingly ignorant sonofabitch I ever met in my life."[11] Lou Perini of the Boston Braves, Bob Carpenter of the Philadelphia Phillies, and Bill DeWitt of the St. Louis Browns had petty beefs with Chandler, based mainly on unfavorable player contract decisions.[12] Still, they provided Saigh and Webb with crucial allies to kill Chandler's re-election at the December meetings.

Another mark against Chandler was his decision to assign all of the broadcast revenue from the 1950 World Series to the players' pension fund. The pension fund had been established as part of the 1946 player contract, but only four years later, it became apparent that the fund would need additional contributions to be able to meet its obligations. The owners unanimously approved Chandler's assigning all $975,000 to the fund, and such annual World Series revenues would subsequently fund player pensions. Still, in 1950, Chandler recalled years later, "The owners didn't think too much of that."[13]

Another theory speculated that Chandler actually caused his own downfall when he insisted on an early re-election. The owners resented being backed into a corner, and that gave vent to other offenses that might have been ignored otherwise.[14] The details worked themselves out quickly and brutally that December. The owners went into an unannounced afternoon executive session and conducted a secret ballot; the vote was 9–7 in favor, three votes shy of the 75 percent needed. As Chandler pointed out, "They didn't have to win over the majority to scuttle Happy Chandler. All they needed was to guarantee five negative votes."[15]

That they did, seven actually, leaving themselves with a lame-duck commissioner whose term still had 16 months left. It was the owners' wish that Chandler would accept the inevitable and resign, with a fair buyout. But Chandler was not about to let them off so easily. He told reporters that he intended to finish out his term. "I have never run away from a situation, and certainly I am not disposed to retreat from the one now confronting me."[16] Through Frick and Harridge, the owners issued a statement: "It is the unanimous vote of the sixteen major league clubs that a new commissioner be selected and elected as soon as possible."[17]

Attention was immediately directed again at Frick: "Ford almost was elected to the job some five years ago and is the logical candidate now," *New York Times* columnist Arthur Daley wrote.[18] Bill Corum, from Frick's old newspaper, the *New York Journal-American*, wrote, "Frick has done a bang-up job as president of the National League, as his new four-year contract with that organization at an increased salary would indicate. In addition to all other qualifications, Frick is an experienced baseball man, which is the business that the commissioner runs."[19] Rarely does anyone get a second bite at such a desirable apple, but that appeared to be Frick's good fortune.

No evidence exists that Frick himself participated in any of the machinations that led to Chandler's ouster. Neither Chandler himself nor any other witness to the proceedings implies as much. Frick might have been aware of the revolt, particularly as the meetings approached, though many of Chandler's supporters were also in the dark until the first shot. Realize too that the baseball owners did not need Frick's endorsement or involvement, and given what we know of the ringleaders' mindset, it is unlikely that they would seek either.

Frick also claimed not to be a candidate for the job the second time around. "I have the best job in the history of the National League, and I am quite content to stay with it," he said, when asked directly at a league event.[20] He repeated the claim in June 1951, after Chandler had scheduled his post–All-Star Game exit. He said that he did not want the position and had expressed that to the owners, leading *The Sporting News* to declare him "out of the list of availables."[21]

The owners debated Frick's potential candidacy on the sports pages. Dodgers owner Walter O'Malley supported him: "Frick fills the specifications which I have in mind for selecting a commissioner. These are a judicial temperament, administrative ability, an awareness of public relations, and a firm belief baseball is the national sport and must be sustained as such."[22] Senators owner Clark Griffith, a Chandler supporter, disagreed: "I will oppose Frick because I am against a commissioner out of the ranks of baseball…. I want a strong national figure. I want the big stick. I am against saddling the new commissioner with a board of directors and making just a phoney figurehead out of him."[23]

A *Sporting News* editorial agreed with O'Malley and repeated his description of Frick's qualifications, adding, "Ford Frick, literally right under the owners' noses, it would seem to *The Sporting News*, is the man to lead them out of the existing wilderness."[24] Dan Daniel believed that Frick's expressed reluctance resulted not from false modesty, but from a sober assessment of all that baseball was facing, both internally and externally. "He realizes that the next two years will be of the utmost importance to the game, and would like to stay away from the leadership of the fight against the anti-baseball forces."[25]

A much more important conflict was brewing, of course, as war had erupted in Korea. While the situation did not reach the gravity of World War II, it did threaten complications for baseball. As before, however, Frick and Chandler expressed their full support for the war effort, including provision for active players who were drafted. No one considered the situation as threatening toward the continuation of play.[26]

Baseball might have been in a holding pattern in the commissioner's office, but offseason business issues still pressed. Frick called a January league meeting to discuss broadcasting. The minor leagues were complaining that radio, not television (yet), was cannibalizing their attendance. So the owners agreed to ban radio broadcasts in minor league towns on game days; previously, it was a matter of individual farm teams consenting. "I don't mind saying it's a terrific problem," Frick had said going in. "We're going to get together and outline a program with every intention of protecting the minors as much as we can. We've got to help minor league baseball. We'd be silly if we didn't." Frick also announced that he would set up a National League radio department to deal with such issues.[27]

Just a few months later, Frick was bullish on the potential of radio and television—at least in early 1951. "I believe they have been unjustifiably blamed for many ills which, in fact, have been the result of failure by owners and front office people to properly publicize baseball," he said. "Our game is wonderful entertainment, but it is a commodity which is in competition like everything else and must be sold to the public." His thoughts on protecting the minors, however, had softened. "They have their own problems this year ... and are in a better position to make their decisions," he said.[28]

Frick also pressed forward with plans to celebrate the National League's 75th anniversary. He originally planned to use Steve Hannagan, whose agency had done such excellent and cost-effective work on the Hall of Fame promotion. But thrift flew out the window this time around. With Frick's support, Chandler awarded Hannagan a $50,000 contract with a $100,000 expense account in 1950. The owners protested and the contract was cancelled—an embarrassment to both men.[29]

The pre-season festivities showed more restraint and less gimmickry than either the Hall of Fame Centennial or Frick's 60th anniversary celebration for the National League, with its birthday parties in each league city and throwback uniforms. The teams planned their own anniversary, but it was not the centralized spectacle Frick had put together in 1936.

This "diamond jubilee" celebration consisted of a ceremony marking the placement of a commemorative plaque at the Broadway Central Hotel, where the league was founded in 1876. Beyond the usual speeches, the highlight was the assembling 14 Hall of Fame members, including Ty Cobb and Rogers Hornsby. Also present at the ceremony were former league president John Heydler, whose retirement 17 years before had elevated Frick to the job, and 91-year-old Arlie Latham, the oldest former major leaguer, who had first played during the league's fifth year of existence in 1880. Even at that age, Latham was still working—as a press box attendant at the Polo Grounds and Yankee Stadium.[30]

The celebration was also noteworthy because of a congratulatory note sent by President Harry Truman. "May the sun never set on American baseball," he wrote. "All Americans can join the guests in wishing the league, and the sport it has helped so much to develop, many more years of uninterrupted activity. I am most enthusiastically among them." The sentiments indicated that Truman was giving the "green light" to baseball much as Roosevelt had in 1941.[31]

Sadly, the Broadway Central eventually decayed, and a section of the hotel collapsed in 1973, leaving its 150 public-assistance guests homeless. The plaque identifying the hotel as the site of the National League's founding had disappeared long before.[32]

The New York baseball writers invited the recently deposed Chandler to speak at their annual dinner. Chandler accepted, though he at first declined to speak. His brief talk was described as "a tense moment," but provided no additional fireworks. "The present crisis in baseball will soon pass," he said. "Men of good will and honest purpose will see to that. Fortunately for all of us the integrity of the game is not involved. Just as we earnestly seek peace in the world, we must seek and obtain peace in baseball." Frick introduced the Hall of Famers who had come for the National League anniversary, adding nostalgia and much-needed distraction to the evening.[33]

It was only two days after Chandler announced an owners meeting for March 12, a month away, that the *New York Times* reported that Ohio Governor Frank V. Lausche would be the next commissioner.[34] A four-member owners committee began the search process, but only one candidate was considered at the March meeting: Chandler, who again could muster only nine of the 12 votes needed to assure his re-election. Chandler accepted the owners' decision, but asked only that they wait until he had informed his family to make a formal announcement.[35]

Following his rejection, Chandler announced no plans to resign. He told reporters that he would examine his options while waiting for the owners to make their next move. "They haven't got anybody, have they?"

he asked. The owners predicted that they would be ready to select Chandler's successor by the All-Star Game.[36]

Confident in their growing influence, the players disrupted the owners' plans by demanding a role in the process. Freddie Hutchinson, player representative for the American League, suggested that if they were ignored, they would hire their own commissioner and suggested that Chandler himself would make an excellent candidate. His comments had their intended effect on the owners, many of whom did not deal well with their authority being questioned. Frick declined a reporter's offer to read the proposal: "I don't want to hear anything about it—no comment."[37]

The owners met in June and agreed to a proposed severance package for Chandler that would allow him to resign on July 15, following the All-Star Game, and would guarantee his salary until April 30, 1952, when his term and his contract would officially end. Until a new commissioner could be named, baseball would be run by its executive council: Frick, Harridge, owner representatives Tom Yawkey of the Red Sox and Warren Giles of the Reds, and George Denman, acting secretary treasurer.[38] Thus, Frick—ever the dutiful soldier—for a second time would be called on to help lead the game he loved, while the owners debated whether to make the change permanent or to once again deny him the top spot.

Chandler did indeed step down on July 15, nine months shy of completing his seven-year term, and the Executive Council, Frick included, which guided baseball following Landis's unexpected death, would do the same after Chandler's slow execution. The owners' committee screening candidates announced that they "hoped" to have an election by August 1.[39]

There were threats on the horizon that would not wait for a new commissioner, however. One emerged in May, when Rep. Emanuel Celler claimed that Congressional hearings were needed to determine the future of the reserve clause, especially in light of the Gardella suit. Though Gardella had settled, court decisions had left open the possibility of a court challenge to the clause. Celler, chairman of the House Judiciary Committee's Special Sub-Committee on Monopolies, suggested hearings to determine whether it deserved legislative protection or elimination.[40]

After delays, Celler announced that the hearings would open on July 30, with players, owners, and baseball officials called to testify. The hearings promised lively testimony, not only because Celler stipulated that questions could cover a wide variety of topics, but also because the hearings would begin after Chandler's term as commissioner had ended, leaving him free to speak candidly.[41]

Speaking at the Hall of Fame ceremonies, Frick sounded optimistic.

Addressing his remarks to "people who profess to see the death knell of baseball as we know it," he declared that "baseball can't be hurt" by the hearings. Instead, he said, "I believe a better game will come out of the hearings. I believe the committee will clear away the mists and open a new highway for baseball through the years ahead."[42]

For the soon-to-be commissioner, the challenge was daunting. For Chandler, a Congressional hearing meant hobnobbing with his old colleagues on familiar ground. For Frick, the ground was not familiar, though he would get plenty of practice, with 14 appearances the next 14 years.[43] Frick was the second witness to appear before the Celler committee, following Ty Cobb. After reading from his 8,000-word statement, the majority of which was a history of the reserve clause, Frick withstood hours of questioning by committee members, spread over two days. The first day, he read from his statement, which defended the reserve clause. Frick defended the policy, saying it was needed to "insure fair and honest competition and to preserve public confidence in baseball's honesty and integrity." He compared baseball contracts to other long-term agreements, "which is nothing unusual where distinctive personal services are contracted for."[44]

The second day, questioning centered on baseball's nonexistent expansion into new markets. To committee members, it represented an unfair limiting of competition. The most direct questions, not surprisingly, came from California Rep. Patrick J. Hillings, whose district included much of Los Angeles County. Hillings, aided by Celler, pressed Frick on why major league baseball had not made it to California, despite booming population and commercial growth. Frick's evasive answer combined an unsatisfying replay of organized baseball's responses to earlier overtures by the Pacific Coast League with vague speculations about future prospects.[45]

Frick also faced questions the second day about the reserve clause—mainly the unprecedented five-year penalties handed down to Mexican League players. Frick objected to Celler's use of the term "blacklisted" to describe the players (though it was accurate in context), but mainly defended the commissioner's right to discipline players who broke league rules.[46]

The committee heard an additional week of testimony in October, which allowed players and team officials to participate. As a reflection of his enhanced leadership role, Frick made a return appearance during the second week of hearings. The second time around was briefer, with less grilling, but Frick did acknowledge that "a great deal of good has come from these hearings, whether there be legislation, regardless of what your report is. I believe baseball has profited very much from this discussion ... on things that we can correct probably within our own organization."[47]

In an apparent effort to do just that and respond to the committee's displeasure with the slow process by which new and growing cities could gain major league baseball franchises, Frick proposed a new "open" designation for minor leagues like the Pacific Coast League. The proposal assumed that expansion via new franchises was impractical—an assumption that would be disproven—and that organized baseball would be better served by creating new major leagues out of prospering minors like the PCL. One of the provisions raised the draft price of players from $10,000 to $15,000, allowing the leagues to keep some of their better players.[48]

Not everyone bought Frick's West Coast strategy. *Los Angeles Examiner* columnist Vincent X. Flaherty sniped, "Mr. Frick knows the Coast League isn't going to become a third major league now, or in the next 50 years.... All he netted himself with his most recent babble was naught but resentment from the thousands of California baseball fans who want real big league baseball and won't trifle with a fraudulent imitation." He predicted, "When major league baseball comes to Los Angeles this town will draw five million fans during the first season."[49]

Ultimately, the subcommittee report accepted organized baseball's defense of the reserve clause in its May 1952 report. The reported stated, "Experience points to no feasible substitute to protect the integrity of the game or to guarantee a comparatively even competitive struggle." The committee recommended against legislative action and referred future evaluation of the reserve clause's legality to the courts.

Briefed on the report during a meeting with owners, Frick replied, "I don't mind telling you that our session, in my new offices in Rockefeller Center, developed considerable jubilation because the Celler committee had given the reserve clause a clean bill of health and admitted that it was essential for the conduct of our enterprise."[50] His official statement did include one nostalgic observation that would seem delusional today, but was Frick's reality back then: "The committee recognizes further that Baseball is not fundamentally operated for profit; that most of the men who operate Baseball are primarily interested in the game itself and must look to a winning club rather than dollars as a recompense for their investment and efforts."[51]

By successfully communicating their image of baseball as a sport and not a business (as reflected in Frick's statement), sports historian William B. Anderson notes, Frick and baseball's other leaders practiced successful public relations. Even Chandler, in his testimony where he groused about greedy owners who ran baseball like a business, indirectly supported baseball's agenda by framing that attitude as a departure.[52]

Because of the Celler subcommittee hearings, the owners delayed their meeting to discuss and perhaps select the next commissioner until August 7. While they did not come to a decision at that meeting (which Frick and Harridge did not attend), the owners did cut the list of 40 candidates down to 11. They also agreed to meet two weeks later to discuss the selection process further.[53]

Frick came close to being passed over for the job a second time, when the owners agreed to name Major General Emmett "Rosie" O'Donnell, a 44-year-old World War II hero, as commissioner. The appointment would have been a surprise, but the owners were sold on his credentials, his relative youth, and his support of baseball. The appointment was derailed by President Truman, who considered O'Donnell indispensable to the strategy in Korea.[54]

The owners learned about Truman's decision at the August 21 meeting, and all they did was further reduce the list of candidates from 11 to five. Although the finalists' names were not reported, it was assumed that Frick was one of them. The owners also announced a formal joint meeting of both leagues for September 20 in Chicago to make its selection of a commissioner. The date allowed the 30 days' notice specified by baseball's rules.[55] The extended process might have seemed torturous to Frick, though the challenges facing baseball might have tempered his expectations and hopes.

A surprising yet tantalizing reported finalist was General Douglas MacArthur, who had been removed from command of the United Nations command earlier that year. One report listed the five finalists as MacArthur, Lausche, Frick, Warren Giles, who was president of the Cincinnati Reds, and President Dwight Eisenhower's younger brother Milton, the president of Penn State University.[56] A July 1951 Gallup Poll showed MacArthur as the most frequently mentioned choice for commissioner, ahead of former U.S. Postmaster James Farley and Frick.[57] MacArthur removed himself from consideration, however, with an aide telling reporters, "As far as I know, the general has never given serious thought to the baseball commissionership."[58]

A week before the September owners meeting, Lausche also withdrew his name from consideration. Lausche considered his responsibilities as governor of Ohio to be too pressing, particularly during a time of conflict such as the country was facing in Korea. The governor would not comment on reports that he was withdrawing because he had demanded a ten-year contract to serve as commissioner, but was turned down.

Years later, when Frick was testifying about integration to Congress, Lausche, in his second term as a senator from Ohio, told Frick that he was within one vote of the post. While considering the job, he went to church and while singing a hymn, saw lyrics that read, "stay at the post." He told Frick, "That's when I decided to go back to Columbus and remain governor." Frick seemed unnerved by the revelation, fumbling a reply about not being aware of the story, but Lausche rescued him and saved the moment by joking, "Would you like to trade jobs with me?"[59]

Lausche's withdrawal left only three active candidates, one of whom was Frick. He continued to put off talk of his becoming commissioner, telling reporters he didn't know who would be elected, "but it won't be me."[60] Even so, as the meeting approached, Frick let it be known that he would accept the job "if they put the finger on me." He repeated, however, "I've never been a candidate for the job, and I haven't talked with anyone about it." He would wait behind in Bronxville while the owners deliberated in Chicago. Going into the meeting, it was believed that Giles was the front-runner, but no candidate had the 12 votes out of 16 needed for confirmation.[61]

That speculation was confirmed. The owners went into executive session on Thursday, September 20, at 12:30 p.m. The voting centered on two finalists, Giles and Frick. Having considered a United States war hero, a governor, and a former Cabinet official and current chairman of the board for Coca-Cola, they debated two baseball insiders. Rather than pit the two candidates against each other, the owners voted "yes/no" on each until one reached the needed 12 "yes" votes. The problem was that neither candidate could garner more than ten "yes" votes, so the voting continued through the afternoon.[62]

Toward late afternoon, some of the owners were ready to adjourn and meet again later. But inspiration came from an unlikely source: 25-year-old Charles Comiskey II, vice president of the White Sox and the youngest man there. "We've got to elect a commissioner today," he said. "And if we don't elect one today, we can't elect either of the men we've been voting on today. We will have destroyed them both. And we'll have to start all over again to try and find a commissioner."[63]

The owners took a dinner break and resumed the voting that evening. The deadlock was finally broken when Giles—who was at the hotel but not participating—sent word that he would withdraw from consideration. "It was obvious to me that it was a deadlock again and that neither of us was going to be elected unless something happened," he said later. "I didn't have any great desire for the job, and that caused me to withdraw."[64] Perhaps he felt that Frick's loyal and productive service as National League president deserved better than two close calls for the top position. To be fair, it should be noted that for all his protestations to the contrary, Frick did not withdraw himself from the deliberations, though he, unlike Giles, was in another city, and we have no evidence that he was contacted at any point during the stalemate.

Just a few minutes after Giles' withdrawal, the owners unanimously selected Frick as the third commissioner of baseball. Earl Hilligan, who handled media relations for the American League, made the official announcement standing on a chair outside the owners' meeting room.[65] Unfortunately, Frick did not answer the phone when they called him. He later explained that he was at a neighbor's house for dinner when the phone rang, and he could not answer it in time. Eventually the Bronxville chief of police had to send a squad car to find Frick and convey the message.[66] By the time they caught up with him, he had returned from dinner and was getting ready for bed.[67] When Frick finally returned the call, Charley Segar, Frick's public relations director at the National League office, answered, "Hello, commissioner."[68] Segar then handed the phone to Giles, who spoke to Frick and informed him of his appointment.[69] Frick later identified the neighbor he was having dinner with as Bill Thompson, a Manhattan business analyst.[70]

Frick's first duty as commissioner was to issue an immediate statement. He confessed to surprise at the sudden news, then stated, "I can only ask for the cooperation of the owners, fans and players. I have the best wishes of the owners, for all of them—the full sixteen—were on the phone fine minutes ago. I will do the best I can, but it is a big job."[71]

To no one's surprise, the New York sportswriters praised Frick's appointment. Red Smith wrote,

> Ford Frick was such an obvious choice ... that it is difficult to understand how the men who own the game could have postponed their decision as long as they did. Hardly anybody except the owner of a baseball team in the major leagues could be so purblind, so befuddled, so irresolute, so light of foot as to avoid making this move for more than eight months.[72]

Bill Corum added, "Baseball never has needed a leader more than now and it couldn't have found a better one than Ford C. Frick.... When a man has character, a good mind, an unblemished reputation, works hard at his job and has succeeded in every job he has ever had, what else can be required of him?"[73]

"They made a sound if not spectacular choice," wrote Joe Williams. "I've known Frick for years and I can assure the fans of the country their favorite pastime is in excellent hands."[74] Of course, his good friend Dan Daniel also praised him: "That Frick will administer the monitorship of the game justly, fearlessly, without bias, and with a thorough knowledge of the regulations is certain. That he will stick to the rules and make no personal interpretations after the manner of his predecessors, also may be assumed without fear of contradiction by him."[75]

The Sporting News also gave its official approval. "In selecting Ford Frick, the magnates acted wisely, for they not only picked a leader thoroughly schooled in the administration of the game and acquainted with its problems, but one of high personal integrity," the official editorial read. "Few in baseball are better fitted for the post than Frick."[76]

The appointment also allowed the New York journalists to take some farewell swipes at Chandler. "[Frick] will not be around singing at banquets, reciting Edgar Guest's poetry to junior high schools and posturing in hotel rooms and ball parks," Ken Smith wrote. Williams added, "If anything, Chandler got too powerful for himself. He had begun to play one club owner against another. His talent for politics which had made him a distinguished senator proved his downfall in baseball."[77] For his part, Chandler was unimpressed by Frick's appointment. "When the clubs pushed me out in 1951, they had a vacancy and they decided to keep it," he would say.[78]

Chandler, like others, also criticized Frick for his focus on the owners in his gratitude and his responsibilities. "That was an unfortunate remark," Chandler said. "The commissioner is elected to protect the players and public and to see that the owners live up to all the rules and regulations."[79]

Chandler knew what his successor was getting into. As sports writer and author Michael Shapiro described the organized baseball minefield Frick was about to enter, it was

> a domain that for decades had managed to endure as the nation's game, despite the absence of a prevailing organizational logic, a vision for the future, a governing voice, or a conscience. It was an enterprise run as a patchwork of fiefdoms, divided between two leagues that had very little to do with each other. Team owners operated with impunity; long ago they had drained virtually all authority from the office of commissioner, a position they had grudgingly accepted in the wake of the scandal that erupted after the fixing of the 1919 World Series.[80]

Speaking on his own behalf in his first interview, Frick was humble but direct.

> I didn't seek this job; didn't particularly want it, but now that I have it, I am going to give it the best I have and I'm going to be the commissioner 24 hours a day. I'm not saying that to let people know immediately that I feel I am the big boss, ready to crack down on everything and anybody, but that I am aware of the requirements of this job.[81]

10

Reconstruction

Ford Frick's first official action as commissioner, which surprised no one, was to announce that he would relocate the major league office to New York City. "I expect I'll move the commissioner's offices from Cincinnati to this city," he said the next morning from his National League office. "This is my home and at the moment, I see no reason for changing it." Even then, the caution set in as he added, "However, I'll discuss that with the executive council." He also announced that he would not assume the top position until he had been replaced as league president, with the council continuing to run baseball until then.[1]

Warren Giles' reward for stepping aside was being named president of the National League. As president and general manager of the Reds, Giles had a secure job with nice pay, so many speculated he would turn down the offer. After a few days to consider, he accepted it, effective November 1. Giles also announced that he would move the league office to Cincinnati—the opposite of Frick's plans for the commissioner's office.[2]

As baseball turned its attention away from the prolonged search and focused on other issues, the leagues agreed on a change in broadcast policy that would have far-reaching consequences. Noting the Justice Department's distaste for sweeping broadcast regulations, the leagues repealed the rule that required radio and television stations within a 50-mile radius of a minor league ballpark to stop broadcasting games 30 minutes before game time. While the change certainly heightened the danger for minor league attendance, it showed the major league's realization that television needed to be promoted, not restricted.[3] Certainly "the shot heard 'round the world"—Bobby Thomson's pennant-winning home run for the Giants—weighed into the owners' decision, becoming the first such baseball moment broadcast nationwide. The coverage conveyed the excitement of both Thomson's clutch swing of the bat and a medium that promised to share such moments with audiences coast to coast.[4]

10. Reconstruction

Almost as soon as Frick occupied the commissioner's office, the players came to him and the Executive Council with fresh demands. They included a ban on getaway day night games, fewer doubleheaders after night games, and a return to a 12:50 a.m. curfew for night games. Ralph Kiner, National League player representative, said the demands were necessary because of the effects of night games. "We feel the players' careers have been reduced by almost 50 percent today by such things as night baseball and the problems it produces," Kiner said.[5]

Frick also had some proposals of his own. He challenged the owners to come up with a system that would not only aid expansion by laying out a path for upper-tier minor league teams, but also allow other minor league towns to move up to higher classifications.[6] The plan would require the cooperation of the majors and the minors—and that would doom it to inaction. Frick would soon learn that even as commissioner, he would enjoy no more respect from the owners than he did as league president. And issues such as expansion would be addressed only when the owners were convinced that their individual interests could be accommodated.

Many of Frick's baseball writer friends held a dinner in his honor at Toots Shor's (his favorite restaurant) on October 29. Famed columnist Grantland Rice even contributed a poem to the festivities. It was included in the program:

> Here is Commissioner Christopher Frick
>   Lord of the leather and king of the ash
> Out from the multitude, Frick is the pick,
>   Named as the tyrant to handle the lash.
> Here is the boss of the game that we love
>   From spikes to the bludgeon, from basehits to glove.
> Here's to our hero, Commissioner Frick.
>   Sultan of swatters and owners to boot.
> You'll find he is ready to handle the stick.
>   Up with the glasses—and pass the salute.
> Here's one for the road to a regular guy
>   Who can stand up and look a mad world in the eye.
> The roar of the millions comes out from the stands.
>   Our troubles are fading—the heart is gone.
> The tumult and shouting—the waving of hands
>   Have wiped our hearts clean while the big game is on.
> His head waits in judgment—his hands hold a brick.
>   Our Lord High Commissioner—Christopher Frick.

At the dinner, Frick drew his line of authority more clearly. "There is a serious misapprehension afloat that the men who own the ball clubs are crooks, connivers, masters of skullduggery," he said. "The fact is, they are honest men, eager for the right, engaged in honest business in an honest way." Thus, he declared, "I am not a commissioner for the purpose of sitting on high and judging people and keeping them walking a straight line."[7]

With such remarks, early on Frick was setting the agenda for his tenure as commissioner. He would be an umpire, not a policeman in the tradition of Landis and, to a lesser extent, Chandler.[8] Frick would uphold the best interests of baseball, but he also recognized the organizational structure set in place by his employers, the owners, and those times he did step in would be tempered by that realization.

The umpire vs. policeman analogy was not original to Frick. The concept of a restrained commissioner's role was actually advanced in a memo developed by an owners' committee. The committee, chaired by Cubs owner Philip Wrigley, prepared a confidential memo that was not released until it was included in the Celler subcommittee's 1952 report. "Some people think that the main role of the commissioner is that of wielding a club to force a state of righteousness on a group of potentially wicked and irresponsible owners," the memo explained. Wrigley's committee recommended a public relations effort to explain the commissioner's role to baseball fans and players.[9]

At the December meetings, Frick also showed his approach when a tie vote came before him concerning a proposal to reduce major league rosters from 25 to 23. The National League supported it, while the American League opposed it. When Frick polled the owners, they also split, 8–8. So Frick cast his ballot against the new roster limit and, he pointed out, in favor of the status quo. "The votes were split, and I declined to cast a tie-breaker in favor of a change, because that would have been contrary to the policy which I have adopted by my administration," he said.[10]

In other decisions passed by the owners at the December meetings, his plan for future realignment of the major and minor leagues—as revised at work sessions in November—was accepted, and the open classification for the Pacific Coast League was approved. The players' proposals regarding night games on getaway days and before doubleheaders were approved, but the 12:50 a.m. curfew was not.[11]

Before spring training in 1952, Frick allowed himself a vacation, and he and Eleanor enjoyed a Caribbean cruise in February.[12] Relaxation at home was also a priority; Frick told one interviewer that he did not have a television set yet: "too distracting." He and his wife preferred reading, frequently with the radio off.[13]

Frick's first spring training as commissioner included a memorable meeting with future Hall of Famer Eddie Mathews, then a young infielder for the Braves. Frick was standing in the Boston outfield with sportswriter

Whitney Martin and Braves publicity staffer Billy Sullivan (later founding owner of the New England Patriots), when Mathews bowled over all three chasing a fly ball. Sullivan was knocked unconscious and had to be carried into the clubhouse, while the young player ended up with a broken nose. Frick suffered no injuries, but it was reported that he was more concerned with protecting his glasses.[14]

Even as commissioner, Frick continued his annual pre-season column. But the tone changed noticeably. He made no predictions about pennant races for both leagues, as he did when league president. In fact, his only specific prediction was that the number of baseball players involved in the Korean War would double, from 1,800 to 3,600. Perhaps that conflict, mentioned first, tempered pennant race fever. Frick also noted the increasing popularity of youth leagues and the Pacific Coast League's prospects to become a major league. Beyond that, he simply stated, "We seem to be headed toward another good season with prospects of close races in both major leagues."[15]

Frick made his first decisive contribution to the rulebook in 1952, albeit informally, when he specifically ruled that women would not be allowed to play professional baseball at any level. His actions were precipitated after the Harrisburg Senators, a Class B Inter-State League team, signed a local softball player, Eleanor Engle. The Harrisburg general manager claimed that he signed Engle because "she can hit the ball a lot better than some of the fellows on the club."

George Trautman, president of the minor leagues, was neither amused nor impressed. He called the signing a "travesty" and refused to approve the contract. Frick was not quoted in the articles (a time when his policy of delegating such assignments to lower-level officials paid off), but Trautman assured reporters that Frick agreed with his assertion that signing women to play was not in the best interests of baseball.[16]

In 1960, Frick would also turn down a female umpire for a minor league game. As a promotional gimmick, Allentown (Pennsylvania) team owner Max Hess hired highly ranked local softball pitcher Maureen Galvin to help call the Binghamton-Allentown game on August 24. Binghamton management contacted Frick, who vetoed the idea, saying the game was "too important" to both team's playoff chances to allow a woman to umpire.[17]

An ongoing struggle for Frick and the teams focused on a uniform opening date for spring training. The 1946 agreement with players set a March 1 date.[18] The teams had been cutting corners for years, however. The Cubs "invited" their players to a conditioning camp at Catalina Island to take advantage of the requirement that "no bats, balls or gloves" will be used. That, plus teams using major league players for February minor league camps, caused Happy Chandler to issue a stern reminder about the March 1 starting date going into the 1950 season.[19]

Still, it was acknowledged that pitchers and catchers could benefit from some extra work, so the players agreed to relax the March 1 provision at the mid-summer meeting, as long as the teams agreed to delay exhibition games until the second Saturday in March.[20] After he took over as commissioner, Frick reminded owners that the March 1 date had not been rescinded, and that earlier starts required player consent. He demanded copies of all team invitations, to assure that the teams were not using coercion to abuse the loophole.[21]

By July of 1952, Frick had eased the March 1 deadline, announcing that pitchers and catchers could report a week earlier. Despite the players' request, he also announced that the exhibition season would open the first Saturday of March, a week earlier than the players had proposed.[22] That decision effectively finalized the spring training debate, leaving baseball with the system currently in use: battery mates arriving around February 20, and all other players on March 1.

In retrospectives following his first year in office, Frick acknowledged his lack of activism and his preference for the background. Even he might have been concerned, however, when he was denied admittance to a World Series game after forgetting his ticket. "Oh, yeah," the gate attendant responded. "Hundreds of blokes like you have tried, but not one got away with it. Move on!" It's hard to imagine something like that happening to Chandler or Landis.[23]

Frick did take the lead in addressing a player's moral issues. On the final day of the 1952 season, White Sox outfielder Jim Rivera was arrested on a charge of rape. Rivera claimed the relationship was consensual, and though a grand jury agreed, declining to indict, public outcry remained strong. Frick had already come to the defense of Rivera, who served a five-year prison sentence for attempted rape from 1944 to 1949. When St. Louis civic and religious groups protested Rivera's playing for the Browns late in the 1951 season, Frick stated, "If the purpose is punishment, then he has already been punished. If the purpose is cure or improvement, then this man has a greater chance to make good being allowed to live as others live. Since Rivera came into baseball his conduct has been beyond question. If in the future he shows that he has not profited by his experience, this office will take action."[24]

The future arrived just over a year later. After summoning Rivera to his office for a long discussion, Frick announced that he would respect the grand jury's decision and allow Rivera to play for the White Sox (he had been traded to Chicago mid-season), but he would be on probation. During that time, the White Sox would "assume full and complete responsibility for his conduct and behavior off the field and on." Frick cemented the team's responsibility by prohibiting them from waiving or trading Rivera for one complete season; the only options would be suspension or retirement.

In announcing his decision, Frick said, "This is the first time a commissioner ever had to make a decision on a morals charge."[25] It turned out to be the right call. Rivera would become one of the White Sox's most popular players of all time, remaining with the team until 1961 and entertaining fans with his reckless speed in the outfield and on the base paths.[26]

Frick would face another complicated morals issue in 1958. Ed Bouchee of the Phillies, who had finished second in the 1957 Rookie of the Year voting, was arrested in his hometown of Spokane in January, on a charge of indecent exposure. The victims were girls, ages six and 10.[27] Bouchee, who was married with one child and one on the way, pleaded guilty and was placed on probation for three years after agreeing to seek psychiatric treatment at a facility in Connecticut.[28]

After Bouchee completed treatment and spent some time in Philadelphia working out, the team requested reinstatement. Frick said he conducted a complete investigation, including interviews with Bouchee's teammates, the presiding judge, and a psychiatrist not involved in the case. The judge, in sentencing Bouchee to probation, had described the case as one calling for treatment, not punishment.

Frick also sent investigators to talk to opposing players. "The verdict was strong and unanimous 'Let Bouchee return to the Phillies, let his trouble be forgotten,'" Frick said. He decided to reinstate Bouchee. "He had been seized with a terrible compulsion, and now he is free of it, and, subject to probation for three years, he is back on the Philadelphia player list," he announced.[29]

Bouchee played in the major leagues for five more years and did not have another such incident. He was traded to the Cubs in 1961 and drafted by the Mets after that, though the Mets dropped him a couple of months into their inaugural season. He played in the minors briefly, retiring in 1963. Like Rivera, he proved worthy of the faith Frick had placed in him and had demonstrated that, criticisms aside, Frick seemed to know when to take a risk on a player.[30]

In the 1952 off-season, Frick proposed rule changes on two knotty issues, though he was motivated more by the Celler committee's findings than any personal proactivity: excessive bonuses paid to unproven players, and trading/waiver policies that allowed teams to "buy" players for late-season pennant drives and shuffle others back and forth to the minor leagues. However, he left the decision to the owners.

The owners were not as concerned about the bonuses as what happened afterward to the players who did not succeed. Earlier attempts to limit the practice failed from lack of enforcement. Under the new rules approved at the December major league meetings, a free agent signing for more than $4,000 would have to stay with the major league team for two seasons. A player who signed for less would have to be kept on a minor league roster for an entire season. The rule was intended to discourage high-dollar signings, mainly through an increase in fines for owners who broke the rules. The new rules also banned under-the-table gifts or cash to family members.[31] The owners, by passing the rule, confessed to an inability to stop the practice on their own.

The waiver rule, also passed at the meetings, closed a loophole that the Yankees had exploited masterfully. Under the previous rules, the only way a player could change teams after the June 15 trading deadline was to be waived. Under that system, an American League team could bid on and purchase a National League player, usually a castoff, who had cleared waivers, but an American League team could not. The same was true for National League teams and players waived by American League teams. The Yankees had used the rule to its advantage, adding veteran National League players off waivers to help a late-season pennant run, before other teams could bid on them.[32]

Under the new rules, the player would have to clear waivers in both leagues. If more than one team wanted the player, he would go to the team with the worst record, thereby eliminating bidding and keeping successful franchises from getting richer. Some owners also suggested that the trading deadline be moved back to July 31 (where it is today), but that change was not made. An amendment also banned recalls of players optioned after July 31, to prevent teams from shuffling players back and forth between the majors and minors. Recalls in case of injury were allowed, with the commissioner's approval.[33]

While the bonus and waiver rule changes got most of the attention, the owners also addressed franchise relocation, another Celler committee concern. Under the new rules, if either league wanted to relocate a team to a city where that league had a minor league franchise, permission from the other league was not required. Under the previous rules, unanimous consent was required in the league making the change, with majority approval from the other league. The within-league approval rules were also relaxed. The vote would not have to be unanimous, but would require only five of eight votes in the National League, and six of eight votes in the American. The change set the stage for the franchise relocation craze over the next five years.[34]

The action was timely, not only for owners seeking greener pastures, but also for baseball itself, which could no longer maintain the geographic inertia of the past fifty years. Through population shifts, five cities with more people than Cincinnati (Los Angeles, San Francisco, Baltimore, Minneapolis/St. Paul, and Buffalo) did not have major-league franchises. St. Louis, Philadelphia, and Boston were struggling as two-franchise cities.[35]

Another 1950s headache, television, also got the owners' attention. Heading into the meetings, Cardinals owner Fred Saigh proposed the first version of what would soon be standard business practice: shared television revenues. Recognizing that smaller market teams such as his were at a financial disadvantage to the Giants and Cubs, he demanded a percentage of their television receipts when his team appeared on their home broadcasts. Otherwise, he threatened to exercise his right to decline having the game broadcast.[36]

Most major league teams were broadcasting all of their games on radio, home and away, by this time, and each team handled its own broadcasting, except for the World Series. But television presented a new set of financial and technological obstacles for the away team, thus providing a temporary but substantial advantage for the larger markets. Saigh's proposal, surprisingly, met with support—not only from smaller market teams such as Pittsburgh and Cincinnati, but also from Cubs owner Philip Wrigley, who agreed to Saigh's proposal. Frick did not include Saigh's proposal on the agenda because it was a matter for individual teams to work out with each other—a familiar response, even if television presented some unique, far-reaching perils that could have been discussed.[37]

Following Saigh's actions at the league winter meetings, Frick appointed a committee of team owners and league officials to develop policies for broadcasting games. The committee included minor league representation and was chaired by Frank Shaughnessy, president of the International League.[38] At its first meeting, the committee responded to minor league officials' allegations that television was destroying their attendance by commissioning a survey to report on the damage alleged. "Then we shall be in position to decide on a remedy," said George Weiss, Yankees general manager.[39]

Saigh's involvement in the issue, and anything related to baseball, ended after he pleaded no contest to income tax evasion and was sentenced to

15 months in prison in 1953.⁴⁰ Saigh had been indicted in April 1952 on five counts of income tax evasion involving both his personal and his corporation's income.⁴¹ Frick had allowed Saigh to continue working with the team while his case was decided.

Following his plea, and after meeting with Frick and Giles, Saigh announced that he would remove himself from participating in team activities, in advance of selling the team as quickly as possible. Frick, visibly shaken, said, "This has been the toughest thing I ever had to do, but there just was no other way it could be done." Many felt Frick's actions were particularly difficult because Saigh had led the ouster of Chandler, so in some ways Frick owed his job to Saigh.⁴²

The situation led to the club's purchase in late February by the Anheuser-Busch brewery, which would own the team until 1996.⁴³ At Frick's recommendation, the brewery formed an intermediary company to own the Cardinals, so that the team would not be directly controlled by a brewery.⁴⁴ Frick also dissuaded the new owners from naming their home field Budweiser Stadium. Instead, the team honored their owners by naming it Busch Stadium—its name today. The change did not placate the Women's Christian Temperance Union. "Busch is not much of an improvement," said Mrs. D. Leigh Colvin, WCTU president. "You could toss up the three B's. Call it Beer Park, Budweiser Park or Busch Park and they all mean the same thing."⁴⁵

A year later, speaking from the Senate floor, Senator Edwin Johnson of Colorado proposed a law that would cause teams owned by beer companies to come under anti-trust scrutiny. He acknowledged that the bill was specifically targeted at Busch and the Cardinals.⁴⁶ Johnson alleged that Busch, through the team and its radio network, was attempting to establish a "beer monopoly" that would overwhelm local breweries.

He also criticized Frick. "Personally, I do not think the commissioner measured up to his high responsibilities when he permitted Anheuser-Busch to purchase the St. Louis Cardinals," he said. He added that he hoped his bill would "awaken the commissioner to his responsibilities and cause him to restore the good reputation and good standing of professional baseball in America."⁴⁷

Frick responded to Johnson's attacks on him and Busch by expressing disappointment that Johnson, president of the Class A Western League, would use such tactics. He criticized the proposed bill, saying, "I cannot conceive of any Congress passing discriminatory legislation which is pointed at one partner, to the exclusion of other partners. Even if such legislation is passed, I do not see how it would solve the major problem."

10. Reconstruction

Casting Johnson's attack in a broader context, he added, "Half our problem is a fear complex. The time has come for us to get together, and make our own decisions and see what reaction comes from Washington." In defense of Busch, he added, "Baseball people are not a lot of crooks. They are not looking for loopholes, for chances to perpetrate skullduggery." He did not comment on Johnson's specific accusations against him, and Johnson did not respond to Frick's statement.[48]

Frick and Busch did not face Senate subcommittee questioning until May. The March hearing featured a long statement from Johnson, and the main attraction of the April hearing was Joe Garagiola discussing his planned broadcasting career. During Frick's time before the subcommittee, he was asked about his role in convincing Busch not to name the Cardinals' home field Budweiser Stadium. "I still don't think I have the authority to say to Mr. Busch, 'You have got to change the name of your real-estate holdings or else,'" Frick said. "It was more a case of moral persuasion, not authority."[49]

Frick also challenged Johnson's characterization that baseball had been "prostituted" into "the adjunct of the brewing business," calling the statement "a little too broad."[50] Johnson's law faced opposition, led by Illinois Senator Everett Dirksen, and did not see further action after the hearings.

The first shots in the relocation-expansion explosion of the 1950s were fired as spring training was about to begin. For months beginning in 1952, a group of highly placed baseball fans in Milwaukee, eager for the St. Louis Browns to relocate there, had been prevailing on Boston Braves owner Lou Perini, who also owned the Braves' minor league franchise, the Milwaukee Brewers of the American Association. Perini, however, refused to consider the city's offer of $500,000 to relocate the Brewers to Toledo, as even the governor and state legislature urged, which would allow the Browns to move to Wisconsin for the upcoming 1953 season.[51]

Frick concurred with Perini. "I am not opposed to transferring of major clubs to other cities," he said. "But I think the idea of moving a major league franchise right now is perfectly nonsensical. You just can't do those things in a few hours. There is too much at stake."[52] On March 12, Perini even suggested a new rule allowing major league teams to move to minor league cities only between October 1 and the December league meetings, a rule change that Frick supported.[53]

But a mere two days later, that is exactly what Perini did. Instead of allowing another team to move in, Perini offered his own team, the Braves, who had always struggled in Boston against the more popular Red Sox.

News broke Saturday of National League owners meeting the next week to approve Perini's relocation of his Braves franchise to Milwaukee, in time for the upcoming season. Harridge also announced an American League owners' meeting to discuss moving Veeck's St. Louis Browns to Baltimore.[54] After 50 years of franchise stability, through two commissioners and two world wars, the geography of baseball was starting to explode. Frick's only statement on Saturday contradicted his earlier feelings about franchise relocation and betrayed weariness with what threatened to become an ordeal: "Move if you are going to. If not, shut up."[55]

Frick and the owners involved met Monday to go over the relocation process, in anticipation of league meetings the next two days. Frick reiterated his preference for such moves to happen more slowly, and even reiterated his support for the idea Perini had proposed and then disowned, for such moves to happen only after the season. He also acknowledged that in the current situation, waiting could prove more disastrous than moving ahead.[56]

The Browns' relocation to Baltimore hit an unexpected snag when five out of eight American League team owners voted against the move, fearing that it could not be completed in time.[57] Perhaps the owners were respecting Frick's expressed opposition to such moves.

On the other hand, Perini's request to move his team was approved the next day, setting off celebration in Milwaukee, which anticipated the arrival of major league baseball in less than a month.[58] A crowd of 12,000 fans greeted the players at the train station, and an additional 60,000 cheered them at a welcoming parade. Its first year in Milwaukee, the team drew more than 1.8 million fans, who gave players gifts from sausage and Wisconsin cheese to clothing, televisions, and even cars.[59]

A couple of weeks later, Frick was supporting the Boston move. "The cases were not at all similar," he said in an April interview. "There was no displacement of East-and-West balance in Boston's shift [author's note: really?]. There was no hitch in Lou Perini's shift, because he owned the Milwaukee franchise already, and the American Association was agreeable to the territorial change."[60]

Still, the process had to concern Frick. Critics had predicted that he would be powerless against the owners, and that seemed to be the case. He expressed his opposition to short-sale franchise relocations, and team owners ignored him. Even worse, an abstract opinion about the future of other two-franchise cities sent sports writers scurrying to Phillies owner Bob Carpenter. To the reporters, Frick had as good as announced that the Phillies would be moving—a prospect Carpenter angrily denied.[61]

Frick and the team owners were initiating a new era in the relationship between teams and cities, according to sports economists Dennis Coates and Brad Humphreys. Previously, the owners built and owned their stadiums. But in this case, as well as the moves of the Browns from St. Louis to Baltimore in 1954 and the Athletics from Philadelphia to Kansas City in 1955, cities lured teams by offering cheap rent for publicly owned stadiums. The Braves paid $1,000 for their first two years at Milwaukee's County Stadium.[62]

Even before he become commissioner, Frick was a strong opponent of gambling and initiated a crusade against it heading into the 1947 season. In remarks delivered at that year's writers' dinner, he called out players who were friends with gamblers, noting that such characters "too often are permitted the run of our ball parks ... and access to our clubhouses."[63]

Tellingly, he even enlisted the help of sports writers: "If you have evidence of wrong-doing, it cannot be of value to you as a rumor, but should be submitted for action. The door of the commissioner of baseball is open to you every day." To combat the intrusion of gamblers, Frick posted a sign at all National League clubhouses, including spring training facilities: "Positively no admittance to dressing rooms. Players and active working press only. By order of Ford Frick, president, National League."[64]

Thus, the Brooklyn Dodgers responded quickly in 1949 when catcher Bruce Edwards received a letter attempting to fix a game. The letter was turned over to the commissioner for investigation. Frick announced that no further action was required, because investigators had determined that the writer was, in Frick's words, "a mental case."[65]

In 1951, Frick accepted an appointment to Attorney General J. Howard McGrath's advisory committee of sports leaders, who were charged with helping stamp out illegal gambling. The committee met with President Truman at its September 1951 organizational meeting and planned a conference for the next month on the influence of gambling in sports.[66]

The committee demanded a "full scale Congressional investigation" into sports gambling at both the college and pro levels, with new laws. The committee in particular wondered whether the practice of awarding athletic scholarships made a college athlete particularly susceptible to bribes from gamblers, because he "begins to view his ability in a commercial vein. Such thinking provides a ready field of growth of the seeds of irregularity and illegality."[67]

After a couple of years as commissioner, Frick wondered if his anti-gambling crusade was working. His investigators reported players patronizing bars and restaurants that were known headquarters for bookies.

While he claimed no evidence against specific players, he announced, "The players who regularly visit the gambling nests will be told directly and personally to end the practice." Frick added, "It's a damn sight better to head off the players with a warning like this, before they get into the kind of trouble that calls for drastic action, such as expulsion."[68]

Such was Frick's distaste for gambling that he forced Yankees pitcher Eddie Lopat to cancel one of two exhibition games in Las Vegas, part of a 1954 post-season barnstorming tour Lopat had organized. "The commissioner told me that he did not want a lot of ball players hanging around Las Vegas on a Saturday night," Lopat said. "He wants us to move in, play, and get right out of town." Lopat considered it a "radical decision," but said he would abide by it.[69]

In 1955, he even opened an investigation into a good-natured pregame race between catchers Del Rice of the Cardinals and Rube Walker of the Dodgers—more of a "slow-off" than anything. Teammates good-naturedly threw money in a pot, yielding no more than $50. Frick demanded an explanation from managers Eddie Stanky and Walter Alston. Although nothing came of the situation, it definitely showed on which side Frick would choose to err.[70]

During Frick's first two seasons in office, for all of the attention and developments afforded television and franchise realignment, there were few if any proposals that related to player welfare. The perception was spreading that Frick, unlike Chandler, was an "owners' commissioner" instead of a "players' commissioner." An All-Star break meeting where Frick and the two league presidents had "'amicably received' but tabled" player demands, only reinforced that perception. The players responded by announcing that they had hired an attorney, J. Norman Lewis, to represent them in their dealings with the league.[71] Labor relations in major league baseball was entering a new era.

If Frick was stung by this player repudiation, he did not say so publicly. As usual, he offered no official comment but did acknowledge several telephone conversations with Lewis. He might have felt that publicly criticizing Lewis's hiring would have eroded player relations even further. Instead, his league presidents responded. "The players can do more for themselves than any outside representative, no matter how able that outsider may be," Warren Giles said. "If the players delegate to anyone outside their own ranks any of their rights to discuss and negotiate individually, they are surrendering a privilege that has been very valuable to them."[72]

Predictably, sports writers came to Frick's aide. *The Sporting News* ran a front-page headline ("Players Rap Hiring of Mouthpiece") that both denigrated the hire and implied strong opposition. The article quoted players who were both skeptical toward the idea and hostile, like Mickey Grasso of the Washington Senators: "I'm definitely set against a lawyer representing us. I see it this way: We have enjoyed good relations with the owners in the past. I don't think we ought to ask them for outlandish demands."[73]

The Sporting News' support was consistent with its pro-organized baseball editorial philosophy. The journal had positioned itself as "the official record of baseball," partially through a troublingly close relationship with baseball's leadership for decades. A *Sporting News* editor had even drafted the 1903 agreement forming the National and American leagues. Thus, its staff and correspondents could be counted on to present editorials and even perspectives within its reporting that reflected the leaders' agenda.[74]

Red Sox owner Tom Yawkey, also a member of the executive council, was sharper in his criticism. He criticized Ralph Kiner and Allie Reynolds, the leading player representatives, for the hiring process, reinforcing the claim that many of the other player delegates were not informed of the change. He also defended Frick. "I strongly resent any inference that [Frick] doesn't represent the players as much as he does the owners. Ford Frick is one of the fairest men I have ever met.... I know that his sole aim is to give everybody a square deal. I am for him 100 percent and I'll back him till Hell freezes over."[75]

Reynolds also deflected perceived criticism toward Frick.

> We didn't intend this to be a slap at Commissioner Frick's office or the owners. But we were in dire need of legal advice.... Our main aim is to improve the relationship between the players and the owners. We hope this move will help to bring our players' organization closer together and that we will be able to put out a coordinated effort.[76]

Kiner concurred. "Commissioner Frick has been very co-operative with all the players," he said. "He's done a lot to help us individually and collectively, and he's done it without telling the world about it." He added that Frick promised the players a generous infusion of World Series money to shore up the pension fund: "He has told us that we'll get every penny of it—and he means it."[77] Lewis did accompany Reynolds and Kiner to the executive council meeting on August 24. Frick did not allow him to attend the actual meeting, since he was not a member of the council, but he and the league presidents did confer with Lewis and the players after the meeting, where several proposals were discussed. Frick asked that the proposals not be made public, Lewis noted in talking to reporters after the meeting.[78]

The next day, however, Lewis did bristle at his exclusion from the executive council meeting. He claimed that the commissioner's attorney had invited him to the meeting and that he was unaware of Frick's statements to reporters that Lewis would never be allowed to attend such meetings. He also declined once again to outline the proposals offered, though reports quoted other sources, who said they included an increase in the minimum salary from $5,000 to $8,000.[79]

As if to promote Frick as a friend of the players, thus undercutting the players' concerns, *The Sporting News* ran a front-page article soon after, praising the major league pension program and presenting Frick as its protector. "There is no other industrial pension plan operating in the United States that is comparable," the article proclaimed. It noted that players could retire at age 50 with a $100/month pension and could sign up for the program after only 60 days of major league service.

The writer, Roscoe McGowen, implied that players were seeking outside legal counsel because they did not appreciate their benefits. He added, condescendingly, "It is a bit difficult to understand why," because Frick had distributed a booklet explaining the plan. It's no surprise that McGowen's article included interviews with insurance experts conducted in the office of Charley Segar, now secretary-treasurer of major league baseball.[80]

If the reader somehow missed the point, McGowen threw in a sidebar with anecdotes demonstrating how Frick had helped players get their benefits. "It has been said, and believed by some ball players, that they need a commissioner 'because the owners have one.' The following is offered in evidence that the players already have a commissioner in Ford Frick."[81]

Quickly, Lewis seemed to come around to the players' perception of Frick. Lewis declared "no more acrimony" between himself and Frick. "I am satisfied that everything will proceed on a smooth scale from now on," he said. "The commissioner and I are very intent upon arriving at some solutions for players' problems to the reasonable satisfaction of the players, the commissioner, the club owners, the league presidents and baseball generally."[82]

All involved had become so amiable that Lewis was invited to the September quarterly meeting between the players and the Executive Council, along with both league attorneys. Frick said, "I always have said the players have a right to be represented on legal matters, and certainly the pension plan falls into that category."[83]

Owing perhaps to Lewis's presence, the players "gained more concessions than they had in the past eight years," the *New York Times* reported. The players gained an increase in meal money and moving expenses for trades, a reduction from ten to eight years for veteran status, and reimbursement equivalent to hotel costs for a player living on his own during spring training. Issues of minimum salary and pension increases, however, were deferred until the league meetings.[84]

At the same time, it was announced that the St. Louis Browns would indeed be moving to Baltimore after all for the 1954 season, but without owner Bill Veeck. Frick's involvement in the move is noteworthy in that it was nonexistent—or at least it seemed that way. The shift was handled completely by Harridge and American League owners.

Veeck had evolved into an annoyance in his efforts to stay competitive in a two-team town. Veeck and Chicago White Sox general manager Frank Lane had exercised an escape clause effectively abolishing the American League agreement assigning all broadcast rights to the home team.[85] Like Saigh, he was trying to work a deal to get a percentage of television revenues for games against major market teams. When they hesitated, he exercised his option and declined permission for the games to be televised at all.[86]

Those team owners responded by declining night games when playing the Browns in St. Louis, costing Veeck valuable attendance.[87] That deepened his financial hole, particularly after his relocation attempts in the 1953 season drove away the St. Louis fans. Veeck appealed to Frick, but as was his policy, the commissioner declined involvement in a squabble between individual teams.[88]

Soon after the Browns' relocation to Baltimore was voted down early in 1953, with neither sympathy nor help from Frick or any other league official, Veeck also surrendered on the television battle.[89] By September, Veeck was gone as Browns owner. The owners again turned down his relocation to Baltimore, though they approved the move two days later, after Veeck had sold his interest in the team to a group from that city. Although the opposition owners claimed concern for the team's financial stability, it is difficult to eliminate Veeck's unpopularity as a factor.[90]

To the outsider, it seemed that Frick was staying out of the fight. Others have subsequently claimed that Frick, in fact, wanted Veeck out of baseball and prevailed on the owners both to deny his franchise relocation and then to ease him out of club ownership. Frick supposedly resented Veeck's innovative ideas on eliminating the reserve clause and sharing revenue, along with his abrasive public persona. In March 1953, it meant denying Veeck the stature of being the first owner to relocate. Nine months later, it meant removing the thorn from Frick's side,[91] though Veeck would seek a measure of revenge nine years later.

11

Old Problems, New Problems

For most of Frick's first term, the minor leagues' struggle proved to be the most stubborn problem, as leagues and teams folded nationwide. The popularity of televised baseball was moving fans from the small-town grandstands to their living rooms, threatening the existence of the majors' talent pipeline.

As James Walker and Robert Bellamy point out in their excellent history of baseball on television, the minor leagues' decline could not be blamed on television, though it did contribute. They cite other factors, including the overexpansion of the minors after World War II, changes in transportation that made it easier to drive to a major league park, the shift of major league teams from inner city to suburban stadiums, and even air conditioning, which made summertime television preferable to sweating in the bleachers.[1]

At the February 1953 baseball writers' dinner, Senator Edwin Johnson, who was not only president of the Western League but also on the television committee Frick had appointed, interjected a serious note. Referring to television money as baseball's "thirty pieces of silver," he threatened that if Congress ever held antitrust hearings again, "I will testify that baseball is a cruel and heartless monopoly, motivated by avarice and greed."[2]

As a senator, Johnson had some tactics he could use to help minor league teams, and he put them to use. On March 20, he proposed a law allowing minor league teams to ban radio and television broadcasts of major league games in their territory.[3] In testimony before Johnson's subcommittee, Frick endorsed the proposed law. He claimed that organized baseball had tried to introduce such a policy on their own in 1949 to protect the minor leagues, but the Justice Department had labeled it an illegal restraint of trade. "The major leagues cannot exist without the minor leagues," Frick testified. "Television and radio have unquestionably created baseball interest. We can only go by attendance figures. I think they will demonstrate to you that this thing can be overdone." His fear was that "baseball, because it is a sport, must give its product to television stations or radio stations here, there or elsewhere ... without regulation and without restriction when they know that to do so is to destroy the game."[4]

Walker and Bellamy note that in that same hearing, Frick also said, "we have no objection to television going into towns that want to see baseball where baseball is not being played or where baseball is being played." To them, that demonstrated the tightrope Frick walked, between protecting the minors and maintaining a laissez faire on business-related issues.[5]

The committee heard from only one broadcaster, the president of the National Association of Radio and Television Broadcasters, Harold Fellows. He submitted a letter opposing the law, stating that it "would be contrary to the public interest" to limit public access to major league baseball on television. Johnson closed the hearings expressing optimism that the bill would become law.[6] The Johnson threat would fade, however, as the owners began to see the benefits of local and nationwide game broadcasts,[7] and Johnson left the Senate to become governor of Colorado.

The problem had already generated a procession of committees and reports. In January 1953, Frick had appointed a committee, chaired by International League President Frank Shaughnessy.[8] In true bureaucratic fashion, the committee's first action was to commission a survey of television's effects on the minors.[9] It was a timely move, given Johnson's legislation to curb major league broadcasts in minor league cities.

As the committee conducted its survey, Frick acknowledged television's continued devastation of minor league attendance. "Without the minors, the majors could not exist five years," he said. "If there are no minors, the entire structure will collapse—majors, little leagues and everything." At the same time, he would not discuss the first "Game of the Week" nationwide broadcast that would be starting that season—another threat to the minors. In fairness to Frick, during that period the networks arranged such games with individual teams, and not major league baseball.[10]

The irony was not lost on Charley Young, sports editor of the *Albany (New York) Knickerbocker News*. He pointed out that the "Game of the Week" would be blacked out in the major league away team's city, but "piped into minor league cities." He added, "With due respect to Commissioner Frick and Harridge and Giles, they don't know what the minors need."[11] Frick said he had read the article but declined comment.

The committee did not make a report at the December meetings.

After those meetings, however, Frick appointed another major/minor committee, this one to discuss an update to guidelines regulating how players were signed and then controlled in the minor leagues. The minors' complaint was that the existing rules unfairly distributed talent, creating an inferior product for some franchises.[12] The latter committee met for two days in January and reported progress, with another meeting scheduled for February 1.[13] Following the February meeting, chairman Branch Rickey predicted another meeting in March, but no concrete actions before the December meetings.[14] The committee's proposals were on the agenda for the mid-year meetings, but were tabled until December.[15]

In the interim, Frick conveyed to the Justice Department a plan to create a major league-wide "Game of the Week" broadcast. It was forecast to bring in $2 million, allowing Frick to use half of that to subsidize the minor leagues. The government turned down the idea, however, on antitrust grounds; league-wide broadcasting contracts would not be permitted until 1961. So that delayed that strategy.[16]

A survey of minor league team officials suggested several solutions that related to controlling player and other costs, limiting major league control to 40 players, and controlling major league broadcasts into minor league towns. No major league owners returned a survey, and Frick also declined, saying that because his office only enforced the rules and did not create them, it would not be proper for him to participate.[17]

By September 1954, at least some minor league owners had lost their patience and announced they would file a $50 million lawsuit against Frick and all 16 major league teams. The lawsuit claimed that television encroachment had cost the minor leagues tens of millions of dollars, "and the major leagues have benefited greatly financially by disregarding our territory, giving away free major league ball." Frank D. Lawrence, owner of the Portsmouth, Virginia, team, was one of the main organizers of the lawsuit, and he claimed that former U.S. Attorney General James P. McGranery had agreed to represent them.[18]

The minor league team owners passed a new working agreement, as suggested by the majors-minors committee, at their meetings in early December, and sent it along to the major league meeting the next week. The owners threw in another resolution of their own, confining broadcasts to a 50-mile radius from the home team.[19]

At their December meetings, the major league owners rejected the broadcast radius resolution. Frick explained that any rules limiting television would invite antitrust scrutiny from the Justice Department. However, they did agree to changes in the working agreements which would

11. Old Problems, New Problems 169

require them to cover more of the minor leagues' expenses, including spring training and manager salaries—which would benefit the minors by $3,000 to $5,000 per club. "This is by far the most important piece of legislation passed at these meetings," Frick said. "It can well be the means of survival for many clubs in lower minor-league categories."[20]

Heralding a new era of international sports diplomacy, Frick and his wife joined the New York Giants on an 18-game tour of Japan, Okinawa, the Philippines, and Guam after the 1953 World Series. Frick's involvement demonstrated that the trip was about more than baseball; the Eisenhower administration considered it key to their diplomatic strategy for the region, as the fighting in Korea was coming to an end.[21] Before the opening game, Frick read a goodwill message from Eisenhower, pledging friendship and peace.[22]

Frick and his wife actually left the entourage in Japan for a 17-day global tour of their own. They headed west, visiting China, India (including the Taj Mahal), Beirut, Paris, and London before returning to New York.[23] Among the souvenirs they brought back was a 700-year-old Samurai armor set, to be presented to Eisenhower as a gift from Japanese baseball fans.[24]

Although the Japan tour was hailed as a diplomatic success, no such tours were planned the following year. An unsettled economy in 1954 left promoters reluctant to schedule tours to the region. That, plus unspecified "financial disagreements" from the 1953 tour, caused Frick to bar major league players from visits to Japan in 1954.[25] It was learned later that several players complained after the 1953 trip, noting that while they were not paid for their participation, they played before sellout crowds, leading them to conclude that someone was making a lot of money at their expense.

Frick was ready to allow another tour of Japan in 1955 which involved the Yankees and was sponsored by the Mainichi newspaper chain. A rival chain, Yomiuri, also wanted to sponsor a baseball team tour, but Frick expressed his opposition to competing barnstormers, and Yomiuri agreed to wait until the 1956 post-season. Frick and his wife, Eleanor, planned to join the team on this tour as well.[26] Although the players again would not be paid for their voluntary participation, they were allowed to bring their wives along on the trip. Three newlywed players—Eddie Robinson, Andy Carey, and Johnny Kucks—used the trip for their honeymoon.[27]

Ford and Eleanor remained with the tour for only a week in Japan before flying to Hong Kong for a four-day vacation before returning to the United States. Frick declared the Japanese players as "not ready for the

American leagues yet" as he departed.²⁸ After his return, he announced his support for annual tours of the country, with the competing newspaper chains alternating sponsorship.²⁹

Following his return from the first trip, and perhaps inspired by the new horizons, Frick promoted the idea of territorial expansion, repeating comments he had made in Honolulu at the beginning of the tour. "Conditions have changed all over the country and there are many cities that want and can support major league baseball. Our problem now is to work out a way to meet this demand," he said. One holdup was that Frick, lacking a blueprint, assumed that the only way to do this was to anoint existing Triple-A clubs as major league franchises; in Honolulu, he gave the requirements as a sufficiently large stadium and major league-caliber players.³⁰ The concept of an expansion draft for a new franchise was foreign.

Frick and major league baseball's other leaders got encouraging news after he returned: The U.S. Supreme Court upheld an appeal to its 1922 ruling in the Federal Baseball case that baseball was not subject to antitrust laws. The ruling upheld the reserve clause, among other practices. Subsequent lower court rulings had convinced some that the Court would reverse the 1922 ruling, but they were wrong. The Court was ruling in the case of George Toolson, a minor league pitcher who rejected a demotion from Class AAA to Class A and tried to catch on with another team in a higher league. He was "blacklisted" from all other teams and filed suit as a result.³¹

While most baseball officials were celebrating the ruling, Frick was more pensive and forward-looking in his response.

> This vote of confidence puts it squarely up to us to end any practices that might border on deceit, no matter how trivial. It also gives us a springboard to overcome the No. 1 problem facing us today: baseball must re-survey itself and make territorial changes to keep pace with the economic and population shifts in this country in the last fifty years.³²

For Frick, the decision gave organized baseball the clarity to pursue such changes. At the same time, he warned,

> From now on the responsibility is ours of modernizing baseball: of stepping from the past into the changing present and making sure always that our decisions and our policies are based on honesty, on fairness, on true sportsmanship, and with every consideration to the best interests of the fans and the players and those others who make baseball our great national game.³³

That philosophy was reflected in a private, unpublished letter Frick wrote to the team owners soon after his return from Asia. The letter also displayed his style in dealing with owners: not prescribing specific action, but merely drawing their attention to issues that he felt demanded a response. The issues he mentioned mirrored the Celler committee concerns: expansion and realignment of teams; more opportunities for players to advance, in particular through liberalized draft policies and fairer minor league player control; broadcasting policy, especially as it related to the survival of the minor leagues; stadium construction and improvement; and the need for a centralized promotional effort.[34]

Dan Daniel resurrected the letter five years later and published it for the first time, to demonstrate Frick's attempts at visionary leadership and to illustrate, by consequence, the limitations he faced with the owners.[35] Columnist Red Smith saw the letter and hoped that it would lead to some self-examination on the part of owners and some fair examination toward Frick.

> From time to time, Ford Frick is attacked as a do-nothing commissioner, a stooge, a puppet. Most of this criticism comes from outside baseball, but not all of it. Now and then this same complaint is made—off the record, of course, by some of the very men to whom the commissioner addressed his call for action on November 11, 1953. Pretty near any day now, they'll get around to reading it.[36]

So little had been accomplished, and the only tangible development—West Coast baseball—was motivated by immediate gain rather than long-term strategy. If major league baseball—and Frick's authority—remained the same, it was as much because of his self-imposed lack of firm leadership as the owner's self-interested actions.

As the December 1953 league meetings approached, the autumn goodwill between Frick and the players disappeared. Norman Lewis pressed for an increase in pension benefits for players and questioned whether they were getting all the money they should within the current agreement. He pointed out that the policies guiding the pension called for a committee that included the player representatives to administer the fund; the committee had not met for three years, he claimed.[37] Frick offered to talk to the players in Atlanta while he was there for the minor league meetings. He did not invite Lewis to either that meeting, however, or the major league meetings in New York.[38]

When the players arrived for the meeting, they insisted that Lewis be included. After Frick declined, noting that the league's attorneys were not there either, the players walked out. Frick acknowledged his earlier allowance for legal representation, but he claimed that in this case, he was fulfilling his role as commissioner "to summon anyone before me I wanted to in the interests of baseball without any outsiders present."[39]

The players' demand, that more of the anticipated income from television be committed to the pension plan and thus increase its benefits, did not sit well with the owners. Perhaps they wanted to throw some shade at the players in light of the Toolson decision; it is more likely that they were still caught up in antiquated notions of athletes' rights compared to other workers. In any case, Frick announced after the non-meeting that baseball's operators would consider a resolution eliminating the pension program at their meeting the next week.[40]

This was not just a heel turn in response to the players walking out, Frick insisted. The resolution had been introduced at the meeting in September, though kept confidential. "The council's reason was that it felt the club owners were fed up with the constant bickering over the pension fund despite the fact that the owners still bear 70 percent of the cost of its upkeep," he said.[41]

The Sporting News reporting continued to promote the owners' agenda with belittling descriptions of the players' position. It too described the owners as "fed up with the players' ever-increasing demands" and noted that Frick "stood firm," though not fully recovered from an illness that caused him to be sent home until the league meetings the next week.

A Page 2 editorial, even more strident, endorsed Frick's reasoning for excluding the attorney from the pension discussions. It also warned the players that fans—"thinking that major league players 'never had it so good,' and wondering why they would jeopardize all this by demands for even greater pension benefits"—would not support them. Like Frick, the journal warned that declining attendance and shaky franchises threatened baseball's future.[42] Apparently only the players and their attorney saw television as the pot of gold it would become.

Other journalists were not as supportive of Frick, however. Ed Pollock, long-time columnist for the *Philadelphia Bulletin* (and frequent Frick critic) noted that to baseball fans, many of whom in 1953 were beneficiaries of attorneys and collective bargaining, Frick's actions were unnecessary and confrontational. "Baseball gained nothing and lost a great deal," he wrote.[43] Pollock's call was more accurate, as things turned out.

In fact, the commissioner's relationship with sports writers was evolving, and the player meeting fiasco might have marked the beginning of the end. Smith described an anecdote from a couple of months before, following Frick's exclusion of Lewis from the August meeting. Frick was seated near a table of sports writers at Toots Shor's. "These were guys who had bitten at Ford here on the calf and there on the arm … within the last week or so," he noted. When someone tried to break the awkwardness by asking Frick if he had read a column on the topic, Frick said,

"I have given up reading you [in the plural sense, Smith noted] in the past couple of weeks."[44] The laughter lessened the tension but did not change the perception that the friendship was cooling.

Even so, Frick's understanding of the news media and its role kept him from being unnecessarily prickly about such criticism. His long-time assistant, Frank Slocum, recalled one article that was so critical, he feared his boss's seeing it. After he worked up the courage to show it, Frick said, "Yes, and I have no complaints. Like the good newspaperman he is, the writer checked every fact with me first."[45]

Regarding the pension plan, Frick had publicly stated his preference that it be maintained in its current form. If the leagues split on the question, he would exercise his tie-breaking privilege and vote to maintain. The owners did not give him that option, however, as they appointed a committee to study whether to scrap the pension plan and start over. So irate was Frick at this departure from his anticipated resolution that he turned the post-meeting press conference over to Giles and Harridge. The committee would comprise general manager (and former player) Hank Greenberg from Cleveland and team president John Galbreath from Pittsburgh. At the same time, the owners did increase the minimum salary from $5,000 to $6,000, the first increase in seven years, as a goodwill gesture.[46]

Ex-commissioner Happy Chandler inserted himself into the debate. Chandler had committed the proceeds of baseball's $6 million, six-year contract with Gillette to the pension. While he claimed to be staying out of the dispute, he did advise the players not to go into any meeting without an attorney. He offered no comment about Frick's stated support for the pension, but the report noted, "His off-the-record comment indicated he bore no love for Frick."[47]

A month later, Chandler was back. In an interview, he claimed that all of the World Series television money was intended for the players' pension fund. "It's a horrible thing they are doing to the players," he said. "The job of the commissioner is to protect the players. I don't know what the present fellow is doing, but he's wrong. He could lose the confidence of the people and the players."[48]

An annoyed Frick invited sports writers to his office, where he handed out copies of the pension plan explanation and report given to players. He pointed out that the plan, as developed by Chandler, did not assign World Series television money to the pension plan, but to a central account that funded several obligations, the largest of which was the pensions. Frick did not address Chandler's criticism directly, but simply said, "The facts are all there. Any conclusions you gentlemen arrive at are your own."[49]

Lewis joined in the fun, also criticizing Frick for talking about the current pension plan while the players were hoping to negotiate adjustments. "The very things we are bargaining about are mentioned in the commissioner's report as finished business," he said. "It looks like the decision already has been made. What's the use of trying to work out something?"[50]

Wedged between the intransigence of the owners and the increasing activism of the players, Frick struck back in his speech at the annual New York baseball writers' dinner. He almost didn't attend the dinner because of his continued illness, but his health improved and he prepared his thoughts. The baseball office would not release the text until hours before, to keep it from being published before it had been delivered.

He outlined the challenges facing baseball, summarizing it as "a crisis born of attempting to operate a 1954 machine with an 1890 motor." He also referred to the various problems that baseball was addressing, particularly television. As he gave his philosophy of baseball leadership, he spoke directly to both sides of the squabble. "I believe that all men in baseball, players and operators alike, must give more thought to their public responsibility and less to their selfish interest," he said. "I believe there has been too much idle talk; too much gossip; too much pontification unhampered by fact; too many hasty proposals without thought to effect or result."

The speech was a hit and got a standing ovation. The *Times* report called it "perhaps the strongest speech he has made since taking office." Daniel wrote that he "walloped the players and their lawyer, he walloped the Department of Justice, ... he took a crack at major league owners ... and he smote the majors."[51]

And he did it while struggling with health issues. After having to head back home for a couple of days' rest during the December 1953 meetings, he admitted to an "aggravating, but not serious ailment." He complained, "It's getting on my nerves, makes me feel irritable. Getting so I snap at people who work with me and they probably wonder what kind of a so-and-so I turned out to be."[52]

By March, reports of his continued health struggles generated rumors of his imminent resignation, which he angrily denied. He explained that he had picked up "an infection from a bug" during his global travels that caused him to be sent home in December and almost made him miss the writers' dinner. "I finally got it out of my system after a two months' fight and I feel much better now," he claimed.[53]

11. Old Problems, New Problems

The players and owners did set aside their acrimony long enough to negotiate a new pension agreement to begin in 1956. Under the agreement, 60 percent of all World Series and All-Star Game television and radio receipts would be designated for player pensions. The players would be represented on the plan's administrative board, which would oversee the pension instead of the commissioner.[54]

One columnist credited the successful negotiations to Frick's and Lewis's absence—both from the negotiations and in the new structure.[55] Fans today will note that neither side could foresee the flood of money from regular season games, both at the national and local level, but in the 1950s, the big events were the best bet, financially. The owners in both leagues approved the new plan at their meetings in March, but added that they did so "with reservations." They did not elaborate on what that meant.[56]

The agreement also included the stipulation that Lewis's $40,000 in attorney fees would be paid through the Commissioner's Central Fund. That might seem presumptuous on the players' part, but realize the alternative: For the players to pay an attorney would require the formation of a dues-paying organization—a union. The owners were probably more accommodating to paying Lewis than risking unionization. Still, in the agreement, it was agreed that future attorney fees would be paid directly out of the pension fund.[57]

One result of all the drama in Atlanta was that the players, after walking out of their meeting with Frick, began the process of forming the Major League Players Association. Its leaders consistently denied that they were forming a union—a prospect so unpopular among fans that it could create public relations issues. The AFL-CIO was similarly unimpressed and would not allow the MLPA to join for several years, noting the group's lack of cohesiveness in its early days after its 1954 charter.[58]

The players presented their latest demands to Frick during the 1954 World Series Executive Council meeting—this time, without the Frick vs. Lewis drama. Frick met with Lewis and the players "informally" to discuss their proposals, which included a raise in the minimum salary to $7,200, and then the players presented them to the council later, without Lewis present. They also proposed a deadline of December 1 for unconditional releases—any later than that unfairly limited the released players' options, they claimed.[59] The proposals would all be denied at the baseball winter meetings. The players had also requested the freedom to negotiate directly to play winter ball in Caribbean leagues, but the owners refused that as well, keeping them under the team's authority for such opportunities. The owners did agree to move up the date to receive contracts from February 1 to January 15—two weeks instead of the two months the players requested.[60]

The next shoe dropped in the franchise relocation craze with the 1954 sale of the Philadelphia Athletics and their move to Kansas City. Once again, Frick was not involved in the move, calling it an American League matter. He might have weighed in, considering that the franchise was sold to Arnold Johnson, who also owned Yankee Stadium.[61] The fire sale trades of A's prospects to the Yankees, including Roger Maris, would become a baseball-wide joke later in the decade, while seriously threatening the "best interests of baseball" that Ford was empowered to protect.

Instead, Frick signed off on the purchase, using the rationale that Johnson's interest in the Yankees was strictly as landlord of their stadium.[62] So removed from the negotiations was Frick that he met Johnson only through a chance encounter in the hotel lobby after the meetings. "And that's how the commissioner of baseball, the No. 1 man in the game, and the man who had bought a franchise and who had owned Yankee Stadium for a year, got together," wrote Robert L. Burnes of the *St. Louis Globe-Democrat.*[63]

A few days before the December meetings, Frick met with the owners for a private dinner. He outlined the challenges facing baseball, both long-term and short-term. A copy of the speech remained in his files, giving insight into his personal approach in dealing with the owners who employed him and created the work environment you'd expect from 16 different bosses, all wealthy business leaders. The speech is marked "December 1953," but its historical references (the Philadelphia A's move, the status of the Liberty broadcasting lawsuit) more properly place it in December 1954.

He outlined two short-term problems: litigation, mainly the broadcasting-related lawsuits baseball was facing, and player relations, particularly the looming possibility of a full-blown players' union. "I hear talk today of a player union. Gentlemen, don't kid yourselves," he warned in the speech. "We have a company union right now. And unless the move is headed off you will have a real union in another two years."

The three long-term challenges Frick listed included financial, with related discussion of relocation and expansion; the minor league problem; and radio and television. Addressing all three, Frick did not provide much guidance, but did cite geographic data and minor-league franchise survey results to the owners. Toward the end of what must have been a long speech, he also threw in three more long-term problems—player control (as related to draft and contract rules), incentive, and public relations—but could not devote much time to any of them.

What is telling about this speech is what it reveals about Frick's philosophy toward his role. "The commissioner has no authority, nor does he propose to force legislation or arbitrarily change rules," he said in his introduction. In describing broadcasting-related litigation issues, he added, "Those are matters of policy which the Commissioner is not authorized nor qualified to determine. Those are questions which you men as club owners and operators must face and decide." Particularly in issues needing some forecasting and vision, the owners might have appreciated some specific guidance from Frick. But that was not his style, especially on the broader issues that require a CEO's vision and leadership.

Frick addressed the public relations issue—and once again harkened back to his newspaper/publicity days—when he announced that he and team PR officials had planned a "Let's Play Ball" week for March 19–26, 1955. The plans included government proclamations at all levels, promotional tie-ins with sporting good companies, and multimedia story strategies encompassing newspapers, magazines, radio, and television. Such a pervasive, coordinated strategy was the first of its kind and showed Frick's media relation skills at work. He revealed that the strategy was developed at a January meeting that was publicized as training for the team PR directors.[64] He did succeed in getting President Dwight Eisenhower (more of a golfer) to declare March 19–26 as "Let's Play Ball Week."[65] Beyond that, no reports from the week emerged, so any assessments of its long- or short-term effects would be pure speculation.

A year later, Frick was also as excited about a television special NBC would broadcast the Sunday before Opening Day. It would be hosted by TV personality Art Linkletter and combine sports with Hollywood-style entertainment. The "cavalcade" would feature such celebrities as Jayne Mansfield and the cast of "Damn Yankees," plus baseball names like Leo Durocher and broadcaster Mel Allen.[66]

Frick bragged, "I want this to be one of the finest things that the American people have seen on their television screens. We have top script writers, actors and actresses working on the program." *Cleveland Press* columnist Franklin Lewis was not as optimistic. He groused about plans to use "ham actors trying to make like baseball players," and expressed amusement at how the sport had overcome its previous rogue image: "Gee, remember when baseball players were ruffians who chewed tobacco and went into the seats to chase big-lipped character assassins?"[67]

The show became an annual event on NBC. Gene Kelly, an acknowledged baseball fan, hosted the 1957 version. The featured entertainer, Janis Paige, was panned for her lack of baseball knowledge—she identified one player as playing for the "Philadelphia Pirates" and assigned Ernie Banks to the White Sox. A young singer named Tony Bennett sang in a quartet with Paige, Kelly, and ventriloquist Paul Winchell. The program featured a player from each team (two Dodgers and Yankees) and several Hall of Famers and showed highlights such as the last three outs of Don Larsen's perfect game the year before.[68]

Baseball broadcasts, however, were not as popular with Frick. He, like most fans, was annoyed by commercial interruptions. What was worse, in his opinion, was the way announcers would work sponsors into game moments. Mel Allen was notorious for calling Yankees home runs "Ballantine blasts" or "White Owl Wallops." Red Barber gave a nod toward sponsor Procter and Gamble, referring to a change-up pitch as an "Ivory floater." Frick eventually ordered commercial references limited to between-innings spots, but it was a tough ban to enforce, since sponsors were determined to get as much exposure as possible for the increasing amount of money they were paying.[69]

As National League president, Frick had lobbied for the return of the spitball and even tried to get it added to the agenda for the 1949 December meetings, though the American League would not consent.[70] "Our pitchers need some help," he said. "Every time the Rules Committee holds a meeting, they take another sock at the hurlers."[71] Will Harridge disagreed. "I believe it would be a serious mistake to restore the spitball because it would let down the bars to every other form of trickery employed by the pitchers years ago."[72] The issue did not come up.

Six years later, securely in the commissioner's office, Frick felt ready to take up his spitball crusade again. The rules committee had met a few days before, and while he praised their changes, he added, "They could have gone farther and given the pitchers some much-needed help. Personally, I would like to see the return of the spitball, which is nowhere near as odious, mysterious, all-powerful or dangerous as most people think it is."[73]

Joe Cronin, general manager of the Red Sox and a member of the rules committee, was not a supporter. "Where is the line to be drawn?" he asked. "Is the 'spitball' just a saliva ball or is it a ball half-covered with slippery elm or licorice or tobacco? If the spitter came back, the ball would be half-brown and half-white after a few pitches."[74]

Visiting with the Phillies at their spring training camp, Frick once again promoted the spitter. "Why, with this lively ball, and with everybody swinging, it's gotten so that a pitcher's afraid to lay the ball in there," he said. The results he envisioned, however, might not engage many fans.

"There might not be so many home runs, but the game would be just as good—maybe better. The old-timers went for a lot of singles hitting to the opposite field, and that's what would happen again."[75]

Former Dodgers pitcher Preacher Roe came clean about throwing the spitball in a July 1955 *Sports Illustrated* article with Dick Young, a year after Roe retired. "But the Commissioner, I don't think he'd mind. Fact, I hear he wants the spitter back," Roe said. "I'm sort of pleased that Mr. Frick has got that healthy attitude about my pet pitch. Makes me feel I was right all along." He claimed that the pitch was no more dangerous than any others, and even demonstrated some of his techniques for adding moisture to the ball.[76]

If the response of his two league presidents was any indication, Frick's crusade was doomed. "Legalizing the spitball would not make the game any more attractive as an entertainment," said National League president Warren Giles. "To attempt to reduce the hitters' effectiveness by restoring freak pitching would be tampering with the game." Harridge repeated his arguments that legalizing the spitball would open the door to other forms of cheating.[77]

A nonscientific *Sporting News* survey found a surprising lack of opposition. Just more than half of those polled (mainly pitchers and coaches) supported the spitter, while about a third opposed and the rest had no opinion. Pee Wee Reese, Roe's former Dodgers teammate, said, "I don't think legalizing the spitter would make much difference. They never stopped throwing it anyway."[78]

Some of the strongest opposition came from Washington owner Clark Griffith, who called Frick's idea "just the latest piece of nonsense I've been reading" and expressed disappointment in Frick, "who has been in our game for a long time and should have known better." Having started his playing career in the 1890s—decades before the pitch was outlawed—Griffith could remember when the spitball was legal. He claimed it was impossible not only to hit, but also to field, if the unfortunate infielder encountered the wet part.[79]

Frick's crusade soon ended. Heading into the major leagues' mid-season meeting, *The Sporting News* canvassed the Playing Rules Committee and found that only two of the nine members of baseball's Supreme Court favored allowing the pitch. It remained forbidden—and a continued source of speculation and accusation.[80]

At the same mid-season meeting, the leaders heard the preliminary results of the research Frick had commissioned. Continuing his modernization strategy, he had hired the Stephen Fitzgerald Co. to conduct a nationwide survey over the 1955 season. "The survey will go into everything that has to do with baseball," he said. "The Fitzgerald firm will interview baseball writers, housewives, fans in the bleachers, girls down for a coffee break—well, just about everybody who might be cognizant of our problems and ready to give us advice on their solution." He cited television, game length, and the minor leagues as issues where baseball leaders could learn something from fans.[81] He went so far as to distribute a survey for fans, via the Associated Press, which newspapers then could print. Fans were instructed to mail them to his office in Rockefeller Plaza.[82]

The response to the idea from many baseball leaders was more 1890s than 1950s. Dodgers owner Walter O'Malley noted an earlier survey that found the average fan attended a game and a half a year. "A survey among fans thus might get a lot of opinions from people who see a game and a half a year." Consensus was that baseball recognized its problems already, and that action was needed. "It would be most unwise for the heads of the game to let their problems grow while they're waiting for the research firm's report," a *Sporting News* editorial chided. An anonymous club owner complained, "What does an outside research firm know about the problems of baseball?"[83]

Preliminary results from the more than 10,000 respondents showed strong support for baseball—93.7 agreed with the statement that it was "America's game"—though younger respondents were less enthusiastic. About half said their interest had increased, and another 39 percent said it had stayed the same. The main reasons given for not attending games were parking (reflective of transportation trends and bad news for downtown stadiums), television availability, and the slow pace of games.[84]

The long-game accusations had supporting evidence. The Associated Press found that from 1930 to 1955, average game time had increased from 1 hour, 58 minutes to 2 hours, 29 minutes. The increase was not attributed to radio or television, but to various ways players and managers slowed the proceedings.[85]

Frick had floated a proposition of his own to the owners, in an interview with *The Sporting News*, and it contradicted the criticisms that had stereotyped him. Armed with the fan surveys, Frick wondered whether it was time for major league baseball to change the commissioner's role from adviser and adjudicator to more of a policy maker—centralizing in the position leadership what had been assigned to 16 squabbling team owners.[86]

Frick had floated a similar proposal the year before: to centralize baseball, majors and minors, under the commissioner's office. His plan involved locating all league offices in New York, with the National League moving from Cincinnati, the American League from Chicago, and the minor leagues from Columbus, Ohio. Such a system, Frick suggested, would allow baseball to adapt more quickly and nimbly to face its many challenges.[87]

With this new proposal, the issue was authority as much as centralization. Challenges such as the ongoing television battles, particularly with the Justice Department, necessitated a more nimble structure, he said. Frick, as usual, gave owners the authority to act on the proposal, citing his current role, but was forward enough to say he preferred the commissioner having more authority.

He outlined the basics at a private dinner during the meetings. Baseball would establish a board of directors, including two owners, the league presidents, and the commissioner. The commissioner would function as the CEO. He did not press for a decision on the proposal but instead called a special meeting for February 5, 1956, to discuss it further.[88]

It's a good thing he didn't press the owners at the December meeting, because they were in a "do-nothing" mode—confirming Frick's assessment—and no fan surveys, minor league resolutions, or player demands could budge them. They dismissively rejected almost all of the players' demands: a raise in minimum salary to $7,200; eliminating restrictions on winter baseball; starting the World Series on a Thursday to assure a Sunday date, with expected high attendance; and to be kept fully informed of broadcast negotiations that would affect their pension. The owners did agree to allow players to report voluntarily to spring training before March 1, but consensus on that rule change was long assumed.[89]

The players, of course, were angry at the owners' action and frustrated at a system that allowed them to submit proposals only once a year, at a closed meeting that discussed other business. They met with Frick on December 15 and demanded that their proposals be considered once again, at the February meeting. Frick agreed to put the demands on the agenda once again, but remained pessimistic about the prospects.[90]

Later that same day, Frick made a second, more popular proposal, this time after meeting with baseball writers. He suggested that the BBWAA institute a third award, for pitchers only, and that it be named for Cy Young. He cited Robin Roberts' six 20-win seasons—which earned him zero on the MVP cred scale—as evidence.[91] At their February meeting, the owners approved both the pitching award and Frick's idea to name it after Young, who had just died in November 1955 and still holds the major league record for most wins at 511. Selection for the award, like the MVP, was assigned to the baseball writers.[92] The BBWAA also approved the award at a meeting before the All-Star Game. At the outset, only one award, covering both leagues, would be presented.[93]

The owners were not as positive toward the players' ideas. They once again rejected the minimum salary raise. They did, however, promise an internal salary study, and Frick, who handled the negotiations for the All-Star Game and World Series broadcasting rights that generated the pension funding, promised to keep the players informed personally. "It looks as if we had made some improvement," said American League player representative Bob Feller, putting on a brave face. "I hope these committees meet. They can't meet soon enough."[94]

Nothing was announced regarding Frick's proposal for a change in the structure of baseball and the commissioner's role. By June, however, several team owners did express an interest in expanding Frick's power by giving him authority to veto owner decisions.[95] Previously, his power was limited to casting a tiebreaking on issues where the two leagues differed. A *Sporting News* editorial supported the change, noting that Frick had earned the authority, citing performance in "a five-year span which may have produced more taxing situations than Landis and A. B. Chandler faced in a total of almost 30 years."[96] Whether the idea was rejected outright or consigned to internal-study limbo, the owners apparently told Frick the same thing they told the players: business as usual for now.

One 1957 report, citing conflict between Frick and George Trautman, claimed that Frick was planning to oust Trautman and assume control of the minor leagues, certainly an expansion of his authority.[97] The report came out of Albany, New York, a hotbed of minor league activism, and seemed based in frustration more than fact. Frick quickly denied the report as "completely, unequivocally and categorically false" and expressed strong support. "I have full confidence in Mr. Trautman's ability to perform what is a most difficult and complicated job," he said. "I think Mr. Trautman is equally confident of the utmost co-operation from this office."[98]

12

To the West Coast

As he began to focus on the 1956 season, Frick cut loose with a prediction that made sense, even if it landed far out of the "actually happened" zone. He predicted that a third major league was imminent. In his opinion, the moves of the three previous seasons had solved pressing problems, and no further realignment was necessary. The solution was a third league that could include teams on the West Coast (Los Angeles, San Francisco), in Texas (Houston, Dallas), and toward the upper Midwest (Minneapolis–St. Paul, Montreal). In fact, he avoided naming specific cities, respecting his own ban on idle franchise talk.[1] The idea certainly made transportation and geographic sense, even if it required a level of vision and proactivity never exhibited by the owners.

The real thing was not as fast-moving. Game length, identified as a prime concern in the fan survey, was a prime focus of major league baseball heading into the 1956 season. The American League instituted a rule that if a manager visited the mound more than once during a game (as opposed to an inning), the pitcher had to be removed from the game.[2] Warren Giles opposed a similar move for the National League, considering such conferences an important part of game strategy, though he did instruct umpires to move the managers along.[3]

Frick did not take sides, saying only, "I will watch with great interest this season the new American League rule." Frick was not convinced that new rules were the solution. He was convinced that if managers and umpires were educated on how long, drawn-out games were driving down both stadium attendance and television ratings, they would take the steps to accelerate the proceedings.[4]

One of the later ideas to speed play, proposed by the Rules Committee and approved by Frick, set a 20-second time limit between pitches with the bases empty. The committee had paired that rule change with another that would prevent the batter from leaving the batter's box after the pitcher had come to a set position.⁵ Once spring training started, however, the new rules left players and managers confused and upset, as they were with most rule changes. They felt it could encourage pitchers to "quick pitch," another rules violation, leaving umpires in a judgment call dilemma.⁶

In the annual pension plan report, Frick tried to temper the players' hopes that the new World Series and All-Star television contracts would be a boon to their retirement. Norman Lewis had predicted that the rights could snare as much as $5 million, according to the experts he had talked to. Frick dismissed that and other quotes as "loose talk." He added, "My investigation and negotiations indicate that the rights are very valuable but that networks and sponsors are not contemplating the extraordinary bids predicted by some." He repeated his pledge to get the best deal possible for "players, fans, and clubs."⁷

For all of those warnings, Frick turned out to be a better negotiator than prophet. The World Series and All-Star Game contract between NBC and major league baseball came in at $16.25 million over five years—more than $3 million a year. He acknowledged that with the new contract, the pension plan would be able to offer "even more liberal benefits." *The Sporting News* was less restrained, noting that Frick "not only assured the fans of a wonderful free show, the players in the majors of the best pension plan ever drawn up, and the club owners of a tidy extra nest egg, but he gained his own job assurance."⁸ Even his frequent nemesis Lewis agreed, "The commissioner did an excellent job."⁹

Times columnist Arthur Daley sounded an indignant note at the players' newfound rewards—a thread that would amplify as athletes' pay surged the rest of the century. He dismissed claims that the liberal pension plan would draw more young talent into the sport: "Maybe so, but gifted financiers don't ordinarily become major league ballplayers. No one named Rockefeller ever made the big time." Daley made a better point wondering whether the money also should have gone to help the minor leagues (a suggested beneficiary of the bonanza team owners were getting from local contracts) or to retired players, who would not benefit from the new and improved pension.¹⁰

The new pension benefits that resulted from the more lucrative television contract were impressive. Benefits would increase 75 percent, from $100 to $175 per month for ten-year players, and from $50 to $88 per month for five-year players. The plan also added insurance, hospitalization, and disability benefits. Frick said the plan was "as generous as anything ever written for any group of men in America." Speaking for the players, Bob Feller said, "The generous pension scheme now going into effect will make baseball all the more attractive to the youngsters of America."¹¹

12. To the West Coast 185

Editorial support still stressed the supposed generosity of the owners. "Obviously, the players never had it so good," gushed *The Sporting News*. "They may be thankful not only to the club executives and fellow players who worked out the details, but to the Providence which placed them in the majors at this time." The editorial made no mention of the good fortune of the owners benefiting from the infusion of television money, or the notion that the players, with their athletic ability and hard work, actually deserved the money.[12]

The owners were not as generous as the broadcast contract. They turned down a request from the player representatives to increase the minimum salary from $6,000 to $7,500. Frick explained that the pay raise was turned down for two reasons: (1) the average rookie salary was $6,700; and (2) owners would have to pay the higher minimum salary to players sent down to the minors—an additional unwanted expense. The owners did leave the door open for more discussion on the increased salary and agreed in principle to an annual meeting with all team owners and player representatives.[13]

Still, Frick definitely profited; the re-election talk had already begun. In May, he was more than two years away from the end of his first term, but that did not prevent the first report predicting a second term. *The Sporting News* included a brief that claimed such a renewal was on the agenda for the joint session that month,[14] though no news came of that. The May meetings would be the first of quarterly sessions Frick had proposed, with only two club representatives attending. The added sessions would decrease the colossal agenda of the December meeting, which included trade talks and other distractions that limited their effectiveness.[15]

Joe Williams, columnist for the *New York World-Telegram Sun*, claimed to have taken a survey of owners, players, and journalists, about whether Frick deserved a second term. He claimed 100 percent support from the owners, less positive sentiment from the players, and a majority vote of confidence from writers—though some complained he "played his cards too close to the vest and, inferentially, that he was a confirmed company man." Williams' call was that Frick's position was "stronger than ever. His re-election is a mere formality."[16]

The big news coming out of the May meetings was not Frick's renewal, but that the major leagues might finally move toward an open draft. That might sound surprising, but that was not how teams signed young talent before 1956. Previously, every amateur player was a free agent, with the hotter prospects drawing high bonus offers from bidding teams and the minor leagues filling out their rosters by signing the leftovers. The system not only made the rich teams richer in talent, but also encouraged outlandish bonuses for unproven talent and unethical behavior by teams and prospects.[17] The open draft proposal, however, was unanimously rejected by a committee.[18]

Other earlier proposals to help the minor leagues had subdued the outward panic, at least for the 1955 season. But Dodgers owner Walter O'Malley had an idea for a more permanent solution. He proposed giving half of the "Game of the Week" income—$3 million—to the minors. It was a replay of the same idea turned down by the Justice Department a year and a half earlier. O'Malley said he believed the contract could be structured to survive federal scrutiny. Frick could only protest that the proposal was "news to me" and was not on the December meeting agenda.[19] The owners did endorse O'Malley's plan,[20] but in January O'Malley reported that broadcasting negotiations had stalled and would be picked up later.[21]

Not to stop moving, Frick appointed a six-member committee of team owners to study ways of helping the minors, including the most effective way to spend an expected infusion of $500,000 from the owners. "Our discussions did not involve financial aid entirely," Frick said. "There are legislative matters which will help in the long run." The committee was expected to announce its proposals at the December meetings.[22]

A more promising idea to help the minors emerged from the committee's September meeting, where it was revealed that an amendment would be proposed to require major league clubs to reduce their rosters to 28 by opening day, rather than a month later. Formerly, the teams were allowed to keep as many as 40 players on their roster the first month of the season, with most carrying 30 to 32. Having minor-league rosters at full strength from the opening of the season would increase local interest and press coverage, advocates claimed.[23] The owners accepted the proposal in December.[24]

The financial help was also taking shape. While O'Malley replayed a familiar theme—putting the players to work in providing the $500,000—by suggesting 20 All-Star Games in different minor league cities, his plan was quickly scrapped. Instead, as Frick announced in October, the plan was approved for the money to come from the team owners, with it being administered by yet another committee Frick would name and supervise.[25]

By November, Frick had appointed the six members of the committee, with a meeting scheduled for the middle of the month. (If Frick could not control the owners, he could at least keep them occupied.) He announced plans to hire an administrator to oversee the account. Frick stressed that the administrator would have "the cold and detached attitude of a banker, who must pass on loan applications without prejudice." He expressed a preference to help responsible teams that were having difficulties, as opposed to those who simply claimed they could not start the season without extra money or a group that wanted backing for a new league.[26] In December, Bill DeWitt, assistant general manager of the Yankees, was approved as administrator of the fund.[27]

The rescinding of the "College Rule" provided the most controversy at the December 1956 meetings. Adopted by the major leagues but annually rejected by the minors, the rule banned teams from signing college players beginning their sophomore year, until either their class graduated or they reached the age of 21, with exceptions allowed for financial hardship. Frick supported the decision to rescind the rule as of February 1, but for a good reason. "I asked for the adoption of this resolution," he said, "not because I am opposed to a college rule. In fact, I would like to see a workable rule adopted. But since the minor leagues have no college rule, it was a joke for the majors to have one since they were merely signing college players through the back door."[28]

College coaches like Ethan Allen of Yale were outraged by the decision and did not buy Frick's claim that the problem lay with the minor leagues. "We were informed through the grapevine that the majors had instructed their minor league representatives to vote against the rule."[29] With the old rule gone, Frick challenged the college coaches to propose a new rule, adding that it would not be wise for major league baseball to propose anything until then. One college conference commissioner pointed out that the college coaches had done just that—proposing an amendment allowing contact between players and teams in the off-season—but the minor leagues had vetoed their idea at their meeting in December, which led to the rescinding of the rule by major league owners.[30]

The debate became personal, as in face to face, when Frick spoke to the Executives' Club of Chicago in February. Big Ten Commissioner Kenneth L. "Tug" Wilson asked how the minor leagues could reject the rule without the majors approving their actions. Frick replied, "The man who made the speech which killed passage of the rule ... is not in any way associated with the majors." Frick was referring to Leslie M. O'Connor, Commissioner Landis's former secretary and Frick's former colleague on the Executive Council. O'Connor had evolved into an opponent of Frick's after taking over as president of the Pacific Coast League. Frick concluded, "Once this bickering is ended, I think we can work out a rule. But it isn't a one-way street."[31]

O'Connor would remain a thorn in Frick's side throughout his tenure as PCL president. While testifying before the Celler committee in 1957, in the midst of the Giants/Dodgers rumor-nado, he blasted Frick's "do-nothing" policy in response to the PCL's plea for help in coping with the possible consequences of a move. Along the way in his testimony, he also suggested that Congress eliminate the reserve clause and bring all professional sports under antitrust scrutiny.[32]

In 1957, the Supreme Court issued a ruling in Radovich v. NFL that denied pro football the antitrust exemption baseball enjoyed. The court acknowledged that this seemed to afford baseball special treatment, but stressed—as it had in the 1953 Toolson decision—that the remedy needed to come from Congress, not the courts. So Patrick Hillings, the Californian who had grilled Frick about expansion during the Celler hearings, and Celler himself introduced bills to remove baseball's antitrust exemption. Celler considered it an issue of equal treatment, while Hillings, no doubt still vexed at the lack of major league baseball in his state, vowed to "break up the horsehide cartel which has allowed a small group of men to dominate and control America's National Pastime."[33]

Frick declined comment on the court's decision and encouraged other baseball representatives to follow suit. That frustrated Celler's efforts in developing legislation, and he fired back. "It's what one would expect from the czar of a tightly knit organization like baseball," he said. "It only proves the need for overhauling the entire organization of baseball and ripping out all restrictive covenants like those that set up the commissioner and the reserve clause."[34]

Maybe Frick had a point. Around that time, C. Leo DeOrsey, an attorney on the Senators' board of directors, suggested in the media that baseball come under antitrust exemption, revise its reserve clause, and form one large 16-team league with franchises in Los Angeles and San Francisco. The comments drew immediate pushback from Frick, who said, "I don't think we can take too seriously the observations of a man who has been in baseball less than three months and professes to know the answers to all of baseball's problems." Even Senators president Calvin Griffith, who had taken over the team after his father died in 1955, chimed in, "I want it fully understood that Mr. DeOrsey was not speaking for me."[35]

In response to the turmoil in Washington, Frick called a special meeting of all team owners. Reports from the meeting indicated that Frick had appointed yet another committee, this one comprising himself, his two league presidents, and minor leagues head George Trautman. Frick emerged from the meeting and declared, "We're not scared. We're not frightened.

But we are going to defend ourselves because we think we are right." As he described baseball's strategy, it would be that baseball was indeed a business as well as a sport, but it was not a business that required antitrust oversight.[36]

Frick denied that the committee had been appointed, during an interview a couple of days later. He said that the owners had passed a resolution "expressing confidence that the commissioner's office could handle anything necessary which may arise in connection with the bills pending in Congress." He also said he was looking to retain experienced legal counsel in Washington, to help in the event of Congressional hearings.[37]

The hearings came quickly. Frick and several other baseball players and league officials appeared before Celler's committee in mid–June of 1957, to discuss the proposed anti-trust laws. One report described Frick as "more forceful and assured than in his first appearance as a witness here six years ago." He made a strong, sincere defense of the reserve clause and baseball's antitrust exemption, presenting profit/loss statements for the New York franchises to support his assertion that baseball was not a big business.[38] In his opening statement, he laid it out: "It is my opinion, for reasons which I will explain, that any legislation which would place professional baseball completely under the antitrust laws would seriously injure professional baseball with no offsetting benefit to the public."[39] Whether because of Frick's testimony, or because of internal strife among Judiciary Committee members, none of the bills submitted made it out of committee. The House did pass a bill partially extending antitrust privileges to other sports, but it never made it out of committee in the Senate.[40]

By the summer of 1957, rumors of franchise relocation to California had reached a boiling point, blowing the lid off Frick's directive to limit franchise shift or expansion discussions to the off-season. In the years following World War II, the demand for major league baseball in exploding metropolitan areas west of Missouri had grown. Since Chandler's tenure, baseball's response had been to delay, combining vague expansion promises with veiled threats to keep the Pacific Coast League in line.

In August and September of 1947, Frick had accompanied Chandler and Will Harridge on a week-long tour of West Coast baseball cities. In Los Angeles, Chandler had stated, "I am in favor of every section of the country having major league baseball, if they can support it," but he refused to get more specific, angering local media and fans.[41]

Chandler had tried to turn his words into action, floating a proposal at the 1947 December meeting to create two ten-team leagues by bringing the four strongest PCL franchises (Los Angeles, San Francisco, Oakland, and Hollywood) into the majors.[42] The proposal fell into the same thorn bush that would thwart progress for the next ten years: prohibitive rules that equated elevating a minor-league franchise to stealing it from its established league, and the pre-doomed notion that the easiest way to bring major league baseball to the West Coast was to make the PCL a third league—but only when it was completely ready. The National League actually supported Chandler's idea, but the American League owners blocked it.[43]

While on the West Coast in 1948, Frick accompanied the New York Giants and Pittsburgh Pirates, who were barnstorming against Pacific Coast League teams. Ostensibly there to study television broadcasting techniques, he was reported to have predicted, "The big leagues will be out here in two years."[44] The trip included attendance at the inter-league games and at dinners that honored him and visiting players and press.[45]

The removal of Chandler as commissioner was also perceived as a blow to West Coast major league aspirations.[46] The 1951 Celler hearings would provide some motivation, if not to act, at least to appear that they were, leading to the PCL being granted its elevated "open" status. Early in his term as commissioner, Frick was pointing to that as the most reliable pathway to major league baseball in the West.[47]

Unfortunately, the specifics of the plan Frick referenced to the Celler committee not only dimmed the PCL's hopes, but also demonstrated the impracticality of the "one league at a time" approach to expansion. The requirements included a stadium capacity minimum of 25,000; only Los Angeles and San Francisco met that standard. The policy, approved at the December league meetings, reflected Frick's preference for evolutionary over revolutionary change—letting the West Coast teams grow into a major league.[48] The plan invited revolutionary change, however. Even as some PCL owners were claiming that Frick's standards were "within easy reach,"[49] it was becoming clear for others wanting to move baseball westward that franchise relocation would have to be their strategy.

Frick continued to endorse the PCL-to-major plan, even predicting during a spring 1952 visit, "The Coast league will become a third major within possibly five to ten years." The statement was in part a response to Warren Giles, who had expressed doubt that any other West Coast cities besides Los Angeles and San Francisco could score a franchise. "Los Angeles and San Francisco are big league cities now.... The fans out here deserve big league ball. Asking them to wait until the other PCL cities can qualify is like telling two fellows in a block they can't buy a Cadillac until all their neighbors can afford one," Giles said.[50]

12. To the West Coast

By the 1950s, both the Dodgers and the Giants were in trouble in New York City. Conventional wisdom might have held that New York could handle three franchises, but neighborhood demographics said otherwise. Both teams, unlike the Yankees, struggled in substandard stadiums within declining neighborhoods that offered dismal prospects for expansion and little parking for the suburban fans willing to drive. The conventionally wise assumed the Dodgers and Giants would never leave New York City. They were wrong.[51]

By 1952, the struggling Browns were also ready to move, the first club to threaten West Coast relocation, and Frick sought to squelch it. He warned that "hit-and-run" relocation would create a team with exorbitant travel expenses and uncertain attendance.[52] Yes, he once again threw out expansion and third-league prospects. But it is important to note that Frick, with his affinity for committees, never appointed one for this pressing issue. Thus, if events would move in directions he did not approve, it was because he let them.

According to a *New York Times* report, the issue was being discussed below the radar, at the league level, by a committee of five AL owners. The report claimed Frick as an ally, noting his statement after the owners limited franchise moves to the October 1–December 1 window: "There is no reason now why a club cannot move its franchise elsewhere if it so desires."[53] As the leagues discussed the Browns' pending move to Baltimore (or *anywhere*), Del Webb, a committee member, urged the league to consider moving two franchises to the West Coast. "Having only one team on the coast would not be good," he said. "We have got to shift two franchises in the same league to reduce the problem of transportation, and possibly its costs, and to make it easier on the schedule."[54]

The Browns were ready to move, but the men leading the California baseball crusade wanted the Dodgers. Walter O'Malley told an August 1953 Executive Council meeting that he had been contacted by a rich and powerful Los Angeles man. "This man, whose name I cannot reveal, assured me that if the Brooklyn club were transferred to Los Angeles, a modern, commodious stadium would be built for it," O'Malley said. "The man who wrote to me said that Los Angeles was very eager, and ready, to come into the majors, but would not just accept any old club."[55]

By May 1954, Frick had enough of owners discussing realignment offers on the sports page and called for an end to it. "Statement after statement now is appearing in the newspapers in which this baseball man or that makes definite prediction as to changes in our major league lineup even to the point of naming cities." How much did Frick want this to stop?

His statement concluded, "You are hereby put on notice that such statements specifying possible cities will be interpreted by this office as conduct detrimental to the best interests of baseball and will be so handled."[56]

That didn't stop Frick himself from talking to a Los Angeles reporter a couple of months later—though he declined to be specific, "otherwise, I would be violating my own gag order." Frick told Al Wolf of the *Times* that "no major league club is going to be moved to any city lacking an adequate place to play." He defined adequate as "a seating capacity of at least 35,000, plus proper parking and transportation facilities."[57]

Frick said the same thing to a delegation from San Francisco in October 1954, with a more specific focus. Noting a $5 million stadium bond issue on the ballot in November, he told them, and the voters, that if they passed the bond issue, "you will have overcome the biggest hurdle in the path to major league baseball." During the discussion, Frick agreed that San Francisco fans did not like his "third league" idea. "They want to see clubs like the Giants, Yankees, Cleveland and Brooklyn. What would be wrong with a ten-club league? It isn't suicide; it's perfectly feasible."[58]

San Francisco voters approved the ballot proposal authorizing the bond issue, causing O'Malley to predict that westward expansion would come up at the December 1954 meetings. Consensus was that the National League was ahead of the American on this issue, even with Webb's lobbying.[59] O'Malley's prediction, however, was premature: no announcement regarding expansion emerged from the December meetings, and in late January, NL owners voted not to consider expansion. They could not make it work financially to their satisfaction, and Frick warned that expansion talk hurt the minor league teams, which the new franchises would uproot. Speculation would cripple teams that were already struggling.[60]

By 1956, both the Giants and Dodgers were proposing new stadiums in New York City. The Giants were supposedly developing a new, 110,000-seat, triple-decker stadium in Manhattan that was equipped for television and radio. The cost would be $20 million, with construction able to begin quickly because the site was a railroad right of way near Times Square.[61] O'Malley had unveiled plans to build an all-weather, geodesic dome stadium at the corner of Flatbush and Atlantic avenues. The design was pioneered by Buckminster Fuller, whom O'Malley had visited at Princeton.[62] Its design also provided an all-weather source of humor to comedians and columnists.

Both O'Malley and Horace Stoneham of the Giants faced considerable roadblocks in their attempts to build new stadiums, so they began to look elsewhere. O'Malley visited Southern California—to pick up a new team plane for the Dodgers, he claimed. Since he just happened to be out there, he allowed his hosts to take him on a personal inspection tour of Chavez Ravine, where the city was planning to build a major league baseball stadium.[63]

O'Malley's first step was to sell the land under Ebbets Field to a real estate developer. That provided the $2.5 million to run a swap of his Fort Worth, Texas, minor league franchise with Phil Wrigley's PCL Los Angeles Angels. Stoneham made a similar swap for a million less, trading his Minneapolis franchise to Tom Yawkey for his San Francisco Seals.[64] O'Malley's swap intensified the narrative—whether as a sign of an impending move or a shot across the bow for slow-moving Brooklyn officials, or both.[65] Los Angeles city officials visited O'Malley in Vero Beach, Florida, during spring training, to persuade him toward the former. They promised a comprehensive proposal that would solve the problems O'Malley was having trying to keep his team in Brooklyn. "We are optimistic as a result of our visit," Los Angeles Mayor Norris Poulson said.[66]

The West Coast focus left other MLB-hungry towns feeling pre-jilted, and Frick spoke in one of them, Houston, in May 1957. Perhaps to assuage their feelings of neglect, he revived the prospects for a third major league and called on the owners to start planning. "You people in Houston have a right to ask for a classification as high and as good as you can support," he said, stressing through his speech that he preferred expansion to relocation.[67]

But that was not how the story was moving. Only a couple of days after Frick's speech, San Francisco Mayor George Christopher went to New York to meet with O'Malley and Stoneham. Publicity about the meeting goaded Frick to turn to 1957's version of social media, firing off a telegram to O'Malley. (Stoneham was an unannounced, last-minute participant.) It read, "I must call your attention to the fact that wide public and newspaper discussion at this time of any franchise transfers is harmful to baseball. No changes can be made during the playing season and any publicity relative to future action is to be avoided by all clubs." As a result, O'Malley, who had just returned from another trip to Los Angeles to inspect his new minor league purchase's facilities, did not participate in the press conference afterward. Stoneham did, fueling speculation that San Francisco was after the Giants, but he did not make further comment.[68]

Immune from Frick's edict and back in San Francisco, Christopher speculated that the two teams' shift would be approved at the major league meetings in July, but not announced until after August 30. Christopher was careful to stress that this was merely his own opinion. Frick could only fume that "this Roman holiday of speculation is harmful to both leagues."[69]

With sports page speculation rampant, Frick still promoted his expansionist agenda. "Shifting of franchises is not a solution," he said. "Moving from one city to another is only like taking from one pocket to put it into the other. It is only a case of juggling within our present structure." He left further action to the owners, reminding them, "We are in the same position as other businesses which have sat tight too long while economy and population boomed in fantastic proportions." The owners, however, seemed content to let O'Malley and Stoneham work out their own details.[70]

Realignment and Congressional committees aside, Frick still had pressing immediate concerns. When late ballot-box stuffing put eight Cincinnati Reds on the 1957 National League All-Star starting team, Frick stepped in. He put Stan Musial at first base instead of George Crowe, Willie Mays instead of Gus Bell in center field, and Hank Aaron instead of Wally Post in right field. Given the controversial nature of the situation, Frick couldn't wait and instead took action three days before the teams were scheduled to be announced. The numbers confirmed Frick's wisdom. Cincinnati fans poured in 550,000 votes during the last week of voting—almost three times what the leading vote-getter had received for the entire previous year's voting.[71]

For his trouble, Frick was burned in effigy by Cincinnati fans. One admitted ballot-box stuffer complained, "I voted 800 times, and I worked hard to get the vote in. If it's the wrong way to choose a team, let them choose it next year." Another saw more sinister motives. "This isn't Russia," he said, "and no one man like Frick should make the decisions."[72]

According to *Cincinnati Enquirer* columnist Bob Husted, the trouble started when Frick, concerned about low fan voting, reached out to newspapers to help. The *Cincinnati Times-Star* agreed to help, but only if Frick granted the afternoon newspaper exclusive rights. Its daily ballot effort was augmented by the Burger Brewing Co., sponsor of the Reds broadcasts. Company reps distributed 350,000 ballots to local taverns.[73] Once the ingredients of the recipe for disaster were there, preparation was a snap.

It seemed like everyone had an idea for how to fix the All-Star Game voting. Frick acknowledged his own distaste for the status quo. Although he confessed to being in no hurry to fix the problem, he offered a couple of alternatives to fan voting: player voting, with no player allowed to vote for someone on his own team; or even selection by the BBWAA, continuing to show excellent media relations savvy. Regardless, he concluded, "I wish I faced no more serious things in the next three years."[74]

12. To the West Coast

One of those headaches—the move by the Dodgers and Giants to California—was apparently a foregone conclusion, with discussion focusing on how to bring a second team back into New York. Frick couldn't predict whether it would happen through another relocation or expansion by elevating a minor league franchise, but he did state, "I simply can't conceive of New York as a one-franchise city." The owners agreed that it would be easier to bring in a National League franchise; the Yankees, as holders of territorial rights, had a much easier time with the concept of New York as a single-franchise town.[75]

Yankees President Dan Topping claimed the authority to veto any franchise, American or National, from moving into his team's turf. He cited the Yankees' 1903 charter, which gave the team the "City of Greater New York." The National League would forfeit their right to the city if the Dodgers, chartered in 1890, moved out of town. Topping was envisioning the television potential as much as the attendance monopoly.

Frick concurred with Topping's opinion, calling it "legally" correct. "But there is more to this than legality," he said. "It would be unhealthy for baseball if there was only one major league team in a city of this size. The charter must be amended when and if the Giants and Dodgers leave." Frick and Will Harridge also maintained that Brooklyn, though consolidated into New York in 1898, could be considered "open territory," outside of the Yankees' domain.[76]

By August 18, Stoneham was ready to fire the first shot and announced that his board of directors had voted 8–1 to relocate to San Francisco for the 1958 season.[77] Frick's only response was to restate his belief that if the Dodgers also followed through on their rumored move, Brooklyn should be considered "open territory," to ease the establishment of a replacement franchise, whether by relocation or by expansion.[78] If Giants fans were expecting the commissioner to intervene on behalf of fans, they would be disappointed. This was an internal team/league matter, not one he was authorized to address. In Montreal for the International League All-Star Game, the best Frick could muster was a repeat of his push for a third major league.[79]

One note of alarm that would later sound ironic came from Dick Young of the *New York Daily News*. Assuming a Dodgers move to Los Angeles, with a season of games at the minor league Wrigley Field, Young complained, "Babe Ruth's revered 60-homer record will be in serious jeopardy of being broken by a shower of cheap fly balls.... Balls jump out of [Little Wrigley Field] like popcorn on the fire." He called on Frick "not to permit the quasi-sacred record to be ravished as a by-product of the money grab." Yes, this is the same columnist who sarcastically asked Frick if he was going to put an asterisk next to Roger Maris's home run record, thus creating the urban legend.[80]

In anticipation of the Dodgers' move, Frick called a joint owners' meeting for October 1, to discuss territorial rights. The purpose was to amend the baseball code to identify Los Angeles and San Francisco as two-team towns, along with New York and Chicago. The issue was as much keeping New York open to the National League as opening the West Coast for American League expansion. The amendment was tabled after O'Malley requested an extra week, beyond the October 1 deadline for franchise moves; the city ordinance approving the sale was denied the unanimous consent to consider it on first reading by the Los Angeles City Council, pushing approval back a week.[81]

The ordinance passed the next week, and the Dodgers announced that they too would be leaving New York. Frick made no statement other than to acknowledge that O'Malley had filed his formal notice of intent to move and that Frick's office had forwarded that notice to the appropriate minor league officials, so that negotiations regarding territorial rights could commence.[82]

Thus Frick looked ahead to the 1958 season and the beginning of his second term. Within his management philosophy, he had responded appropriately to the challenges facing baseball, and the West Coast expansion showed that his beloved sport was adjusting to the demands of a modern, postwar culture. When necessary, he would step in and discipline players, managers, and owners, protecting the best interests of baseball. He showed a particular skill in navigating the hazardous waters of Congress. To fans and (just as importantly) the media, however, suspicion grew as to whether Frick was the leader that baseball needed, or a pliant tool of the owners. It was a suspicion that would not only dog him throughout his second term, but would also taint his legacy.

13

Game Two Begins

Meeting at the July 1957 All-Star Game, the owners rewarded Frick with a second seven-year term, to begin the next year. Some anti–Frick sentiment was reported, particularly in the American League, but ultimately the owners realized that the immediate challenges of the Celler committee necessitated a united front, and Frick was unanimously re-elected.[1]

In his first interview after his re-election, Frick offered no reflection on a decision that would carry him to almost his 70th birthday and bring him to more than 30 years of leadership in organized baseball. Instead, he was in more of a mood to ponder the challenges inhabiting his second term. "The next five years will be the most critical, the most momentous, in the history of baseball," he said, citing issues of franchise relocation and its effects on the minor leagues more than television or labor. "We are going to solve our problems, but we will have to go through trying years before we reach those important solutions."[2]

A *Sporting News* editorial applauded the decision, calling it a "thumping tribute" to Frick. They noted the challenges he faced: "The players' new militancy, two congressional investigations and the complications of franchise shifts and rumors," combined with the "absurd situation in which baseball found itself sued both for broadcasting too much and broadcasting too little." The conclusion wished Frick "many years of health and happiness—and a minimum of headaches—in his service to the game."[3]

Not all the media response was positive. In the July 1958 issue of *Esquire*, sports writer Roger Kahn delivered an assessment of Ford Frick as baseball commissioner as Frick entered his second term. The article was more of a takedown. For all the changes that the pastime was facing, Kahn wrote, "Frick has not led the game of baseball one step further into the twentieth century…. No one who knows Frick would ever accuse him of corruption. His failing is simply that he has found no path down which he can confidently lead."

Unfortunately for Frick, none of the sources Kahn interviewed challenged that notion, including the commissioner himself. J. Norman Lewis, the players' attorney, said, "I don't think Frick makes any significant decision without sounding out the owners first." Former players representative Bob Feller added, "Frick does everything the owners want him to do. Frick is hired by the owners, answerable to them and fired by them. Naturally, he does what he thinks they want."

The interview that could have challenged Kahn's analysis mostly confirmed it. After outlining several proposals to deal with the transitions baseball was facing, Frick turned cautious. "I can suggest changes," he told Kahn. "It is up to the league officials and committees to adopt them." Although he later claimed authority over the game itself and even the status of the owners, the tone of the article was clear.[4] In an additional sting, the article was promoted within a small ad in the June 25 *Sporting News*, and a brief article two pages away from the ad highlighted the critical comments.

A 1957 column about NFL Commissioner Bert Bell reached the same conclusion about Frick. Comparing Frick to Bell and Landis, *Cleveland News* columnist Ed McAuley said, "Wisely or not—and I think not—Ford Frick brought to the commissioner's office a gentler concept of his place in the baseball picture." McAuley noted Frick's preference for cracking down behind closed doors, "But I think it's important to preserve the public view of the office as a stern, hard-hitting law enforcement agency."[5]

Even with his kinder, gentler approach, there was work to be done. Frick turned his attention to cleaning up the mess the Giants and Dodgers had left, particularly for minor league alignment. As seemed his favorite approach to tasks, with sleeves rolled up, Frick called a meeting of minor league officials, with Giants and Dodgers representation, for November 12. The meeting couldn't resolve the damage done to the Pacific Coast League, but Frick said he hoped a proposal could be presented at the minor league meetings in December.[6]

Those meetings produced two changes Frick had championed for years: an end to the bonus rule and a loosening of draft rules. Under previous rules, teams could protect players for up to seven years and could lose only one unprotected player from each minor league club. The result was an old school version of the rich getting richer. Teams like the Yankees, Cardinals, and Dodgers, with their well-developed farm systems, could protect major league-caliber players on their rosters for years while depriving them of a chance at the majors. The new rules lowered the tenure of a protected player to four years and removed the limit to players who could be drafted off one team.[7]

The television issue only got worse for minor league officials. They were leery enough when some major league teams signed a Saturday "Game of the Week" agreement with both CBS and NBC. When the networks announced a Sunday "Game of the Week," the minor leagues exploded in anger. They immediately sent a telegram to Representative Emanuel Celler, chair of the House Judiciary Committee, asking him to re-open the previous year's investigation of baseball.[8] Frick approved. "Believe me, if it were up to me, I'd issue an order at once, barring the Sunday telecasts. But my hands are tied." When he was told that each of the five teams involved in the Sunday contract would receive $100,000, Frick replied, "I hope they are not sleeping well these nights."[9]

Frick and the minor league officials even scheduled a follow-up meeting with his Congressional nemesis, to see if he could offer legislative aid. Celler and his Republican counterpart, Kenneth Keating, were measured in their promise for support. They recommended that the baseball leadership check instead with the Justice Department.[10] Frick had to head back to New York, but the minor league officials did meet with Robert A. Bicks, the No. 2-ranking official in the Antitrust Division. Bicks did no more than listen, but given that the Department was also moving against NFL Commissioner Bell for blacking out a game in the home team's city, they might not have been too optimistic.[11]

Other issues proved stickier. The dispute over New York's territorial rights produced conflicting motions from the two leagues. National League owners wanted to replace both franchises in New York if possible, while the American League wanted free access to the San Francisco and Los Angeles metropolitan areas. Frick ultimately appointed a four-member committee, two owners from each league, to come up with a policy.[12]

The committee returned its recommendations within weeks. It recommended that any city with more than 2,000,000 in population be declared "open territory" for a second team. That rule would include Los Angeles as well as New York, satisfying American League objections. The new rules also set a five-mile limit for the proximity of new stadiums, which eliminated the Polo Grounds, and all of Manhattan, as a future home.[13]

Frick declared himself "delighted with the quick and satisfactory results achieved by the special committee,"[14] mainly because it kept him out of a jam. Without the new rules, if a team had requested to locate in New York, whether by relocation or expansion, it was likely the American League would vote no and the National League would vote yes. Frick's sentiments on the matter were clearly stated, and he could have broken the tie with his vote. But he much preferred that the rules make such a decision for him.

In fact, the territorial rules committee came up with a much simpler rule as a replacement. The new proposed rule simply removed the other league from the decision-making process. Relocations could be approved by the franchise's league and the commissioner. While definitely aimed at returning National League baseball to New York, it would also make it easier for American League to move to Los Angeles or San Francisco. Frick attended the meeting but did not issue a statement, though he could be assumed to approve it.[15]

The owners would eventually let him down with their self-interested squabbling. This time it was Detroit general manager John McHale at the wrench. He wanted the population threshold increased to 2,500,000, no doubt because his city was close to the proposed minimum and he didn't like the idea of competition without compensation. The National League also voted against the new law, preferring to leave Los Angeles as closed territory. So baseball ended up as it often did on such issues: back where it started. Frick refused to acknowledge defeat, noting that the proposal was tabled, not defeated, and that even without a stated rule, he would consider New York open territory for a new franchise.[16]

The move to Los Angeles generated other rule changes as well. The controversy over the home run wall in Los Angeles, described in Chapter 1, resulted in more than just an expressed commitment to protect Ruth's home run record from an easy assault. In response to that, Frick requested that the major league baseball rules committee amend stadium standards with a minimum of 325 feet down the foul lines and 400 feet to center field. His proposal met with near-unanimous approval, with the only regret being that it was too late to affect the 251-foot left-field fence at the Los Angeles Coliseum.[17]

By 1958 Frick finally pulled away from the third league concept, now that West Coast relocation had disposed of Pacific Coast League aspirations. The solution lay instead with each circuit adding four teams. "We would have two twelve-team circuits, six East, six West, with interlocking schedules, somewhat after the manner of the National Pro Football League." He offered no specific ideas for new franchise locations, as was his policy.

In the same interview, Frick displayed a sense of where sports were going that certainly could have sustained a more authoritative approach. First, as fans would be glad to hear, he chided owners who threatened to relocate as a negotiating tool. "One thing I don't like," he said. "I don't admire the method of threatening a city with loss of its club to another major city if this or that isn't done by the municipal authorities." That was the strategy of Powel Crosley, Jr., Reds owner, in his efforts to secure more parking for his stadium. In all fairness to Crosley, parking was nonexistent, but the city would eventually alleviate the situation, and Crosley did not have to follow through on his New York relocation threats.

Frick also signaled the change toward public financing of sports stadiums, alluding to O'Malley's efforts in Los Angeles: "I do not believe that it is possible for any ball club to build its own stadium minus city aid, without the help of condemnation proceedings." He also stipulated that such publicly financed and legislated stadiums should not be for baseball only, but should be "all-purpose, all-weather, all-year domed arenas which could be used for ... other interesting events of wide public concern with important revenue certainties." Los Angeles and San Francisco, of course, were planning the exact opposite.[18]

Frick had championed the all-weather sports palace concept in an article for *This Week*, a popular magazine supplement in Sunday newspapers. As he described it, the arena sounds like old news today—like every indoor arena. But in 1958, when the suspension roof, without posts, was a new idea, it sounded visionary—a source of pride and guaranteed revenue for a city willing to take risks. The first such facility would not open until seven years later: the Astrodome in Houston.[19]

Eventually, after the 1957 Cincinnati ballot-box stuffing, Frick decided to take the All-Star selection process out of the fans' hands. He announced that for the 1958 All-Star Game, the teams would be selected by players, managers, and coaches. The players, voting for opponents only, would select the eight starters, with the managers selecting pitchers and reserves. "The fan poll idea was abandoned only after long consideration and with a great deal of regret," Frick said. He said the new plan would be in effect for a year and then evaluated.[20] It would remain that way until Bowie Kuhn returned the vote to the fans in 1970.

Frick also claimed the fan vote presented logistical issues because millions of votes had to be tabulated. Some fans disagreed with Frick, but the plan received surprising support from fans as well as players and media.[21] Gabe Paul, general manager in Cincinnati, home team of the offending fans, saw no problem in the current system. "There was just more voting here than in other areas," he said. "If the fans of other communities had been given the same voting opportunities as in this area, there would have been greater satisfaction with the results."[22]

One advantage of the players voting was that the selection could take place within a more compact time frame, allowing emerging All-Stars a chance to make an impression. The ballots would be distributed by the managers on June 22 and returned to Frick's office immediately. The player selections would be announced by June 29, with pitchers and substitutes selected in time for the July 8 game.[23]

The All-Star voting results accomplished two objectives. Thanks to the players' involvement, both teams featured deserving selections instead of local heroes and under-performing fan favorites. It also caused a cry for a return to the fan voting that had been rejected so disdainfully the year before. "There is so little to identify the fans with the game, except to take their money at the ticket window or listen to their complaints, that I feel very strongly we should give the All-Star vote back to them," said Frank Lane, Indians general manager. Frick also described himself as not too happy with the new system, "but we'll go along with it and see how it works out. It may be changed next year—I don't know."[24]

At this point, cracks had begun to emerge in the relationship between the player reps and their attorney. It started when the players officially endorsed the law Celler had proposed, altering the reserve clause and bringing baseball under antitrust law.[25] The players' leadership had described the agreement as unanimous, but four players broke ranks and contacted Kenneth Keating to express their support for his competing bill, which would have afforded baseball more protection from antitrust laws.[26] The player representatives ended up rescinding their earlier endorsement of the Celler law, in a move that was seen as a pushback of Lewis's leadership.[27] The disagreement, climaxed by the reversal, sparked a reported anti–Lewis movement. If there was one, it was squelched, as the player delegates voted unanimously to retain Lewis at a meeting the next week.[28]

With or without the players' endorsement, Celler's bill faced tough sledding. What caused concern was the bill's stipulation that activities found to be "reasonably necessary to accomplish the results enumerated in this bill" would not violate antitrust laws. To opponents, the words "reasonably necessary" invited constant court involvement. Celler's bill barely made it out of committee by a 17–15 vote, and when it was scheduled for floor action, four other House Judiciary Committee members introduced a bill close to the one Keating had introduced, with no mention of the troublesome phrase. It offered greater antitrust protection to all pro sports and had the support of Frick and his peers in other leagues. Celler's bill finally passed the House in June, after the words "reasonably necessary" were deleted, and it was sent on to the Senate.[29]

13. Game Two Begins   203

The Senate appeared poised for quick action on the Celler bill, and hearings on the bill began July 9. Along with Frick and other pro sports leaders, the list of invited witnesses included Ted Williams, Mickey Mantle, and Stan Musial. (They would testify the first week, to sync with the All-Star Game, which was being played in nearby Baltimore.) Even Happy Chandler was invited to join the fun.[30]

In his testimony before the Senate Antitrust Subcommittee, Frick focused on the television restrictions required by antitrust laws. He claimed that without some limit of major league broadcasts to avoid conflict with minor league home games, the end was near. "Minor league towns are being wrecked," he said. "We have got to be able to meet that problem head on, or within ten years it won't be a problem. There will be no television problem because there will be no baseball." By his calculations, the minors were at a minimum level to provide the talent to sustain the majors.[31]

When Celler testified before the committee, his input was sufficient to sink the bill. He cited Frick's lack of authority as a point of peril. "Ford Frick, for example, cannot control the baseball owners. He admitted it to the committee," he thundered. "His office is too frail a reed for us to rely on." That, plus "Frick's own statement shows that money, not the welfare of the minor leagues, determines the club owner's actions in the TV question."[32]

From that point, for all the earlier quick work, the bill went no further. The subcommittee voted to table it, and the Senate adjourned without taking further action, so the bill died. It did not come up before the next session, or any other, so it would represent the closest Congress has come to placing baseball specifically under antitrust law.[33]

A bill was introduced to Congress in 1961 that would have granted all pro sports the same antitrust exemption enjoyed by baseball. Sponsored by Keating and Democratic Senator Philip Hart of Michigan, the bill had the support of Washington attorney Paul Porter, who predicted that Frick would support it as well.[34] The bills were reported by the Antitrust Subcommittee to the full Judiciary Committee, without hearings, but the Judiciary Committee merely discussed the bills without further action.[35]

By 1958, it became apparent that Frick was slowing down for his second term. He traveled less for the special occasions that had drawn him before; he had Warren Giles handle the festivities in St. Louis on June 7–8 honoring Stan Musial's 3,000th-hit, for example. New, stiffer penalties for beanballs, following a near brawl at a Pittsburgh-San Francisco game in May, were decided on and announced by his two league presidents, regardless of the "best interests of baseball" involved.[36]

He also canceled the joint league meeting following the 1958 All-Star Game, leaving the two leagues to debate realignment and expansion issues on their own, claiming that there was nothing on the agenda that could not wait until December. As it turned out, at the American League meeting—note, one that Frick was not leading—Washington Senators owner Calvin Griffith asked for permission to move his franchise out of the nation's capital, a move that the other owners swatted at but could not eliminate.[37] Frick later described himself as "opposed to any change" in Washington. He added, "I believe that the nation's capital always should have a major league ball team, and that the American League should continue here."[38]

With all of the issues baseball was already facing, and the new uncertainty in Washington from the Senators, both politicians and the franchise, Frick called an owners' meeting in Chicago for September 8 and 9. Six of the teams would be represented anyway for the World Series meeting; why not bring the rest in and talk?[39]

As so often happened at these meetings, nothing really happened. The owners did vote to move up Opening Day by four days and endorsed reinstatement of a bonus rule—mainly to discipline the unchecked spending on untested players that they could not themselves control. At that meeting, Griffith temporarily halted his discussions of a franchise move. But no new policy or vision on expansion or realignment was announced, and yet another committee was appointed to come up with new bonus and draft policies.[40]

The Sporting News tried to apply a brave face to the proceedings, noting that with the dynasty power of the Yankees and the emerging consistency of the Braves, perhaps baseball did need to cool the expansion talk and build some competitiveness among the existing teams. Arthur Daley of the *New York Times*, by contrast, reinforced the emerging frame: that Frick, "a sound-thinking, but powerless man, by choice or by law could do nothing to curb greedy owners who have only one measuring device: What's in it for me?"[41]

Frick and the owners faced a new hazard at the Chicago meetings: air conditioning. The *Chicago Daily News* printed a complete transcript of the joint meeting the next day. Consensus was that Bill Furlong, a young reporter on the byline, was able to gain a clear "audio" of the meeting in an adjoining room. An Associated Press report said officials were so angry that they were considering withholding advance notice of future meetings. Dan Daniel, noting that the source for the threat was not Frick, defended the action as solid enterprise reporting and advised the owners to police themselves in the future.[42] A *Sporting News* editorial expressed admiration for Furlong; he scooped his veteran colleagues, who were waiting at another hotel for the official post-meeting press conference. But the editorial also groused about the impropriety of reporting a private meeting and called on the BBWAA to develop a code of ethics.⁴³

The pain in Frick's side was real, and it was not caused by an intrusive media. Eight days before the 1958 World Series, he underwent an emergency appendectomy. There were no complications, but Eleanor Frick put him on the disabled list for at least the first two Series games. "He won't go to Milwaukee," she told a reporter. "Maybe a younger person can become active sooner after such an operation but Ford isn't so young anymore." The 63-year-old had not missed a World Series game since being elected National League president in 1934.⁴⁴

Frick ended up missing the entire Series, entrusting game administration to his top assistant, Charley Segar, but Frick still did his job. Watching the game at home, he saw Yankees pitcher Ryne Duren give the choke gesture to umpire Charlie Berry. As soon as he returned to the office, he announced a $250 fine for Duren. The pitcher claimed he could not remember making such a gesture, but apologized and said that he would pay the fine "with a big smile" after his team's World Series victory.⁴⁵

Frick was a regular attendee at World Series and All-Star games, though an appendectomy caused him to miss the 1958 World Series (National Baseball Hall of Fame Library, Cooperstown, New York).

For the 1958 off-season, sufficiently recovered, Frick joined a group of players traveling to a new destination: Venezuela. Although players had been spending the winter in Latin America for decades, the State Department and business leaders thought it might be wise to send an official tour there, given the growing Communism-inspired rumblings in Central and South America. Ford and Eleanor made the trip by cruise ship, with most of the players and other representatives meeting them there via plane.[46] The tour and its clinics were a great success, both for baseball and for the federal government. Baseball's friend in Congress, Kenneth Keating, preparing to transition from the House to the Senate, pledged his support even to expanding the program.[47]

Frick also had a proposal for expanding opportunities for players to join Caribbean and Latin-American leagues, and that became a hot topic after Fidel Castro led a rebellion in 1959 that overthrew the Batista regime. Several American players were literally caught in the crossfire, as was Cleveland general manager Frank Lane. None were harmed, though they were confined to their hotels, which were guarded by rebel forces who were friendly toward the players.[48]

For the immediate situation, Frick did not recall the players from Cuba because they were there on their individual team's authority. But he did give the teams permission to withdraw their players (among them future Dodgers manager Tommy Lasorda) without violating the agreement with the Cuban leagues. Many players chose to stay. In the days immediately following the overthrow, many expressed optimism that Castro would be supportive of all things American, including baseball.[49]

At the January 31 meeting, owners endorsed Frick's proposal, allowing Latin-American players unlimited rights to play winter ball in their land of birth. American players would still be limited to their first two years in the majors. To Frick, the rule was particularly needed as a goodwill policy, in view of the unrest in Cuba. The rule still mandated an equal balance between Latin-American and American players on each team's roster.[50]

Another strategy to improve U.S.–Central America relations, while also helping the minor leagues, featured a series of 1959 games between Texas and Mexican League teams. Teams from both leagues crossed the border to play a total of 36 games against their counterparts. Frick attended the opening game in Austin as the "official representative" of President Eisenhower, and Senator Lyndon Johnson sent greetings and congratulations. The American players were allowed to enter Mexico on tourist visas, without passports, though lack of communication caused some to be delayed at the border.[51]

13. Game Two Begins

Soon the situation reversed in Cuba. As the 1960 season drew to a close and players started their winter league plans, the situation in the Caribbean had deteriorated to the point where Frick declared Cuba off-limits to American players. "The situation in Cuba has reached a point at which I no longer want to be responsible for the lives and welfare, and financial return, of American players there," he said. The situation in the Dominican Republic was also unstable, but not to the point where Frick felt it necessary to keep Americans out.[52]

By January 1961, relations with Cuba would deteriorate to the point where the United States broke diplomatic relations with the island nation. The concern for Frick and the league presidents centered on whether Cuban players still in the country would be allowed to return for the 1961 season. With the situation still uncertain, and President-elect Kennedy yet to take office, all Frick could do was wait to learn the fate of the eight players (including three headed to the newly relocated Minneapolis franchise).[53]

The players got the December 1958 meetings off to a rousing start with their demand that owners allocate at least 20 percent of all revenues for salaries. The concept is a component of most pro sports collective bargaining agreements today. NFL players receive from 47 to 48.5 percent of revenue, and the percentage for NBA players hovers between 49 and 51 percent. But for baseball owners in 1958, the idea of players demanding a specific percentage of their revenue as pay seemed outrageous. Even today, baseball does not have a salary cap.

The owners voted down the proposal, with a vote and accompanying rhetoric that showed unusual solidarity and anger. Most spoke anonymously. "I don't want to get mixed up in this mess," one said. "But the players are moving closer and closer to forming a union. That 20 percent gag is union stuff." Red Sox owner Tom Yawkey publicly complained about the "constant jockeying" and confessed to thoughts of leaving baseball. He added, "I've put a lot of money into this game. I did it voluntarily. I never asked the players to share my losses."[54]

The players were not much happier; they voted to drop J. Norman Lewis as their counsel on March 24, 1959, ending a six-year relationship that had greatly benefited the players. Lewis, having bigger fish to charge by the hour, was gracious in his exit. "The players have decided by reason of their achievements up to now they no longer need a permanent attorney under contract," he said. "There was no acrimony and everything was settled amicably." Lewis said he did not know if the players were pressured by the owners. "But I am sure a lot of people on the other side of the fence are well-pleased," he said. "I don't think I ever would have won a popularity contest with them. You know, every now and then I put a burr under them."[55]

Sources told reporters that the end did not come amicably, as Lewis claimed, but was the result of player anger—particularly by Robin Roberts—over Lewis's statements during the antitrust hearings the previous summer.[56] Others (including Marvin Miller, executive director of the MLBPA from 1966 to 1982) claim that the players felt so threatened by the owners' pushback on Lewis's 20 percent of revenue proposal that they dumped Lewis, following the expressed wishes of their bosses.[57]

As a replacement, the players chose to retain a public relations specialist, Frank Scott, rather than legal counsel. After a few months, the players recognized that they did need an attorney and retained Robert Cannon, a Milwaukee judge, as their legal representative late in 1959. Attractive in his resume was that his father, Raymond Cannon, had come surprisingly close to organizing the players into an effective union in 1922.[58] In that regard, Robert Cannon was far from being his father's son and would gain a reputation as more of an effective campaigner to succeed Frick than a strong players' representative.

From the start, Cannon seemed determined to create peaceful relationships with the owners. It was reported that Cannon would not make demands of the owners and would never speak for the players. His capacity would be strictly advisory.[59] Thanks to Cannon and the players who followed his lead, Frick and the owners would enjoy a period of labor peace for the duration of Frick's term, though the simmering issues would explode in the years soon after.

Although they had turned down the player demands, the owners approved the new draft rules at the meeting. All minor league players would be available in an unrestricted draft after one year in the minors, with no limit on the number of players who could be drafted from each team's farm system. However, the owners approved the new rule for only one year, to be confirmed by a follow-up vote. The owners also approved a waivers-free interleague trading period between November 21 and December 15. Frick did not like the idea, citing the maintenance of interleague distinctiveness and rivalry, but he lacked the authority to stop it. Instead, he said he would ask reconsideration of the decision at the July league meetings.[60] The owners would reaffirm the rule then as well, citing the possibility of high-profile trades that would spark fan interest.[61] The interleague swap period proved popular with fans, sports writers, and, to a varying extent, team owners and management, many of whom urged its continuation.[62]

13. Game Two Begins

The most important action taken was not the adoption of any proposals, but the appointment by Frick of a four-man committee (including Walter O'Malley) to come up with a plan to deal with expansion. Frick had suggested specific attention to the issue five years before, but as the next chapter details the emerging threat of a third league with a franchise in New York was enough to budge the owners from their self-interested inertia.[63]

Frick had more success helping the minor leagues come up with a realignment plan, the sad consequence of television-inspired contraction. Such was the upheaval and protest that the minor leagues representatives almost left the meetings without a plan, which could have proven disastrous given their struggles. Frick, however, invited minor league presidents to his suite for a discussion, and they emerged with a renewed sense of cooperation, approving a tough but necessary realignment plan.[64]

When it came to the rules of baseball, Frick was more direct and decisive. The Texas League directors had voted to eliminate the four pitches of an intentional walk, to speed up games, but Frick wired the league president, Dick Butler, and informed him that the proposal violated the rules, which required actual pitches. He told Butler his league could test the idea during exhibition games and report back, but could not implement it for actual league games.[65]

Major league baseball had considered such a rule change, Frick noted, but ultimately decided against it. Games featured an average of one intentional walk per game, and eliminating the pitches shaved only 65 seconds from the game length. "It isn't the length of a game that fans find unpleasant," he said. "Rather, it's the dead spots. People want action." He considered attacking those dead spots a wiser strategy.[66]

Another era ended for Frick at the January meeting, as the American League owners elected Joe Cronin, Red Sox general manager, as their new league president. His long-time colleague, William Harridge, had announced his retirement at the December meetings, effective February 1, 1959.[67] Harridge had been in the position for 28 years, taking the job four years before Frick became the NL president. Their association had spanned World War II, the Executive Council following Landis's death, and Frick's own ascension to the commissioner's office. Cronin was unanimously approved and received a seven-year contract.[68] As was his prerogative, Cronin moved the league office from Chicago, Harridge's hometown, to Boston.[69]

Frick was back at the witness table in February, but this time it was federal court, not a Congressional hearing. He testified as a defendant in a lawsuit filed by Frank Lawrence, a former minor league team owner. Lawrence had filed suit in October 1954, charging that Frick and other baseball officials had destroyed his operation through the major leagues' television policy. Frick agreed that television broadcasts had hurt the minors, but claimed that he could do nothing about it, given the Justice Department's stance that such controls resembled antitrust violations.[70]

The judge dismissed Lawrence's lawsuit, mainly on the technicality that Lawrence cited Rule 1(a), which banned teams from violating each other's geographic properties. The judge ruled that Lawrence had applied it incorrectly to broadcasts, though the judge also admonished Frick to fix the television problem. Frick expressed relief at the ruling and stressed his commitment to help the minors. "I would like to see something written, either by Congress or the Justice Department, enabling us to regulate it," he said. "If they'd only give us some way to do it, we could save a lot of grief. As it is, we cannot help the minors as much as we'd like to."[71]

Frick announced in early May that the players' representatives had suggested a second All-Star Game to benefit a pension for older players, who were not covered under the current plan. The owners supposedly would use their 40 percent of the television contract to fund amateur baseball, including youth leagues. The Executive Council, in approving the suggestion, urged Frick to find a suitable date within the 1959 season, if possible.[72] With Lewis out of the way, the owners would be able to make the players work harder for their benefits, while the owners contributed less of their growing profits. What is curious and troubling is that the players themselves seemed to accept the concept.

Frick denied that the second All-Star Game was a money-grabbing ploy by the owners, though he declined to comment specifically on how the money would be used. A second 1959 All-Star Game seemed impractical, but Frick was certain that it would be worked into the 1960 schedule. Some, including Dan Daniel, were already criticizing the idea for diluting the All-Star Game concept. "If two All-Star contests are scheduled, no matter how splendid the causes why not three? And if three, why not four?" Daniel asked.[73] *The Sporting News* joined in opposing the concept. An editorial predicted the plan "would weaken, if it did not destroy, the public interest in the battle of the best.... The stunt sounds like one of those over-hustling efforts which conceivably might kill the golden goose."[74]

Frick had returned from his 1958 Venezuela trip two days early after Eleanor became ill (nothing serious). He arrived just in time for a press conference by a committee appointed by New York Mayor Robert Wagner.

The committee, headed by attorney Bill Shea, announced their endorsement of a third major league, which would bring a new franchise to New York, and construction of a new stadium to host it. An outraged Frick declared, "Baseball is not going to be sledge-hammered into putting a club into New York because of a threat of a third league."[75]

Frick commented further in an interview with Daniel, who described his temper as "disbelief and mystification, mingled with resentment." He recalled meeting Shea once, with no mention of such a plan. "Why did Shea bypass me?" he asked. "I would like to see two majors of 12 clubs each, with East and West sections. But if New York were to head up a third major, I would accept that."

His description of the difficulties awaiting the New York proposal barely veiled the threats. "You don't pick eight cities and merely announce that you have a third league. There are baseball laws about such matters," he said. "Where would they get the players at this time? The money, the cities, the parks? Does Shea realize that no player would be willing to go into his third league? Who would want to give up pension rights?"[76]

Harry Grayson, sports editor for the *Newspaper Enterprise Association*, wasn't buying it. He called the response "typical": "Frick lets the situation get out of hand and then attempts to counter with a weak punch." Grayson could not believe O'Malley and Stoneham had left New York without a baseball game half of the season and claimed "any baseball commissioner other than the fence-straddling Frick would have reacted immediately."[77]

A backtracking Shea was deferential in his reply. "The reason we haven't yet gone before Mr. Frick is that up to now we have had nothing concrete to offer," he said. "I am working on a package.... When we have that package assembled, all neat and with bona fide guarantees attached, we'll go to the commissioner and ask him how we go about coming into the baseball picture as a third major league." Shea added that if Frick turned him down, they would consider operating independently.[78] Still, Shea and his associates could hardy be blamed for going around Frick. As the dual West Coast relocations demonstrated, he was an available resource, but hardly the gatekeeper.

The Shea committee's work to bring a second team to New York also gained the owners' attention. They held a secret meeting at Pittsburgh owner John Galbreath's farm near Columbus, Ohio, on May 21, 1959, and emerged with the announcement that they too were ready to form a third eight-team league, with Frick outlining the requirements for the new franchises. No mention was made of how talent would be provided to these new franchises, whether through an expansion draft or other means.[79]

In a follow-up article, Daniel cited Frick's leadership on the third major league issue as an example of his strong authority on such issues. Frick agreed. "I want to take credit for what happened at Columbus," he said in a rare moment of humblebrag. His claim was based in substance more than style, because of his statement's clarity in "laying down requirements for major league status, and for furnishing eligible cities with a reasonable program in an orderly and practical manner without destroying our present structure and without the bitterness and disruption of a baseball war."[80]

Columnists like Daley were not impressed. He labeled the owners' "mighty noble and unselfish gesture" a Trojan horse. He predicted that a third major league would present a weak, inferior product to fans—particularly those in New York City—for years. "A sincere move toward expansion would remain within the framework of the two leagues. But this one is a cynical invitation to disaster."[81]

But a third league would indeed emerge, and its announced arrival, led by a revered and intimidating name in baseball, would soon dominate Frick's second term.

14

The Third League

Criticism and opposition (even from team owners like Bill Veeck and Tom Yawkey) notwithstanding, Frick announced on June 8 that a second All-Star Game would indeed take place in 1959, in Los Angeles four weeks after the first game, on August 3. The game would include no "All-Star" break, despite the travel complications; games were scheduled for the next day. A 5 p.m. start time would allow East Coast fans earlier viewing.[1]

Frick admitted the second game was motivated by money but cited the benefits to the pension plan, which could expand to help older players, and other programs supported by organized baseball.[2] That did not stop the media and many players from ridiculing the idea. Players wondered whether there should be two Kentucky Derbies or two Rose Bowl games, and Baltimore manager Paul Richards said he would push for two Christmases. It turned out that only nine of 16 major league teams supported the game, based on a player vote. Two opposed, and five could not come to a decision based on the information provided.[3]

Player sentiment seemed split toward the second All-Star Game. Some, like Don Drysdale, believed it was a good idea, poorly presented. "It's for a great cause," he said. Mickey Mantle said, "I like it. I'll play anywhere, anytime they tell me. That's how I make my living." Frank Malzone of the Red Sox, who had a doubleheader in Kansas City the next day, groused, "This is phony and I'm going to be dragging my tail tomorrow." Al Kaline wondered about teams involved in pennant races risking their players for a later-season All-Star Game. Frick seemed prepared for defeat: "I don't think they're for it," he said of the players. "However, it's their game and they'll have to make the decision. If they vote against it, I'll drop the game."[4]

The 1960 double-feature All-Star Games took place on July 11 in Kansas City and July 13 in New York, with the same players participating in both. Attendance at Yankee Stadium was disappointing, and the second game lacked drama and excitement. Harvey Kuenn of the Indians had supported both games, but the experience caused him to request an immediate vote of the Players' Association to eliminate the second game. Frick repeated his promise to follow the players' wishes.[5] Kuenn and most baseball fans were shocked, then, when the players voted to support a second All-Star Game by a six-to-one margin. Only Kuenn's team, the Indians, voted against the second game. The extra $180,000 for the pension plan was cited as the most influential factor.[6]

Frick continued the surprise, issuing a statement: "It is the feeling of the owners and many of the players that after 1961 the schedule should revert to the old plan of one All-Star Game per year." The players protested that the question was still open, but on this issue, it seemed that Frick was willing to apply strong, specific leadership.[7] The 1961 games would be played on July 11 in San Francisco and July 31 in Boston, Frick announced.[8]

The players restated their support for two All-Star Games through their representatives, who endorsed it at their 1961 mid-season meeting. Bob Friend of the Pirates, National League player rep, argued that the fans supported two games and that, with expansion to 20 teams, it would be 20 years between hosting All-Star Games for league cities. He did not have to mention the pension plan boon.[9] The players conveyed their wishes at a joint meeting of club owners and player reps during the World Series, but Frick was careful to point out that when the committee approved the plan, the vote was unanimous.[10]

To reiterate their support, the player representatives held yet another meeting, in Miami right before the owners' meetings, where they reported ten-to-one support among the players for the idea. They presented their arguments to Frick, Giles, Cronin, and the owners, who promised to discuss them.[11] The owners did in fact approve the second All-Star Game for 1962, but the American League owners overwhelmingly voted to return to one game beginning in 1963.[12]

Before leaving town for a tour of Japan following the 1962 season, Frick met with the player representatives and Robert Cannon. He confirmed that the Executive Council had also recommended a return to a single All-Star Game in 1963, with a final decision to be made at the December meetings. Frick told the players that the Council had promised to come up with a solution for dealing with the reduced pension contributions.[13] The solution turned out to be a greater share of All-Star Game television proceeds, from 60 percent to 95 percent, and in November, the players agreed to drop the second contest. The owners concurred, their generosity eased by skyrocketing network revenues.[14]

The continued emergence of a third major league was the dark cloud to the financial silver lining. In early July 1959, Bill Shea and his associates were granted some unexpected Congressional help by Senator Estes Kefauver, chair of the Senate's Antitrust Committee, and Emanuel Celler. Kefauver had filed a bill that did not eliminate the reserve clause but did reduce the number of players any pro league could control. He offered hearings on the bill in the context of the efforts to form a third league, Shea said. Shea declined, and Frick condemned Kefauver's bill, saying it would "prevent a third league and do more harm to baseball and other professional sports than anything I can think of."[15] Even Vice President Richard Nixon chimed in, favoring the third league and suggesting franchises in Havana, Montreal, and Mexico City during a *Today* show interview.[16]

The movement was gaining momentum, as evidenced by the raft of negative articles in the July 1 *Sporting News*, no doubt with Frick's blessing. They included a front-page banner piece by Dan Daniel on the lack of talent facing the new league,[17] a history of the failed Federal League efforts in 1914 and 1915,[18] a brief quoting Cronin as saying the third major would "wipe out the minors,"[19] and an editorial listing the financial problems facing such an undertaking[20] (which was next to a skeptical column reprinted from the *Washington Star*[21]). The only effort to balance coverage was an interview with Branch Rickey—a name that would soon figure prominently—claiming that there was plenty of major league talent out there, and that any new league would be able to provide a competent product.[22]

Frick could not ignore the challenge, however, so he appointed a seven-member advisory committee at the 1959 All-Star Game meetings. He later announced that he would meet with Shea and his group in mid-August. "The meeting will be entirely exploratory," he cautioned.[23]

The shot was formally fired on July 27, when Shea announced the formation of the Continental League, with franchises in Houston, Toronto, Denver, St. Paul-Minneapolis, and of course New York. Shea announced that the new league would begin its first season in April 1961, and that the New York franchise would play at a new stadium, on the World's Fair grounds in the Queens borough.[24] The Denver franchise group was headed by Edwin Johnson, who had criticized the major leagues strongly—both as a U.S. Senator and as president of the Western League.[25]

Kefauver had scheduled his committee's hearings for the same week as the Continental League announcement. Frick used that as his opportunity to comment on the upstart effort, and his tone was measured and non-combative. He declared that plans to meet with Shea and his colleagues were "on the level," and he made it sound like he considered the

Continental League to be providing the spadework for the third major Frick had championed over the past few years.

Frick realized that hostility toward the new league was likely to create a bidding war that would ultimately hurt baseball. "The quickest way for the new league to get players is to come into organized baseball, have their own working agreements, have some ownership clubs," he said at Kefauver's committee hearings. "Then they have got a place where they can put their players for development."[26] He also took the opportunity to warn the committee against new laws, such as Kefauver's, that would handicap such efforts."[27]

Following those hearings, when the Continental League leadership arrived at their meeting with Frick and the advisory committee on expansion, they brought a powerful new member: Rickey, who at 77 years old had just been elected league president. In part because of that, the meeting went swimmingly. "We want your cooperation," Rickey said. "We need your cooperation. We demand your cooperation."[28]

At the end, Frick issued a statement supporting Rickey and company's efforts, but remained reticent on promises to help the upstart too much.[29] To some critics, Frick's stated support throughout the process was disingenuous—an effort to prevent the League from going independent and starting a bidding war—but as long as Frick and organized baseball portrayed themselves as inviting, the Continental League had no choice but to play along.[30]

By September, antitrust legislation in Congress was a confusing mess, but that did not exempt Frick from more committee appearances. The House was considering six versions of the bill Celler had proposed the previous year, bringing baseball under limited antitrust scrutiny. A seventh bill exempted all professional sports from antitrust laws. Kefauver had withdrawn his bill and had introduced a second one, which did not mention baseball, but still provided other sports more freedom other antitrust law. This bill would level the playing field between baseball and other sports, Kefauver said, while giving Congress more time to deal with baseball.[31]

Testifying before the House, Frick found himself battling broadcasting executives who complained that proposed blackout rules were excessive and unfairly denied major league baseball to too many viewers. They also denied that baseball was responsible for the minor league's problems. In retreat before committee members who seemed to side with the broadcasters, Frick still pushed for limited blackout authority.[32]

Frick was summoned back before the House subcommittee two days later to answer questions about the Continental League, whose establishment and survival would allay Congress's concerns that baseball was unnecessarily blocking expansion. Frick testified that the league would need a few years to get on its feet, and that limitations imposed by antitrust laws would impede its growth. No further action was taken on any of the House bills, and Kefauver's second bill was reported favorably to the Senate Judiciary Committee, where it would be considered the next year, though Keating had indicated his opposition to it.[33]

As the 1959 World Series progressed, Senators owner Calvin Griffith re-launched trial balloons to move the national pastime from the nation's capital to Minneapolis. Frick stated his opposition to the move and his inability to do anything about it. Still, his words were uncharacteristically strong. He said, "Cronin agrees with me that Griffith's plan should be knocked in the head for the good of baseball." Frick noted that the Senators had been a profitable team, but Griffith simply wanted to make more money, and he implicitly criticized Griffith's management: "If Griffith can't operate successfully in Washington, a fine baseball town, how can we assume he can operate well in Minneapolis after the novelty wears off?" The Senators owner simply stated the attitude of the owners for years when he replied, "Frick doesn't have a vote. We don't have to pay any attention to him."[34]

Griffith ultimately decided to stay in Washington, at least for the 1960 season. He canvassed his fellow American League owners and realized he lacked the votes he thought he had after a similar survey a couple of weeks earlier. Sources credited Frick's opposition as a major factor. His argument against moving the team from a one-franchise city that also happened to be the nation's capital was convincing.[35]

By 1959, the major leagues were still struggling to meet the growing nationwide demand for top-tier baseball with 16 franchises, and the Continental League was a welcome, though risky, proposition. So the American League took the wheel and announced an intention to expand to ten teams in 1961, with Los Angeles and Minneapolis as the rumored additions. Frick was not in a commenting mood. "I'm not going to get into any controversy," he said. "I'm for expansion and I don't care how it's done." Shea felt the development undercut the Continental League's efforts. "They were supposed to cooperate with us," he said, "but here they are, going in the opposite direction, doing everything to impede us."[36]

Rickey knew exactly what was going on and sent Cronin a sharply worded telegram warning Cronin about meddling through his league's expansion plans and inviting him to visit Continental League cities, at the league's expense, to resolve "this confusion." Rickey demanded a meeting; what he got was a phone call from Frick. The commissioner proposed a meeting with Rickey (who was pleasantly surprised Frick would call him), but their schedules couldn't mesh. "Neither of us wants this thing to go haywire," Frick said. "You know what I mean by that." Rickey did.[37]

What transpired instead was a modern war of words for Frick, with Shea providing the firepower and Rickey the more statesman-like stature, though still infused with fire and vinegar. "Our founding cities agreed that vague promises of American League franchises had proved a surprisingly effective means of forestalling the early completion of Continental League membership," Shea said. A later statement added, "We sat down in good faith with these gentlemen and thought they had entered into a co-operative plan with us. Evidently, we were mistaken." With the verbal brawn of Churchill, Rickey discussed the worst-case scenario of major league expansion, which to him represented a repudiation of earlier promises to cooperate. "It would be a case of survival or surrender, and we propose to survive," he said. "In the event we were forced to undertake survival, it would be a quick and a more economical procedure."[38]

Frick was forced to assume both roles for major league baseball. "Up to now, I've tried not to say anything, and up to now I've succeeded fairly well, but I don't know how much longer I can hold out. Frankly, I cannot understand this continual sniping." He frequently repeated his pledge: "We will be happy to give the Continental League our blessings as soon as it is prepared to organize in a manner that conforms to the standards that we and the Continental League have agreed on."[39] To Rickey, no doubt, it was a familiar scenario: Frick insincerely outlined a rational meta-proposal, while the owners did whatever they micro-wanted. And the fans munched popcorn while the sportswriters posted the daily battles.

At the December meetings, expansion imploded. The National League owners declared that they were not interested in expansion "at the present time" and cast their lot with the Continental League plan. The American League owners wanted to add only one franchise, in Minneapolis, with a ninth NL franchise in New York and interleague games for the odd men out. Perhaps that curious, impractical idea, rather than the concept of ten-team expansion itself, caused the owners to hit the pause button.[40]

Frick noted the implications for the new league. "Now that the National and American Leagues have restated their positions as announced last May, the Continental League continues to have the opportunity of proceeding with its announced program," he said. "The commissioner looks forward to such positive action as will permit them to qualify for major league status."[41]

Even Congress was drawn into the Rickey vs. Frick popularity contest. On January 5, Rickey visited in Washington with Keating, who promised his support, legislatively and personally, for the new league's efforts.[42] So of course Frick scurried to the capital the next week for his own face time with the senator. The commissioner reiterated his support for the new league's efforts, as long as they were conducted within the conditions outlined by the owners. Keating offered to serve as an unofficial mediator, realizing that any role in enhancing the national pastime would also enhance his stature as a possible Republican vice presidential nominee.[43] Frick was stung. "Mediator of what?" he asked his press box friend, Daniel. "Is there any dispute that requires mediation? Have Rickey and Shea abolished my job as commissioner?"[44]

As part of his lobbying, Frick accepted a speaking engagement at the Washington Touchdown Club, but failed to score points. Frick spoke strongly, recalling his many appearances before Congressional committees. "I hope Congressman Celler and Senator Kefauver are as tired of seeing me as I am of testifying," he said. Then he added, "Expansion is coming, but it will not come by fiat, by pressure or by the threat of legislation." In the audience, Kefauver was not impressed, declared to a reporter that Frick had "disparaged Congress," and said, "He did not help baseball."[45]

Frick and Rickey started meeting in February to make the process more face-to-face. The meetings were more arcane process, with moments of fiery talk. Crucial topics like minor league territorial demands or player drafts were off the table, Frick said, until the league met the stated stipulations. He launched into a lengthy, dry review of those requirements.[46] At one such meeting, Rickey recalled, "I tried somewhat desperately to get a word in edgewise. He was voluble beyond understanding.... Finally, I said, 'Will you let me say a word?'"[47] At the end of this particular meeting, Frick said to Rickey, "You've got a tough job. I don't know whether you can do it or not." Rickey shot back, "Don't try to scare me."[48]

For Frick's leagues, there was much more good news. Soon after this meeting, Frick announced another renewal of the television contract for the All-Star Game and World Series. The new agreement increased the annual rights fee from $3.25 million to $3.75 million, an increase of 15 percent, with a $250,000 fee for a second All-Star Game. It included a renegotiation clause if a third major league began play. Although the player representatives were not present at the press conference announcing the new contracts, they reportedly approved.[49]

But television was not all rewards for baseball. Just a few months after the contracts were announced, Frick was given a script for an upcoming drama, "Black Sox Scandal," which would open the fall season of the "Du Pont Show of the Month" for CBS on September 30. Frick reportedly did not like the script, but his concerns were temporarily addressed when the segment had to be canceled because one of the former players (later identified as Eddie Cicotte), would not consent to his name being used.[50] Although producer David Susskind insisted that Cicotte had blocked the project, criticism centered on Frick, who was portrayed as using strong-arm tactics, as custodian of a popular CBS content source, to censor television drama. In that vein, he did indeed function as a czar making arbitrary decisions.[51]

Four weeks later, the Black Sox scandal drama re-emerged, literally, as CBS announced that a new series, "The Witness," would focus on "Shoeless Joe" Jackson and not mention Cicotte or any other surviving White Sox players.[52] "The Witness" was a live, unscripted program that would simulate hearings involving well-known criminals from the past: Lucky Luciano, Al Capone, Ma Barker, and even Huey Long. A committee of actors would question a guest performer portraying the personality of the week.[53]

The Shoeless Joe episode of "The Witness" was broadcast on January 28, 1961. By all accounts, the format did not work; Lee Allen, historian for the Baseball Hall of Fame, called it "a production horrible beyond belief."[54] Interviewed after the broadcast by *New York World-Telegram* columnist Joe Williams, Frick admitted that he had not watched the show and had not been alerted to its scheduling by CBS. "Not that they would be obligated to," he said. "We have no authority in this field, other than to see that our games are properly presented. It is our right, however, to protest against misrepresentation and falsification, and this we do, most vehemently." Frick did have a theory as to why it was broadcast in January rather than the fall. "My guess would be the economic climate is less hazardous now," he said. "When I took the matter up with them originally, some important sports programs had yet to be negotiated. They may have feared repercussions."[55]

The show itself was replaced midseason. The only long-term effect of the controversy was that the screenwriter on both projects, Eliot Asinof, was sufficiently attracted to the subject matter that two years later, he would publish *Eight Men Out*, considered one of the best baseball books ever.[56]

Although still early in his second term, Frick had been considering retirement, columnist Dick Young claimed. Young reported that Frick originally planned to retire in 1959, but abandoned the idea to see baseball through expansion and Congressional action related to broadcast regulation.[57] Soon after, Frick confirmed those plans to his good friend, Dan Daniel, but later rather than sooner. He said he planned to take both leagues to 12 teams and get Congress to pass legislation allowing baseball and other sports more freedom in developing broadcasting policy. "Then Mrs. Frick and I will start our travels around the world," he said.[58]

As the Continental League set about putting together its minor league system, it found out just how technical Frick's technicalities would be. Frick at first vetoed an agreement between the new league and the Class D Western Carolina League, because the new teams had not yet been approved as organized baseball teams.[59] The league was ready to play a 112-game schedule in 1960 under its Continental parent, which was not scheduled to inaugurate play until 1961. Frick did not like the "innovative" (Rickey's word) concept of a league-to-league agreement.[60]

The Continental League was forced to withdraw temporarily, and the Western Carolina League returned to organized baseball.[61] Rickey once again involved Congress, inviting two senators (including Kefauver) to discuss the situation with Frick. Kefauver reminded the commissioner that Congress was looking closely at baseball's monopolistic practices.[62] Duly threatened, Frick suggested that each WCL team apply to baseball as an independent club, and then the teams could set up arrangements with the Continental League.[63] By May, the WCL and CL acquiesced with Frick's wishes, setting up working agreements between each minor and major league team (pending those teams actually playing, of course).[64]

Shea once again complained about Frick's obstructionist tactics and threatened to call on Congress for help.[65] Frick discounted Shea's complaints. "I wonder if it wouldn't help a little if we had fewer complaints, less alibi-ing, and a little more positive action," he said.[66] In Los Angeles for World Series ceremonies, Frick and the Dodgers' brass cited as an example the Continental League's refusal to accept the Dodgers' terms for taking over the Dodgers' Montreal franchise ($150,000 up front, $75,000/year in stadium rental), because it was "excessive."[67]

An April 1960 vote by the New York City Board of Estimate, authorizing the construction of a baseball stadium in Flushing Meadows and the issuance of bonds to pay for it, brought the Continental League's plans for a New York franchise that much closer to fruition. Frick was impressed. "It's a good thing, a fine move toward the realization of the Continental League," he said. Most observers agreed that the league had made important progress that would help the other franchises as well.[68]

In 1960, Kefauver introduced yet another bill, even though his bill and Keating's bill from the previous year were reported favorably. This bill also offered limited antitrust protection to pro sports, with a specific new wrinkle aimed at baseball. He limited the number of players who could be controlled by teams to 100, with all but 40 eligible to be drafted during the off-season. The limit was considered a favor to the Continental League, and Frick lashed out, claiming the bill "would eliminate minor league baseball."[69]

Kefauver claimed that major league teams unfairly controlled too many players, limiting athletes' ability to succeed. Frick and his supporters disputed Kefauver's claim that some teams had as many as 450 players under contract. Frick promised to fight what he called "a vicious piece of legislation," adding, "If we're operating illegally, send us to jail."[70]

Kefauver's subcommittee hearings on May 18–19 provided the fireworks expected and more. Rickey said, "Without this legislative clearance, there can never be any expansion of the game." Listing the many occasions when, in his opinion, Frick made promises and then broke them, Rickey claimed Kefauver's bill was necessary to "remove the power of money" that was controlling baseball. Without it, the subcommittee would be "a pallbearer at the funeral of professional baseball in America."[71]

Shea went further, telling committee members his league might be forced to "a raid, or some kind of a war over players' contracts." Speaking of major league owners, he added, "My thinking is that they are pushing us to such a point, to see whether we would have the courage to do it."[72] Frick gave his usual patient statement and unwavering testimony, demonstrating how the bill would ruin the structure baseball had built over the past century.[73]

The real star of the hearings was Edwin Johnson. Now a consultant for the Continental League, he ridiculed Frick as a puppet of the major league team owners. He also disputed the commissioner's claim that he was protecting the minor leagues. "During this commissioner's regime, the minor leagues have gone from universal prosperity to universal poverty—like a bum on skid row. Personally, I don't pay much attention to a doctor whose patients are all in the cemetery."[74] At the end, Frick, who considered him a friend, said, "Ed, I wouldn't take that from anyone but you."[75]

Kefauver's bill barely made it out of committee. Two amendments were proposed and defeated. One would have eliminated the section limiting roster protection and included baseball in the sports given limited antitrust protection. The other would have limited the draft of unprotected players to the American and National Leagues, thus minimizing the Continental League's rights. Although both amendments were defeated, the committee reported the bill to the Senate without recommendation.

As the Senate debated the bill, Frick and Rickey carried on their own debate in the press. Frick wired the senators and warned that the bill as amended confused the player development issues; it seemed to give the Continental League the right to draft off major league rosters, while being exempt from other such rules, such as signing high school players. Rickey accused Frick of threatening the senators. Frick denied that; *The Sporting News* compliantly ran the text of his telegram verbatim.[76]

The amendment including baseball with the sports getting limited antitrust protection passed in the Senate, but immediately thereafter, Colorado Senator John Carroll, a Continental League supporter with a franchise in his state, moved to recommit the bill to the Judiciary Committee, to study it further. Carroll might have hoped that would result in a bill more to his faction's liking. Assigning it to committee limbo had the opposite effect: The bill was never heard from again.[77]

Frick, informed of the development by a sportswriter in Philadelphia, said, "That's the best news I've heard in a long time." That the bill being studied provided baseball with equal antitrust protection "was exactly what we wanted."[78] Rickey was disappointed but clear in his strategy: If the bill did not pass at the next session and negotiations with baseball continued as they had been, his league would operate independently beginning in 1961. If the bill did pass, the league would open play in 1962, to allow time to work out the details with organized baseball.[79]

Frick continued his crusade against gamblers in his second term. During the 1958 season, he confirmed that he had put together a team of investigators to stamp out gambling in major league baseball. The staff members focused on fans as much as players and cooperated with local police in attacking offenses.[80]

In his memoirs, Frick identified former federal agent Buck Greene as the point man for his anti-gambling crusade. "His appointment was never publicly announced, but his identity became known to many officials and players," he wrote. Frick said Greene presented statistics showing that in 15 years of working in cooperation with local law enforcement, Greene was responsible for 839 arrests—usually in and around ballparks.[81]

When Detroit outfielder Al Kaline announced an investment in a horse racing stable, Frick declined action until he had all the facts, but the lack of a ringing endorsement was clear. After team president Bill DeWitt explicitly expressed his displeasure, Kaline withdrew his investment. "My life is baseball and I don't want to embarrass anybody," he said.[82]

Vic Power of the Indians also got Frick's attention after he joked with a broadcaster about playing in the second All-Star Game after pleading heat exhaustion in the first one. But his joke, "I'll bet you $100 [AL manager Al Lopez] doesn't play me in the second game," did not sit well with Frick, who grilled Power on the exchange almost immediately, at the second game. Power was cleared of both gambling and loafing.[83]

Frick did not confine his efforts to the players. His investigators uncovered gambling in the bleachers at Chicago's Wrigley Field. They turned the information over to Chicago police, who conducted an undercover investigation of their own. Twenty fans were arrested in a fifth-inning sweep of a July 23 game. The operation was so efficient that many fans didn't realize what was going on.[84]

A convicted gambler in Philadelphia who claimed to have lent money to baseball players presented Frick with a more ominous challenge. The information emerged at the trial of café owner Harold Friedman, who had been convicted of attempting to bribe former Phillies pitcher Humberto Robinson the year before.[85] Friedman produced a letter, allegedly from a player, thanking him for a loan. The district attorney in the case forwarded the details to Phillies general manager John Quinn, with a request that he inform the commissioner. Frick acknowledged the letters and promised to investigate, though he would not comment further.[86] This was consistent with Frick's usual handling of such issues; either he found the letter to lack credibility or he discussed the issue with the players privately.

The suspension of NFL players Alex Karras and Paul Hornung for gambling in 1963 did not concern Frick. He felt his office took the necessary precautions to head off trouble. He acknowledged individual private conferences with players and frequent warnings to avoid certain locations and individuals. "But never once has there ever been an accusation of any ball player throwing a game or betting against his own team during the 12 years I have been commissioner," he said, knocking on the top of his desk.[87]

When it involved owners, however, Frick was far less concerned. John Galbreath, owner of the Pirates, owned a thoroughbred racehorse farm; one of his horses, Chateaugay, won the 1963 Kentucky Derby. Yankees owner Del Webb built casinos, and he even held a mortgage on one. Frick tried to point out the particular challenges for the player in directly affecting the quality of the game, thus requiring greater vigilance. To many fans and media, the main distinction seemed to be that the owners were his bosses.[88]

The worst news for the Continental League came out of the 1960 All-

14. The Third League

Star meetings, when the National League owners voted to expand to ten teams for the 1962 season. *The Sporting News* made the right call: new franchises in New York and Texas, either Houston or Dallas. The *New York Times* predicted teams in New York and either Toronto or Minneapolis, with Houston and Los Angeles speculated as joining the American League, which had announced no expansion plans. Frick acknowledged the expansion talk, without specifics. "The National League vote clears the air," he said. "It does two things. It makes expansion a reality and it also gives the Continental League a chance to qualify if it fulfills its obligations to baseball."[89]

Some praised Frick's approach to expansion. He had been calling for it for years, but it took the prospect of a third major league and several visits to Congress before the owners caught up with him. "It's probably better this way," he said. "You know, when you try to blackjack folks into doing what you know is good for them, you win no thanks for yourself. Let them find out the hard way and they are all satisfied." Such an approach can also be evidence of weak leadership, but it was Frick's consistent philosophy.[90]

The strategy also resulted in the demise of the Continental League. Rickey and Shea met with the major league expansion committee. As the negotiations once again dragged on, Braves owner Lou Perini changed the game. He asked Shea and Rickey if they would accept four of their teams being the four expansion franchises. A brief caucus later, they agreed, and the Continental League was no more. The plans called for New York and Houston going to the National League and Toronto and Minneapolis–St. Paul to the American, with the other four franchises promised primary consideration for future expansion.[91]

The American League owners were not so keen on the four-up transfer. They had their eyes on Los Angeles as an expansion target, and it was not part of the Continental League. Yankees owner Dan Topping, seeking some leverage with the National League's pending expansion into his city, pressed Frick to declare Los Angeles "open territory" for a second franchise. Frick concurred, saying, "I believe Los Angeles to be just as much entitled to a second club. People should get as much baseball as they will support."[92] That would enable Topping to swing a New York/NL for Los Angeles/AL quid pro quo, should it come to a vote. As the AL would later discover, Frick's sentiments on what was and wasn't open territory would not be enough to justify a move to Los Angeles.

On October 17, 1960, the National League made it official, adding franchises in New York and Houston, both former Continental League members, for the 1962 season.⁹³ It was not surprising that the National League announced its expansion while Frick was vacationing in Puerto Rico, showing his support for Caribbean baseball by throwing out the first pitch at the San Juan team's winter league opener.⁹⁴

The American League announced its expansion plans on October 27. The National League might have grabbed the initiative and the two most attractive Continental League franchises, but Cronin and his owners had a counter-strike of their own. First, the AL expansion would take place in 1961, just a few months away, not 1962. Minneapolis-St. Paul did end up with a team, in a convoluted swap that allowed Griffith to move his Washington team to Minnesota, but kept Congress happy by immediately locating another franchise there. The second franchise, however, ignored the Continentals and targeted the open territory of Los Angeles.⁹⁵

Frick again was an interested spectator. "I haven't seen anything officially yet," he said. "There are so many angles to be considered, such as ball parks and what to do regarding players, that I cannot make any comment until I have talked to the people involved officially."⁹⁶

Oliver Kuechle, sports editor for the *Milwaukee Journal*, expressed the frequent sentiment toward this and other examples of Frick's leadership style. "Can anybody imagine Judge Landis in his days as commissioner taking such a helpless position?" he wrote. Kuechle was troubled by remarks that reflected Frick's lack of involvement with the process. "Ford Frick, as commissioner of baseball, should have been in on the ground floor on any discussions which involved expansion," he wrote. "What can be more crazy than to expand as the American League has with the start of the next season less than six months away?"⁹⁷

Continental League franchises feeling jilted were of no concern to Frick. He was told that the American League owners had considered the priority for former CL franchises as a recommendation and voted it down. His greater concern was the AL's compressed expansion schedule—especially as it related to a more complicated November 28 free agent draft that would include ten franchises from one league and eight from the other.⁹⁸

Frick's involvement at this point would deepen, particularly for the American League. While the National League had a year and a half to integrate two franchises with established owners, the American League was starting from scratch in one-third of the time. The authority for qualifying owners in time for the free agent draft fell to him.⁹⁹

Frick expressed those concerns to the two league presidents at a meeting on November 1, when the commissioner began slogging through the details. Giles and Cronin promised to work together on future expansion decisions. "Baseball can't afford not to let its right hand know what its left hand is doing," Frick said. "If the leagues go off at tangents, they might get at arm's length, and build up feeling that would not be in the best interests of cities which hope to become major." Frick ruled that the new AL teams would be ineligible for the November 28 draft, because they had not been in existence for a year, as the rules stated, but he also predicted the owners would allow extra considerations to help them out.[100] He also froze AL rosters until after the draft, to prevent teams from dumping marginal players on the new teams to free up roster space.[101]

Frick made a similar move in 1961, when the National League expansion draft was held, though with the more relaxed time frame. The draft was held right after the season ended, rather than in December.[102] One drawback of the earlier expansion draft date was that it took place before the annual free agent draft, when teams would unload their less desirable players. Thus, the owners were allowed to dump those players into their expansion draft allotment, making the talent pool for Houston and New York a lot shallower, as those teams' subsequent performance would demonstrate.

The risks of Frick's hands-off strategy became apparent soon after the amicable Giles-Cronin meeting, as National League dissatisfaction with the American League became clear. Los Angeles had invited O'Malley and the NL to their city; the AL showed up later, uninvited. O'Malley had paid to indemnify the Pacific Coast League and to make the Coliseum a temporary baseball park; the AL showed up later.[103] Plus, the compressed time frame seemed designed to rush everyone past the difficult details. Perhaps if Frick had been involved in the planning from the start, these problems could have been avoided. Instead, it was left to him to scramble, jetting cross-country for quick turnaround trips to clean up the AL's mess.[104]

Frick was creating his own obstructionist rumblings, threatening to block all expansion until the owners amended Rule One, which barred any team from entering another's territory without the unanimous consent of all teams in both leagues. At least one "no" vote on the AL's move into LA could be expected, so Frick was adamant on the rule change preceding any expansion-related decisions.[105]

O'Malley enjoyed watching the American League squirm in the corner it had painted itself into, and created a tighter squeeze when he announced his opposition to a second Los Angeles team. His leverage in negotiating was strengthened by Frick, who agreed with O'Malley's demands.[106] With Griffith having vacated Washington for Minneapolis, and an owners' syndicate approved for the replacement franchise, the AL entered full scramble mode, suggesting a nine-team league in 1961 with interleague play. The catch was that the National League would also have to jump to a ninth team, with Houston the likely choice to enter a year early.[107]

The American League owners were not pleased with Frick's reluctance to allow them to expand so quickly and pushed back. They expressed their anger at a November 16 meeting; Webb wondered if it was Frick's business to intervene before the proposal was ready. Though angry and eager for Cronin to express their displeasure, they also agreed to wait on accepting a Los Angeles ownership bid until the situation with O'Malley could be resolved.[108]

So Frick intervened even more. First, he brought Cronin and Giles to his office for two days of meetings to craft acceptable amendments to Rule One—with concessions to O'Malley as part of the acceptability test. Those concessions included a payment to O'Malley of $450,000 and an agreement that the new franchise would play in Wrigley Field, not the Coliseum, for its first two years.[109]

The traveling drama moved to St. Louis for the December league meetings. First, the National League officially scuttled the American League's nine-team plan. Even an offer from the Yankees to have the NL New York franchise enter a year early and play in Yankee Stadium did not sufficiently sweeten the pot. Then a group of owners led by Gene Autry, "the singing cowboy," was approved for the AL California franchise. O'Malley realized that if push ever did come to shove, Frick would side with the AL's amendment to Rule One that would enable a ten-team AL for 1961.[110]

Thus it was resolved at the major leagues' joint meeting on December 7. The owners unanimously agreed to an amendment to Rule One that Frick endorsed for the long term. It provided that a new franchise seeking to share territory pay the team already there half of its original location costs plus $100,000. That would net O'Malley a reverse housewarming gift of more than $300,000 from his new neighbors. The National League owners then joined the American League in approving the AL's plans for 1961.[111]

Frick realized the kindness O'Malley had extended by saving Frick the awkwardness of publicly siding with one league—in other words, taking a stand—and publicly acknowledged his help. "If it hadn't been for the cooperation of Walter O'Malley, baseball would have been in one of the damnedest messes ever seen," he said.[112]

14. The Third League

In his version of a post-game interview, Frick confirmed his leadership style. First, he revealed that once in St. Louis, he had withdrawn from the negotiations and allowed the two league's owners to work it out for themselves, keeping him informed. He also insisted that he "never was on the spot." To his view, the owners were and had responded to the challenge.[113]

Frick also worked with Giles and Cronin to negotiate a rule change allowing the new National League teams to establish farm systems for the 1961 season to begin developing talent, an arrangement banned under the existing rules. The rule change was approved by a mail vote, which Frick preferred to a special meeting. "I'm all for avoiding any meetings at this time if at all possible," he said. "These meetings have the darnedest way of kicking up fresh trouble when you least expect it and putting us right back with a problem on our hands."[114]

15

Expansion

If there was one issue where Frick's silence and lack of input was unforgivable, it was the continued lack of integrated housing in Florida during spring training. Some of the nicer hotels in cities like Bradenton and St. Petersburg, reluctant to offend their wealthy Old South patrons, would refuse to allow African American players to stay at their hotels and even gladly direct them and their teams elsewhere.[1]

In January 1961, Wendell Smith re-entered the fray. The African American journalist, who had championed Jackie Robinson's entry into the majors, published a column decrying the lack of progress in integrating Florida spring training. Titled "Spring Training Woes," it described the humiliation most African American players faced in Florida. Some hotels even banned the players from *visiting* their teammates at the "whites only" hotels. Factor in segregated restaurants, and it was obvious: the main thing tolerated in Florida was institutionalized racism.[2]

The absurdity reached its height when the St. Petersburg Chamber of Commerce sponsored a "Salute to Baseball" breakfast in March 1961, and African American players were excluded from the invitation list. City and team officials claimed that the slight was unintended, but to those players, it was consistent with the treatment they endured in Jim Crow Florida.[3]

The Sporting News dusted off its pre-integration tone in addressing the discrimination. "Baseball has not sidestepped any issue and, in fact, has been a leader in the fight to end segregation," an editorial stated. "At the same time, we do not believe that baseball is under any obligation to be a crusader or martyr in this issue." Dan Daniel, in a column, tried to offer the clumsy argument that African American players were better off than their counterparts 50 years earlier, who endured much worse conditions at a time when baseball was not as popular.[4]

Speaking to the Bradenton Chamber of Commerce—in the very city that would not allow Hank Aaron to stay with his teammates—Frick left the moment unseized. He said the segregation problem affecting spring training "will solve itself." He reminded his audience, "Baseball has shown the way toward integration, and too much publicity will set it back."[5] Frick's stated policy as commissioner, which could be evaluated as official policy, was for teams to "not become involved in any sort of controversial racial or religious question."[6] It was a cowardly and disappointing retreat from a man who had spoken so forcefully toward his own players 14 years previous.

The state Chamber of Commerce got involved where Frick wouldn't, soon after spring training. Its Professional Baseball Committee, sensing a growing mess if segregated housing caused the state to lose its attractiveness as a spring training site to Arizona, passed a resolution urging the communities involved to work out the problems as quickly as possible.[7]

Even Robert Cannon, labeled as a do-nothing players' attorney, was more proactive on the issue of segregation than Frick and the owners were. At a mid-season players' meeting, Cannon revealed, the players approved a letter expressing their concerns. The attorney also said "there might be more certain clubs could do" in ending segregation in player housing. Another evidence of player initiative on race issues was the involvement of two African American player representatives—one of them Bill White of the Cardinals, future president of the National League.[8]

Testifying before the Senate Commerce Committee in 1963, Frick claimed that all such segregation problems had been pretty much solved—not only spring training accommodations, but also minor league limitations in Southern states that banned interracial sporting events. "Baseball today is completely integrated," he told the committee.[9]

Frick praised the example of Little Rock, Arkansas, which had repealed its law against interracial teams. He did not address the plight of Richie Allen, the first African American player for the city's Phillies farm team. Allen was still banned from eating in a restaurant with his white teammates and had to endure racial epithets from fans in the stands and from protest signs, as well as threatening messages left on his car.[10]

Although a *Sporting News* editorial gushed over Frick's performance,[11] columnists like John Drebinger of the *New York Times*, who had witnessed the attitudes toward players like Allen over the years following integration, sarcastically noted, "He could have laid it on a bit thicker."[12] Drebinger, unfortunately, was likewise mistaken on the more recent history; his column on the return of minor league baseball to Little Rock emphasized the surface positive (integrated grandstands) and ignored the deeper racial hatred-generated threats that would plague African American players for decades.[13]

The second 1961 All-Star Game in Boston didn't help the two-game faction. Rain forced Frick to call the game after nine innings, leaving a 1–1 tie. Even Yankees ace Whitey Ford pleaded with him during a rain delay, "You got to call it, Mr. Commissioner. The fast ball doesn't hop in this kind of weather." Frick did call the game only 30 minutes after the rain delay, leaving fans grumbling, particularly when the skies cleared an hour later.[14]

The game was memorable to Frick's grandson, Ford II, for another reason: He ended up with a foul ball hit into the commissioner's box. Frick was eager for his grandson to share baseball experiences, and having the game in Boston—where his son, Frederick, lived and worked—provided such an opportunity. Frick's top assistant, Charley Segar, actually caught the foul ball and turned it over to the boy. That didn't stop young Ford from boasting about how he had caught the ball to the driver of the limo the box party shared, drawing a humorous correction from Segar.[15]

Frick the grandfather was eager to provide such opportunities for both of his grandkids to experience his beloved game, with unique benefits and experiences. Ford Frick II remembers the 1959 Hall of Fame ceremony, when his grandfather sent him to the game in the care of Ty Cobb—a prospect that contradicts modern images of the baseball legend. Ford's sister, Kelly Frick Richards, also remembers accompanying Cobb and Frankie Frisch to the Hall of Fame games—complete with player critiques, off-color jokes, and quick apologies by the "babysitters."[16]

On August 28, Frick appeared yet again before the House Antitrust Subcommittee. The topic was the landmark Sports Broadcasting Act of 1961, which allowed professional sports organizations like the NFL to negotiate television contracts without violating antitrust laws. The law was spearheaded by Pete Rozelle, the dynamic, young, second-year commissioner of the National Football League. His league's new television contract with CBS had been blocked by U.S. District Judge Allen Grim, who ruled that the contract fell under a similar ruling he had issued in 1953. Rozelle chose Congress over the Supreme Court as the way to fix it. He chose well.

For all his stated preferences for such a law, Frick did not play a major role, either at the subcommittee hearing or in its actual passage. At that point, individual major league teams handled their own television contracts. Frick had sought legislative help on blackout policies, particularly

15. Expansion

to protect the minor leagues earlier. But for these particular hearings, his appearance was brief and later in the day. He acknowledged that baseball might be interested in such arrangements, but for the time being, the bill had his support mainly because it explicitly protected baseball's antitrust status.[17]

All in all, it took Congress only 72 days to consider and pass the law allowing league-wide television contracts.[18] The Sports Broadcasting Act sailed through the House and Senate Judiciary Committees and was passed by voice vote on September 30, 1961—yet another sign of the growing influence of televised sports. In terms of the current status of television sports rights—a multibillion-dollar phenomenon affecting sports at all levels—it stands as one of the most important pieces of sports legislation ever passed by Congress.

In retrospect, the law did more than provide Rozelle and the NFL with a means of explosive financial success. As Rozelle's profile rose, Frick's suffered by comparison. With the new television contract and his successful

Frick (left) with NFL Commissioner Pete Rozelle and NBA Commissioner J. Walter Kennedy (right) (National Baseball Hall of Fame Library, Cooperstown, New York).

lobbying of Congress, the 35-year-old Rozelle had captured the media's attention. Frick, at 67, seemed more hidebound. As the major league expansion plans settled into 20-team game action, following two years of owner-induced drama, Frick seemed content to allow baseball forces to play themselves out for the time being. He spent much of his time tinkering with a minor league reorganization proposal. His interviews about baseball carried the urgency of a board game or hobby.

Given those contrasting styles, sports journalists openly wondered if football would soon supplant baseball as the most popular sport among fans. An Associated Press poll found sports writers and broadcasters evenly split on the issue. "I'm not alarmed that pro football is going to take baseball's place," Frick said. "Actually, baseball has more than doubled its attendance in the last 20 years, so why should people say we are slipping?" His interviewer did not challenge his use of attendance during World War II as a benchmark. The commissioner did agree that the game needed "pepping up." His prescription: "fewer delays and home runs."[19]

He performed similar mathematical gymnastics in comparing attendance figures for the previous 34 years. Frick split the period in half and pointed out that total attendance had more than doubled—from almost 150,000,000 to more than 300,000,000. Again, that the earlier split (1929–1945) included the Depression and World War II, and the later split encompassed the postwar economic boom, was not addressed. Instead, he crowed, "Anybody looking at these figures who says people are losing interest in baseball just doesn't know what he is talking about."[20]

Frick also hyped increases in participation. Little League started just after World War II in Pennsylvania. By 1964, almost two million boys were playing Little League baseball. Similar gains were seen in American Legion, Babe Ruth, Colt, and Pony Leagues. Over the same period, high school baseball had grown from 4,000 to 13,530 teams, he claimed, with more than 700 college teams beyond that.[21]

A fellow veteran, Joe King of the *New York World Telegram*, penned yet another appraisal that affirmed Frick's leadership style. "Technically, Ford has no more jurisdiction to form baseball policy than the general manager of, say, International Harvester, who is hired to administer the policy defined by his board of directors." He also praised Frick's preference to table a proposal that the two leagues disagreed on, rather than cast the tie-breaking vote, as was his organizational responsibility.[22]

Frick still had to step in from time to time, for the whimsical as much as the arcane. He fined Casey Stengel $500 for appearing in a Rheingold beer ad wearing his baseball uniform, which violated policy. Frick ordered

15. Expansion

a stop to the ads, which featured Stengel in a bunting pose in front of an attractive model. "If Casey is going to teach bunting, he should be a little more careful to keep his eye on the ball. It's behind him in the picture," Frick quipped.[23]

Frick also contributed to another icon's legacy when Stan Musial announced his retirement. He suggested that Musial's Hall of Fame plaque should read, "Here stands baseball's happy warrior; here stands baseball's perfect knight." Those words now adorn Musial's statue outside of Busch Stadium in St. Louis.[24]

The 1961 home run outbreak had led to a revival of the spitball debate. Frick was not late to that game, but this time around he picked up a strategic ally: Joe Cronin. "There's nothing bad or dangerous about the spitter," Cronin said. "I had to bat against both and I'll tell you a good knuckleball is much harder to hit than a spitball."[25] Cronin encouraged the Rules Committee to bring the pitch back.[26] Frick added his endorsement for the rule change, which would be considered by the committee at its next meeting, as requested by Chicago White Sox general manager Ed Short. Frick in particular liked it as a weapon in psychological warfare. "The most effective spitball is the one that the pitcher doesn't throw," he said. "The threat of a pitcher throwing a 'spitter' and going through the motions leading up to it promises to keep the batter from digging in at the plate."[27]

The Rules Committee dismissed Frick's and Cronin's idea by an 8–1 vote, with Cal Hubbard, American League supervisor of umpires, casting the only ballot in favor. Calvin Griffith, Twins owner, had stated his support for the change earlier but retreated to the majority when it was time to be counted.[28] Committee chairman Jim Gallagher did acknowledge complaints by pitchers about the shrinking strike zone but said it was not discussed, and a proposal to expand home plate from 17 to 19 inches was defeated.[29]

Some felt that Frick was angling for a reconsideration of the spitball rule, or at least more control over the process, when he named his secretary-treasurer, Segar, as chair of the Official Rules Committee in October 1962.[30] *The Sporting News* applauded the appointment, noting his reputation as "a thorough student of the game to the point of being a stickler for adherence to the rules." The editorial acknowledged the possibility that Segar's day job would present a conflict of interest at times: "a remote possibility, but it is worth considering."[31]

A year later, in lieu of the spitball, Segar and the rules committee complied with Frick's desire to help pitchers by expanding the strike zone for the 1963 season. It had been shrunk in 1950 to "between the batter's armpits and the top of his knees." The more spacious strike zone added as much as 12 inches to the zone by returning it to its earlier dimensions: "between the top of the batter's shoulders and his knees when he assumes a natural stance."[32]

The new zone did its job. Frick's office released statistics that showed strikeouts increased by about six percent, while walks decreased by about 12 percent. A serendipitous consequence of the change was reflected in a decreased game length of six minutes in the National League and 12 minutes in the American League.[33]

Even after the 1958 realignment, it had become obvious that additional, more drastic work would be necessary to stabilize the minor leagues. In 1961, Frick began to float a proposal that would reduce the number of classifications. The minor league teams were resistant at first, and the committee working on it was stalemated.[34]

On May 18, 1962, Frick and his committee were ready to present their minor league realignment plan. It reduced the number of classifications from six to three, with 100 teams competing in 15 leagues (from a high of 438 teams competing in 59 leagues soon after World War II), starting with the 1963 season. For a nostalgic conservative like Frick, it must have been painful legislating out of existence the small-town baseball he cherished, but such was the new reality.

"We approved a broad, general plan to stabilize a sound minor league system, adequate to take care of our player development needs," Frick said after the meeting where the owners unanimously adopted the plan. He promised a more detailed matrix, with leagues, teams, and affiliations identified, by the December meetings.[35]

Another potential casualty of the reorganization was the National Association, which had overseen minor league baseball for decades. It was rumored that at the December meetings, the association would be abolished and the minor leagues brought under the commissioner's office. Frick would not comment on that, preferring to avoid the issue until the actual plan was ready and in place, to avoid distractions.[36]

The plan was praised for bringing stability to a minor league system whose entrepreneurial yet random style had clicked in an earlier time, but proved chaotic when discipline was needed.[37] For Frick, it provided evidence of the strong leadership and vision he supposedly lacked. But in a television age, the majors had the public's attention. Only five sports writers covered the Chicago meetings where the plan was adopted[38]—also evidence of the contraction that was beginning to confront the newspaper industry.

The farm system directors were not as impressed by the plan. When Segar presented it at a special September meeting of the minor league leaders, they threw it back. It was not a good idea to leave them out of the loop during the plan's development. After rejecting it, they formed their own committee to come up with a better plan.[39]

The realignment plan was passed at the December 1962 meetings. It retained Frick's idea for three minor league classifications (AAA, AA, and A) instead of six, eliminating the B, C, and D levels. It called for 104 clubs instead of the 100 that Frick proposed. Making the deal more palatable was the majors' offer to pick up almost all player development costs, leaving the minor league teams to cover mainly their local administration costs, an investment valued at upwards of $10 million per year.[40]

By the next season, it was obvious that the AAA level could not support three leagues, and the American Association was forced to disband temporarily. In the midst of the turmoil, George Trautman, long-time president of the minor leagues association, died on June 24,[41] and although vice president Frank Shaughnessy was named acting president, the minor league owners clearly looked to Frick for leadership. Frick, ignoring the earlier rebuff, responded with a framework for the 20 AAA teams involved that would scrap the two ten-team leagues and replace them with a geographically sound 12-and-eight split, emphasizing reduced travel costs.

Frick tried to keep his plan secret until it was approved, but it was later revealed. Dallas-Forth Worth and Oklahoma City would leave the Pacific Coast League (which would also make geographic sense) and join the International League in a Southern Division that would include Richmond, Jacksonville, Atlanta, and Little Rock. The Northern Division would comprise current IL franchises in Syracuse, Buffalo, Toronto, Rochester, Indianapolis, and Columbus. The PCL would be left with Denver, Seattle, Spokane, Tacoma, San Diego, Portland, Hawaii, and Salt Lake City.[42]

As usual, the minor league owners fussed and deadlocked until the last minute before finally accepting Frick's 12-and-eight plan, with one change: The PCL grew to 12 teams, adding Little Rock and Indianapolis, and the International League returned to its preferred size of eight teams. The PCL also adopted Frick's suggestion for geographic sanity, forming two six-team divisions to reduce travel costs.[43]

Expansion underway, Frick predicted more to come, and soon, forecasting 24 major league teams by 1965 and a realignment of the minor leagues. "I can see three cities ready for the majors right now," he said. He declined to name the candidates, "because I get into trouble with those I leave out."[44] Frick felt that the ten-team leagues would prove inefficient and would affect the caliber of play, making expansion to 12 teams more of a necessity.[45] He also thought future expansions would work more easily, given the leagues' pledge to work together more than they did in 1960.

The apparent success of expansion had the team owners wanting more and publicly pushing Frick to expand to 12-team leagues as soon as possible, even by 1964. In his usual style, Frick deferred to the owners on that, though he warned that expansion required time. While Frick liked the idea of six-team divisions, he didn't want more than one extra round of playoffs. "In the meantime, let's digest what we have eaten before tackling another dinner," he cautioned. "Let us plan carefully, so that we make no mistakes in the next expansion move."[46]

The owners ignored Frick's call for expansion proactivity, so he became more direct after the December meetings, challenging them to at least come up with a plan that would avoid the shoddy approach in 1960. "I am a firm believer in an organized and definite procedure so far as possible," he said. "I am hopeful that the owners will get together within a short time and determine their expansion program."[47] His policy of leaving such initiatives to the owners meant, of course, that they would do nothing until years past Frick's retirement.

As technologies improved, Frick and his office were drawn into drama related to cheating accusations. It all started when the Associated Press ran an anonymously sourced article that claimed Bobby Thomson's "Shot Heard 'Round the World" in 1951 was enabled by stolen pitching signs.[48] The article provoked a lively discussion of the moralities and practicalities of sign stealing, but the debate did not go much further than that. Frick promised to forfeit any game where "evidence of artificial aid could be presented," but said no more.[49]

In 1959, thanks to an 80-inch lens NBC had introduced, broadcasters Mel Allen and Phil Rizzuto were even able to call pitches correctly. Frick asked NBC to stop using the lens, and the network, lacking the power television holds over the league today, acquiesced. Dick Young wondered why Frick didn't simply ban television from the dugouts.[50]

The debate intensified in July 1962, forcing Frick to dismiss as "a lot of bunk" charges by Milwaukee manager Birdie Tebbetts that the Chicago Cubs were stealing pitching signs from center field and relaying them to batters. The charges set off a swarm of charges, counter-charges, and confessions among the various teams. Frick promised to get baseball's Rules Committee to insert a strong rule against the practice, though he wondered about the practicality of the practice.[51]

Frick faced public ridicule during the 1962 season when Bill Veeck published his autobiography, *Veeck as in Wreck*. The book featured a chapter in which the multi-stop team owner unloaded years of frustration on Frick, or as Veeck referred to him, "baseball's version of the Battle of Bull Run."[52]

Throughout his chapter on Frick, Veeck piled accusation upon accusation: that Frick maneuvered him out of his St. Louis Browns ownership as a condition of the move to Baltimore, and that he prevented Veeck from buying the Philadelphia Athletics (allegations discussed in Chapter 8). The truth is that Veeck endeared himself to almost no one, owner or official, except baseball writers, with his poorly conceived ultimatums and publicity stunts. Frick might have favored those owners who were easier to work with, but Veeck seemed to concentrate his blame on the commissioner.

The words were still shocking in their hostility. "This is why I have always opposed Frick. Not because I dislike him but because I believe him to be inept," Veeck wrote. "Because he has done almost nothing without prodding to address himself to the problems of baseball or the structure of the game."[53]

Veeck's book was a best-seller, but not everyone praised it. Arthur Daley called him "a literary bulldozer," adding simply, "This reporter disagrees vehemently with his blistering of Frick."[54] Bob Burns of the *St. Louis Globe-Democrat* noted that while he "paints himself as the bare-foot boy with the Horatio Alger touch who was kept under thumb by the rich magnates of baseball," he was instead "the front man for a syndicate composed of men of substantial wealth."[55]

Although Frick did not specifically reference Veeck's book, at around the same time it was reported that he had "lost patience and endurance insofar as putting up with unfounded and unwarranted attacks on the game are concerned." The statement relied on vague allusions to "critics who dig up fancied abuses and are ever ready to take a crack at the game, the players, and the club owners." Chester Smith, sports editor of the *Pittsburgh Post-Gazette*, who had felt the commissioner's wrath at times, was not convinced. "It is difficult to buy the idea that baseball is being beset by traducers who are only trying to untrack the game," he wrote. "It is true, too, that baseball has its bugs which crawl out of the walls occasionally.... [I]t all means the presence of a vigilance that is both vital and valuable."[56]

If Frick thought his capricious owner issues departed with Veeck, he was mistaken. In December 1960, Charles O. Finley bought the Kansas City Athletics and soon occupied the time and emotional energy Frick had regained post–Veeck. Most of Finley's hijinks fell under Frick's "league matter" deferral (to his relief), but Finley frequently prevailed on the commissioner in his crusade for self-profiting justice.

When Finley bought the team, he proclaimed himself a Kansas City hometown owner with no plans to move the team.[57] Before the end of his first season, Ernie Mehl of the *Kansas City Times* reported, Finley was looking elsewhere, particularly Dallas. Mehl's columns so angered Finley that between games of an August doubleheader, he held an "Ernie Mehl Appreciation Day—Poison Pen Award for 1961"—in absentia, it turned out —that involved a truck driving around the field carrying billboards that showed a Mehl character at a typewriter and a bottle of poison ink. Frick was so mortified that he telephoned Mehl to apologize, both personally and on behalf of baseball.[58]

Although Frick officially tried to stay out of Finley's ongoing franchise relocation soap opera, he could not avoid yet another trip to Washington to testify before Congress. He was there to talk about yet another antitrust exemption bill, but the committee members were more interested in talking about Finley. Frick agreed with opinions that the courts would uphold baseball's efforts to keep Finley in Kansas City, but declined more specific comment because of the legal technicalities.[59]

Finley also caused Frick headaches heading into the 1964 season, when he moved part of the Municipal Stadium right field fence in to match the 296-foot distance at Yankee Stadium. He was convinced that the short fence, more than a shrewd front office and good players, was the secret to the Yankees' success. Both Frick and Joe Cronin immediately ordered Finley to follow baseball's rules, which set the right field fence at 325 feet. "There's no appeal in this," Frick growled. "There's no hearing, no appeal, no nothing." Finley could only comply, though he still gained a 13-foot-closer advantage.[60] On the field, however, the team responded by losing 105 games and finishing last in the American League.

Finley did not move his franchise until after Frick's term ended, but the Kansas City owner still dragged him into the spectacle. During spring training of 1965, Baltimore general manager Frank Lane, who was Finley's first GM in Kansas City, predicted that Finley would move his team to Milwaukee as soon as the Braves moved out. "He's drooling at the mouth," Lane said. Finley complained to Frick, alleging that Lane's comments had damaged the credibility of Finley's "good work" in Kansas City. Once Lane assured the commissioner that he had been talking on his own behalf and not representing an official Orioles policy, Frick declared the matter closed with no additional action.[61]

15. Expansion   241

In 1962, the 162-game schedule turned out to be a problem for the players as much as the record books. They requested a return to the shorter schedule, citing travel fatigue with teams on the West Coast and in Texas. They actually found a sympathetic ear with Frick. "It just hasn't worked out well," Frick said of the new schedule. "Hardly anyone has been satisfied with it." He requested that his schedule experts come up with some alternative ideas, even including inter-league play.[62]

The idea of American and National League teams playing, as proposed by Frick, would have worked with fans. His schedule reflected a 40-game inter-league stint at midseason, around the All-Star Games. It worked out to 157 games, but even five fewer games meant fewer doubleheaders and a couple more off days. The National League owners voted it down at their mid-season meeting, and inter-league play did not become a reality until 1997.[63]

Frick later backed away from the idea. He claimed that he was actually stating his support for inter-divisional play when baseball expanded to 24 teams but was misunderstood. "I have always maintained that the two leagues should keep themselves apart as much as possible," he said, citing his opposition to expanded interleague trading. Of course, the schedule debate dealt with the current roster of 20 teams, not 24, but Frick was not asked to clarify that discrepancy.[64]

Another 162-game record controversy dogged Frick in 1962 as Maury Wills of the Dodgers challenged and then broke Ty Cobb's stolen base record. Frick re-issued his credo that Wills would have to break Cobb's record in 154 games to gain full ownership, even though Cobb had actually played in 156 games because of two tie games that were replayed under the old rules.

In rejecting Wills' 156-game claim, Frick went so far as to specifically inform Wills that he would have to steal three bases on September 21, his 154th game, to lay claim to the record. "All this time I've been under the impression that it was 156 games," Wills said, dejected. "I wish I'd known earlier. I've stolen three bases in one game many times but that's asking a lot."[65] Wills confused the debate even further by surpassing Cobb's record in his own 156th game.

Frick would have none of it and resisted the asterisk discussion as well. He ruled that Cobb's and Wills' records would appear in the record book, along with two pre–1900 players who had stolen more bases in fewer games than Cobb had. "Some people say a season is a season, regardless of its length. That's an invalid argument," Frick said. "I feel duty-bound to protect not only the past but the future."[66]

Wills disputed the timing of Frick's announcement more than the decision. "I wouldn't have minded so much had Frick made his ruling earlier," he said. "But why did he wait until the last day?" Wills felt that if he were aware of the urgency, he would have broken the record sooner.[67] Ultimately, Frick backed down. "It's a record," he proclaimed after Wills stole his 104th base to end the season. "Whether we say it's a record in 162 games or not, there's no question. It's a new record, the most bases ever stolen in a season."[68]

Given the continuing turmoil in Central and South America, the State Department was interested in planning an off-season players trip, with the emphasis on clinics and teaching as well as games against national teams.[69] Frick's office staff lined up 45 players who were willing to go. Ultimately, the trip was canceled because of government turmoil—in Washington. Excessive costs for two entertainment tours of the region, one featuring renowned actress Helen Hayes, caused such an uproar in Congress that the tours were set aside for the time being.[70]

A 1962 tour of Japan by the Detroit Tigers (the Yankees had declined) was still on the schedule, and Frick and his wife were a part of this tour as well. Frick's departure was delayed after torrential rains in San Francisco caused a three-day delay in the World Series. The idea was for the entourage to leave right after the World Series. Instead, Frick sent the Tigers off to Hawaii, saying, "We'll catch up as soon as we can."[71] Frick also had to waive the rule banning exhibitions until after the World Series ended, much to the relief of Hawaii Governor William Quinn.[72]

The constant Series rain, which also dogged the Series in New York, added a phrase to press box lore. During a rain delay there, with players, fans, and media begging for a cancellation, Frick proclaimed, "It's clearing in Jersey." For years after that, during any New York rain delay, someone in the press box could be heard to yell that.[73]

Traveling with Joe Cronin and his wife, the Fricks made it to Hawaii two hours before the Tigers flew to Japan. Still, they allowed themselves two days to relax on Waikiki Beach before catching up to the tour in Tokyo. The Fricks, experienced world travelers, would host the Cronins on their first world tour, with stops in Bangkok, Singapore, Cairo, Athens, Rome, Paris, and London. The itinerary generated rumors that the trip was also an orientation for Cronin to take over as commissioner when Frick retired.[74] They hadn't even left Hawaii before Frick quashed those rumors. "When I do [retire], I will make an announcement," he said. Cronin labeled the reports as "hogwash."[75]

The retirement talk refused to relent. In December 1962, it was even reported that, although Frick still had three years to go until his term ended, owners were already talking about possible successors. Popular candidates inside baseball included Cronin, Lee MacPhail (Larry's son), and Buzzie Bavasi, whose close friendship with Frick's family posited him as the closest thing to a family successor. Outside of baseball, they mentioned Robert Cannon, Kenneth Keating, and even former Vice President Richard Nixon.[76]

Frick would finally outline his exit strategy in August 1963, more than two years ahead of schedule. He said he planned to retire at the end of his contract, which he said was on October 1, 1965. His objectives until then were to continue to fix the minor leagues (including a revival of the AAA American Association, which had just disbanded) and to oversee another possible round of expansion. On issues that seem quaint decades later, he also acknowledged that night All-Star Games were a possibility, but vetoed any World Series games being played under the lights.[77]

Soon after returning from the Japan tour, Frick spoke out against a move by the St. Petersburg City Council to name the spring training grounds there "Casey Stengel Field," a change from its previous name, "Miller Huggins Field." Injured that his old golf buddy was snubbed, Frick said, "Huggins did a lot for St. Pete, which was his winter home, and there is no valid reason for taking the honor contained in the training field name away from him."[78] Dick Young derided Frick's sentiments as "maudlin mush." He noted that Stengel, in accepting the honor, told officials, "If you get an excellent man in two years, you can give it back, if it'll give you a good ad. I'll never get mad, even if I turn over 18 times in my grave!"[79]

Robbie Robison, head of the St. Petersburg Chamber of Commerce baseball committee and proponent of the name change, was forced to defend it in print and on the *Today* show. He acknowledged getting Frick's letter and claimed a friendship with the commissioner. At the same time, he attributed the outrage to "a small group of Miller's personal friends" and expressed his preference that Stengel's contributions to the city during his years as Yankees manager be honored.[80]

The council's decision grew complicated when that group of friends noted that the plaque honoring Huggins said the field "forever shall be known as Miller Huggins field." The council voted to re-rename the field "Huggins-Stengel Park," with the earlier Yankees manager getting top billing and matching plaques honoring both.[81]

Frick had called a January meeting of public relations officials to develop a proactive plan to battle pro football's supposed inroads into baseball's popularity. The result was a multimedia strategy that included television (a 30-minute program plus shorter clips that could be dropped into game broadcasts), radio clips, film highlights, and even a couple of books. The organizational media focused not only on drawing fans to stadiums and broadcasts, but also on boys continuing to take up the national pastime. The project allowed Frick to assume the role of spokesman, a role he preferred to the commissioner's other tasks, particularly where young people were concerned.[82]

Among the media products was a booklet, *Baseball—The Game, the Career, the Opportunity*. It actually counseled young boys toward a career in baseball, with chapters outlining the supposed practicalities. "Of all the phrases that have been used to describe the United States, none has lasted as long, or proved as accurate, as 'The Land of Opportunity,'" Frick waxed. "The young man who has the interest, and the athletic skill, will find in baseball a worthy and rewarding experience, both tangible and intangible, not to be found anywhere else."[83]

Frick did draw the line on a proposal for a baseball version of the ESPYs—a post-season awards show on television that would announce winners for Most Valuable Player, the Cy Young Award, and the Rookies of the Year. His motive was to protect newspapers. He felt that the gradual announcement of the awards provided his former colleagues with copy to write and copies to sell. To lessen the impact on both the awards and newspaper circulation was a bad idea.[84] The television special idea originally drew widespread support, but the baseball writers, who selected the awards, especially Dick Young, came around to Frick's perspective, and the idea was shelved.[85]

Frick faced an early-season outcry in 1963 surrounding, once again, balks. During spring training, Warren Giles had again ordered National League umpires to make pitchers come to a complete stop for one second before throwing to the plate, as major league rules stipulated: "I don't want you to be balk happy, but I want it enforced," as he said.[86] By May 6, NL umpires already had called a record 96 balks, already beating the previous record by 20, compared to four in the American League.[87]

Realizing what this disparity promised in the World Series and All-Star Game, Frick called Giles and Cronin to a balk summit at his office for May 7. There they agreed that, while pitchers still had to come to a perceptible stop during their motion, the umpires did not have to time it out to one second. The relaxed rule was consistent with Frick's desire to give pitchers some help in baseball's home run-happy phase. National League managers were happy that they did not have to give Wills and other fleet base runners any more advantages.[88] The rules committee concurred and officially pulled the plug on the "one-second" measure a week later.[89]

Frick also mended the relationship between major league and college baseball around this time. For the two years following Frick's rescinding of the college rule in 1956, the relations between the two remained tense. By 1958, college coaches were making it clear to pro scouts that they were not welcome on campus and refused to give them any more access than was afforded by a ticket of admission. "We feel we've had exceptionally shabby treatment at the top, that is, from Commissioner Frick," said Michigan State head coach John Kobs. "We do not believe Frick ever has been very sympathetic to our situation or has been much interested in the majors reaching an agreement with us."[90]

Within two months, however, negotiations had reopened, and as often happens where delicate diplomacy is required, it was initiated at lower levels of authority. Four young major league general managers (including Lee MacPhail) met with four representatives of college baseball in Detroit, with a mind toward healing the rift. Although Frick was not a part of the meeting, he not only was aware of it, but also helped to set it up.[91]

By January 1960, the coaches were reporting that the negotiations had indeed been fruitful and that they were close to agreeing on a rule that would ban the signing of college players until after their sophomore year.[92] At the December meetings, both the minors and the majors agreed to a rule change that banned the signing of players during the academic year.[93] At their annual meeting the next month, the coaches applauded the action and sent a thank-you letter to the officials who had worked it out.[94]

Frick soon proposed the amendment mentioned earlier, prohibiting the signing of freshman and sophomore college players. "We are trying to cooperate with the colleges and help their baseball program all we can," he said. "We also feel that if a boy starts in college and completes two years before signing a contract, it will be a lot easier for him to go back and finish his education."[95] The rule was approved by both the majors and, finally, the minor leagues soon after Frick proposed it.[96]

A year later, organized baseball and colleges were ready to take their relationship to the next level, through the cooperative establishment of summer leagues that would provide college players with local jobs and a great opportunity to hone their baseball skills. Frick and the owners liked the idea because it developed their future talent even more. College coaches liked it because they were less likely to lose their players to the pros.[97]

Frick and the college officials involved had to work quickly to jump through the requisite NCAA hoops in time for the leagues to begin play in the summer of 1963. Although organized baseball made a $50,000 contribution to the foundation overseeing the league, Frick and anyone working for a major or minor league team could not participate in any form. The first league, a pilot program, had six teams in central Illinois communities, with college baseball coaches running the teams.[98]

The leagues turned out to be a success, both in popularity with fans and their effectiveness in developing future All-Stars—no small consideration, given the uncertain position of the minor leagues. The summer baseball program was talking expansion as well, anticipating leagues in Pennsylvania, North Carolina and New England—where the established and popular Cape Cod Summer League would soon join the cooperative arrangement with the major leagues.[99] In 1964, baseball agreed to greater financial support of a wider geographic assortment of the leagues, including one in western Canada.[100]

Related to current All-Stars, the system of having the players choose the team worked well enough, though they turned out to be just as bad as fans at choosing established stars over lesser-known players having great seasons, and sentiment grew to return the job to the fans. The players themselves were among those making the push, believing it would "engender more interest in the game." The players found an ally in the public relations directors Frick had mobilized. He had asked them for ideas to promote the game; fans voting for All-Stars was high on the list.[101]

Even the nation's emerging computer industry offered to help. Frick complained that it took 30 people counting 12 hours a day for three weeks to tally the ballots. A computer programmer from Minneapolis suggested that baseball use one of those newfangled machines, with coded ballots that would be transcribed into punch cards. It would save time and money, he claimed.[102] Frick rejected the idea—at least for the 1964 season—declaring it impractical. "The teams chosen in the past few years by the players have been regarded as truly representative and that method of selection has been retained," said Frank Slocum, speaking for the commissioner's office.[103]

In 1964, Frick appointed a three-man committee—himself, Robert Cannon, and Houston public relations director Bill Giles, to study returning the vote to the fans, as the players had repeatedly requested.[104] But it would not happen until 1970, when Bowie Kuhn brought it back.[105]

The explosion in televised sports was benefiting baseball as much as any other sport, but as it spread from a local to a nationwide phenomenon, it became obvious that some teams were benefiting more than others. Pete Rozelle and the NFL had long fixed that problem, sharing all national television contracts equally and centralizing nationwide negotiations. The baseball owners' innate parochialism and greed delayed them, but eventually they came around to the concept as well.

As they did, it was reported that they were discussing with the networks the possibility of a nationwide Monday night game.[106] The plan was abandoned for the 1964 season when baseball could not put together a satisfactory schedule, so they planned to try again the next year.[107] One factor working against baseball's proposal was that it allowed only a month for bids—a tough time-frame for television networks that would have to juggle complex prime-time schedules.[108]

At their July 1964 meeting, the owners were told the details of what was being called the "Monday Night Spectacular." Comments by Tigers owner John Fetzer, who also owned four radio stations and five television stations, sound presciently like they refer to "Monday Night Football": "It is a radical concept to try to use prime evening television for sports," he said "It has not been done yet, by any sport, on a regular basis." He described a single nationwide broadcast with no blackouts. The only difference with the later concept was that baseball planned to broadcast a later game to West Coast stations because of the time difference.[109]

By November, the proposal was in trouble, and Fetzer announced that it had been shelved for the 1965 season. He claimed that NBC and ABC both indicated an inability to clear programming time to accommodate a prime-time baseball game.[110] It's not too much of a stretch to infer that the owners' shortsightedness and territoriality were also issues, and as close as baseball came to "Monday Night Baseball," they once again would yield the initiative to football.

16

Exit Strategy

While Charlie Finley was entertaining with his high-profile relocation theatrics, the Braves repeated their 1953 maneuver, quietly finessing a move while another media-obsessed owner unpopular with his peers (Veeck previously) was doing it wrong. Anonymous sources confirmed that the Braves were ready to move to Atlanta, where the city promised an $18 million, public-financed stadium and a broad regional television network, for the 1965 season. The sources also expressed confidence that the other owners would approve the move.[1]

Frick's only comment was his usual—that any owner could move a franchise as long as he followed the rules in getting the required approvals within the proper time frame.[2] He even displayed indignation over the criticism he faced for not doing anything to stop or even delay the move. He cited his oft-quoted, oft-derided response that it was a "league matter" and quoted the relevant rules, including the one that stated that none of those rules "shall be considered or construed to be detrimental to baseball," the only spur for Frick to take action and one that the owners had severely limited his freedom to invoke.[3]

Frick expounded on that philosophy to a *Milwaukee Journal* writer, his words providing little comfort to the city's baseball fans. He did encourage owners to think carefully before leaving a city. "But no perpetuity is guaranteed to any city," he said. "As far as my stepping in, that's silly. I can talk to people quietly and maybe have some influence, but nobody can tell a man where or how he should spend his money. That's the law of the land."[4]

Many in baseball disagreed. Speaking in Milwaukee a few years later, Cleveland general manager Gabe Paul said, "If we had had a commissioner who would have been willing to take the ball, Milwaukee would never have lost its franchise. Any commissioner can prevent the transfer of any franchise." Paul at the time was speaking in favor of a strong commissioner to replace Frick's replacement, William Eckert.[5]

16. Exit Strategy

In response to protests by Representative Henry Reuss of Wisconsin, Frick promised to use "every effort to make sure that the Braves and the National League give extra consideration to every angle, including the Milwaukee angle, if the Braves submit to the league a proposal to transfer the location from Milwaukee." Those familiar with Frick's approach to such owner moves recognized how little hope that promise represented.[6]

The passion of Milwaukee fans even moved Frick to encourage the Braves owners to consider selling the team to a Milwaukee-based group. He promised a local sportswriter that he "would insist that if it is the present owners' decision to move, they should give the Milwaukee people an opportunity to buy the club and keep it there." William Bartholomay, Braves chairman of the board, stoked the fans' fading hopes by claiming that he and other stockholders would be taking some time to "think things over and review the situation."[7]

Regardless of Frick's or Bartholomay's assurances, the Braves' proposed move grew increasingly complicated. Milwaukee County officials got a local judge to issue a restraining order, forcing the team to honor the last year of its stadium lease, and a federal judge refused to hear an appeal.[8] Seeing the writing on the courtroom wall, and perhaps heeding Frick's warning about increased vigilance toward their public image, the owners voted to make the Braves stay in Milwaukee for one more season, with the move to Atlanta pre-approved.[9]

In the interim, the baseball fans in Milwaukee were doing everything they could to keep a team there. That included a proposal from six members of the House of Representatives—from Wisconsin, New York, and Texas (all Democrats)—urging Frick to expand baseball immediately and add teams in Milwaukee, Buffalo, and Dallas-Fort Worth. While Frick endorsed immediate planning toward expansion, he told them, "I do not believe ... that expansion can be attained overnight nor accomplished by Congressional edict; nor can it follow a specific plan as contained in your statement."[10]

A new kind of franchise transfer involving the Yankees in 1964 caused Frick a new set of problems, because the new owner was the Columbia Broadcasting System: CBS. The purchase caused criticism among fans, media, and even owners. Judge Roy Hofheinz, president of the Houston Colt .45s, said, "The day CBS finally purchases the Yankees will be the blackest day for baseball since the Black Sox scandal." Frick disagreed. "I asked if the identity of the Yankees would be maintained under their new ownership, whether there would be a conflict of interest on the part of CBS ... and whether the deal would have any effect on competitive bidding for baseball's television rights," he said, declaring himself satisfied on all counts.[11]

American League owners approved the sale, even after Frick was advised by his personal attorney and a National League attorney that the transaction would invite Justice Department scrutiny. Instead of delaying a vote, the AL adopted two resolutions: one approving the sale and the other encouraging the owners and their attorneys to help bring any government investigations to a satisfactory conclusion.[12]

One of the main conflict-of-interest problems for Frick was that several owners and players were CBS stockholders. Frick's personal attorney, Paul Porter, provided him with a legal opinion that, to comply with organized baseball's rules, no team owner could also own stock in CBS, even though the network had set up a separate company to run the Yankees. Relying on strict interpretation of conflict-of-interest rules in court decisions and FCC rulings, Porter recommended that Frick direct all owners to sell any CBS stock.[13] The chair of the firm that ran the Orioles had to resign from the board of directors of CBS and place his 39,500 shares of stock into a non-voting trust.[14]

The same day that American League owners conducted their vote, Frick met with an unnamed staff member from the Justice Department who was fact-finding to help his superiors determine whether to file an injunction against the purchase. Frick repeated his statement from when the sale was announced, but the representative had a more direct question: Was Frick concerned by the purchase? His memo of the meeting stated, "The Commissioner's answer was that of course he was concerned as he would be concerned with any move which might reflect upon the standing of baseball."

For Frick, as with everything, the practical solution lay in the hands of the owners. If they did their job and were diligent when television contracts were considered, the issues would be minimal. He deferred to Porter on the legal issues. Porter was concerned that the Toolson case, which ignored the issue of baseball's antitrust exemption, would be used as a defense of the sale, and if both were shot down, baseball would suffer more than CBS. But the CBS attorneys pledged not to do that, so the legal concerns were also dealt with.

At the end of the 90-minute meeting, the representative, much like Frick, deferred to others on what would happen from there, though his opinion was that any action taken by his superiors would focus on the Yankees purchase and not baseball's antitrust status.[15]

Frick also was called to a hearing before the Senate's antitrust monopoly subcommittee, his 14th appearance before congressional committees in 14 years as commissioner. Accompanied by Cronin and John Fetzer, he assured the senators that the sale itself did not create a conflict of interest and that the owners were coming up with guidelines to address the new reality of larger corporations owning teams.[16] It appeared that the Senate would take no further action based on the sale, particularly after the Justice Department announced during the hearings that it had concluded its investigation into the sale with no recommendation to stop it.[17] Fourteen appearances later, after 14 years of the Supreme Court waiting for Congress to take the lead, while Congress waited for the Supreme Court to rule, baseball still was exempt from antitrust laws.[18]

On Tuesday, August 4, 1964, Frick sent a letter to the 20 team owners, announcing that he would retire as baseball commissioner when his contract expired, which he said was on September 21, 1965. "It's just what I've said all along; now I've just made it official," he said. His retirement letter added, "I will be leaving with a horde of golden memories which the years can never dim."[19] Although he would turn 70 before his term ended, Frick agreed to stay in office until his successor was chosen and even extended his projected retirement date beyond the World Series, at the request of the owners.[20] He also let them know that he would gladly and graciously step down immediately if a suitable candidate were hired earlier.

Having made his exit official, Frick bluntly expressed his ideas on the commissioner's authority at a November 1964 summit to discuss the issues facing baseball. He urged the owners to restore to the post the strong authority that had been granted Judge Kenesaw Mountain Landis when the post was created in 1921. He also exhorted the owners to look at themselves as the source of many of baseball's problems.

Frick claimed that he testified before Congress 14 times in his 14 years as commissioner of baseball (National Baseball Hall of Fame Library, Cooperstown, New York).

So long as the owners and operators refuse to look beyond the day and hour; so long as clubs and individuals persist in gaining personal headlines through public criticism of their associates; so long as baseball people are unwilling to abide by the rules which they themselves make; so long as expediency is permitted to replace sound judgment, there can be no satisfactory solution."[21]

Some saw Frick's statement as courageous and applauded the speech's content. "Judge K. M. Landis would have been proud of his once-removed successor," wrote Russell Schneider, *Cleveland Plain Dealer* columnist. "Frick finally asserted himself ... to his employers, the 20 major league club owners.... More important, he told them flatly that baseball has a bleak future indeed unless the owners and operators take stock of themselves and literally pull their heads out of the ground."[22]

Others applauded the speech, but their main criticism was that Frick waited so long to deliver it. In their opinion, Frick could have helped baseball avoid the problems that had plagued it and maintained its position as America's favorite sport, if he had only challenged the owners earlier. As columnist Melvin Durslag of the *Los Angeles Herald Examiner* wrote, "He has delivered to the owners a manifesto of great dimensions, perfect in every respect except one—its timing.... But strong, persuasive suggestions by Frick years ago very likely would have resulted in responses favorable to the game. His is a case of making the right speech at the wrong time."[23]

Others, like Leonard Koppett, found his speech true, but still self-justifying and too much too late. "The outgoing commissioner ... simultaneously gave the club owners a verbal spanking and himself an excuse, both by implication," he wrote. Still, he acknowledged, "Frick's declaration, even late, may turn out to be his greatest service to the game."[24] The owners in both leagues responded by agreeing to Frick's recommendation and promising to amend baseball rules to restore full, Landis-level powers to the commissioner—though whether they would follow through was anyone's guess.[25]

The owners responded to the pessimism by confirming their promise at the December meetings, restoring two amendments to the baseball rules that also restored absolute power to the commissioner's office. The first waived their rights to legal recourse, and the second removed the clause dictating that no owner action could be considered detrimental to baseball. Frick did not comment further on the change beyond indicating that he had no plans for any drastic actions before his retirement, leaving it to his successor to wield the newly granted hammer.[26]

Early on, Frick stayed out of the process to replace him. At a Topps trading cards event, he did suggest a triumvirate to address baseball's multifaced challenges: "the chairman of the Federal Communications Commission, the president of Allied Van Lines and the chairman of the Judiciary Committee of the U.S. Senate."[27]

16. Exit Strategy

In a January 1965 interview, Frick allowed himself the luxury of beginning to think about his retirement. He predicted that 30 years after leaving his journalism career, he would return to his typewriter ("just for the fun of writing") or something else that was "useful." He made no brash predictions of his successor—only that he would be "young and vigorous," and a Renaissance man straddling baseball, public affairs, and law.[28]

Frick was in a mood to discuss his legacy with veteran New York sports writer Tommy Holmes at his final All-Star Game. "I can tell you what gives me satisfaction," he said. "This has been a revolutionary period in baseball. There have been troubles and problems which we have not only survived but overcome." He listed increased attendance and improved stadiums as signs of baseball's excellent health and vitality. "We haven't done everything as well as we should have," he said. "But I am convinced that our batting average has been high and our generally positive approach has accomplished constructive results."[29]

As the owners searched for his successor, he continued his reflections.

> Today, the commissioner's office deals largely with corporate problems—moving franchises, ownership by larger corporations, laws before Congress, financial arrangements, things like that. I think we're 75 percent over the hump in solving the problems of recent years, because procedures have been set up to handle them. But the new commissioner will have to deal with them.[30]

Sports writers were also thinking about Frick's retirement and legacy. Their views were predictably diverse. Some, like Jim McCulley of the *New York Daily News*, were supportive. McCulley felt that Frick had not gotten proper credit for seeing baseball through its most turbulent period.

> No man in baseball, in my memory, has been so maligned as Ford Frick. He has been sniped at by the press, by belligerent and selfish owners, by foolish players, and by some Johnny-come-latelys in and around the sport, who have the silly notion that it's the 'in' thing to do—knock the commissioner. This type knocks big men, hoping to gain some quaint king of status for themselves.[31]

One of Frick's final accomplishments was among the most important and certainly the most underrated: the establishment of a major league free agent draft. The commissioner and others had advocated the draft as an alternative to the bonus bidding madness that pervaded baseball. The owners, leery of anything that might threaten possible strategic advantages, had resisted him. But after noting the success of football and basketball drafts, the owners came around.

The American League had begun to investigate the possibility of a free agent draft for all unsigned players in 1961, to bring order to the chaos. The concept was attractive, but Frick had spent enough time at the Congressional committee table to know that it would be wise to study the legality of such a move under antitrust law. To sports writers covering the mid-season meetings, Frick would acknowledge only that the major leagues were studying such a draft.[32]

At the December 1961 meetings, the owners did not discuss a draft, but they did approve a new bonus rule. Previous rules had attempted to limit the size of bonuses. The new rule made it more difficult for teams to protect bonus players and decreased the cost of drafting first-year players from minor league rosters. Frick said that would make owners think twice about signing too many players to large bonuses—and took him off the hook for enforcing bonus limits.[33]

Just a few months into the new system, Frick declared it a success, "The new bonus rule has proved itself to be air-tight, foolproof, firm against the loophole seekers who made a mockery of such regulations in the past." The prospect of losing a player signed to a large bonus after only one season discouraged the owners from their previous high spending, he said.[34]

Frick had introduced the draft concept as part of a larger package of changes in 1962, but it was not considered, leading some to fear that once again, the owners were seeking short-term stop-gaps over long-term solutions.[35] Walter O'Malley derided the draft proposals as "socialism," noting their goals of encouraging parity by allowing lower-placed teams to draft first. He did not address the capitalistic advantages of players having the ability to go to a team that valued their services more and would give them greater opportunities to advance.[36]

At a meeting in January 1964, the owners were more interested in the idea and authorized Frick, Giles and Cronin to submit a proposal for a draft.[37] With that authorization, Frick spent spring training talking about the draft with team officials, managers, and players, to get their input. One specific concern Frick heard centered on how long teams could maintain the rights to players they had drafted. "What the limited time will be is the $64 question," Frick said. "There are many questions to be answered. But it can be done and it will be done somehow."[38] Frick returned from spring training optimistic that a draft could be put together by the next spring. He described the March meetings in Arizona and Florida as "fruitful."[39]

Walter Byers, executive director of the NCAA, said his organization was opposed to the concept of a draft on moral grounds; it unfairly limited an athlete's negotiating to one team. But he also recognized the concept

16. Exit Strategy

was spreading at such a rate that he couldn't stop it, so he promised not to work against it, as long as baseball teams agreed not to draft college players until after they graduated.[40]

Still, the owners hesitated. Some wondered whether a draft, coupled with the reserve clause, threatened congressional inquiry and Justice Department scrutiny. At the major leagues' summer meeting, the owners tabled the proposal and urged Frick to propose amendments to the current first-year rule. The 10–10 vote caused some to doubt whether the draft proposal would be discussed at the December meetings.[41]

Frick persisted and worked through the team general managers, calling an October 1964 post-season summit at a Pennsylvania mountain resort. Frick and the GMs approached the varying proposals in the context of their value to baseball in general, not to specific teams. Given that perspective, the team officials voted in favor of a free agent draft.[42]

The indirect approach worked. When Frick met with the owners two weeks later, he found much more support for the draft. Perhaps the sudden support could also be attributed to the stirring speech Frick made to the owners about the commissioner's limited authority. Whatever the case, the owners recommended that Frick bring his plan to the December meetings, where passage suddenly seemed certain.[43]

From there, the sailing was smooth. The minor leagues approved the draft in their meetings.[44] The next night, the major league owners endorsed it. The vote was almost unanimous; the Cardinals held out in opposition until the end. Under the original proposal from Frick, the majors would hold three drafts: in January, June, and September.[45] A single draft would be instituted later. However, for the owners to fall in step behind Frick on an idea they themselves did not embrace was a late-game victory for the commissioner.

Baseball's first free agent draft took place June 8–9, 1965, and from all indications it ran smoothly. Rick Monday was the first top overall draft pick; he was a sophomore outfielder for Arizona State University at the time. Frick had met with team officials the night before, and that was credited with avoiding many of the problems. Years of trial and error in pro football and basketball helped as well. Frick's staff even provided film highlights for some of the top selections.[46] With so many players in the draft, the main problem occurred when teams drafted the same players, with a slight misspelling in one team's selection. In cases where it was not immediately detected, Frick would later rule on which team would get the player.[47]

College coaches were not thrilled that baseball's draft included players who had not completed their eligibility. Organized baseball was not interested in negotiating the point, so they worked through Congress instead, tacking on an amendment to yet another antitrust bill that barred the signing of college players for those four years. The bill did not pass, and baseball's liberal draft eligibility standards would continue to cause tension between the two.[48]

The draft did necessitate other changes. The first-year regulations, when combined with the draft, created an unforeseen consequence where players could have been picked off a team's roster fairly soon after being drafted and with little opportunity for the team to evaluate them. Buzzie Bavasi, now general manager of the Dodgers, suggested doing away with the first-year rule, since the draft itself was solving the problem of uncontrolled bonuses. Frick agreed with Bavasi's proposal,[49] and at their midsummer meeting, both leagues did as well, eliminating the rule.[50]

While on the 1963 Japan trip, Frick used the time to conclude some international business, baseball style. He and his counterpart in Japan, Yushi Uchimura, agreed to a framework of rules governing the exchange of players between the two countries. Frick and his owners were particularly concerned when Joe Stanka, a pitcher for the White Sox, spurned his stateside team for a better offer in Japan—a disturbing display of autonomy for a player in the early 1960s. "I feel sure our agreement will prevent recurrence of the Stanka episode," Frick said. He also predicted that the agreement would lead to Japanese players in the U.S. major leagues.[51]

The solid relationship Frick had built with Japan's baseball organization ceased to exist in February 1965, following a dispute involving the first Japanese pitcher to play in the major leagues. Masanori Murakami pitched 15 innings, all in relief, for the Giants in 1964. He then signed contracts with the Giants and his original team, the Nankai Hawks, for 1965. The Giants claimed ownership, and even his Nankai team owner was quoted as agreeing. But his general manager refused to allow his return.

In a letter Frick sent to all owners, he treated Murakami like any other player, regardless of nationality. He wrote, "[T]his office must hold that Pitcher Murakami has violated his contract. He is placed on the Disqualified List insofar as American baseball is concerned and the Nankai Hawks are estopped [sic] from negotiations with any members of Organized Baseball Leagues in the United States."[52]

Part of Frick's frustration resulted from a lack of contact with Japanese baseball commissioner Yushi Uchimura, who did not reply to Frick's attempts at negotiation. Carl Hanta, an American coach with the Nankai team, met with Frick, as did Stanka, who pitched with the Hawks for five years. They

16. Exit Strategy

failed to convince the commissioner that Nankai had been deceived by the Giants. Finally, Frick announced that relations between the two countries would be severed, at least concerning baseball, until the situation could be cleared up.[53] On the other side of the Pacific, Murakami announced that he had no intention of playing for the Giants and had signed with the Hawks "of my own free will."[54]

Frick's letter didn't stop there. He added, "The Commissioner must further hold that if, in the face of this documentary evidence, there still is insistence on the part of the Nankai Hawks Baseball Team to ignore all agreements, all understandings and all dealings and negotiations between Japanese and American baseball are cancelled."[55]

Thus, the consequences of this slapfight extended beyond one player and two teams vying for his services. Frick claimed that the disagreement complicated future post-season barnstorming tours of Japan. "I dislike saying this very much, but the proposed trip of the Pirates to Japan next fall will be jeopardized if the Federation does not fulfill its obligation in the Murakami case," he said while on his final tour of spring training camps.[56]

The drama played out in the Japanese media as well, with interviews of Murakami's heartbroken parents wondering if he could ever come home and insinuations that the Giants had used the language barrier to their advantage.[57] Soon after Frick's ultimatum, Murikami announced was willing to return to the Giants for the 1965 season, under certain conditions. Commissioner Uchimura said he would seek a compromise to allow the pitcher to return home and resume his career there in 1966. Frick, as always, referred such negotiation-related issues to the Giants' front office.[58]

By May, the Giants were facing serious bullpen issues, and Horace Stoneham was ready to negotiate. With Frick's approval, he sent Uchimura a cable agreeing to allow Murakami to return to Japan in 1966 if he would help rescue the Giants' bullpen in 1965. The agreement also ended the suspension of relations between the two nations' baseball organizations.[59]

As if to stress that baseball had plenty of international suitors, Frick and his wife joined the Cleveland Indians on their pre-season tour of Mexico, with games in Monterrey and Mexico City. While there, Frick and Joe Cronin received citations from former Mexico President Miguel Aleman, recognizing their efforts to improve relations between the two nations.[60]

The Japan baseball officials then fired their next shot by cancelling the Pirates' post-season tour. The officials complained that the Pirates' inferior drawing power threatened to make the tour a financial disaster. "The Pirates are unknown in Japan and we did not want to risk going into the red," said Kanzo Hashimoto, a promotion director for the Yomiuri newspaper that was sponsoring the tour. Other reports noted that Yomiuri representatives had tried to sidestep Frick and negotiate directly with Walter O'Malley to get his Dodgers to tour instead, but O'Malley declined.[61] The misstep was forgiven in the wake of the Murakami situation being resolved.

Even with the passage of the Sports Broadcasting Act, the major leagues were slower to embrace the concept of shared revenue. Local radio had transitioned seamlessly into local television, and owners, particularly in large markets, were reluctant to share the wealth and yield to nationwide contracts with equal shares.

As a first step in that direction, Calvin Griffith, owner of the Minnesota Twins, proposed in 1963 that visiting teams get a cut of the home team's television revenue on a per-game basis. Previously, it was considered fair and equitable that the Yankees kept all the television money from their home games, and Griffith's Twins kept all the money from theirs, though the amounts were quite different. Even in the limited nationwide "Game of the Week" broadcasts the networks were setting up with baseball, the home teams got the money.[62] Given the ingrained self-profiting culture, it is not surprising that National League president Giles expressed skepticism that any such revenue-sharing plan could work in baseball as it did in other pro sports.[63]

When Frick announced the first complete network package with ABC for the 1965 and 1966 seasons, the rights fees were spread across 19 of the 20 franchises. (The Yankees were still tied to a contract with CBS.) Each team would get $625,000 over the two years of the contract. For someone who at one time was troubled by the possible domination of baseball by television, Frick was much more sanguine. "Conceivably, for example, there can be three telecasts at once coming into the New York area for fans, the Yankees, the Mets and the ABC game."[64]

Thus, in a telling juxtaposition, Frick's last season as commissioner was the first for truly nationwide regular-season baseball broadcasts negotiated by the league rather than individual teams. The ABC network put together a Saturday "Game of the Week" schedule. It was a ratings disappointment: the Yankees were still tied to CBS, and the most successful franchise had the most popular commentator in Dizzy Dean. Plus, the owners did nothing to adjust their home schedules to help the broadcast; their only response was to welcome the $300,000 per team payment.[65]

What set the ABC game apart was its Roone Arledge-directed innovations: the instant replay, slow-motion, and stop-action that were making their college football broadcasts so popular. The new stuff impressed most fans, with one exception. Frick warned, "Speaking broadly, baseball shouldn't give the TV fan more information than it gives the guy who paid $2.50 or $3 for a seat at the park." He didn't completely dismiss the camera wizardry, "but I don't think they should overdo it." He felt the tricks were better suited to football, "a mass game, where you need to isolate the action. Baseball is an open game, where you can see everything that's going on."[66]

On some issues, Frick did more than critique. When Leo Durocher, while doing analysis for a May 8 game, started "stealing" the catcher's signals, Frick was not pleased. But when the broadcast included cameras in the dugouts, he moved quickly, banning the practice.[67] The dugout cameras also drew protests from print journalists, who considered it an unfair advantage for television, since the camera operators could hear bench talk and relay the information to the control booth.[68] The writers were told that the cameras had been banned as well, but broadcasters kept seeking ways around the directive (cameras in the actual dugout, but separated by a cardboard partition), so the writers kept complaining.[69]

As Frick's final season drew to an end, there was no tour with tributes at major league stadiums. The baseball writers threw a farewell party at the Dodger Stadium Club during the World Series. The emphasis was on light fun, and Frick told his former colleagues, simply, "This is one of my happiest occasions." The most newsworthy comment came from O'Malley—an appropriate speaker, given his unofficial status as baseball's most powerful owner. "This farewell may be a trifle premature," he joked, noting the struggles to replace Frick.[70]

As a nice gesture from inside "the family," the official 1965 World Series program was dedicated to Frick. The picture showed Frick, his son, Fred, and his grandson, Ford II, enjoying a sandlot moment—posed but also genuine. The dedication repeated the familiar accomplishments of Frick's tenure and closed, "and now the Commissioner has decided to retire.... Perhaps now and then he can sneak out and umpire a Little League game.... Maybe he can spend some time curing that hook off the golf tee ... but whatever he chooses to do, he has earned his retirement and he has left the sport he loves in a mighty healthy state."[71]

As the World Series ended, Frick's tenure did not. Given his offer to remain in office until his successor was chosen, the owners were taking their time working through the list of candidates. At their meeting on October 19, they merely reduced the candidate list from 18 to ten, and four of those eliminated withdrew themselves.[72] By the second day of deliberations, the owners were still far from a decision, so they decided to put it off until their December meetings. Some reports claimed the list remained at ten, but a *Chicago Daily News* reporter secretly listened in the room next door and put the number at seven finalists. (Spoiler alert: Their final choice was not one of the seven.)[73]

In the meantime, Frick was called on to testify one last time, but not before Congress. He was deposed in Milwaukee County's unsuccessful lawsuit against the Braves' owners and their efforts to move the team to Atlanta. Frick reiterated his approach to such matters—that he left those decisions to individual owners, with the leagues handling approval. He repeated his opinion that Milwaukee was an excellent candidate for expansion, with the caveat that no, it was not his decision.[74]

To Dick Young, Frick's media gadfly, the testimony was also indicative of Frick's loyalty to organized baseball. To those who expressed shame at Frick's powerlessness to stop franchise moves, Young retorted, "Ford Frick is no dope. He realizes how bad this makes him look. But he is performing his final service for baseball, he is taking the weak-leader rap.... To say otherwise would lay baseball open to charges of collusion, and action by the Justice Department."[75]

A second round of questioning did not go so well. Frick was constantly prevented by his own attorneys from answering questions on what he knew about the Braves' plans to move and his opinion of whether it was good for baseball. Sadly, the impression it left, as he prepared to leave office, was of a powerless, silent, ineffective commissioner, unable to stop greedy owners from bulldozing the fans.[76]

Even after his retirement, Frick was called on to give depositions in the case. A few days after his final baseball meetings, he testified regarding supposed promises to give Milwaukee an expansion franchise. His simple "no" answer was repeated to questions from the other direction—whether there was an active plan to keep major league baseball *out* of Milwaukee.[77]

Judge Elmer Roller actually ruled against the Braves' move in April 1966 and ordered the team to return to Milwaukee unless baseball announced an expansion franchise for the spurned city[78]—an impractical order that was never enforced. Far from doing the major leagues a favor, Frick's testimony about the ease of expansion was considered damaging. The decision quoted Frick's surprisingly strong statement supporting the fans over the owners: "[I]f we refuse to consider the interest of the public in the development of our game, if we insist on being completely monopolistic in our organization, we will lose all the public esteem which presently exists. We will pave the way for the breakdown of the structure."[79]

Right before the December meetings, the owners announced their choice to replace Frick: 56-year-old retired Air Force General William "Spike" Eckert. Making light of his anonymity, New York Daily News sports writer Larry Fox dubbed him "The Unknown Soldier."[80] The owners appointed Lee MacPhail as Eckert's chief administrator, to provide experienced help and perhaps to keep an eye on him, as he eased into a new, unfamiliar position. Eckert, one of the original nominees, had removed his name from consideration initially but agreed to restore it later. Thus his appointment was something of a shock.[81]

Years later, Dick Young claimed that Cronin was the owners' choice to take over for Frick, but they panicked at the last minute, given the response to the Braves' proposed Atlanta move, and felt they needed someone with strong Washington connections, so they chose Eckert.[82] Ultimately, Eckert would continue the baseball commissioner's losing streak in comparison to Pete Roselle and all that he was accomplishing in football.[83]

Frick had to come to Eckert's rescue at his introductory press conference. The journalists there peppered him with questions about the issues he would be facing. Eckert had no specifics, but the journalists kept pressing. Finally, Frick cut in. "Gentlemen, you are not being fair," he said. "General Eckert cannot be expected to answer such questions and should not be subjected to them. The files on Milwaukee are voluminous and have been compiled over a two-year period. Give the man a break."[84]

Frick met briefly with Eckert soon after his appointment. "I told him a few things to watch out for," Frick said, always gracious. "But I didn't offer him any thousand-dollar advice. He didn't offer me a thousand dollars so I didn't give him the advice." He confirmed that he

Frick was forced to stay in office a couple extra months in late 1965, as the owners kept searching for his successor (National Baseball Hall of Fame Library, Cooperstown, New York).

would lead the major league meetings one last time before turning the reins over to Eckert on December 4.[85]

The meetings went as smoothly as any during Frick's tenure. The most pressing issue on the agenda was a policy concerning rainouts, and even there the owners put off a decision. The two leagues also came to an agreement on rules against fraternizing on the field—a full-circle moment, considering that was one of the first issues Frick addressed as National League president.[86]

After what business there was transpired, the owners shooed reporters and the lone television camera out of the room and had a private farewell ceremony for Frick. From the hallway, the media detected speeches by Cronin and Phillies president Bob Carpenter, along with an appropriately sustained ovation. The reporters were allowed back in so Frick and Eckert could give them the official report on the meeting.

As he finished, Frick stood up and wished the reporters a merry Christmas. The significance of the moment dawned on everyone, and Frick laughed. "That's right," he said. "This is the last meeting I'll preside over. I guess you could call it my last official act in office."[87]

With that, Frick's 31 years of leadership in organized baseball came to a close, and he walked out of the room as the first commissioner to leave office on his own initiative.

17

Extra Innings

Although Frick had often talked of leaving New York after retirement and returning to Colorado, he remained in Bronxville and would never leave there. "It isn't a big house, but it is comfortable and has nice grounds," he told columnist Joe Trimble. "Since word of my retirement got around, I have had many callers asking to buy it. But it isn't for sale. I'm going to stay around for a while."[1]

It turned out to be an excellent base of operations. For the first few months after his retirement, Frick's main responsibility was to enjoy, or endure, the inevitable banquets and tributes. American League President Joe Cronin and National League President Warren Giles announced that the Rookie of the Year Award would be named for Frick. "Commissioner Frick at all times evidenced interest in the welfare of the young player and it is most fitting that his name be associated with these awards," Giles said.[2] (It would be renamed for Jackie Robinson in 1987, to mark the 40th anniversary of baseball integration.)

At the end of January, Frick was awarded the Dr. Robert Hyland Award for meritorious service to sports, by the St. Louis chapter of the Baseball Writers' Association of America. It gave Frick the opportunity to share memories of the city from his days covering baseball, like "the old press box at Sportsman's Park, where fans flicked bottle caps at your ears if they didn't like what you wrote." He also turned poignant. "I believed in the honesty of the game when I started," he said with some emotion. "After all of the vicissitudes, I still believe in it. The players are getting better and so is the game. And I retire with that feeling in my heart."[3]

In retirement Frick was able to increase his involvement with the Baseball Hall of Fame and chaired the Veterans Committee. One of his first actions was to initiate and oversee a secret election by mail to enshrine long-time manager Casey Stengel in the Hall before the required five years passed. Frick traveled to Florida to make the surprise announcement at a

Mets spring training game. The news sparked a loud celebration both in the stands and on the field, and drew an emotional, grateful response from Stengel, who thought he was there to present a plaque to the Mets.[4] The deception worked so well that several baseball writers missed the actual announcement. Thinking it was a minor ceremony, they stopped to fish along the way, though they did catch the after-party.[5] Later that year, Frick was also named chairman of the Hall's board of directors.[6]

The years were filled with other typical tasks and activities of someone in his position. He was appointed head of a committee trying to bring the 1976 Winter Olympics to Denver.[7] The extent of Frick's involvement was not clear, though the effort was successful at first. Denver was awarded the 1976 winter games, but a combination of voter discontent and environmental concerns caused the city to forfeit the opportunity.[8]

He also was hired as a consultant for the City of New York's Manpower and Career Development Agency by Mayor John Lindsay in 1967, charged with helping business leaders "to open up opportunities and career lines for unemployed and underemployed New Yorkers."[9] Again, no record exists of the fruit of his work with the agency. He was named to the Babe Ruth League's Hall of Fame in 1968—in gratitude more for his help in fund raising than for his protection of Ruth's home run record.[10] He was elected to the Babe Ruth League's board of directors in November 1969.[11]

His successor, Eckert, would last only three years before being forced into retirement by the owners in December 1968, their admission that they had picked the wrong man. While Frick played no role in the drama, he nonetheless was assigned part of the blame. "Frick's long tenure ... was perhaps too quiet," one sports writer noted. "Problems piled up under the surface, baseball lost ground to the rapid growth of professional football and the game's entire structure began to weaken."[12] That perspective seemed to imply that Eckert or Frick could somehow corral the owners who were creating these problems and resisting any steps to solve them.

Leonard Koppett took a more realistic view. He noted that Frick and Eckert were strictly administrators for the owners' policy, even as the owners' bickering stymied their efforts. "Their jobs depended on the daily politicking of keeping various factions happy," he wrote. "Frick succeeded for fourteen years, Eckert failed after three, but neither was in a position to perform objectively or productively for the industry—or game—as a whole."[13]

Frick resigned as chairman of the Hall of Fame Veterans Committee on January 7, 1970, but for a good reason: At its next meeting, the committee considered, and approved, Frick's induction into the Baseball Hall of Fame. It was fitting that the news was announced at the 47th annual baseball writers' annual dinner, where Frick had entertained and been entertained since Dinner One. "I am terrifically flattered," he said. "When one is in a profession and is lucky enough to move up and reaches the culmination of what the sport has to offer, you naturally feel very proud. But I also feel very humble."[14]

Not everyone was impressed. Even after almost 20 years, Happy Chandler was still bitter. "Next thing you know they'll be voting in Charlie McCarthy. He's a dummy, too, you know," he said. "All he ever did, for goodness sake, was 'saw logs.' Why, he slept longer in office than.... Rip Van Winkle."[15]

Not satisfied with insults, Chandler also wrote a letter to *Sporting News* publisher C. C. Johnson Spink, calling "simply not true" an article's contention that Frick deserved partial credit for baseball's integration. "In fairness, it must be thanks to Rickey, Robinson and Chandler." Frick, always gracious, declined to comment.[16]

Frick made his last trip home to Indiana in the spring of 1970, for Rome City High School's 60th class reunion.[17] A thank-you letter to cousin Harold Frick and his wife, Virginia, showed he still appreciated his roots, despite having moved away 55 years earlier. "A visit to the peace and quiet of the Indiana I once knew is like a breath of cold air to a drowning man," he wrote. "I came away with a great sense of pride in our Indiana heritage—and most particularly in my Indiana friends and relatives."[18]

A few weeks later, on July 27, Frick was inducted into the Hall of Fame he helped found, along with pitcher Jesse Haines, who played for the Cardinals from 1920–1937; outfielder Earle Combs, who played alongside Babe Ruth with the Yankees (1924–1935); and Cleveland Indians player-manager Lou Boudreau (1938–1952). "More than anybody else, Ford Frick has brought us here today and through the years," said commissioner Bowie Kuhn in inducting Frick. "He is the father of the Baseball Hall of Fame. It was his foresight and determination that brought it into existence."[19]

Frick's acceptance speech served as the perfect farewell to the pulpit the game had given him. The moment definitely was overwhelming. "You know, through the years, officially and semi-officially, I have appeared on this rostrum many times and I never seemed to be at a loss for words," he said. "Now suddenly, when I most hoped I could be eloquent and pointed, I find that words fail me."

Noting the accomplished former baseball players surrounding him was equally humbling. "I recognize the physical contributions they have made to baseball as players on the field when all I could do was sit at the desk and talk about baseball and do the best that I could to direct it and love baseball," he confessed. "If those are qualifications, then I accept them very happily."[20]

"Anything that connects yesterday to today and today to tomorrow is important, because it means continuity," he said, ever the baseball evangelist. "Baseball will continue to grow because it exemplifies what is perfect in men. But without memories of the past, there could be no dreams of the future. Without those yesterdays, there could be no bright tomorrows."[21]

The next year, Satchel Paige was admitted to the Baseball Hall of Fame, but not without a struggle, part of which Frick created. Shortly before his retirement, in 1964, Frick had opposed adding Paige to the Hall. "We can't alter the rules for old Satchel," he said, a bit patronizing. "In fact, I think we have been too lax in the past on the admission of players to the Hall. If you make one exception, you have to make many."[22]

Kuhn invited Frick to a meeting, along with Paul Kerr, Hall of Fame president, in early 1970 to discuss how to respond to calls for the inclusion of Negro leagues players in the Hall. Frick and Kerr argued that the players did not meet the admission requirement of ten years in major league baseball, and admitting them would water down the Hall's standards. No records exist defending Frick's circular logic: It was the very racism they were trying to reverse that denied the players a major league career and thus enshrinement in the Hall.

Dick Young, also invited to the meeting, reacted angrily to Frick's arguments. Kuhn recalled Young's response to Frick as being unnecessarily angry, even to the point of being rude. Young recalled the meeting and Frick's resistance, "not because they were black, but because they had not played in the major leagues. He could not see it was the same thing."[23]

Young's response and the overall tenor of the meeting caused Kuhn to abandon the idea and later appoint a special committee of Negro leagues experts, who would oversee a special exhibit honoring the players. In essence, Kuhn proposed to segregate the Negro leagues players to a separate hallway as a solution to the Jim Crow discrimination that affected their eligibility for the Hall.[24] The decision predictably drew protests, and the Hall of Fame board of directors approved Kuhn's follow-up proposal for those honored to be allowed admission directly into the Hall, with Paige the first so honored.[25]

A few weeks after the Hall of Fame ceremony, while working on his memoirs at home, Frick suffered a severe, and quite scary, fall. His kneecap was shattered and had to be replaced, and his face and head were badly cut. The injuries threatened to delay the project since he could not use a typewriter, but he promised to find a secretary to help once he left the hospital.[26] By February, Frick reported that surgery to replace the kneecap was successful, and he was able to get around much more easily—and resume work on the memoirs.[27] By March, he had recovered to the point that he was able to attend an annual Hall of Fame banquet in Bradenton, Florida, during spring training.[28]

From time to time, he would be called on to comment about some baseball controversy or historical moment, and usually by one of his old-school friends. He defended Kuhn, who was criticized for mishandling the 1972 players' strike, with familiar logic. "It simply is not the function of the office to intercede in such matters as the strike," he said. "I was involved in situations that the public thought I should get involved in and I was criticized for saying it was a 'league matter.' That's what this was, entirely between the players and the clubs in the two leagues."[29]

Frick was able to return a career-long favor to the writers, in part, by lobbying the Hall of Fame to recognize living recipients of the J. G. Taylor Spink Award, given annually to recognize sports writers, during the Hall of Fame ceremonies—"to let writers walk in the garden while they could still smell the roses," as columnist Bob Broeg put it.[30]

The first two to benefit from the public recognition, in 1973, were Fred Lieb, who wrote about baseball for several newspapers over his 60-year career, and Dan Daniel, long-time writer for the *New York World-Telegram and Sun*. It was particularly gratifying for Frick to see Daniel recognized in that way; he had served as Frick's Boswell, chronicling Frick's 31 years in baseball administration. The third honored, J. Roy Stockton of St. Louis, was awarded posthumously, as most previous honorees had been.[31]

In March 1973, Frick's book, *Games, Asterisks, and People: Memoirs of a Lucky Fan*, was released. Those hoping long-simmering frustration would lead Frick to unleash a controversial takedown of baseball owners were once again disappointed. This was not an autobiography, filled with rigidly researched detail and critical reflection, but memoirs from an affable man who did not practice public shaming.

Perhaps the saddest chapter in the memoirs is the one where Frick discusses the role of the commissioner. Of all the observations to begin the chapter, he states, "The commissionership of baseball is a very lonely job."[32] That was the first impression from the former sports writer who enjoyed the professional fraternity of ink-stained wretches and from the former league president who loved interacting with players, managers, and umpires.

According to his granddaughter, Kelly Frick Richards, during his 14 years in baseball's top job, he found fellowship from his neighbors in Bronxville and especially from his office staff. "His office staff loved him," she said. "He treated them so well; they mattered as people. Frank Slocum and Mary Sotos [his personal secretary for almost 30 years]—why would his granddaughter know their names?"[33] Slocum, son of Bill Slocum—Frick's fellow ghostwriter for Babe Ruth—served as the commissioner's assistant for 13 of his 14 years in office. He later served as the first executive director of the Baseball Assistance Team, a charitable organization endowed by Major League Baseball to provide confidential assistance to former players in particular need.[34] Even the wait staff at Toots Shor's, Frick's daily lunch stop, provided a measure of friendship denied him by virtue of his position.

Veteran St. Louis baseball writer Bob Broeg, in his column about the book, claimed "it is indeed really more than the casual thoughts of a man whose modesty saw himself as a fan first, baseball official second and as an authority third." At the same time, he confessed, "I just wish he would have taken off his velvet gloves, but if he had, obviously, he wouldn't have been true to himself."[35]

The Sporting News' official book review, which appeared three months later, was written by Joe Pollack, who was restaurant and theatre critic for the *St. Louis Post-Dispatch*. Pollack, a former sports writer, went easy on Frick. "In Frick's more than 30 years, a lot of things transpired," he noted, adding, "Few of them get any sort of deep look or interpretation from Frick, despite his supposed involvement." The review acknowledged how Judge Landis did not fare well under Frick's critique of his obstructionism toward integration. But beyond that, Pollack assigns respect for Frick, "in this warm and loving book by a man who has been most happy with a long and enduring love."[36]

Other reviews were kind to both Frick and the book. Red Smith combined Frick's book with Harold Peterson's *The Man Who Invented Baseball* to discuss the game's supposed origins. About Frick's work he noted the author's 50-plus years in baseball and added, "If in that time he ever discovered a flaw in the game, in its owners, administrators, players or umpires, in the ball or the bat or the bases, he does not mention it in his memoirs." Smith also critiqued Frick's downplaying of the anti–Jackie Robinson strike of 1947 and defended the article by Stanley Woodward that covered it.[37]

Dick Young's review picked out many of the book's anecdotes (particularly those that involved Young himself). Playing off the salacious news in 1973 of Yankees Fritz Peterson and Mike Kekich swapping wives and families, Young contrasted that with Frick's perspective. "He is the Walt Disney of the written word, pushing family entertainment, avoiding sensationalism and controversy, refusing to exploit shock value."[38]

There is evidence that Frick sincerely tried to complete more writing projects in retirement, though nothing came of them. While working on his memoirs, he did mention another book project, about "the lore and legends of the Ute Indians." It had been a lifelong interest, dating from his days in Colorado, but nothing came of it, and no remnants seem to exist in what few papers he left to his family.[39]

He did leave behind two chapters of a revealing book project: a fictional biography of a major league baseball player, titled *Big Leaguer*.[40] No date exists on the manuscript, but from its condition, it clearly appears to have been written later rather than earlier in Frick's life. It was presented as a first-person account, "as told to Ford C. Frick." The implied role of Frick as ghost writer might seem ironic, given his professional history, but it also provided some rhetorical distance from what turned out to be a surprisingly impolitic look at baseball, considering the author.

The ballplayer in Frick's book is never named, and the one teammate mentioned is a childhood enemy who becomes his big league teammate, a stereotypical Italian character nicknamed "Tony Bananas." The teammate dies young, of complications from an old World War I injury—a loose piece of shrapnel in his lungs. While Frick extols the manhood and courage of major leaguers, he also implicitly criticizes a system that treats players as chattel, even though as commissioner he fought to preserve the reserve clause that promoted such treatment.

If the plot revealed Frick's attitude toward baseball, his writing style reflected his admiration for the writers he worked with in the 1920s. The risky technique of using an athlete as narrator, given their literary shortcomings, was also used by one of his more esteemed contemporaries, Ring Lardner, in his 1916 book, *You Know Me, Al*. The themes of courage and manhood were explored in *The Sun Field*, a 1923 book by another New York colleague, Heywood Broun. And of course the concept of players as property formed the reality of the 1919 Black Sox scandal, which received its best literary treatment in Eliot Asinof's 1963 nonfiction book, *Eight Men Out*. (*Shoeless Joe*, the W. P. Kinsella novel that inspired the film *Field of Dreams*, was published after Frick's death.)

But sadly for Frick, the writer's pen yielded no tangible results outside of his memoirs. If Frick had looked forward to retirement as an opportunity to get back to his first vocation, the distractions—first of the ceremonial trappings of a retired sports executive and later of declining health—deprived his work of the audience it had enjoyed in the 1920s.

Right before his own book came out, Frick participated in one of the interviews that produced Jerome Holtzman's excellent oral history of sports writing in the Golden Age and beyond, *No Cheering in the Press Box*. No doubt it was very satisfying to Frick that Holtzman would list him within the company of Dan Daniel, Fred Lieb, John Drebinger, Red Smith, and Shirley Povich.

Frick's chapter stands apart because it is personal history and career reflection more than sports beat anecdotes. It also could be argued that Frick was more candid and honest (and salty) to Holtzman than he was in his own memoirs. He spoke more candidly about ghost writing for Babe Ruth and even said, "I tried to protect the Babe because his record should stand until it's honestly beaten." And he reiterated his claim that the lot of the commissioner was a lonely life.[41]

At some point after his book was published, Frick suffered a series of strokes that by early 1977 had left him "partially paralyzed and unable to speak," according to Holtzman.[42] Perhaps the cruelest irony for Frick was that his developing health problems deprived him of the social contact he enjoyed and replaced it with the isolation he despised as commissioner.

His granddaughter, Kelly Frick Richards, wonders if he was suffering from the same condition, progressive supranuclear palsy, that would lead to her father's death 14 years later.[43] His grandson, Ford Frick II, remembered visiting his grandfather during this time, and particularly his departing words to the grandson whom he had squired to so many baseball events: "Remember me."[44]

Family, fans, and sports journalists did indeed remember Frick after his death on April 8, 1978, at the age of 83 after a month-long hospitalization. A private funeral service and interment of his ashes followed.

Kuhn, who attended the service, also saluted him. "Through 31 years as a baseball leader he brought the game integrity, dedication and a happy tranquility far removed from the turbulence of today."[45]

"He was a good man but he will be remembered chiefly as a reluctant leader," Red Smith wrote. "This was due not so much to irresolution as to the way he viewed his job. He didn't think baseball needed a house dick and didn't consider himself one."[46]

Frick was recognized by the Hall of Fame—whose existence caused him so much satisfaction—with the establishment of the Ford Frick Award

17. Extra Innings

to honor excellence in baseball broadcasting. The first two recipients were Mel Allen and Red Barber, who were honored at the Hall of Fame ceremony less than four months after Frick died.[47]

So how should Frick be remembered? The powerless, compliant owners' servant is a tempting analogy. Perhaps it would be better to consider whether Frick simply stayed close to his journalism roots. He was not there to make things happen. He was there to gather information, analyze it, and present it in a way that informed his audience—the owners, in this case.

The word "media" fits well within Frick's role as commissioner. In its common usage, the term signifies journalism's role in the middle—between sources (events, information) and audiences. As commissioner, Frick functioned in the middle—between players, owners, fans, and the media. And he stood alone in their crossfire.

At some point after his memoirs were published in 1973, Frick suffered a series of strokes that left him unable to speak. His last words to his grandson: "Remember me" (National Baseball Hall of Fame Library, Cooperstown, New York).

But he wasn't really alone. He spent virtually his entire professional life in a close relationship with the game he loved. If, as commissioner, all Frick had to hold onto was the game of baseball, then that was enough. And he lived and died a happy man for it.

Chapter Notes

Introduction

1. Frank Graham, "Big League Owners Hired a Newspaperman," *New York Journal-American*, September 24, 1951.
2. Jimmy Cannon, "Frick Exemplifies Baseball's Innocence," King Features Syndicate, February 5, 1970.
3. Roscoe McGowen, "MacPhail Offers New Inter-League Series Plan," *New York Times*, October 26, 1939, 36.
4. Dan Daniel, "Frick Devised Contract Reform in '36," *The Sporting News*, July 31, 1946, 3–4.
5. Ford Frick, "Radio Editorial, WOR & WINS—1932," personal papers.
6. Ford Frick, "Baseball Has Its Musical Angles," *Music Journal 14* (July–August 1956) 6: 11–12, 32. The article also mentioned the musical talents of baseball players and Bing Crosby's part ownership of the Pittsburgh Pirates.
9. *Ibid.*
10. Ford Frick, *Games, Asterisks, and People: Memoirs of a Lucky Fan* (New York: Crown, 1973), 154.
11. Larry Moffi, *The Conscience of the Game: Baseball's Commissioners from Landis to Selig* (Lincoln: University of Nebraska Press, 2006), 51.
12. Frick, *Games, Asterisks, and People*, 155.
13. Joe King, "Mantle, Maris Spark Gate Boom," *The Sporting News*, July 26, 1961, 8.
14. Arthur Daley, "The Pause That Refreshes?," *New York Times*, September 19, 1961, 40.
15. C. C. Johnson Spink, "Writers Back Frick's Homer Decision," *The Sporting News*, August 9, 1961, 1, 4.
16. *Ibid.*
17. Anita Bernstein, "Question Autonomy, With an Asterisk," *Emory Law Journal* 54 (2005), 239–260.
18. Walter Bingham, "Assault on the Record," *Sports Illustrated*, July 31, 1961, 8–11.
19. Hy Hurwitz, "Mick 'Wouldn't Want Mark If It Was Set in 155 Games,'" *The Sporting News*, August 9, 1961, 4.
20. "Yanks' Homer Derby Goes West and Berra Ponders a New Pitch," *New York Times*, August 22, 1961, 34.
21. Spink, "Writers Back Frick's Homer Decision," 4.
22. Hurtwitz, "Mick 'Wouldn't Want Mark,'" 4.
23. "Now's Time for N. L. Decision," *The Sporting News*, August 9, 1961, 8.
24. Richard J. H. Johnston, "Homer Record After 154 Games Won't Count With Fan on Street," *New York Times*, September 21, 1961, 42.
25. Rosenfeld, *Roger Maris: A Title to Fame*, 77.
26. Harvey Rosenfeld, *Still a Legend: The Story of Roger Maris* (Lincoln, NE: iUniverse, 1991), 86–87.
27. David Halberstam, *October 1964* (New York: Fawcett Columbine, 1995), 159.
28. *Ibid.*, 163–164.
29. Charles Allen Jr., "The Man Behind the Asterisk: Another Side of Maris," *New York Times*, September 29, 1991, S13.

Chapter 1

1. William Barry Furlong, "That Sixtieth Home Run," *New York Times Magazine*, August 20, 1961, 53.
2. Rube Samuelsen, "Frick Swipe Speeds Action on L.A. Park," *The Sporting News*, January 22, 1958, 5.
3. Dan Daniel, "250-Foot Home-Run Distance Obsolete," *The Sporting News*, May 7, 1958, 12; "Coliseum Homers Viewed as Farce," *New York Times*, April 30, 1958, 37.
4. Arthur Daley, "Protecting the Records," *New York Times*, October 23, 1960, S2.
5. Howard M. Tuckner, "Frick, Giles and Tests of Ball Can't Explain Homer Increase," *New York Times*, August 3, 1961, 16.
6. Harvey Rosenfeld, *Maris: A Title to Fame* (Fargo, ND: Prairie House, 1991), 61.
7. Dan Daniel, "Majors Hint Move Toward Free-Agent Draft," *The Sporting News*, July 5, 1961, 5–6.
8. "Ruth's Record Can Be Broken Only in 154 Games, Frick Rules," *New York Times*, July 18, 1961, 20.

30. Bill Veeck with Ed Linn, *Veeck—As in Wreck: The Autobiography of Bill Veeck* (Chicago: University of Chicago Press, 1962), 240–242.
31. "Was Frick Out of Bounds in Making Rule? Dan Asks," *The Sporting News*, August 9, 1961, 4.
32. Rosenfeld, *Still a Legend*, 140.
33. Jack O'Connell, personal e-mail, January 18, 2014.
34. Oscar Kahan, "Scribes Back Off—Threat to Protest Fades," *The Sporting News*, December 13, 1961, 8.
35. Dan Daniel, "Weary Bombers Fuel Motors for Attack on Cincy," *The Sporting News*, October 4, 1961, 8.
36. Dan Daniel, "Cronin Stirs Up Rhubarb, Raps Frick Homer Ruling," *The Sporting News*, September 20, 1961, 9.
37. John Drebinger, "Record of Maris Has No Asterisk," *New York Times*, December 23, 1961, 18.
38. Mark Armour, *Joe Cronin: A Life in Baseball* (Lincoln: University of Nebraska Press, 2010), 273.
39. Maury Allen, *Roger Maris: A Man for All Seasons* (New York: Donald I. Fine, 1986) 24.
40. "Maris Finishes Second to Babe's No. 1," *The Sporting News*, September 27, 1991, 10.
41. Dan Daniel "Frick Proposes Record Book for 162-Game Chart," *The Sporting News*, 14.
42. "No * Will Mar Home Record, Says Frick with ++ for Critics," *New York Times*, September 22, 1961, 38.
43. Frick, *Games, Asterisks, and People*, 155.
44. Allen Barra, "The Myth of Maris' Asterisk," Salon.com, October 3, 2001, accessed December 11, 2013.
45. Rosenfeld, *Maris: A Title to Fame*, 69.
46. Leonard Koppett, "Home Run Timetable: Lost in Its Own Footnotes," *New York Times*, July 21, 1964, 36.
47. Leonard Koppett, *Koppett's Concise History of Major League Baseball* (New York: Carroll & Graf, 1998), 307–308.
48. Louis Effrat, "Maris, Frick Make Hit Speeches, Then Strike Words From Record," *New York Times*, January 27, 1962, S15.
49. Mickey Mantle and Herb Gluck, *The Mick* (New York: Doubleday, 1985), 208.
50. Marty Ralbovsky, "After Decade, Maris Resents Asterisk," *New York Times*, 49.
51. George Vecsey, "Roger Maris: No Asterisk," *New York Times*, December 16, 1985, C11.
52. Ken Rosenthal, "Moments Baseball Would Rather Forget," *The Sporting News*, July 29, 2002, 16.
53. Tom Clavin and Danny Peary, *Roger Maris: Baseball's Reluctant Hero* (New York: Touchstone Books, 2010), 261–262.
54. Deane McGowen, "Yanks Face Top Batter Today," *New York Times*, May 17, 1963, 54.
55. Allen, *Roger Maris*, 189–190.
56. Oliver E. Kuechle, "Ford Frick Takes the Bull—by the Tail," *Milwaukee Journal*, June 10, 1963.
57. Murray Chass, "Maris Without Ruth? It's a Possibility," *New York Times*, August 2, 1991, B15; Murray Chass, "Maris's Feat Finally Recognized 30 Years After Hitting 61 Homers," *New York Times*, September 5, 1991, B12.
58. "Maris 'Asterisk' Might Go But Ruth's Name Won't," *The Sporting News*, August 12, 1991, 5.

Chapter 2

1. Dan Daniel, "Frick, New National League Head, Born Poor Farm Boy, Received First Big Break When New York Called Him," *The Sporting News*, November 15, 1934, 5.
2. Mary Jane Lepird, personal interview, August 8, 2012, Brimfield, IN.
3. Jerome Holtzman, *No Cheering in the Press Box* (New York: Holt, Rinehart and Winston, 1973), 200.
4. Carl Heim, "Preface." This is a prepared speech with the subtitle, "Presentation to Ford Frick, Commissioner of Baseball, of the Award as 'Hoosier of the Year' by the Sons of Indiana in New York, at Toots Shor's Restaurant, New York City, Friday Night, April 25, 1952."
5. Lepird, personal interview, August 8, 2012.
6. Holtzman, *No Cheering in the Press Box*, 200.
7. Frick, *Games, Asterisks, and People*, 33–34.
8. Robert F. Kelley, "An Old Ball Player Makes Good," *New York Times*, December 11, 1934, 30.
9. Ford Frick, *Games, Asterisks, and People*, 5.
10. Holtzman, *No Cheering in the Press Box*, 199.
11. Ward Morehouse, "Ford Frick: He Isn't Trying on Landis' Toga for Size—Yet," *The Sporting News*, January 25, 1945, 3.
12. Daniel, "Frick, New National League Head."
13. "Address by Ford Frick, Centennial Celebration, Indiana Alpha Chapter, Phi Kappa Psi Fraternity, Greencastle, Indiana," June 5, 1965, Baseball Hall of Fame Archives.
14. Carl Heim, "Preface."
15. Holtzman, *No Cheering in the Press Box*, 199.
16. "Ford Frick's Stay in Walsenberg is Recalled," from personal papers.
17. Robert E. Kelley, "An Old Ball Player Makes Good," *New York Times*, December 11, 1934, 30.
18. Holtzman, *No Cheering in the Press Box*, 199.
19. Kelley, "An Old Ball Player Makes Good."
20. Rud Rennie, "Ford Frick—President," *Baseball Magazine*, January 1935.
21. Terry Housholder, "Ford Frick Dies at 83," *Ligonier Advance-Leader*, April 11, 1978, 1.
22. Nancy Christofferson, "Frederick Cowing: Businessman, Stockbroker, and Mason." http://www.huerfanojournal.com/node/4182. Retrieved November 27, 2013.
23. "Marriage," *Colorado Springs Gazette*, September 19, 1916, 10.

24. Dr. Lloyd C. Shaw, undated and untitled clipping. The article is included in a Frick family scrapbook and appears to have been published in the *Colorado Springs Gazette* when Frick was appointed commissioner in 1951.
25. "Frick Started Climb to New Post as Local Sports Scribe," *Colorado Springs Gazette*, September 21, 1951, 14.
26. Tom McLaughlin, "Looking Them Over," *Colorado Springs Gazette-Telegraph*. The date on this clip is uncertain, but it appears to be from 1951, when Frick was appointed commissioner.
27. "Frick in Baseball Since School Days," *New York Times*, September 21, 1951, 39; Holtzman, 206.
28. Robert Follansbee and E. E. Jones, "The Flood of June, 1921, in the Arkansas River, at Pueblo, Colorado." *Proceedings of the American Society of Civil Engineers* 47, no. 10 (December 1921): 769–774.
29. Guy E. Macy, "The Pueblo Flood of 1921," *The Colorado Magazine* 17, no. 6 (November 1940): 201–211.
30. Arthur O. Ridgway, R. G. Hosea, and George G. Anderson, "Papers and Discussions: The Flood of June, 1921, in the Arkansas River, at Pueblo, Colorado," *Proceedings of the American Society of Civil Engineers* 47, no. 9 (November 1921): 535–560.
31. *Ibid*.
32. Macy, "The Pueblo Flood of 1921," 205–206.
33. "How Aeroplane Made Trip to Pueblo Flood," *Colorado Springs Evening Telegraph*, June 4, 1921, 1.
34. Danny Summers, "Baseballs, Kangaroos, and Ford Frick." *Pikes Peak Courier*, February 5, 2014. http://pikespeakcourier.net/stories/Baseball-kangaroos-and-Ford-Frick,144481. Accessed June 13, 2014.
35. Ford C. Frick, "Telegraph Reporter Sees Death and Ruin from an Airplane," *Colorado Springs Evening Telegraph*, 1.
36. *Ibid*.
37. *Ibid*., 2.
38. *Ibid*., 1.
39. "Telegraph Gives World First News and Plane Photos of Pueblo Flood," *Colorado Springs Evening Telegraph*, June 6, 1921, 6.
40. "Airplane Views of Pueblo Flood," *El Paso County Democrat*, June 10, 1921, 5.
41. J. G. Taylor Spink, "Ford's Flood-Tide," *The Sporting News*, May 18, 1944, 1–2.
42. Ford C. Frick, "Cowboys Never Threaten and C.C. Uses Second and Third String Men Registering Year's Record Win," *Colorado Springs Telegraph*, February 26, 1922.
43. McLaughlin, "Looking Them Over."
44. Robert F. Kelley, "An Old Ball Player Makes Good," *New York Times*, December 11, 1934, 30.
45. Frederick G. Lieb, "Flashbacks—Ford Christopher Frick," *The Sporting News*, October 28, 1943, 2.
46. Jimmy Mann, "150-Pound Scrapper," *St. Petersburg Times*, May 6, 1964, 37.
47. Frank Graham, "They Wound Up with One, However," *New York Journal-American*, September 24, 1951.
48. "Steered to Fame by Printer," *The Sporting News*, December 4, 1957, 7; Spink, "Ford's Flood-Tide," 1–2.

Chapter 3

1. Ford Frick, *Games, Asterisks, and People: Memoirs of a Lucky Fan* (New York: Crown, 1973), 42.
2. Frank Graham, "Ford Missed Sunshine of Colo. Springs on Arrival in N. Y.," *The Sporting News*, December 4, 1957, 7.
3. Ward Morehouse, "Ford Frick: He Isn't Trying on Landis' Toga for Size—Yet," *The Sporting News*, January 25, 1945, 3.
4. Jerome Holtzman, *No Cheering in the Press Box* (New York: Holt, Rinehart and Winston, 1973), 207.
5. Frick, *Games, Asterisks, and People*, 85–86.
6. Holtzman, *No Cheering in the Press Box*, 207.
7. Tommy Holmes, "Dashing First Baseman, Quarter Mile Runner, Teacher and Writer," *Brooklyn Eagle*, November 9, 1934.
8. Frederick G. Lieb, "'Horse Sense' Policy Pledged by Frick," *The Sporting News*, October 3, 1951, 3–4.
9. Robert H. Boyle, "Perfect Man for the Job," *Sports Illustrated*, April 9, 1962.
10. Dan Hall, "Lieb Writes of '25," *St. Petersburg Times*, March 5, 1950, 33.
11. Frank Graham, "They Wound Up With One, However," *New York Journal-American*, September 24, 1951.
12. "Frick Tells Scribes of Responsibilities," *The Sporting News*, December 11, 1941, 13.
13. Frick, *Games, Asterisks, and People*, 71.
14. American Society of Newspaper Editors, *Problems of Journalism*, vol. 7 (Washington, D.C.: ASNE, 1929), 26.
15. *Ibid*., 99.
16. Frick, *Games, Asterisks, and People*, 35.
17. Ford Frick, "My Greatest Diamond Thrill," *The Sporting News*, February 10, 1944, 9. For the record, his greatest thrill as of 1944 was when Ernie White of the Cardinals shut out the Yankees, 2–0, at Yankee Stadium in Game Three of the 1942 World Series. The Yankees had not been shut out in a World Series game since 1926.
18. Frederick G. Lieb, "Flashbacks—Ford Christopher Frick," *The Sporting News*, October 28, 1943.
19. Warren Brown, *Win, Lose, or Draw* (New York: Van Rees Press, 1947), 121.
20. Holtzman, *No Cheering in the Press Box*, 206.
21. Christy Walsh, *Adios to Ghosts* (self-published, 1937), 5–7.
22. Michael K. Bohn, "Knute Rockne's Un-

timely Death: An Early Airline Crash 80 Years Ago," *McClatchy Tribune Information Services*, March 31, 2011.

23. Robert W. Creamer, *Babe: The Legend Comes to Life* (New York: Simon & Schuster, 1974) 271–274.

24. Walsh, *Adios to Ghosts*, 25.

25. Creamer, *Babe: The Legend Comes to Life*, 273.

26. http://sports.nyhistory.org/bill-slocum-sr/

27. Holtzman, *No Cheering in the Press Box*, 210–211.

28. Fred Lieb, *Baseball as I Have Known It* (New York: Coward, McCann, & Geoghegan, 1977), 152–153.

29. Walsh, *Adios to Ghosts*, 22–23.

30. Creamer, *Babe: The Legend Comes to Life*, 273.

31. Louis Effrat, "Traynor Debunks Tale Frick Wrote," *New York Times*, October 5, 1960, 49.

32. Leigh Montville, *The Big Bam: The Life and Times of Babe Ruth* (New York: Doubleday, 2006), 300; Holtzman, *No Cheering in the Press Box*, 6–7.

33. Robert W. Creamer, *Babe: The Legend Comes to Life*, 186.

34. Arthur Daley, "Honoring an Alumnus," *New York Times*, January 12, 1966, 68.

35. Bob Wolf, "He's Boss," *Milwaukee Journal*, January 15, 1956.

36. Christy Walsh, *Adios to Ghosts!*, 16.

37. Babe Ruth, "Keep an Eye on the A's Outfield," *New York Evening Journal*, March 29, 1933, 23.

38. Babe Ruth, "'I Feel Great and Ready to Go,' Declares Ruth," *New York Evening Journal*, March 23, 1933, 23.

39. Lee Allen, "Famed Old-Timers Get Together," *The Sporting News*, August 10, 1968, 6.

40. Jerome Holtzman, "Introduction" to *Babe Ruth's Own Book of Baseball* (New York: A.L. Burt, 1928), viii–ix, 274.

41. Louis Rubin, "Babe Ruth's Ghost," *Sewanee Review* 101, no. 2 (Spring 1993): 240–248.

42. Ford Frick, *Sports Memories That are Sports Records* (New York: Richfield Oil Corporation of New York, 1931).

43. "Ford Frick's Broadcast!" *New York Evening Journal*, July 7, 1933.

44. Creamer, *Babe: The Legend Comes to Life*, 273.

45. Frick, *Games, Asterisks, and People*, 36.

46. "An Understudy for Lazzeri." The bibliographic information for this item is not given, beyond the title, but a handwritten note gives the date as July 3, 1930.

47. Ford C. Frick II, telephone interview, November 18, 2015.

48. Ford C. Frick, "'Mail-Order' Morse: A Story of Hearts and Diamonds," *Liberty*, April 21, 1928, 33.

49. Ford C. Frick, "'Gangway! I'm Coming Through!'" *Red Blooded Stories*, January 1929, 57–66.

50. Ford C. Frick, "Baseball Anthology," undated clipping.

51. Bob Addie, "Addie's Atoms," *The Sporting News*, October 19, 1968, 14.

52. Ford C. Frick, "They've Got to Be Right," *Saturday Evening Post*, January 26, 1935.

53. Ford C. Frick, "Who Will Win the National League Pennant?," *Liberty*, April 20, 1935.

54. Ford C. Frick, "Baseball Will Find You!," *The All-America Sports Magazine*, June 1935.

55. Robert F. Kelley, "An Old Ball Player Makes Good," *New York Times*, December 11, 1934, 30.

56. Holmes, "Dashing First Baseman."

57. Charles C. Alexander, *Breaking the Slump: Baseball in the Depression Era* (New York: Columbia University Press, 2002), 33.

58. Frick, *Games, Asterisks, and People*, 108–109.

59. Harold Rosenthal, "Broadcast Again Puts $1,500,000 Into Series Kitty," *The Sporting News*, September 16, 1953.

60. John Carvalho and Loren Hawkins, "We Know the Name; Do They Know the Game? 'Celebrity' Articles About the 1924 and 1932 World Series," *Journal of Sports Media* 1, no. 1 (Spring 2006): 73–89.

61. Orrin Dunlap, "Spectators Are Banned," *New York Times*, March 18, 1934, X11.

62. Holtzman, *No Cheering in the Press Box*, 211.

63. Ford Frick, "Radio Editorial, WOR & WINS—1932," personal papers.

64. Lewis E. Lawes to Ford Frick, 24 October 1933.

65. Lewis E. Lawes to Ford Frick, 21 December 1933.

66. Holtzman, *No Cheering in the Press Box*, 211.

67. *Ibid.*, 211–212.

68. "Keeps White Tie and Tails at Office to Go to Opera," *The Sporting News*, February 13, 1952, 3.

69. John Spink, "Why Not? It's Worth It!" *The Sporting News*, October 26, 1922, 4; William B. Anderson, "Crafting the National Pastime's Image: The History of Major League Baseball Public Relations," *Journalism & Mass Communication Monographs* 5, no. 1 (Spring 2003): 22–23.

70. Holtzman, *No Cheering in the Press Box*, 212.

71. Joe Vila, "Terry 'Rides' Carey at Writers' Feast," *The Sporting News*, February 15, 1934, 5.

72. "Tributes Paid Walt Johnson and Carl Hubbell," *The Sporting News*, February 15, 1934, 8.

73. Hy Turkin, "New Features in Green Book," *The Sporting News*, March 8, 1950, 18.

Chapter 4

1. Ford Frick, *Games, Asterisks, and People* (New York: Crown Publishers, 1973), 54–55.

2. Jerome Holtzman, *The Commissioners:*

Baseball's Midlife Crisis (New York: Total Sports, 1998), 94.

3. John Drebinger, "Club Owners of the National League Elect Frick as Successor to Heydler," *New York Times*, November 9, 1934, 29.

4. Tommy Holmes, "New Baseball President Becomes Successor to John A. Heydler," *Brooklyn Eagle*, November 8, 1934.

5. "Frick and Traband," *The Sporting News*, November 15, 1934, 4.

6. John Kieran, "Touching the Bases," *New York Times*, November 9, 1934, 29.

7. Frederick G. Lieb, "Ex-Scribes Write Game History as Officials," November 24, 1948, 7–8.

8. Robert F. Kelley, "An Old Ball Player Makes Good," *New York Times*, December 11, 1934, 30.

9. Dan Daniel, "Frick New National League Head, Born Poor Farm Boy, Received First Big Break When New York Called Him," *The Sporting News*, November 15, 1934, 5.

10. Tommy Holmes, "Dashing First Baseman, Quarter Mile Runner, Teacher and Writer," *Brooklyn Eagle*, November 9, 1934. The *New York Times* reported his salary at $20,000/year.

11. Dan Daniel, "Frick, New National League President, Received First Big Break," *New York Telegram*, November 15, 1934.

12. Ward Morehouse, "Ford Frick: He Isn't Trying on Landis' Toga for Size—Yet," *The Sporting News*, January 25, 1945, 3.

13. "Dan Daniel, Writer and Baseball Expert 50 Years, Dies at 91," *New York Times*, July 2, 1981, D18; Jerome Holtzman, *No Cheering in the Press Box* (New York City: Holt Rinehart and Winston, 1973), 1–14.

14. Michael Shapiro, *Bottom of the Ninth: Branch Rickey, Casey Stengel, and the Daring Scheme to Save Baseball From Itself* (New York: Times Books, 2009), 102–103.

15. "Leaders in Sports Aid Welfare Units," *New York Times*, June 25, 1935, p. 17; "Bronxville Legion Gives Annual Fete," *New York Times*, June 22, 1936, 21.

16. Ford C. Frick, "Frick Sees 5 Clubs in Race for Flag," *New York Times*, January 6, 1935, 57; Ford Frick, "Baseball Outlook Pleases Frick; Great Advance for 1935 is Seen," *New York Times*, April 14, 1935, S5.

17. Drebinger, "Club Owners of the National League Elect Frick," 29.

18. Dan Daniel, "Frick Tosses 'On-the-Record' Feed to Set Record," *The Sporting News*, March 16, 1949, 26; Tom Swope, "Wives Hold Own National League Party," *The Sporting News*, March 16, 1949, 26.

19. Dan Daniel, "Yanks Make Offer for Manush, Meyer," *The Sporting News*, November 15, 1934, 2.

20. "Frick and Traband," *The Sporting News*.

21. "Baseball Writers Honor Frick at Dinner; Landis Is Among the 140 Guests Present," *New York Times*, December 6, 1934, 29.

22. John Kieran, "Sports of the Times," *New York Times*, December 7, 1934, 32.

23. John Drebinger, "Heydler in Unprecedented Plea Urges Players to Best Effort," *New York Times*, April 11, 1933, 24.

24. Jesse Berrett, "Diamonds for Sale: Promoting Baseball During the Great Depression," in *Baseball History 4: An Annual of Original Baseball Research*, ed. Peter Levine (Westport, CT: Meckler, 1991), 54; John Kieran, "Sports of the Times," *New York Times*, April 21, 1936, 30.

25. Gerald Holland, "Baseball and Ballyhoo," *American Mercury*, May 1937, 82–83.

26. Ibid.

27. "League Will Celebrate," *New York Times*. April 24, 1936, 25.

28. "Cubs Twice Beat Bees, 1–0 and 8–4," *New York Times*, June 26, 1936, 24.

29. Frick, *Games, Asterisks, and People*, 215.

30. David Pietrusza, *Judge and Jury: The Life and Times of Judge Kenesaw Mountain Landis* (South Bend, IN: Diamond Communications, 1998), 415–416.

31. Dan Daniel, "The Wise Leadership of Ford Frick," *Baseball Magazine*, April 1949.

32. Dan Daniel, "Chapman Gives Lie to Yankee Dislikes," *The Sporting News*, December 13, 1934, 3.

33. John Drebinger, "Braves' Future and Dog Racing to Be Aired at Meeting Today," *New York Times*, January 18, 1935, 30.

34. Rory Costello, "James Gaffney," SABR Biography Project, www.sabr.org/node/27111. Accessed August 4, 2016.

35. Roscoe McGowen, "Dog Racing Asked for Braves Field," *New York Times*, January 13, 1935, S1.

36. Ibid.; David George Surdam, *Wins, Losses, and Empty Seats: How Baseball Outlasted the Great Depression* (Lincoln: University of Nebraska Press, 2011), 289.

37. Paul Shannon, "Dogs Chase Braves Out of Park, as Yawkey Bars Use of Fenway," *The Sporting News*, January 17, 1935, 1.

38. Burton A. Boxerman and Benita W. Boxerman, *Jews and Baseball, Volume 1: Entering the American Mainstream, 1871–1948* (Jefferson, NC: McFarland, 2007), 121.

39. John Drebinger, "National League Meeting Called to Decide on Future of Homeless Braves," *New York Times*, January 15, 1935, 24.

40. Minutes, National League Special Meeting, January 18, 1935, Baseball Hall of Fame and Museum, Cooperstown, NY. The direct exchange between Fuchs and Adams occurs between pages 44 and 72.

41. "Baseball Assured at Braves Field," *New York Times*, January 29, 1935, 26.

42. John Drebinger, "Rule Permitting Night Baseball With Restrictions Passed by National League," *New York Times*, February 6, 1935, 25.

43. "Ruth Will Draw 500,000 Fans to National League, Says Frick," *New York Times*, March 17, 1935, S5.

44. James P. Dawson, "Braves, With Ruth, Conquer Yankees in the Ninth, 3–2," *New York Times*, March 17, 1935, S1.

45. David George Surdam, *Wins, Losses and*

Notes—Chapter 4

Empty Seats (Lincoln: University of Nebraska Press, 2011), 290.

46. "No Place Open in Major Leagues for Ruth, Poll of Clubs Reveals," *New York Times*, June 4, 1935, 27.

47. "Ruth, Recipient of Life-Time Pass, Expresses His Appreciation to National League for Gift," *New York Times*, September 5, 1935, 27.

48. Montville, *The Big Bam*, 344.

49. Roscoe McGowen, "Ruth Signed as Coach of Dodgers at Reported $15,000 for This Year," *New York Times*, June 19, 1938, 63.

50. Wayne Stewart, *Babe Ruth: A Biography* (Westport, CT: Greenwood Publishing Group, 2006), 114.

51. "Fuchs, in Post Since 1925, Quits as Head of Braves," *New York Times*, August 1, 1935, 16.

52. John Drebinger, "National League Takes Over Affairs of Braves at Meeting of Club Owners," *New York Times*, November 27, 1935, 25.

53. "Goldman Makes Baltimore Bid," *New York Times*, November 28, 1935, 43.

54. "Offer by Quinn to Buy Braves with Adams's Backing Reported," *New York Times*, December 7, 1935, 23; "Braves' Case Statements," *New York Times*, December 11, 1935, 30; John Drebinger, "Deals for Foxx and Simmons Confirmed; Braves Franchise to Quinn," *New York Times*, December 11, 1935, 30.

55. Charles C. Alexander, *Breaking the Slump: Baseball in the Depression Era* (New York: Columbia University Press, 2002), 118.

56. Jack Malaney, "$350,000 Reported Sale Price of Bees," *The Sporting News*, December 12, 1940, 8.

57. J. G. Taylor Spink, "MacPhail Lifting Dodger Debts; Bees Likely to Be Sold by Jan. 1," *The Sporting News*, November 7, 1940, 1, 8.

58. Howell Stevens, "Big Money Support for Bees Under New Syndicate Control," *The Sporting News*, April 24, 1941, 1; Associated Press, "Quinn Syndicate Purchases Controlling Interest in Bees," April 21, 1941, 23.

59. David Pietrusza, *Lights On! The Wild Century-Long Saga of Night Baseball* (Lanham, MD: Scarecrow, 1997), 103.

60. Minutes, National League Annual Meeting, December 11–12, 1934, Baseball Hall of Fame and Museum, Cooperstown, NY, 179–211.

61. John Drebinger, "Night Baseball on Limited Scale Adopted by National League," *New York Times*, December 13, 1934, 31.

62. John Drebinger, "Major Leagues Split on Type of Ball and Night Contests," *New York Times*, December 8, 1937, 35.

63. Frick, "Frick Sees 5 Clubs," 57.

64. Alexander, *Breaking the Slump*, 106; Pietrusza, *Lights On!*, 109–115; "Reds' Night Game Draws 25,000 Fans," *New York Times*, May 25, 1935, 9.

65. Pietrusza, *Lights On!*, 120–121.

66. Ibid., 135.

67. John Drebinger, "Giants Will Play Night Baseball Here," *New York Times*, November 15, 1939, 31.

68. Ronald Oakley, *Baseball's Last Golden Age, 1946–1960* (Jefferson, NC: McFarland, 1994), 40.

69. "Making Punishment Fit the Crime" (Newspaper not identified), May 9, 1935.

70. John Kieran, "Sports of the Times," *New York Times*, June 3, 1935, 24.

71. John Kieran, "Sports of the Times," *New York Times*, April 23, 1936, 30.

72. John Kieran, "An Umpire's Life is Not a Happy One, and Yet," *New York Times*, July 4, 1935, F5, F15.

73. "Umps' 10 Commandments as Pronounced by Frick," *The Sporting News*, March 9, 1949, 31.

74. "2 League Umpired Punished by Frick," *New York Times*, August 24, 1935, 8; Joe King, "NL History Hints Frick Will Be Tough Czar," *New York World-Telegram*, September 22, 1951; Doug Feldmann, *September Streak: The 1935 Chicago Cubs Chase the Pennant* (Jefferson, NC: McFarland, 2003), 154–155.

75. Alexander, *Breaking the Slump*, 111–112; "Landis Investigates Wrangle," *New York Times*, October 5, 1935, 9.

76. "Arbiters Are Only Men in Baseball Held to Fixed Wage, He Says," *New York Times*, January 28, 1936, 23; Boxerman and Boxerman, *Jews and Baseball*, 111–115; "Frick Changes Two Rules," *New York Times*, July 12, 1936, S4; John Drebinger, "Gorman Named Business Manager of Dodgers to Fill Quinn's Post," *New York Times*, January 29, 1936, 16; John Drebinger, "Schedule is Ratified and Breadon Named Vice President by National League," *New York Times*, February 4, 1936, 22.

77. "Curb on Umpire Baiting," *The Sporting News*, April 9, 1942, 9; "Umpire Wrangling and Huddle Are Curbed in National League Order to Speed Play," *New York Times*, April 6, 1942, 20.

78. "All This and Suspensions Too," *The Sporting News*, May 14, 1942, 10; "Violators of Umpire-Baiting Rule Warned of Suspensions by Frick," *New York Times*, May 7, 1942, 25.

79. Aya S. Chacar and William Hesterly, "Innovations and Value Creation in Major League Baseball, 1860–2000," *Business History* 46, no. 3 (July 2004): 407–438.

80. "Landis Seeks Curb on Broadcasting," *New York Times*, April 29, 1936, 25.

81. John Drebinger, "Landis Rift With Owners Seen in Defeat of His Proposal," *New York Times*, December 9, 1936, 36.

82. "Dodger Baseball to be Broadcast," *New York Times*, Dec. 7, 1938; "Heavy Program Awaits Three-Day Sessions of Major Leagues Here," *New York Times*, Dec. 11, 1938, 104.

83. Roscoe McGowen, "Giants Will Sell Radio Rights to Polo Grounds Games in 1939," *New York Times*, December 17, 1938, 19.

84. Chacar and Hesterly, "Innovations and Value Creation in Major League Baseball," 422.

85. "Frick Fines Dean, Ripple $50 Each for Starting Battle in St. Louis," *New York Times*, May 21, 1937, 24.

86. Edward F. Balinger, "Dodger Players Riot as Bucks Win, 9–5," *Pittsburgh Post-Gazette*,

May 28, 1943, 16, 18; "Allen Suspended After Flareup," *The Sporting News*, June 3, 1943, 6.
87. "Ford Frick Warns Frisch to Keep Dizzy Dean Quiet After Lifting Suspension," *Reading Eagle*, June 5, 1937, 10.
88. "Frick Bars Dean for Alleged Slur." *New York Times*, June 3, 1937, 30.
89. Roscoe McGowen, "Dean Still Suspended, Threatens $250,000 Suit Against Frick and League," *New York Times*, June 4, 1937, 28.
90. "Reporter Sure He Quoted Dean Correctly; 2 Others Don't Recall Derogatory Remarks," *New York Times*, June 4, 1937, 28.
91. Roscoe McGowen, "Dizzy Reinstated at Stormy Session," *New York Times*, June 5, 1937, 10.
92. Andrew Zimbalist, *In the Best Interests of Baseball? The Revolutionary Reign of Bud Selig* (Hoboken, NJ: John Wiley & Sons, 2006), 62–63.
93. John Kieran, "Sports of the Times: The Great Dizzy Spell," *New York Times*, June 5, 1937, 11.
94. Dan Daniel, "'Acted Hastily on Hornsby,' Breadon Admitted to Frick," *The Sporting News*, June 8, 1949, 15.
95. Joe Garagiola, "Gags? Players' Wit Is Barbed," *The Sporting News*, April 5, 1969, 51–52.
96. Frederick G. Lieb, "Majors Will Miss Fun-Loving Frankie," *The Sporting News*, October 9, 1946, 4, 6.
97. Frick, *Games, Asterisks, and People*, 140–141.

Chapter 5

1. John C. Skipper, *A Biographical Dictionary of the Baseball Hall of Fame* (Jefferson, NC: McFarland, 2000), 1–2.
2. James A. Vlasich, "Alexander Cleland and the Origin of the Baseball Hall of Fame," in *Cooperstown Symposium on Baseball and the American Culture* (Westport, CT: Meckler, 1989), 1–17.
3. James A. Vlasich, *A Legend for the Legendary: The Origin of the Baseball Hall of Fame* (Bowling Green, OH: Bowling Green State University Press, 1990), 32–33.
4. Frick, *Games, Asterisks, and People*, 202.
5. Vlasich, *A Legend for the Legendary*, 38.
6. "Plan Hall of Fame for Diamond Stars," *New York Times*, August 16, 1935, 18.
7. Frick, *Games, Asterisks, and People*, 203.
8. Vlasich, *A Legend for the Legendary*, 41–46; "Writers to Select Stars of Baseball," *New York Times*, December 24, 1935, 20.
9. Vlasich, *A Legend for the Legendary*, 89–90.
10. William B. Anderson, "The 1939 Major League Baseball Centennial Celebration: How Steve Hannagan & Associates Helped Tie Business to Americana," *Public Relations Review* 27, no. 3 (Autumn 2001): 353–366.
11. Ken Smith, *Baseball's Hall of Fame* (New York: Grosset & Dunlap, 1966), 11–12.
12. Robert Winfield, "Baseball's Big Day," *New York Times*, June 4, 1939, XX1; "Notables to Join in Cooperstown Cavalcade Marking Centennial of Baseball," *New York Times*, June 11, 1939, S6; "Centennial Today Depicts Stages in Evolution of Modern Baseball," *New York Times*, June 12, 1939, 26.
13. Bill James, *Whatever Happened to the Hall of Fame? Baseball, Cooperstown, and the Price of Glory* (New York: Simon & Schuster, 1995), 33–34; James F. Vail, *The Road to Cooperstown: A Critical History of Baseball's Hall of Fame Selection Process* (Jefferson, NC: McFarland, 2001), 90–91.
14. James, *Whatever Happened to the Hall of Fame*, 33–34; Vail, *The Road to Cooperstown*, 91–93.
15. Paul S. Kerr to Stephen Clark, August 16, 1944, Ford C. Frick papers, Baseball Hall of Fame and Museum, Cooperstown. NY.
16. Minutes, Baseball Hall of Fame Committee, December 10, 1944, Ford C. Frick papers, Baseball Hall of Fame and Museum Cooperstown, NY.
17. Ethan Allen, "The National League Film Bureau," in *Middle Innings: A Documentary History of Baseball, 1900–1948*, ed. Dean A. Sullivan (Lincoln: University of Nebraska Press, 1998), 184; Anderson, "The 1939 Major League Baseball Centennial Celebration," 353–366; "Stress Technique in Baseball Film," *New York Times*, November 9, 1939, 29.
18. "Baseball Films Planned," *New York Times*, April 23, 1946, 28; "Major Loops to Sponsor Huge Movie Program," *The Sporting News*, April 25, 1946, 1.
19. "Major Stars on TV Film," *The Sporting News*, April 28, 1954, 38.
20. Louis Effrat, "MacPhail Carries Giant-Dodgers Feud to National League Board of Directors," *New York Times*, July 4, 1939.
21. Roscoe McGowen, "Wild Reception Planned Today for Shift in Giant-Dodger War," *New York Times*, July 7, 1939, 20.
22. Roscoe McGowen, "M'Phail's Blasts Add to the Noise," *New York Times*, July 9, 1939, 62.
23. Geoffrey C. Ward and Ken Burns, *Baseball: An Illustrated History* (New York: Alfred A. Knopf, 1994): 273.
24. Roscoe McGowen, "MacPhail Rebuffed, Frick Upheld by National League's Directors," *New York Times*, July 11, 1939, 27; "1940 Game in St. Louis," *The Sporting News*, July 13, 1939, 5.
25. "Action on Magerkurth Criticized by New York," *The Sporting News*, July 20, 1939, 1; "Jurges Suspended 10 Days, Fined $150," *New York Times*, July 17, 1939, 16.
26. "Keeping Umpiring Up to Standard," *The Sporting News*, July 20, 1939, 4.
27. John Drebinger, "Uncle Charlie Calls It a Career," *New York Times*, December 19, 1939, 33.
28. John Kieran, "A Curling Stone Gathers No Moss," *New York Times*, January 13, 1940, 12; "Ford Frick's Rink Wins at Brookline," *New York Times*, January 28, 1940, S3.

29. "Brookline Curlers Win," *New York Times*, January 29, 1940, 23.
30. "Mack and Jones Honored," *New York Times*, January 30, 1940, 28.
31. Arthur Daley, "The Gentle Art of Curling," *New York Times*, January 21, 1944.
32. W. C. Heinz, "Frick Gets in Licks at Old Scottish Game," *The Sporting News*, January 31, 1946, 7. Vincent Lopez contributed the photos to this report.
33. "Showdown Looms on Farm Issue at Baseball Meetings This Week," *New York Times*, December 3, 1939, 99; Edgar G. Brands, "Recodification Plans Leave Out Landis," *The Sporting News*, February 15, 1940, 2.
34. "Dodgers Manager Asks Five-Year Term," *New York Times*, December 4, 1939, 31.
35. "Baseball Chains Score Over Landis," *New York Times*, December 6, 1939, 39.
36. "M'Phail Rebuffed by Commissioner," *New York Times*, December 9, 1939, 19.
37. Brands, "Recodification Plans Leave Out Landis," 2.
38. Louis Effrat, "National League Seeks Revised and Clearer Major-Minor Agreement," *New York Times*, February 7, 1940, 29.
39. "Landis and Major League Owners Compromise on Operation of Farm Systems," *New York Times*, February 14, 1940, 29.
40. Dan Daniel, "National Definitely at Odds With Landis," *The Sporting News*, February 15, 1940, 10.
41. John Kieran, "Runs, Hits and Errors," *New York Times*, June 25, 1940, 30; J. G. Taylor Spink, "'Pass Bean-Ball Rule in N.L.'—Ducky; Frick Favors Helmets," *The Sporting News*, June 27, 1940, 3. "Ducky" was a popular nickname for Medwick.
42. "Frick Proposes Helmets," *The Sporting News*, July 4, 1940, 9.
43. "Game Next Year Voted to Detroit," *New York Times*, July 9, 1940, 26.
44. Steven Gietschier, "Slugging and Snubbing: Hugh Casey, Ernest Hemingway, and Jackie Robinson—a Baseball Mystery," *NINE* 21, no. 1 (Fall 2012): 12–46.
45. Roscoe McGowen, "Plastic Protectors Inside Caps Will Be Worn by Dodger Batters," *New York Times*, March 9, 1941, S1, S4.
46. John Drebinger, "Orengo's Bat Helps Beat Brooklyn, 6–5," *New York Times*, March 17, 1941.
47. "Frick Will Fine Managers $200 if Pitchers Throw 'Bean Ball,'" *New York Times*, August 11, 1942, 23; Tommy Holmes, "Beantown Beaning Orgy Brings Action From League Head," *The Sporting News*, August 13, 1942, 1–2.
48. Tommy Holmes, "Larry Lets Fly a Few Dusters at Own Club," *The Sporting News*, August 20, 1942, 1; Roscoe McGowen, "French Triumphs in Mound Duel, 1–0," *New York Times*, August 13, 1942, 24.
49. Stanley Frank, "Frick Clamps Down on Body-Balls," *The Sporting News*, August 12, 1943, 1–2; Roscoe McGowen, "Durocher Assails Weber's $100 Fine," *New York Times*, August 3, 1943, 15.
50. "'Proof' Is Claimed in Dodgers' Protest," *New York Times*, May 21, 1941, 29.
51. "Frick Throws Out Dodgers' Protest," *New York Times*, May 27, 1941, 31; "Win or Lose Games on Field," *The Sporting News*, June 5, 1941, 4.
52. Ford Frick, "U.S. Uses Catchers' Masks, Not Gas Masks, Frick Observes, Citing Value of Baseball," *New York Times*, April 14, 1940, 79.
53. Ron Briley, "Baseball and the Cold War: An Examination of Values," *OAH Magazine of History* 2, no. 1 (Summer 1986): 15–18.
54. "Draft Again Given Little Attention by Majors," *The Sporting News*, October 10, 1940, 4.
55. Edgar G. Brands, "Organized Ball, in Harmony, Stands Firm Behind Landis," *The Sporting News*, December 19, 1940, 5, 8. At the meeting, Frick was also elected to another four-year term and given "a substantial raise."
56. "Frick Sounds Warning," *New York Times*, December 3, 1941, 35.

Chapter 6

1. Edgar G. Brands, "Majors Gird to Carry On During U.S. Emergency; Vote Funds to Give Equipment to Men in Service," *The Sporting News*, December 18, 1941, 7.
2. "$42,000 in Equipment Begins Moving to U.S. Camps," *The Sporting News*, January 8, 1942, 2; "Service Men to Get Bat and Ball Kits," *New York Times*, December 31, 1941, 23.
3. "Ford Frick Sets an Example," *The Sporting News*, March 12, 1942, 4; John Kieran, "A Big League President Holds Back," *New York Times*, April 10, 1942, 24.
4. "Pvt. Frick Ends Basic Training," *The Sporting News*, April 27, 1944.
5. Personal interview with Kelly Frick Richards, November 23, 2015; "Obituary: Dr. Frederick Frick, a Research Scientist, 75," *Boston Herald*, September 14, 1992.
6. Franklin Delano Roosevelt to Kenesaw Mountain Landis, January 15, 1942, Baseball Hall of Fame, Cooperstown, New York.
7. "Barrow, Stoneham and MacPhail See Policy Vindicated," *New York Times*, January 17, 1942, 10.
8. Richard Goldstein, *Spartan Seasons* (New York: Macmillan, 1980), 15.
9. John Drebinger, "More Night Games Expected by Frick," *New York Times*, January 18, 1942, S1.
10. Dan Daniel, "N.L. Setting Aside 7-Game Light Rule, Seeks Limit of 14," *The Sporting News*, January 22, 1942, 1.
11. "Frick Backs Nugent," *New York Times*, September 23, 1941, 28; Stan Baumgartner, "Short-End Phillies Pick Up Long Green," *The Sporting News*, September 25, 1941, 2.
12. "Drops Plans to Buy Phils," *New York Times*, September 24, 1941, 30.
13. Stan Baumgartner, "No Blues for Nugent,

Who Chants New Tune," *The Sporting News*, January 22, 1942, 2.

14. Stan Baumgartner, "'I'll Sell, but Find Me Buyer'—Nugent," *The Sporting News*, November 19, 1942, 1, 7; David M. Jordan, *Occasional Glory: The History of the Philadelphia Phillies* (Jefferson, NC: McFarland, 2012), 65–66; "Phils' Sale Ordered by League Directors," *New York Times*, November 12, 1942, 35.

15. Red Smith, "The Padres Find a Father," *New York Times*, January 27, 1974, 246.

16. John Drebinger, "Big Leagues Decide on Two All-Star Games But Deadlock on Night Baseball," *New York Times*, February 3, 1942, 25.

17. Dan Daniel, "21 Night Tilts for Nats, Limit of 14 for Others," *The Sporting News*, February 5, 1942, 1, 12; John Drebinger, "Majors Raise Limit of Home Night Games to 14, Except for 21 at Washington," *New York Times*, February 4, 1942, 24.

18. Dan Daniel, "World Series War Aid Plans Laid by Majors," *The Sporting News*, July 9, 1942, 1; Louis Effrat, "Senators' Plea for More Night Games Denied as Landis Casts Deciding Vote," *New York Times*, July 7, 1942, 24.

19. Arthur Daley, "Major Leagues in Armed Forces to Meet All-Stars at Cleveland," *New York Times*, April 18, 1942, 20; Dan Daniel, "Game Broadens Its Aid to War Effort," *The Sporting News*, April 23, 1942, 9.

20. "Night Games' Fate Awaits Army Test," *New York Times*, April 30, 1942, 10.

21. Dan Daniel, "N.Y. in Dark on Arcs; Will Test Twilight," *The Sporting News*, May 7, 1942, 2; "Valentine Denies Banning Night Baseball," *New York Times*, May 1, 1942, 12.

22. "Valentine Orders Cancellation of Night Baseball in City During Wartime," *New York Times*, May 19, 1942, 25.

23. "All Stars to Open Play Here at 5:30," *New York Times*, May 26, 1942, 27. A 5:30 start time was originally announced, but it later was pushed back an hour ("6:30 Start for All-Stars," *New York Times*, June 17, 1942, 29).

24. "'Dimout' Hits Night Baseball on East Coast," *Pittsburgh Post-Gazette*, April 30, 1942, 1.

25. James P. Dawson, "La Guardia Permits Giants and Dodgers to Resume Night Baseball This Year," *New York Times*, January 25, 1944, 22; John Drebinger, "National League Lists 91 Night Games, Increase of 31 Over 1943," *New York Times*, March 6, 1944.

26. John Drebinger, "National League Votes Afternoon Lights, Ends Night-Game Curfew," *New York Times*, December 13, 1949, 47; Dan Daniel, "Majors Grease the Skids for Bonus Rule," *The Sporting News*, December 21, 1949, 5.

27. Dan Daniel, "Gotham Sits Down for Series Size-Up," *The Sporting News*, August 13, 1942, 5; James P. Dawson, "57,305 See Giants Lose to Dodgers When Dimout Stops Ninth Inning Rally," *New York Times*, August 4, 1942, 22.

28. "Big League Clubs to Reduce Travel," *New York Times*, October 8, 1942, 33; Edgar G. Brands, "Majors and Minors Plan Chicago Meets," *The Sporting News*, October 15, 1942, 16.

29. "Baseball Heads Ridicule Proposal to Regroup Big Leagues Next Year," *New York Times*, October 28, 1942.

30. Goldstein, *Spartan Seasons*, 97–99; J. G. Taylor Spink, "Terry Tips Chicago Lid, Doffing Hat to Giants," *The Sporting News*, December 3, 1942, 1, 11; "ODT Asks Majors to Curtail Travel," *New York Times*, December 1, 1942, 29.

31. Edgar G. Brands, "Alternate Sites for California, Florida, Texas Camps Advised," *The Sporting News*, December 17, 1942, 1, 6.

32. John Drebinger, "Frick Expects Baseball Season to Open on Time Despite Training Difficulties," *New York Times*, December 24, 1942, 22; Tom Swope, "Reds Sitting Tight on New Camp Site," *The Sporting News*, December 31, 1942, 5.

33. "Big League Teams to Train Near Home," *New York Times*, January 6, 1943, 20; Edgar G. Brands, "Pitch Camps in North for First Time in Generation," *The Sporting News*, January 14, 1943, 1–2.

34. Dan Daniel, "War Charts Help Slice Travel by 5 Million Man-Miles," *The Sporting News*, January 28, 1943, 1, 6; John Drebinger, "Major Leagues to Set Precedent With Intersectional Games on Two Holidays," *New York Times*, January 21, 1943, 28.

35. Dan Daniel, "3-Day Start at N.Y. Gives Yankees Edge in Series," *The Sporting News*, September 16, 1943, 2; "World Series to be a One-Trip Affair; Starts Here Oct. 5," *New York Times*, September 12, 1943, S1.

36. Minutes, National League Reconvened Annual and Schedule Meeting, February 9, 1943, Baseball Hall of Fame and Museum, Cooperstown, NY, 115.

37. Bazer and Culbertson, "Baseball During World War II," 123; Roscoe McGowen, "Big Leagues Promised Lively Ball in Two Weeks Following Wave of Protests," *New York Times*, April 24, 1943, 19; William B. Mead, *Even the Browns: Baseball During World War II* (Chicago: Contemporary Books, 1978), 78; Tom Swope, "Pepped Up Pellet Fight Led by Giles," *The Sporting News*, April 29, 1943, 14; Warren N. Wilbert, *Baseball's Iconic 1–0 Games* (Lanham, MD: Scarecrow, 2013), 38.

38. Edgar G. Brands, "Major Leagues Get All 'Balled Up' on New Ball," *The Sporting News*, April 29, 1943, 1; "Frick Permits Use of '42 Lively Ball," *New York Times*, April 25, 1943, S1.

39. Goldstein, *Spartan Seasons*, 134; "Ruling on '42 Ball Defended by Frick," *New York Times*, April 27, 1943, 26; Swope, "Pepped Up Pellet Fight," 14.

40. Minutes, National League Reconvened Annual and Schedule Meeting, February 9, 1943, Baseball Hall of Fame and Museum, Cooperstown, NY, 47.

41. Ibid., 63–78.

42. Ibid., 71.

43. John Drebinger, "National League Purchases Phils for Resale to Syndicate of 6 Business Men," *New York Times*, February 10, 1943, 31.

44. Jordan, *Occasional Glory*, 66.
45. Stan Baumgartner, "N.L. Reported to have Sliced Phil Debts in Half for Cox," *The Sporting News*, February 25, 1943, 1, 7; "Phils Sold to Cox, with Group to Get Title on March 3," *New York Times*, February 21, 1943, S1.
46. "Phillies Win Protest," *New York Times*, June 15, 1943, 27.
47. "Cox Plans Plea to Landis," *New York Times*, June 16, 1943, 26; "Rookie Cox Keeps 'Em on Their Toes," *The Sporting News*, June 24, 1943, 4.
48. "Frick Rulings Hit by Phillies Owner," *New York Times*, July 4, 1943, S1; "Johnson Snubs All-Star Invite," *The Sporting News*, July 8, 1943, 2.
49. "Apology Issued by Phils Owner," *New York Times*, July 10, 1943, 9; Don Basenfelder, "N.L. Directors Back Up Frick," *The Sporting News*, July 15, 1943, 18.
50. "Play-by-Play on Landis Probe of Cox," *The Sporting News*, December 2, 1943, 4, 21.
51. John Drebinger, "Ceased Betting on Phils, Says Cox, When He Learned It Violated Rule," *New York Times*, November 24, 1943, 24; "'Made Sentimental Bets,' Declares Cox," *The Sporting News*, December 2, 1943, 21.
52. Stan Baumgartner, "Bob Carpenter, 'My Boy,' to Dad, Kid of Prexies," *The Sporting News*, December 2, 1943, 4.
53. Drebinger, "Ceased Betting on Phils."
54. Dan Daniel, "Bar Against Cox Upheld by Landis After Appeal," *The Sporting News*, December 9, 1943, 8; Daniel E. Ginsburg, *The Fix Is In: A History of Baseball Gambling and Game Fixing Scandals* (Jefferson, NC: McFarland, 1995), 217–220.
55. "Landis Explains Overseas Projects," *New York Times*, August 28, 1943, 7; "Overseas Junket Awaits War Department O. K.," *The Sporting News*, September 2, 1932, 2.
56. "124 Volunteer from N. L.," *The Sporting News*, September 9, 1943, 14.
57. Dan Daniel, "Players Bring Strong Plea From Far North," *The Sporting News*, February 3, 1944, 3; "War Department Calls Off Pacific Tour of All-Stars," *The Sporting News*, October 7, 1943, 5.
58. "St. Louis Head Says Squad of 19 Is Needed—Frick Says Baseball Should Go On If There Are Only 9 Men on a Team," *New York Times*, January 26, 1944, 14.
59. Dan Daniel, "St. Louis Blues Draw Boos from Rickey, Barrow," *The Sporting News*, February 3, 1944, 2; Frederick G. Lieb, "Cardinals' Sam Changes Tune to Confidence," *The Sporting News*, February 3, 1944, 2.
60. "Manpower Supply Looks Ample Enough to Frick," *The Sporting News*, March 9, 1944, 17.
61. "Baseball's Value Cited," *New York Times*, April 27, 1944, 16; Ford C. Frick, "Full Season Seen by League Heads," *New York Times*, April 16, 1944, S1; Goldstein, "Spartan Seasons," 35.
62. Dan Daniel, "Night Ball Fight Stirs Majors' Meetings," *The Sporting News*, July 20, 1944, 1–2; "Night Ball Limit Ends on Weekdays," *New York Times*, July 12, 1944, 14.
63. "Both Majors' and Minors' Executives in Hospitals," *The Sporting News*, October 5, 1944, 1; "Landis Unable to Attend," *New York Times*, October 3, 1944, 17.
64. "Baseball Heads Will Recommend New Seven-Year Term for Landis," *The Sporting News*, November 18, 1944, 20; Edgar G. Brands, "Landis Will Decide On Extending Term to 1953," *The Sporting News*, November 23, 1944, 2.

Chapter 7

1. "Landis Is Praised by His Colleagues," *New York Times*, November 26, 1944, 56; David Pietrusza, *Judge and Jury: The Life and Times of Judge Kenesaw Mountain Landis* (South Bend, IN: Diamond Communications, 1998), 451.
2. John Drebinger, "Council to Succeed Landis Is Expected at Majors' Meeting," *New York Times*, December 10, 1944, S1.
3. "Early Election of 'New Landis' Indicated," *The Sporting News*, January 4, 1945, 10.
4. E. G. Brands, "Majors Name Council to Rule Until New Pact," *The Sporting News*, December 14, 1944, 2, 4; John Drebinger, "Three-Man Council Will Rule Majors," *New York Times*, December 12, 1944, 26; "Majors Set Plans to Pick New Head," *New York Times*, December 13, 1944, 27.
5. Dan Daniel, "Washington Doesn't Plan to Halt Game," *The Sporting News*, January 4, 1945, 1–2; "Roosevelt Stand Seen as Blackout for Pro Athletics," *New York Times*, January 7, 1945, F1.
6. John Drebinger, "Elevation of Frick Looms Next Month," *New York Times*, January 14, 1945, S1.
7. Dan Daniel, "Ford Frick Reported Choice for Landis Post," *The Sporting News*, January 18, 1945, 1–2.
8. Morehouse, "Ford Frick: He Isn't Trying on Landis' Toga for Size—Yet," 3.
9. Dan Daniel, "Game Sees No Hint in Washington of Stop Order," *The Sporting News*, January 25, 1945, 2; "Delay in Naming Baseball Commissioner Expected by Big League Officials in West," *New York Times*, January 21, 1945, 53.
10. John Drebinger, "Frick Says Majors Have a Free Choice," *New York Times*, January 24, 1945, 15.
11. Dan Daniel, "Frick Defends Visit to Capital, After Criticism," *The Sporting News*, February 1, 1945, 2.
12. Frederick G. Lieb, "St. Louis Clubs Won't Attempt All-Kid Teams," *The Sporting News*, February 1, 1945, 17.
13. Arthur Daley, "About Sports Commissioners," *New York Times*, February 2, 1945, 15.
14. "Double Check Endorsed," *New York Times*, January 24, 1945, 15.
15. "Griffith Expects Majors to Operate," *New York Times*, January 25, 1945, 23.
16. "Senator Chandler Goes to Bat to Keep 4-F Players in Game," *The Sporting News*, February 1, 1945, 1.

17. John Drebinger, "Majors Set to Pick Commissioner Here," *New York Times*, February 2, 1945, 15.
18. Roscoe McGowen, "Pick Commissioner Now, M'Phail Asks," *New York Times*, February 3, 1945, 14.
19. Dan Daniel, "Game to Ask Priority to Avoid 'Slacker' Tag," *The Sporting News*, February 8, 1, 2, 4; John Drebinger, "Drive to Fill Post of Landis Hits Snag," *New York Times*, February 3, 1945, 14.
20. John Drebinger, "Majors Ready to Pick Czar Soon, Probably Before Season Is Opened," *New York Times*, February 5, 1945, 18.
21. "Owners in Contact by Telegraph On Choice of New Baseball Czar," *New York Times*, February 7, 1945, 24.
22. John Drebinger, "Four Baseball Men Sift Field for Czar," *New York Times*, February 9, 1945, 19; Carl T. Felker, "Writers Veer to Outsider as Leader," *The Sporting News*, February 15, 1945, 3, 4.
23. "Roosevelt Wants Baseball to Go On," *New York Times*, March 14, 1945, 24; George Zielke, "Game Okayed by FDR in 'Pinch-Hitter' Form," *The Sporting News*, March 22, 1945, 8.
24. "Baseball Leaders Generally Elated," *New York Times*, March 22, 1945, 18; Dan Daniel, "WMC Pitch to Job Hitch Cuts Camp Absenteeism," *The Sporting News*, March 29, 1945, 2.
25. "Majors Receiving Committee Reports on Candidates for New Commissioner," *The Sporting News*, April 5, 1945, 6; "Selection of Baseball Czar Near," *New York Times*, April 1, 1945, S3.
26. "Majors Will Act on Leader April 24," *New York Times*, 23; "Meeting Called on Commissioner," *The Sporting News*, April 12, 1945, 1.
27. Dan Daniel, "MacPhail Calls for Prompt Pick of Leader," *The Sporting News*, April 19, 1945, 1–2.
28. "Writers Try to Tell Results of Meeting," *The Sporting News*, April 19, 1945, 4.
29. "Barrow Refuses Baseball Czar Job," *New York Times*, April 15, 1945, 15.
30. "Major League Moguls Meet Today with Scant Hope of Naming Czar," *New York Times*, April 24, 1945, 27.
31. Dan Daniel, "MacPhail Facing Showdown With Chandler," *The Sporting News*, April 30, 1947, 1–2; James P. Dawson, "Rumors of Strife Stir Major Loops," *New York Times*, April 26, 1947, 17.
32. "Giles' Stand Blocked Frick, Caused Chandler's Election, Says MacPhail," *The Sporting News*, September 5, 1951, 6.
33. Branch Rickey, Memorandum, April 25, 1945, the Branch Rickey Papers, Library of Congress, box 27. In *Late Innings: A Documentary History of Baseball, 1945–1972*, ed. Dean A. Sullivan (Lincoln: University of Nebraska Press, 2002) 4–11. See also William Marshall, *Baseball's Pivotal Era: 1945–1951* (Lexington, KY: University of Kentucky Press, 1999), 18–22.
34. "Game Makes Perfect Choice in Chandler," *The Sporting News*, May 3, 1945, 10.
35. Happy Chandler with Vance Trimble, *Heroes, Plain Folks, and Skunks* (Chicago: Bonus Books, 1989), 188.
36. "Chandler Scores in New York Test," *The Sporting News*, June 14, 1945, 10.
37. "Fan Brings Charges Against Magerkurth," *New York Times*, July 21, 1945, 14; "Assault Charge Dropped," *New York Times*, July 22, 1945, 50; Tom Swope, "Magerkurth Hits Fan, Pays Him $100," *The Sporting News*, July 26, 1945, 9.
38. "Dayton, O., Fans Contribute to Fund to Reimburse Umpire Magerkurth," *The Sporting News*, August 2, 1945, 2.
39. "Warning to Umps," *The Sporting News*, April 2, 1947, 10.
40. Vincent X. Flaherty, "O.B. to Spend $50,000 for Sandlot Promotion," *The Sporting News*, August 23, 1945, 4–5; "Baseball Moves to Make Places for its Returning War Veterans," *New York Times*, August 17, 1945, 13.
41. Goldstein, *Spartan Seasons*, 195.
42. Flaherty, "O.B. to Spend $50,000 for Sandlot Promotion," 4–5; "Baseball Moves to Make Places for Its Returning War Veterans," 13.
43. Dan Daniel, "Navy Runs Into Snag on Pacific Tour Idea," *The Sporting News*, September 20, 1945.
44. "Chandler Angers Baseball Leaders," *New York Times*, October 8, 1945, 22.
45. Art Flynn, "Bombshell Tossed at Chandler Proves Dud," *The Sporting News*, October 11, 1945, 1, 10; "Rumor of Move to Buy Chandler Contract Spiked at Club Owners' Chicago Meeting," *New York Times*, October 9, 1945, 16.
46. "Head for Manila and Tokyo," *The Sporting News*, November 22, 1945, 2; "Players Named for Tour of Pacific," *New York Times*, November 16, 1945, 26.
47. John Drebinger, "Arc-Light Games Leading Problem as Majors Gather," *New York Times*, December 9, 1945, 79.
48. "New Promotional Plan Fails to Get Chandler O.K.," *The Sporting News*, December 13, 1945, 5.
49. Edgar G. Brands, "Majors Back Chandler's Authority Over Game," *The Sporting News*, December 20, 1945, 4, 6.
50. Harold C. Burr, "N.Y. Scribes Pelt Game's Brass Hats with Gags," *The Sporting News*, February 7, 1946, 2.
51. Harold C. Burr, "Border Raid on Dodgers Lifts Rickey's Eyebrows," *The Sporting News*, February 14, 1946, 8; "Olmo Weighs Mexican Bid," *New York Times*, February 6, 1946, 32.
52. "'Boost Comes a Little Late'—Olmo Says He'll Fulfill Mexican Contract," *The Sporting News*, February 28, 1946, 2; "Mexican Leaguers Raid U.S. Teams," *New York Times*, February 19, 1946, 29.
53. Frick, *Games, Asterisks, and People*, 185–189.
54. *Ibid.*, 188.
55. Alan M. Klein, *Baseball on the Border: A Tale of Two Laredos* (Princeton, NJ: Princeton University Press, 1997), 78.

56. Shirley Povich, "Chandler Warns Mexican Jumpers to Return," *The Sporting News*, March 14, 1946, 2.
57. Klein, *Baseball on the Border*, 86–88; L. A. McMaster, "Stephens: 'Mexico OK for Song Writers, But—,'" *The Sporting News*, April 11, 1946, 1; "Stephens Returns to Browns Fold," *New York Times*, April 6, 1946, 22.
58. Harold C. Burr, "Newest Jump by Owen Fails to Jar Rickey," *The Sporting News*, April 18, 1946, 4; Camille M. Cianfarra, "Owen Jumps Back to Mexican League," *New York Times*, April 13, 1946, 20.
59. Art Flynn, "N.Y. Justice Denounces Pasquels in Decision," *The Sporting News*, May 23, 1946, 2; "Curb on Mexicans Granted to Yanks," *New York Times*, May 21, 1946, 26.
60. "Court Postpones Hearing," *New York Times*, May 29, 1946, 26.
61. Klein, *Baseball on the Border*, 98; Tom Swope, "New All-Star Selection Plan Up Before Council," *The Sporting News*, June 12, 1946, 12.
62. Carl T. Felker, "Happy Backs Players' Program, Gives 'Inside' of Breadon Fining," *The Sporting News*, August 14, 1946, 2.
63. "Breadon, Cardinals' Head, Confers with Pasquel of Mexican League," *New York Times*, June 21, 1946, 28; Frederick G. Lieb, "Breadon Visit Paves Mexican Peace Path," *The Sporting News*, July 3, 1946, 1–2.
64. "Breadon Explains $5,000 Fine, Lifted by Chandler," *The Sporting News*, July 31, 1946, 31; "Breadon Kept Word with Pasquel, Drew $5,000 Fine from Chandler," *New York Times*, July 27, 1946, 25.
65. "Chandler Sympathizes with Quest of Ball Players for Improved Lot," *New York Times*, August 3, 1946, 20.
66. "Frick Loses His Purse Too," *New York Times*, July 10, 1946, 26; "Frick Robbed As He Sleeps," *The Sporting News*, July 17, 1946, 4.
67. Arthur Daley, "The Passing Baseball Scene," *New York Times*, May 25, 1946, 24; Joseph M. Sheehan, "Dodgers Win, 2–1, as Fists Fly Again," *New York Times*, May 24, 1946, 22.
68. Dan Daniel, "Bean Ball Managers Given Dusting-Off by Frick," *The Sporting News*, August 14, 1946, 2; Frederick Turner, *When the Boys Came Back* (New York: Henry Holt, 1996), 183–185.
69. Hugo Autz, "Players Ask to Help Draft New Contract Form," *The Sporting News*, July 24, 1946, 2; "New Uniform Players' Contract to Be Drafted by Major Leagues," *New York Times*, July 19, 1946, 14.
70. "Average Pay $9,500 in National League," *New York Times*, July 24, 1946, 31; "Only 29 National Players Get $5,000 or Less—Frick," *The Sporting News*, July 31, 1946, 4.
71. Dan Daniel, "Frick Devised Contract Reform in '36," *The Sporting News*, July 31, 1946, 3, 4.
72. "Owen's Pardon Plea Is Sent to Chandler," *New York Times*, August 13, 1946, 20.
73. "Chandler Turns Down Owen's Bid and Five-Year Suspension Stands," *New York Times*, August 15, 1946, 31; Dan Daniel, "Mexicans Speed Hunt for Big-Name Players," *The Sporting News*, August 21, 1946, 1–2.
74. Oakley, *Baseball's Last Golden Age, 1946–1960*, 38.
75. Dan Daniel, "MacPhail Blueprint Charts Game's Course," *The Sporting News*, September 4, 1946, 1, 3; "Majors Meet All Player Demands and Set Up New Executive Council," *New York Times*, August 29, 1946, 31.
76. "168-Game Schedule Happily Appears Doomed," *The Sporting News*, September 11, 1946, 10.
77. "168-Game Plan Opposed," *New York Times*, September 6, 1946, 13; "Magnates Pull 'Boner' With 168-Game Card," September 4, 1946, 12.
78. Dan Daniel, "Rising Opposition Dooms 168-Game Schedule," *The Sporting News*, September 11, 1946, 1–2.
79. Dan Daniel, "Television Clause Snags Player Contract," *The Sporting News*, September 25, 1946, 1, 3; Louis Effrat, "Minimum Salaries, Other Reforms Gained by Major League Players," *New York Times*, September 17, 1946, 9.
80. "$175,000 Radio Fee to Pension Fund," *New York Times*, October 14, 1946, 34; Dan Daniel, "Series Dough Assures Pension Plan for Players," *The Sporting News*, October 16, 1946, 2, 8.
81. Marshall, *Baseball's Pivotal Era*, 78–79.
82. Dan Daniel, "Players Win New Concessions from Majors," *The Sporting News*, December 11, 1946, 1–2.

Chapter 8

1. "Writers Re-Elect Daniel," *New York Times*, December 29, 1934, 20.
2. "Not Ted Lewis, But Is Everybody Happy?" *The Sporting News*, February 11, 1948, 2.
3. Wendell Smith, "General Public Must Be Changed," *Pittsburgh Courier*, February 25, 1939, 1, 16.
4. Chris Lamb, *Conspiracy of Silence: Sportswriters and the Long Campaign to Desegregate Baseball* (Lincoln: University of Nebraska Press, 2012), 97.
5. Ford Frick, *Games, Asterisks, and People: Memoirs of a Lucky Fan* (New York: Crown Publishers, 1973), 94.
6. Wendell Smith, "Smitty's Sport Spurts," *Pittsburgh Courier*, March 11, 1939, 16.
7. "Backs Colored Ball Players," *New York Times*, May 17, 1939, 6.
8. "Champions Negro Stars," *New York Times*, January 23, 1940, 30.
9. "Baseball Policy Rapped," *New York Times*, February 3, 1943, 25.
10. Bill Veeck and Ed Linn, *Veeck—As in Wreck* (Chicago: University of Chicago Press, 2001) 171–172.
11. David M. Jordan, Larry M. Gerlach, and John P. Rossi, "A Baseball Myth Exploded: The Truth About Bill Veeck and the '43 Phillies," *Na-

tional Pastime: A Review of Baseball History 18 (November 1998): 3–13; Lamb, *Conspiracy of Silence*, 227.

12. Stan Baumgartner, "I'll Sell, but Find Me Buyer—Nugent," *The Sporting News*, November 19, 1942, 1, 7.

13. The article generated criticism within the baseball community for its harsh treatment of Veeck. Tygiel himself contributed a response in *Baseball Research Journal* (2006 edition, 109–114) that, while still questioning the credibility of Veeck's stated efforts, presented evidence that the anecdote was circulating before 1962 and was not a fabrication that first popped up in the memoirs.

14. Red Smith, "Remembrances of Eddie Gottlieb," *New York Times*, January 13, 1980, S3.

15. Bruce Kuklick, *To Every Thing a Season: Shibe Park and Urban Philadelphia 1909–1976* (Princeton, NJ: Princeton University Press, 1991, 146; David Pietrusza, *Judge and Jury: The Life and Times of Judge Kenesaw Mountain Landis* (South Bend, IN: Diamond Communications, 1998), 421.

16. *Ibid.*, 405–430.

17. Frick, *Games, Asterisks, and People*, 94–95.

18. John B. Holway, *Voices from the Great Black Baseball Leagues: Revised Edition* (Mineola, NY: Courier Dover Publications, 2012), 225.

19. Robert Peterson, *Only the Ball was White: A History of Legendary Black Players and All-Black Professional Teams* (Englewood Cliffs, NJ: Prentice-Hall, 1970), 152–153.

20. "Landis on Negro Players," *The Sporting News*, July 23, 1942, 11. Although an apparently strong and important statement, it was reported in a four-paragraph brief buried in the midst of the box scores page.

21. John Drebinger, "Big Leagues Vote to Stage 16 War Relief Games and All-Star Benefit Again," *New York Times*, December 4, 1942, 32.

22. "Senator Chandler in Talk with Frick," *New York Times*, April 27, 1945, 24.

23. Jules Tygiel, *Baseball's Great Experiment: Jackie Robinson and His Legacy* (New York: Oxford University Press, 1997), 80.

24. "Sound Basis Urged for Negro League," *New York Times*, January 21, 1946, 29.

25. Tygiel, *Baseball's Great Experiment*, 82, 85–86.

26. http://libraries.uky.edu/forms/chandlerrpt.pdf. Retrieved July 2, 2015.

27. Frick, *Games, Asterisks, and People*, 93.

28. Happy Chandler with Vance Trimble, *Heroes, Plain Folks, and Skunks: The Life and Times of Happy Chandler* (Chicago: Bonus Books, 1989), 226–229.

29. Jerome Holtzman, *The Commissioners: Baseball's Midlife Crisis* (New York: Total Sports, 1998), 69.

30. "Rickey Claims That 15 Clubs Voted to Bar Negroes from the Majors," *New York Times*, February 18, 1948, 37.

31. Lee Lowenfish, *Branch Rickey* (Lincoln: University of Nebraska Press, 2007), 449–450.

32. Roscoe McGowen, "Rickey Agrees That Club Owners Might not Recall Anti-Negro Vote," *New York Times*, February 19, 1948, 31.

33. J. G. Taylor Spink, "MacPhail Blasts Rickey in Negro Row," *The Sporting News*, February 25, 1948, 1–2.

34. Dan Daniel, "MacPhail Blue Print Charts Game's Course," *The Sporting News*, September 4, 1946, 1.

35. "Players' Demands Studied by Majors," *New York Times*, August 28, 1946, 33; "Majors Meet All Player Demands and Set Up Executive Council," *New York Times*, August 29, 1946, 31.

36. Tygiel, *Baseball's Great Experiment*, 82–86; Andrew Zimbalist, *In the Best Interests of Baseball? The Revolutionary Reign of Bud Selig*.

37. Don Warfield, *The Roaring Redhead* (South Bend, IN: Diamond Communications, 1987), 203–206.

38. "Cardinal Ace Gets Sid Mercer Award," *New York Times*, February 3, 1947, 25; "Merry Mexican Melange ... of Satire and Song ... Mixed by N.Y. Scribes," *The Sporting News*, February 12, 1947, 56–58.

39. Arthur Daley, "Opening Day at Ebbets Field," *New York Times*, April 16, 1947, 32; Roscoe McGowen, "Double by Reiser Beats Boston," *New York Times*, April 16, 1947, 32.

40. John Paul Hill, "Commissioner A. B. 'Happy' Chandler and the Integration of Baseball: A Reassessment," *NINE: A Journal of Baseball History and Culture* 19, no. 1 (Fall 2010): 28–51.

41. Stanley Woodward, "National League Averts Strike of Cardinals Against Robinson's Presence in Baseball," *New York Herald Tribune*, May 9, 1947.

42. Dick Young, "Baseball's Undirty Old Man," *New York Daily News*, April 5, 1973.

43. Frick, *Games, Asterisks, and People*, 97–98.

44. Harold Rosenthal, "The Story Behind the Story," *New York Times*, May 4, 1997, S9.

45. Stanley Woodward, "Views of Baseball," *New York Herald Tribune*, May 10, 1947.

46. *Ibid*.

47. "Say Cards' Strike Plan Against Negro Dropped," *New York Times*, May 9, 1947, 27.

48. "Robinson Reveals Written Threats," *New York Times*, May 10, 1947, 16.

49. "Cardinal Strike Threat Against Jackie Averted," *The Sporting News*, May 14, 1947, 13; "Report 'Ridiculous,' Declares Breadon," *The Sporting News*, May 14, 1947, 13.

50. Stanley Woodward, *Sports Page* (New York: Greenwood Press, 1968), 82–83.

51. Arthur Daley, "The Passing Baseball Scene," *New York Times*, May 13, 1947, 32.

52. "The Negro Player Steps on the Scales," *The Sporting News*, May 21, 1947, 14; G. Edward White, *Creating the National Pastime: Baseball Transforms Itself, 1903–1953* (Princeton, New Jersey: Princeton University Press, 1996), 192.

53. Tygiel, *Baseball's Great Experiment*, 185–188.

54. J. Nicholas De Bonis, Robert S. Kahan, J. David Pincus, Edgar P. Trotter, and Stephen C.

Wood, "The Baseball Commissioner's Public Communication Role: A Test of Leadership," in *Cooperstown Symposium on Baseball and the American Culture*, ed. Alvin Hall (Westport, CT: Meckler, 1990), 187–211; Lee Lowenfish, *Branch Rickey* (Lincoln: University of Nebraska Press, 2007), 628.
 55. NAACP Assistant Secretary to Ford Frick, May 15, 1947. Frick papers, National Baseball Hall of Fame and Museum.
 56. "Winners Announced for Jefferson Prize," *New York Times*, February 16, 1948, 23.
 57. "Intolerance Group Presents Awards," *New York Times*, April 12, 1948, 23.
 58. Gordon Cobbledick, "Jockeys Ride Every Rookie," *The Sporting News*, May 21, 1947, 14; "Many Letters and Calls Over Chapman's Stand," *The Sporting News*, May 14, 1947, 13.
 59. Roscoe McGowen and Dan Daniel, "Robby Cites Bombers' Lack of Negro; Ability Sole Test for Job, Replies Weiss," *The Sporting News*, December 10, 1952, 3; "Robinson Charges Yankee Race Bias," *New York Times*, December 1, 1952, 31.
 60. "Bavasi Berates Bombers," *New York Times*, December 3, 1952.
 61. "Cautioned on Bias, Robinson Admits," *New York Times*, December 18, 1952.
 62. Michael Gaven, "Jackie Battled Rivals, Umps, Own Pilots," *The Sporting News*, January 23, 1957, 13. The article was a reprint of a two-part report in the *New York Journal-American*.
 63. Jackie Robinson and Charles Dexter, *Baseball Has Done It* (Philadelphia: J. B. Lippincott, 1964), 99.
 64. *Ibid.*, 100.
 65. *Ibid.*, 105.
 66. James P. Dawson, "Frick Re-Elected by National Loop," *New York Times*, July 8, 1947, 30; J. G. Taylor Spink, "Majors Bar Conditional Sales During Season," *The Sporting News*, July 16, 1947, 2.
 67. "National League's House in Order," *The Sporting News*, December 24, 1947, 12.
 68. Sid Keener, "Grandma Talks of Herself in New York," *The Sporting News*, January 14, 1948, 20.
 69. Louis Effrat, "58,339 Acclaim Babe Ruth in Rare Tribute at Stadium," *New York Times*, April 28, 1947, 1, 29.
 70. "Spellman Calls Ruth Champion of Fair Play, a Leader of Youth," *New York Times*, April 28, 1947, 29.
 71. William Marshall, *Baseball's Pivotal Era, 1945–1951* (Lexington: University of Kentucky Press, 1999), 166–211.
 72. Hy Turkin, "Babe Ruth Establishes Foundation to Aid Underprivileged Children," *The Sporting News*, May 14, 1947, 1; "Babe Ruth Foundation Set Up to Aid Underprivileged Youth," *New York Times*, May 9, 1947, 27.
 73. "Truman, Spellman Ask About 'Babe,'" *New York Times*, August 14, 1948, 26.
 74. Robert W. Creamer, *Babe: The Legend Comes to Life* (New York: Simon & Schuster, 1974), 424.
 75. "Nation's Leaders Mourn Babe Ruth," *New York Times*, August 17, 1948, 16.
 76. Oscar Kahan, "Ruth's Recorded Voice Adds Drama to Network Memorials," *The Sporting News*, August 28, 1948, 46.
 77. Dan Daniel, "Frick Suggests Third Major Club in Chicago," *The Sporting News*, August 6, 1947, 1, 6.
 78. "That Old 'St. Louis Problem,'" *The Sporting News* August 13, 1947, 12.
 79. Stan Baumgartner, "Frick Predicts 10-Year Dominance by National," *The Sporting News*, October 8, 1947, 2.
 80. "Exciting Race Forecast by Frick," January 6, 1948, 19; Keener, "Grandma Talks of Herself in New York."
 81. "Necrology," *The Sporting News*, November 19, 1947, 21; "Noble County Pioneer Jacob B. Frick, of Elkhart Twp., Dead," undated clipping.
 82. John Drebinger, "Rejection Is Seen for Elevation Bid," *New York Times*, December 11, 1947, 51.
 83. Stan Baumgartner, "Video Will Bring Camps to Home Fans," *The Sporting News*, March 17, 1948, 1–2.
 84. Dan Daniel, "N.L. Umps Ordered to Halt 'Cheating,'" *The Sporting News*, March 24, 1948, 1–2.
 85. Cy Kritzer, "'Video Imminent Threat to Minors'—Leo Miller," *The Sporting News*, June 2, 1948, 6.
 86. Dan Daniel, "Circuit-Breaker on Video Demanded," *The Sporting News*, June 9, 1948, 1, 6.
 87. Dan Daniel, "Leo's Move Laid to Dodger Tug-of-War," *The Sporting News*, July 28, 1948, 3; "Rickey is Annoyed in Cincinnati When News Is Broken Here Early," *New York Times*, July 17, 1948.
 88. Andrew Goldblatt, *The Giants and the Dodgers: Four Cities, Two Teams, One Rivalry* (Jefferson, NC: McFarland, 2003), 95–96.
 89. "Scottish Curlers Defeat Americans," *New York Times*, January 12, 1949, 35.
 90. Oscar Ruhl, "Diamond Terms Abound in Postal Guide," *The Sporting News*, January 2, 1957, 15.
 91. "National League Head Aids 1949 Heart Drive," *New York Times*, December 13, 1948; "Cardiac Crusade Appeal," *New York Times*, January 8, 1949, 17; "2 Fund Campaigns Endorsed by Mayor," *New York Times*, January 11, 1949, 30.
 92. Dan Daniel, "Cardinal's Talk Stirs N.Y. Diners," *The Sporting News*, February 16, 1949, 11; John Drebinger, "Boudreau and Frick Receive Warm Tributes at Dinner of Baseball Writers," *New York Times*, February 7, 1949, 24.
 93. J. G. Taylor Spink, "Long-Range Views from the 19th Floor," *The Sporting News*, January 26, 1949, 10.
 94. "Long-Term Television Contracts Urged for Minor Loop Baseball," *New York Times*, January 22, 1949, 17.
 95. J. G. Taylor Spink, "Game Faces Biggest Legal Test Since '22," *The Sporting News*, Febru-

ary 16, 1949, 2; "Stoneham 'Glad,' Wants Showdown," *New York Times*, February 10, 1949, 39.
96. "Ban on Major Leaguers Who Jumped to Mexico Lifted by Chandler," *New York Times*, June 6, 1949, 24; Marshall, *Baseball's Pivotal Era*, 243–244.
97. "Frick Promises a Fight to the Finish; Harridge Refuses to Comment on Case," *The Sporting News*, February 16, 1949, 16; "Stoneham 'Glad,' Wants Showdown," *New York Times*, February 10, 1949, 39.
98. Frick, *Games, Asterisks, and People*, 190.
99. "Mexican Jumpers Advised by Frick to Get Clearance from Contracts," *New York Times*, June 8, 1949, 40.
100. Dan Daniel, "Frick Opens Fire on Slipshod Scoring," *The Sporting News*, August 3, 1949, 1, 6.
101. Arthur Daley, "Scoring a Baseball Game," *New York Times*, August 16, 1949, 26.
102. "One Warning Suggests Another," *The Sporting News*, August 10, 1949, 12.
103. Jerry Nason, "Keeping Score on the Scorer," *The Sporting News*, August 17, 1949, 12.
104. "Frick to Provide Umpires for Little League Series," *The Sporting News*, August 17, 1949, 22; "Hammonton Nine Wins Title," *New York Times*, August 28, 1949, S3; Jim Sheen, "New Jersey Team Wins U.S. Little League Crown," *The Sporting News*, September 7, 1949, 21.
105. James P. Dawson, "Giants Devote Day to a Lecture on New Rules by Umpire Stewart," *New York Times*, March 11, 1950, 12; Dan Daniel, "Doubtful Points in New Rules Demonstrated," *The Sporting News*, March 15, 1950, 3–4.
106. Ken Smith, "Looks Like Rough Year for Runners," *The Sporting News*, March 22, 1950, 8.
107. Ray Gillespie, "Variations in Balk Decisions Befuddling Fans," *The Sporting News*, May 3, 1950, 2; "American League Is Not Affected by New Balk Rule, Says Harridge," *New York Times*, April 25, 1950, 44.
108. Bob Broeg "Players Shaping Attack on Bonus Rule," *The Sporting News*, June 21, 1950, 1–2.
109. Jack McDonald, "Frick Plans Strict Balk Observance," *The Sporting News*, March 28, 1951, 15; Barney Kremenko, "N.L. Umps Reminded to Bear Down on Balks," *The Sporting News*, April 11, 1951, 1–2.
110. Hy Turkin, "Lip's Sound Effect Creates TV Storm," *The Sporting News*, May 10, 1950, 2.
111. Harold Rosenthal, "Frick Asks for Curbs on Radio Blurbs," *The Sporting News*, January 14, 1953, 1, 4.
112. Roscoe McGowen, "Wasn't It Dressen Who Predicted He Could 'Handle Russ Meyer,'" *The Sporting News*, June 3, 1953, 7; "Russ Meyer Fined and Suspended for His Outburst at Philadelphia," *New York Times*, May 26, 1953, 36.
113. "Quotes: Philly Fans Aroused by Meyer's Antics," *The Sporting News*, June 3, 1953, 14.
114. J. G. Taylor Spink, "Rickey Given Big Assist in Jackie's Film Story," *The Sporting News*, March 8, 1950, 2.
115. Buzzie Bavasi with John Strege, *Off the Record* (Chicago: Contemporary Books, 1987), 29–30.
116. "Attorney Ray Cannon Dies; Tried to Unionize Players," *The Sporting News*, December 5, 1951, 26. Cowing's obituary is included among several that follow.

Chapter 9

1. John Paul Hill, "Commissioner A.B. 'Happy' Chandler and the Integration of Baseball," *NINE: A Journal of Baseball History and Culture* 19, no. 1 (Fall 2010): 28–51.
2. Happy Chandler with Vance Trimble, *Heroes, Plain Folks, and Skunks: The Life and Times of Happy Chandler* (Chicago: Bonus Books, 1989), 177.
3. Chester L. Smith, "Prices and Chandler Both Up in '48," *The Sporting News*, December 29, 1948, 13.
4. "Sunday Night Game at St. Louis Declined by Rickey, Chandler Says," *New York Times*, June 9, 1950, 31; "Lights Out on Sunday Night Game Billed for St. Louis," *The Sporting News*, June 21, 1950, 2.
5. "Cards, Ignoring Order by Chandler, Ask Hearing on Sunday Night Ball," *New York Times*, 12; "Lights Out on Sunday Night Game Billed for St. Louis," 2.
6. "Cardinals, Ignoring Order by Chandler, Ask Hearing on Sunday Night Ball," 12.
7. Tom Swope, "New Seven-Year Chandler Contract Assured," *The Sporting News*, November 22, 1950, 1, 12; "Chandler Assured of Retaining Post," *New York Times*, November 18, 1950, 19.
8. Andrew Zimbalist, *In the Best Interests of Baseball? The Revolutionary Reign of Bud Selig* (Hoboken, NJ: John Wiley & Sons, 2006), 49–50.
9. William Marshall, *Baseball's Pivotal Era, 1945–1951* (Lexington: University of Kentucky Press, 1999), 379–380.
10. Jerome Holtzman, *The Commissioners: Baseball's Midlife Crisis* (New York: Total Sports, 1998), 80.
11. Chandler, *Heroes, Plain Folks, and Skunks*, 189.
12. Marshall, *Baseball's Pivotal Era, 1945–1951*, 380–381.
13. James R. Walker and Robert Bellamy, Jr., *Center Field Shot: A History of Baseball on Television* (Lincoln: University of Nebraska Press, 2008): 79–81; "Agree on Series Money," *New York Times*, November 9, 1950, 9; "Yankees Acquire Pitchers Muncrief and Peterson in Draft," *New York Times*, November 17, 1950, 45.
14. John P. Carmichael, "Magnates Resented Carmichael's Desire to Know Where He Stood," *The Sporting News*, December 20, 1951, 2.
15. Chandler, *Heroes, Plain Folks, and Skunks*, 189.
16. *The Sporting News*, December 20, 1950, 3.
17. John Drebinger, "Majors Fail to Buy Con-

tract of Chief," *New York Times*, December 13, 1950, 61.

18. Arthur Daley, "More on the Upheaval," *New York Times*, December 14, 1950, 56.

19. "Pro and Con Views of Sport Scribes on Chandler's Ouster," *The Sporting News*, December 20, 1951, 2.

20. "Frick Denies Candidacy for Commissioner's Post," *The Sporting News*, December 27, 1950, 5.

21. Dan Daniel, "Chandler to Step Down in mid–July," *The Sporting News*, June 20, 1951, 1, 8.

22. Joe King, "Frick Fills Requirements, Asserts Dodger President," *The Sporting News*, July 4, 1951, 3.

23. Dan Daniel, "Griff for 'Strong National Figure,'" *The Sporting News*, July 4, 1951, 3, 10.

24. "Frick's Stock on the Rise," *The Sporting News*, July 4, 1951, 12.

25. Dan Daniel, "Majors Differ Widely on Ideas for Leader," *The Sporting News*, July 25, 1951, 7–8.

26. "Draft Tightening Threatens Player Shortage," *The Sporting News*, January 31, 1951, 6.

27. "Frick Sets Parley on Radio Problem," *New York Times*, January 5, 1951, 32; Roscoe McGowen, "Post-Season Play-Off Day Is Voted by National League," *New York Times*, January 12, 1951, 39; "N.L. to Shape Air Policies," *The Sporting News*, January 10, 1951, 2.

28. Stan Baumgartner, "Radio and TV Can Aid Game, Asserts Frick," *The Sporting News*, March 7, 1951, 19.

29. James A. Vlasich, *A Legend for the Legendary: The Origin of the Baseball Hall of Fame* (Bowling Green, OH: Bowling Green State University Popular Press, 1990), 212–213.

30. Dan Daniel, "Hall of Fame Stars Join N.L.'s 75th Birthday Party," *The Sporting News*, February 7, 1951, 4; Roscoe McGowen, "Giants Sign Two Players for Total of Nine Under Contract," *New York Times*, January 10, 1951, 47; John Drebinger, "National League Celebrates Diamond Jubilee at Site of Founding in 1876," *New York Times*, February 3, 1951, 21.

31. Jim McCulley, "Truman Gives Hearty Go-Ahead to Baseball," *New York Daily News*, February 3, 1951, 24.

32. "N.Y. Hotel, Where N.L. Was Formed, Collapses," *The Sporting News*, August 25, 1973, 42.

33. "Baseball Writers to Frolic Tonight," *New York Times*, February 4, 1951, 133; John Drebinger, "14 Hall of Fame Stars Come Back to Frolic with Baseball Writers," *New York Times*, February 4, 1951; Dan Daniel, "Stanky, Harridge Receive Special Awards at Dinner," *The Sporting News*, February 14, 1951, 7.

34. "Ohio's Gov. Lausche to Be Named Chandler Successor, Official Says," *New York Times*, February 10, 1951, 23.

35. Marshall, *Baseball's Pivotal Era, 1945–1951*, 390–391.

36. "18 Leading Candidates for Post Are Identified," *New York Times*, March 13, 1951, 43; "Chandler Asserts He Will 'Stand By,'" *New York Times*, March 14, 1951, 55.

37. "Players' Commissioner Idea Stirs Baseball Heads," *New York Times*, March 21, 1951, 58.

38. "Chandler Signs Resignation Pact, to Become Effective on July 15," *New York Times*, June 22, 1951, 18; Daniel, "Chandler to Step Down in Mid-July," 1.

39. Dan Daniel, "Majors Differ Widely on Ideas for Leader," 7–8; "Chandler Will Step Down Today After 6 Years as Baseball Head," *New York Times*, July 15, 1951, S3.

40. Shirley Povich, "Precedent for Exempting Game From Anti-Trust Laws in Books," May 16, 1951, 7; "Celler Favors Airing of Dispute Over Baseball's Reserve Clause," *New York Times*, May 5, 1951, 30.

41. Dan Daniel, "Inquiry to Lift Veil on Game's Finances," *The Sporting News*, July 4, 1951, 1, 6; "Big Leagues Prepare Groundwork for Showdown on Reserve Clause," *New York Times*, July 9, 1951, 32.

42. Dick Conners, "Better Game to Come Out of Hearings, Says Frick," *The Sporting News*, August 1, 1951, 13; "Frick Defends Baseball," *New York Times*, July 24, 1951, 39.

43. Stuart Banner, *The Baseball Trust: A History of Baseball's Antitrust Exemption* (New York: Oxford University Press, 2013), 115.

44. Organized Baseball: Hearings Before the Subcommittee on Study of Monopoly Power of the Committee on the Judiciary, 82nd Congress, 30 (1951) (statement of Ford C. Frick, President, the National League).

45. *Ibid.*, 80–106.

46. *Ibid.*, 51–52.

47. *Ibid.*, 1057.

48. Joseph M. Sheehan, "Plan Arranged for Minor Leagues to Reach Major Status," *New York Times*, November 15, 1951.

49. Vincent X. Flaherty, "Frick Talks Nonsense About Coast League Ball," *Los Angeles Examiner*, March 26, 1952.

50. Dan Daniel, "Game's Officials in Huddle on Celler Report," *The Sporting News*, June 4, 1952, 1, 4.

51. "Backing of Clause Is Hailed by Frick," *New York Times*, May 24, 1952, 25.

52. William B. Anderson, "Major League Baseball Under Investigation: How the Industry Used Public Relations to Promote Its Past to Save Its Present," *Public Relations Review* 30, no. 4 (November 2004): 439–445; Luther B. Huston, "More Major Leagues Proposed by Chandler in Testimony at Baseball Inquiry," *New York Times*, August 7, 1951, 29.

53. John Drebinger, "Owners Will Meet Here Again Aug. 21," *New York Times*, August 8, 1951, 28; J. G. Taylor Spink, "New Commissioner to be Named August 21," *The Sporting News*, August 15, 1951, 2.

54. J. G. Taylor Spink, "Game Sought General O'Donnell as Boss," *The Sporting News*, August 29, 1951, 1–2, 4.

55. Joseph M. Sheehan, "List of Commissioner

Candidates Cut to Five and Vote Set Sept. 20," *New York Times*, August 22, 1951, 27.

56. "M'Arthur Decision Sought by Owners," *New York Times*, August 26, 1951, S3.

57. George H. Gallup, *The Gallup Poll; Public Opinion, 1935–1971* (New York: Random House, 1972), 1000.

58. "MacArthur Not Likely to Accept Baseball Job," *New York Times*, August 28, 1951, 26.

59. "Lausche Was Frick's Rival for Commissioner in 1951," *The Sporting News*, July 27, 1953, 6.

60. "Lausche Withdraws as Candidate for Baseball Commissioner Post," *New York Times*, September 16, 1951, S1.

61. "Giles and Frick Head Candidates in Baseball Vote Listed for Today," *New York Times*, September 20, 1951, 40.

62. Joseph M. Sheehan, "Frick Elected Commissioner of Baseball for Seven Years," *New York Times*, September 21, 1951, 1, 39; Edgar Munzel, "Giles Slated to Be Named N.L. President," *The Sporting News*, September 26, 1951, 1, 4.

63. Ed Sainsbury, "Young Comiskey Turned Tide by Insisting Magnates Make Selection," *New York World-Telegram and Sun*, September 21, 1951, 33.

64. *Ibid.*

65. Munzel, "Giles Slated to Be Named N.L. President," 4.

66. Whitney Martin, "Frick Knows Way to First in New Job," undated clipping; Harold Rosenthal, "Frick Says Commissioner's Job Means Change in Way of Life," *New York Herald Tribune*, September 23, 1951. The Martin report for the *Associated Press* appeared in many member newspapers.

67. "Police Break the News to Frick as He Prepares for Bed," *The Sporting News*, September 26, 1951, 4.

68. Leonard Lewin, "Frick Tackles Czar, N.L. Prexy Problems," *New York Mirror*, September 22, 1951, 20, 22.

69. Sainsbury, "Young Comiskey Turned Tide," 33.

70. Oscar Ruhl, "Horses and Horse Hides," *The Sporting News*, October 3, 1951, 39.

71. "Diamond Leader Requests Cooperation of Everyone," *New York Times*, September 21, 1951, 39.

72. Red Smith, "He Will Make Mistakes," *New York Herald Tribune*, September 22, 1951.

73. Bill Corum, "Baseball Does Itself Proud," *New York Journal-American*, September 21, 1951, 22.

74. Joe Williams, "Ford Frick's Excellent Pick as Game's Boss," *New York World-Telegram and Sun*, September 22, 1951.

75. Dan Daniel, "Frick Faces Varied Problems," *New York World-Telegram and Sun*, September 22, 1951.

76. "Game Chooses Sound, Experienced Leader," *The Sporting News*, September 26, 1951, 12.

77. Smith, "He Will Make Mistakes"; Williams, "Ford Frick's Excellent Pick."

78. Tom Callahan, "A Commissioner on Deck," *Time*, March 12, 1984, 58. Marshall, *Baseball's Pivotal Era*, 426.

79. Rodger Pippen, "Election of Frick Mistake, Chandler Says in Baltimore," *The Sporting News*, October 21, 1951, 10.

80. Michael Shapiro, *Bottom of the Ninth: Branch Rickey, Casey Stengel, and the Daring Scheme to Save Baseball from Itself* (New York: Times Books, 2009), 20–21.

81. Frederick G. Lieb, "'Horse Sense' Policy Pledged by Frick," *The Sporting News*, October 3, 1951, 3.

Chapter 10

1. James P. Dawson, "Frick Says He Is Planning to Move Offices of the Commissioner Here," *New York Times*, September 22, 1951, 11.

2. "Giles of Reds Accepts Presidency of National League for Term of 4 Years," *New York Times*, September 28, 1951, 44.

3. Dan Daniel, "Majors Toss Radio, Video Control Back to Individual Clubs," *The Sporting News*, October 17, 1951, 4; "Control of Radio Reverts to Clubs," *New York Times*, October 9, 1951, 46.

4. Walker, James R., and Robert Bellamy Jr., *Center Field Shot: A History of Baseball on Television*. Lincoln: University of Nebraska Press, 2008, 86.

5. Edgar G. Brands, "Big League Players Ask for 'Better Deal,'" *The Sporting News*, October 17, 1951, 1–2.

6. Frederick G. Lieb, "Frick Backs Plan for More Majors," *The Sporting News*, October 24, 1951, 1–2.

7. Dan Daniel, "'I Won't Wave Big Stick,' Frick Tells Writers at Party for Him," *The Sporting News*, November 7, 1951, 4.

8. Edgar G. Brands, "Frick to Be an Umpire Instead of Policeman," *The Sporting News*, November 28, 1951, 1, 4.

9. "Game Doesn't Need Policeman, Wrigley Committee Reported," *The Sporting News*, May 28, 1952, 12.

10. Dan Daniel, "Frick Demands Majority for New Laws," *The Sporting News*, December 19, 1951, 1–2; John Drebinger "Majors' Recall Rule Stands; Player Limit Is Kept at 25," *New York Times*, December 10, 1951, 47.

11. Dan Daniel, "Majors Retain 25-Man Limit, 24-Hour Recall," *The Sporting News*, December 19, 1951, 7–8; Drebinger, "Majors' Recall Rule Stands."

12. "Frick on Tour of Camps," *The Sporting News*, February 27, 1952, 29.

13. Ward Morehouse, "Frick Urges Sale of Game to Kids via TV," *The Sporting News*, February 13, 1952, 3.

14. Roger Birtwell, "Rookie Ed Mathews Makes Big 'Hit' with Frick as Outfielder," *The Sporting News*, March 12, 1952, 18; Arthur Daley, "Youth Must Be Served," *New York Times*, March 13, 1952, 37.

15. Ford Frick, "Growth of Sport Encourages Frick," *New York Times*, April 13, 1952, S3.
16. "Trautman Bars Woman Players, Censures 'Travesty' on Baseball," *New York Times*, June 24, 1952, 38.
17. Joe McCarron, "Woman-Ump Gimmick Given Fast Heave-Ho in Frick Edict," *The Sporting News*, August 31, 1960, 37; "Flashback: In 1960, Allentown Nearly Had Pro Baseball's First Woman Umpire," *Allentown Morning Call*, August 23, 2010.
18. Louis Effrat, "Minimum Salaries, Other Reforms Gained by Major League Players," *New York Times*, September 17, 1946, 9.
19. John Drebinger, "Majors Fear Chandler's Bulletin Presages Crackdown on Training," *New York Times*, February 2, 1950, 40; "Chandler Issues Warning Regarding Camp Deadline," *The Sporting News*, February 8, 1950, 9.
20. Dan Daniel, "Players Ask $25 for Road Expense," *The Sporting News*, July 19, 1950, 10; "Minor Leagues Hit by Big Broadcasts," *New York Times*, July 11, 1950.
21. "Frick Asks Major Clubs for Copies of Camp Bids," *The Sporting News*, January 16, 1952, 2.
22. Roscoe McGowen, "Dodgers and Indians Get Approval for World Tour After the Series," *New York Times*, July 8, 1952, 30.
23. "'Oh Yeh! Mr. Frick, So I'm Napoleon,'" *New York Times*, October 6, 1952, 29.
24. David Eskenazi and Steve Rudman, "Wayback Machine: Rajah, Rivera, '51 Rainiers," http://sportspressnw.com/2128720/2012/waybackmachine-rajah-rivera-51-rainiers. Posted March 27, 2012.
25. "Frick Puts Rivera Under Probation," *New York Times*, November 13, 1952, 39.
26. Eskenazi and Rudman, "Wayback Machine: Rajah, Rivera, '51 Rainiers."
27. "Baseball Star Held on Coast," *New York Times*, January 18, 1958, 36.
28. "Bouchee to Be Treated," *New York Times*, March 7, 1958, 49; "Bouchee Put on Probation; Phillies to Aid in Treatment," *The Sporting News*, March 12, 1958, 24.
29. Dan Daniel, "Frick Reinstates Ed Bouchee on Probation Basis," *The Sporting News*, July 9, 1958, 23; Roscoe McGowen, "Bouchee of Phillies Reinstated to Club's Active List by Frick," *New York Times*, July 2, 1958, 34.
30. Jim Price, "Bouchee Dies at 79," *Spokesman-Review*, January 25, 2013.
31. John Drebinger, "Majors Adopt Two-League Waivers, End 24-Hour Recall on Options," *New York Times*, December 8, 1952, 36.
32. Roscoe McGowen, "Baseball Acts to Curb Interleague Deals After Trading Deadline," *New York Times*, October 30, 1952, 43.
33. John Drebinger, "Majors Adopt Two-League Waivers."
34. Joe King, "Path Opened for Browns' Shift to Milwaukee," *The Sporting News*, December 17, 1952, 2; Edgar G. Brands, "Sweeping Changes Okayed by Majors," *The Sporting News*, December 17, 1952, 7.
35. G. Edward White, *Creating the National Pastime: Baseball Transforms Itself, 1903–1953* (Princeton, NJ: Princeton University Press, 1996), 298.
36. "Saigh Urges One-Year Blackout of Baseball TV," *New York Times*, November 27, 1952, 53.
37. John Drebinger, "Cubs Agree to Share Home Television and Radio Money with Cards and Reds," *New York Times*, December 6, 1952.
38. Dan Daniel, "Frick Picks TV Committee, with Shaughnessy as Head," *The Sporting News*, January 7, 1953, 2, 4.
39. James P. Dawson, "Survey on Effect of Television on Minor Leagues to Be Started," *New York Times*, February 3, 1953, 28; "O.B. to Conduct Nationwide Survey on Effect of Radio and TV on Game," *The Sporting News*, February 11, 1953, 8.
40. Ray Gillespie, "Owner Given 15 Months, $15,000 Fine," *The Sporting News*, February 4, 1953, 11, 12.
41. "Saigh Role in Game to Be Up to Frick," *New York Times*, April 24, 1952, 17; "Saigh Confident of Vindication After Indictment on Income Tax Charges," *The Sporting News*, April 30, 1952.
42. John Drebinger, "3-Man Committee to Operate Cards," *New York Times*, January 31, 1953, 19.
43. Bob Broeg, "Busch Plans TV Step-Up by Cardinals," *The Sporting News*, March 4, 1953, 1, 10.
44. Bob Broeg, "New Corporation Organized by Busch to Operate Cards," *The Sporting News*, March 18, 1953, 9.
45. "Frick Cries Over Beer, So Cards Name Park for Busch and Budweiser Goes Down Drain," *New York Times*, April 11, 1953, 11.
46. Bob Broeg, "Johnson's Censure of Busch Policies Gets Quick Replies," *The Sporting News*, March 3, 1954, 3.
47. Jack Walsh, "Johnson, in Senate Talk, Voices Criticism of Frick," *The Sporting News*, March 3, 1954, 2.
48. Dan Daniel, "Frick Calls on Game to Repel Attacks," *The Sporting News*, March 3, 1954, 1–2.
49. Subjecting Professional Baseball Clubs to the Antitrust Laws: Hearings Before a Subcommittee of the Committee on the Judiciary, United States Senate, 83rd Cong. 88 (1954) (statement of Ford C. Frick, Commissioner of Baseball).
50. *Ibid*.
51. C. C. Johnson Spink, "Milwaukee Stalled in Efforts to Switch Browns," *The Sporting News*, March 11, 1953, 6; "Governor and Senate Add Weight to Milwaukee's Franchise Quest," *New York Times*, March 6, 1953, 31.
52. "Browns' Shift Opposed," *New York Times*, March 7, 1953, 20.
53. "Braves Seek Curb on Shifting Clubs," *New York Times*, March 12, 1953, 33; "Perini Had Asked Change in Rule on Franchise Shift," *The Sporting News*, March 18, 1953, 4.
54. J. G. Taylor Spink, "Braves to Milwaukee, Browns to Baltimore," *The Sporting News*, March

18, 1953, 1, 4; "Baseball Weighs Shifting of Browns to Baltimore and Braves to Milwaukee," *New York Times*, March 14, 1953, 18.
55. "Baltimore Elated," *New York Times*, March 15, 1953, S1.
56. "Way Seen Clear for Browns and Braves Shifts Following Baseball Conference," *New York Times*, March 16, 1953, 24.
57. Rodger H. Pippen, "Baltimore Fandom Bewildered and Boiling," *The Sporting News*, March 25, 1953, 7.
58. Lester Smith, "Braves Set Sail on Sea of Red Ink," *The Sporting News*, March 25, 1953, 1, 8; "Milwaukee Plans 7-Day Celebration," *New York Times*, March 20, 1953, 30.
59. Glen Gendzel, "Competitive Boosterism: How Milwaukee Lost the Braves," *Business History Review* 69 (1995) 4: 530–566.
60. Hy Turkin, "Florida Gives Frick Sunny '53 Outlook," *The Sporting News*, April 8, 1953, 20.
61. "Phils Will Stay in Quaker City, Says Carpenter," *The Sporting News*, March 25, 1953, 9.
62. Dennis Coates and Brad R. Humphreys, "Do Economists Reach a Conclusion on Subsidies for Sports Franchises, Stadiums, and Mega-Events?" *Working Paper Series, Paper No. 08–18* (August 2008), International Association of Sports Economists, 2.
63. "Cardinal Ace Gets Sid Mercer Award," *New York Times*, 25; Charles C. Spink, "1,450 Guests at Fun Fiesta," *The Sporting News*, February 12, 1947, 5.
64. James P. Dawson, "Giants Correct Voiselle's Stance on Pitch to Restore Effectiveness," *New York Times*, February 20, 1947, 34.
65. Louis Effrat, "Newcombe Victor With 6-Hitter, 6–0," *New York Times*, August 25, 1949, 27; "Gamblers Approached None in Game; 'No Substance' to Rumors—Mulbry," *The Sporting News*, August 31, 1949, 2.
66. Paul P. Kennedy, "M'Grath Unit Asks Sports Pools' End," *New York Times*, September 14, 1951, 15; "Gambling Probe Committee Includes Harridge, Frick," *The Sporting News*, September 12, 1951, 16.
67. "Federal Probe of Gambling and Bribery in Sports Asked," *The Sporting News*, February 25, 1953, 32; "Sports Bribes Stir Pleas to Congress," *New York Times*, February 17, 1953, 33.
68. Hy Turkin, "Reports on Some Players in 'Joints' Put Frick in Fury," *The Sporting News*, May 6, 1953, 4.
69. Dan Daniel, "Frick Advises Lopat to Cut Barnstorming Layover in Las Vegas," *The Sporting News*, September 15, 1954, 13.
70. Bob Considine, "More Money Than Friends," *New York Journal-American*, May 22, 1955; "Frick Asks for Names in Bets on Foot Race," *St. Louis Post-Dispatch*, May 19, 1955, 48.
71. "Baseball Players Hire Own Counsel," *New York Times*, August 22, 1953, S1.
72. "Players' Aide, Frick to Meet Tomorrow," *New York Times*, August 23, 1953, S1.
73. Carl T. Felker, "Players Rap Hiring of Mouthpiece," *The Sporting News*, September 2, 1953, 1–2, 4.
74. White, *Creating the National Pastime*, 190–192.
75. J. G. Taylor Spink, "Yawkey Declares Player Reps Used 'Wrong Approach,'" *The Sporting News*, September 2, 1953, 2.
76. Felker, "Players Rap Hiring of Mouthpiece," 2.
77. James Enright, "Lewis Won Post as Legal Adviser from Field of 30," *The Sporting News*, September 2, 1953, 4.
78. Joseph M. Sheehan, "Players' Lawyer Confers with Baseball Officials," *New York Times*, August 25, 1953, 26; Felker, "Players Rap Hiring of Mouthpiece," 2.
79. "At Least 12 Proposals Submitted by Players to Baseball Officials," *New York Times*, August 26, 1953, 30.
80. Roscoe McGowen, "Players' Pension Plan Tops All in U.S.," *The Sporting News*, September 9, 1953, 1, 4.
81. Roscoe McGowen, "Frick Helped Ex-Big Timer Regain Pension Privileges," *The Sporting News*, September 9, 1953, 4.
82. "Ball Players' Attorney Reports 'Definite Progress' on Proposals," *New York Times*, September 1, 1953, 26.
83. Frederick G. Lieb, "Players Win New Concessions, But Hit Snag on Pension Hike," *The Sporting News*, October 7, 1953, 8.
84. Louis Effrat, "Council Approves Five Proposals Submitted by Baseball Players," *New York Times*, September 29, 1953, 32.
85. J. G. Taylor Spink, "Move to End A.L. Pact Airing Games," *The Sporting News*, November 5, 1952, 1, 4.
86. Ed McAuley, "New TV Setup May Give Veeck Trading Advantage," *The Sporting News*, November 19, 1952, 13.
87. Ray Gillespie, "Veeck Plans Snag for 'Silk Stocking' Rivals Over Video," *The Sporting News*, January 21, 1953, 8; "Yanks Cards Indians and Red Sox on Night Games Kept From Browns," *New York Times*, February 5, 1953, 28.
88. Edgar G. Brands, "Veeck Appeals to Frick in Battle for Television Divvy," *The Sporting News*, February 11, 1953, 5–6.
89. "Veeck Ends Fight on TV, Radio Issue," *New York Times*, March 24, 1953, 38; "Veeck Surrenders, Okays Televising of Road Contests," *The Sporting News*, April 1, 1953, 21.
90. Robert L. Burnes, "Receivership Threat Sped Browns' Shift," *The Sporting News*, October 7, 1953, 3–4.
91. Jerome Holtzman, *The Commissioners: Baseball's Midlife Crisis* (New York: Total Sports, 1998), 113–114; Zimbalist, *In the Best Interests of Baseball?*, 65–66.

Chapter 11

1. Walker, James R., and Robert Bellamy Jr., *Center Field Shot: A History of Baseball on Televi-*

sion. Lincoln: University of Nebraska Press, 2008, 204–218. They devote an entire chapter to addressing and dismissing the argument. The chapter also provides an excellent description of the challenges facing minor league baseball in the 1950s.

2. Arthur Daley, "Cassandra Speaks," *New York Times*, February 3, 1953, 28; Dan Daniel, "Sen. Johnson Blasts Majors for TV 'Greed,'" *The Sporting News*, February 11, 1953, 19.

3. "Johnson Begins Hearings on Radio-TV Bill, May 6," *New York Times*, May 6, 1953, 4.

4. Broadcasting and Televising Baseball Games: Hearings Before a Subcommittee of the Committee on Interstate and Foreign Commerce, United States Senate, 83rd Cong. 17 (1953) (statement of Ford C. Frick, Commissioner of Baseball).

5. Walker and Bellamy, *Center Field Shot*, 215.

6. Jack Walsh, "Sen. Johnson 'Optimistic' Over Aircast Relief," *The Sporting News*, May 20, 1953, 13.

7. Walker and Bellamy, *Center Field Shot*, 99–100.

8. Dan Daniel, "Frick Picks TV Committee, with Shaughnessy as Head," *The Sporting News*, January 7, 1953, 2.

9. James P. Dawson, "Survey on Effect of Television on Minor Leagues to Be Started," *New York Times*, February 3, 1953, 28; "O.B. to Conduct Nationwide Survey on Effect of Radio and TV on Game," *The Sporting News*, February 11, 1953, 8.

10. "Frick Predicts Doom of Minors Unless Telecasts Are Controlled," *New York Times*, June 28, 1953, S3.

11. Ray Keyes, "Young, Vet Albany Scribe, Lays Game's Ills to Lack of Leadership," *The Sporting News*, June 30, 1954, 13.

12. Harold Rosenthal, "Frick Seeks Greater Use of Player Talent," *The Sporting News*, December 23, 1953, 1–2; "Frick Appoints 9 to Plan Changes in Baseball Laws," *New York Times*, December 20, 1953, S1.

13. Hy Turkin, "Capital Confab to Map O.B. Radio-TV Policy," *The Sporting News*, January 13, 1954, 1–2, 4; "Frick Committee Holds 2D Meeting," *New York Times*, January 9, 1954, 8.

14. "'Modernizing' Committee Holds Five-Hour Session," *The Sporting News*, February 10, 1954, 8.

15. Hy Turkin, "Curb on Campus Recruiting Voted by Majors," *The Sporting News*, August 4, 1954, 7.

16. Dan Daniel, "Frick Spikes Aid-to-Minors Proposal," *The Sporting News*, February 17, 1954, 1–2.

17. Ray Gillespie, "Minors' Poll Shows 5-Point Plan to Cut Costs," *The Sporting News*, August 25, 1954, 13.

18. "Lawrence Organizes Minor Group to Sue Majors for 50 Million," *The Sporting News*, September 29, 1954, 27; "Minors to Sue Money," *New York Times*, October 30, 1954, 20.

19. Brad Willson, "Minors Vote to Curb Broadcasts," *The Sporting News*, December 8, 1954, 5.

20. Harold Rosenthal, "Majors Refuse Minors' Plea to Cut Radio-TV," *The Sporting News*, December 15, 1954, 7–8; Drebinger, "Big Leagues Revamp Working Agreements with Minors," 46.

21. Arch Murray, "Giants in Japan, Trip Hailed as Aid in International Affairs," *The Sporting News*, October 14, 1953, 19; "Giants Get Three From Minneapolis," *New York Times*, October 8, 1953, 39.

22. N. Sakata, "Capacity Crowds Watch Giants in First Four Japanese Games," *The Sporting News*, 17.

23. Oscar Ruhl, "Jimmy Finds Yanks Trail in Mississippi," *The Sporting News*, November 4, 1953, 16; "Frick Views Taj Mahal," *New York Times*, October 27, 1953, 34.

24. "Frick Ends World Trip," *New York Times*, November 7, 1953, 21.

25. Dan Daniel, "Major League Barnstormers to Duck Foreign Tours This Fall," *The Sporting News*, September 8, 1954, 4; "Campy Drops His Plans for Barnstorming," *The Sporting News*, September 29, 1954, 21.

26. Dan Daniel, "Plans Shaping Up for Yankee Team to Play in Japan," *The Sporting News*, August 3, 1955, 1–2.

27. "Yankee Party Departs on Six-Week Tour of Orient," *New York Times*, October 9, 1955, S1.

28. (No title), *New York Times*, October 29, 1955, 14.

29. Dan Daniel, "Frick Okays Annual Japanese Junkets," *The Sporting News*, November 16, 1955, 1–2.

30. "Major Expansion Certain, Frick Tells 'Em in Honolulu," *The Sporting News*, October 21, 1953, 18.

31. J. Gordon Hylton, "Why Baseball's Antitrust Exemption Still Survives," *Marquette Sports Law Review* 9, no. 2 (Spring 1998): 391–402.

32. Hy Turkin, "Path Now Clear for Progress—Frick," *The Sporting News*, November 18, 1953, 1–2.

33. "Baseball Executives Hail Ruling as Tremendous Victory for National Game," *New York Times*, November 10, 1953, 40.

34. Ford Frick, Letter to Team Presidents, November 11, 1953.

35. Dan Daniel, "Ford Sees Capital Meetings as Spur to Majors' Expansion," *The Sporting News*, December 24, 1958, 7.

36. Red Smith, "Call to Action by Frick in '53 Finally Heeded," *The Sporting News*, January 14, 1959, 10.

37. Dan Daniel, "Players Eye Series TV Pot as Means of Pension Hike," *The Sporting News*, November 25, 1953, 2.

38. "Players' Lawyer to Press Fight for Revision of Pension Fund," *New York Times*, November 13, 1953, 30.

39. John Drebinger, "Baseball Players and Frick at Odds," *New York Times*, December 3, 1953, E2.

40. Edgar Munzel, "$7,580,000 Cost Hike Threatens Pension," *The Sporting News*, December 9, 1953, 1–2; Drebinger, "Baseball Players and Frick at Odds."

41. Drebinger, "Baseball Players and Frick at Odds."

42. "Growing Demands Jeopardizing Pensions," *The Sporting News*, December 9, 1953, 2.
43. Ed Pollock, "Baseball Lost a Point When Frick Barred Attorney," *Philadelphia Bulletin*, December 9, 1953.
44. Red Smith, "Frick Not Bitter at Newsmen," *New York Herald Tribune*, September 2, 1953.
45. Arthur Daley, "Honoring an Alumnus," *New York Times*, January 12, 1966, 68.
46. John Drebinger, "Big Leagues Take Steps Toward Ending Player Pension Plan in 1955," *New York Times*, December 10, 1953; Edgar Munzel, "Greenberg, Galbreath Seek to Save Pensions," *The Sporting News*, December 16, 1953, 5–6.
47. "Players Asked Chandler for Advice," *The Sporting News*, December 16, 1953, 5.
48. "Chandler Blasts Baseball Owners," *New York Times*, January 20, 1954, 37; "Happy, in Chi as Semi-Pro Boss, Raps Frick, Owners," *The Sporting News*, January 27, 1954, 24.
49. Dan Daniel, "Frick Opens Books on Pension Plan; Big Contrast in Player, Owner Funds," *The Sporting News*, January 27, 1954, 5; Roscoe McGowen, "Frick Outlines Pension Operation in Action on Heels of 'Sniping,'" *New York Times*, January 22, 1954, 33.
50. "Lewis Criticizes Report by Frick," *New York Times*, January 26, 1954, 22.
51. Dan Daniel, "Frick Warns Against Attempting 'to Run '54 Machine on '90 Motor,'" *The Sporting News*, February 10, 1954, 1, 6; John Drebinger, "Frick Criticizes Players, Owners and Courts in Baseball Dinner Speech," *New York Times*, February 1, 1954, 27.
52. Oscar Ruhl, "Mathews' Switch to Outfield Predicted," *The Sporting News*, January 13, 1954, 14.
53. "Frick, His Health Improved, Denies He Plans to Resign," *The Sporting News*, March 24, 1952, 2.
54. Roscoe McGowen, "Players' Representatives and Baseball Officials Agree on Pension Plan," *New York Times*, February 17, 1954, 36; Hy Turkin, "Players Strike it Rich in New Pension Terms," *The Sporting News*, February 24, 1954, 1–2.
55. "Frick-Lewis Feud Bypassed in Pension Deal," *The Sporting News*, February 24, 1954, 14.
56. Dan Daniel, "60–40 Pension Plan Agreement Okayed by Major Leagues," *The Sporting News*, March 24, 1954, 6.
57. Dan Daniel, "Players' Lawyer to Be Paid by Central Fund—Reynolds," *The Sporting News*, June 30, 1954, 4.
58. Michael Schiavone, *Sports and Labor in the United States* (Albany, NY: State University of New York Press, 2015), 19.
59. Dan Daniel, "7,200 Minimum Salary Tops New Player Demands," *The Sporting News*, October 6, 1954, 8.
60. John Drebinger, "Big Leagues Revamp Working Agreements With Minors," *New York Times*, December 8, 1954, 46.
61. John Drebinger, "Athletics' Transfer to Kansas City Wins Final American League Approval," *New York Times*, November 9, 1954, 33; Lanse McCurley, "House of Mack—A House Divided," *The Sporting News*, November 10, 1954, 1, 6.
62. Ernest Mehl, "Persistence Won Obstacle Race for Kaycee," *The Sporting News*, November 17, 1954, 4–5.
63. "Quotes," *The Sporting News*, December 22, 1954, 16.
64. Hugo G. Autz, "Frick Flashes 'Go' on March 19–26 as Nationwide Boom for Baseball," *The Sporting News*, February 2, 1955.
65. "Start of 'Let's Play Ball Week' Is Proclaimed by Eisenhower," *New York Times*, March 19, 1955, 17.
66. Richard F. Shepard, "Coward Put Back in Ford TV Show," *New York Times*, March 24, 1956; "90-Minute Show to Salute Game, April 15," *The Sporting News*, March 7, 1956, 16.
67. *Ibid*.; "Quotes," *The Sporting News*, March 21, 1956, 17.
68. Dan Daniel, "Stars, Comedy and Songs in Fast-Moving 'Salute,'" *The Sporting News*, April 24, 1957, 24.
69. Dan Daniel, "Frick Asks Curb of Commercials During Aircasts," *The Sporting News*, March 9, 1955, 8; Pat Harmon, "Frick Restores English Language," *Cincinnati Post*, May 3, 1956.
70. John Drebinger, "National League Votes Afternoon Lights, Ends Night-Game Curfew," *New York Times*, December 13, 1949, 47.
71. Dan Daniel, "Majors Split Over Spitter, Poll Shows," *The Sporting News*, December 14, 1949, 13.
72. Edgar Munzel, "Spitter Would Lower Bars to Trickery, Says Harridge," December 7, 1949, 18.
73. Turkin, "Path Now Clear for Progress—Frick," 2.
74. Oscar Ruhl, "That Something Extra That Makes Stars," *The Sporting News*, December 16, 1953, 11.
75. Art Morrow, "'Bring Back Spitter to Rescue Pitchers'—Frick,"
76. Dick Young, "'The Outlawed Spitball Was My Money Pitch,'" *Sports Illustrated*, July 4, 1955, 18–21, 60–61.
77. "Same Sound Reasons Exist for Spitter's Ban, Says Giles," *The Sporting News*, March 16, 1955, 2; "Spitball Return Would Open Door to Cheating—Harridge," *The Sporting News*, March 16, 1955, 2.
78. Herb Heft, "Players, Coaches, Pilots Favor Spitball," *The Sporting News*, March 23, 1955, 1–2.
79. Shirley Povich, "Restore the Spitter? 'You'll Be Sorry—' Griffith Warns," *The Sporting News*, April 6, 1955, 1–2.
80. J. G. Taylor Spink, "Rule-Makers Oppose Spitball Return," *The Sporting News*, August 10, 1955, 1–2.
81. Dan Daniel, "Frick Employs Research Firm to Survey Game," *The Sporting News*, May 25, 1955, 4; "Baseball Survey Due," *New York Times*, May 18, 1955, 37.
82. "Fans to Prescribe Baseball Remedy," *New York Times*, June 26, 1955, S3.

83. "Solutions Needed, Not More Evidence," *The Sporting News*, June 1, 1955, 12; John Carmichael, "Frick Study Plan May Be Hot Potato," *The Sporting News*, June 1, 1955, 12.
84. "Survey Shows Parking, TV Keep Fans at Home," *The Sporting News*, August 10, 1955, 5; "Slow Games Irk Baseball Fans, Survey Ordered by Frick Shows," *New York Times*, August 2, 1955, 27.
85. "Majors Will Act to Reduce Long Games, Frick Declares," *The Sporting News*, August 24, 1955, 4.
86. Dan Daniel, "Frick Suggests Policy-Shaping Role for Office," *The Sporting News*, November 30, 1955, 1, 4.
87. Cy Kritzer, "Combine Major and Minor Rule—Frick," *The Sporting News*, June 2, 1954, 1–2.
88. Edgar Munzel, "Widen Commissioner's Power, Frick Urges," *The Sporting News*, December 14, 1955, 11.
89. John Drebinger, "Majors Continue Bonus Rule and Reject Players' Demands," *New York Times*, December 7, 1955, 52; Munzel, "Widen Commissioner's Power," 11.
90. Joseph M. Sheehan, "Baseball Players Protest Owners' Rejection of Demands," *New York Times*, December 15, 1955, 55; Dan Daniel, "Frick Tells Players Owners Again Will Consider Demands," *The Sporting News*, December 21, 1955, 8.
91. "Young Award Proposed to Honor Ace Pitcher," *New York Times*, December 16, 1955, 39; "Hurlers Need Award of Own, Says Frick, Citing Roberts," *The Sporting News*, December 21, 1955, 2.
92. Dan Daniel, "Pitchers to Have Own MVP Award in Future," *The Sporting News*, February 15, 1956, 9; John Drebinger, "Majors Reject Player Pay Rise," *New York Times*, February 5, 1956, S1–2.
93. Fred Lieb, "Separate Award for Top Hurler Voted by Writers' Association," *The Sporting News*, July 18, 1956, 15.
94. Carl Lundquist, "Majors Stand Pat on Minimum Pay, but Plan 'Review,'" *The Sporting News*, February 15, 1956, 9–10; Drebinger, "Majors Reject Player Pay Rise," S2.
95. Edgar Munzel, "More Power Sought for Commissioner," *The Sporting News*, June 27, 1956, 1–2.
96. "Commissioner Needs More Power," *The Sporting News*, June 27, 1956, 12.
97. Charley Young, "Big Leagues Gunning for Trautman's Job?," *The Sporting News*, May 22, 1957, 1, 6.
98. Charles Young, "'Oust Trautman' Report Strongly Denied by Frick," *The Sporting News*, May 29, 1957, 37.

Chapter 12

1. Carl Lundquist, "'Third Major League Coming,' Says Frick," *The Sporting News*, March 7, 1956, 3.
2. Hy Hurwitz, "World's Series Film Shows How Huddles Slow Play, Says Cronin," *The Sporting News*, January 25, 1956, 5.
3. "Giles Opposes Rule Curbing Hill Huddles," *The Sporting News*, April 4, 1956, 2.
4. William R. Conklin, "Commissioner Frick Gives Needle to LP Baseball Games," *The Sporting News*, April 15, 1956, S3.
5. Edgar Munzel, "Rule-Makers Move to Speed Games," *The Sporting News*, November 28, 1956, 1–2.
6. Edgar Munzel, "Officials, Players Rap Speed-Up Rules," *The Sporting News*, March 27, 1957, 1, 4.
7. Dan Daniel, "Frick Spikes Players' TV Gravy Dream," *The Sporting News*, May 9, 1956, 1–2.
8. Carl Lundquist, "Everybody Scores on Commissioner's Aircast Grand Slam," *The Sporting News*, July 11, 1956, 6.
9. "'Excellent Job,' Says Lewis, Occasional Critic of Frick," *The Sporting News*, July 11, 1956, 6.
10. Arthur Daley, "It's Now a Dream Job," *New York Times*, July 6, 1956, 24.
11. John Drebinger, "Majors Approve New Five-Year Player Pension Plan with Improved Benefits," *New York Times*, February 2, 1957, 15; Oscar Ruhl, "Players' Pension Plan Now 'Finest Anywhere,'" *The Sporting News*, February 13, 1957, 7.
12. "New Incentive for Careers in Game," *The Sporting News*, February 13, 1957, 12.
13. John Drebinger, "Baseball Clubs Reject Pay Rise," *New York Times*, February 3, 1957, S1, S4; Oscar Kahan, "Athletes' Pitch for Increase to $7,500 Denied," *The Sporting News*, February 13, 1957, 7–8.
14. "Move on Foot to Give Frick Second Seven-Year Contract," *The Sporting News*, May 23, 1956, 4.
15. "Speed-Up Applied to Council Table," *The Sporting News*, May 23, 1956, 12.
16. "Quotes," *The Sporting News*, February 20, 1957, 17.
17. Dan Daniel, "'Free Agent Draft' Planned to Aid Minors," *The Sporting News*, June 6, 1956, 1–2.
18. Clifford Kachline, "Revision Group Rejects Plan for Draft Pool of Free Agents," *The Sporting News*, October 24, 1956, 21.
19. Dan Daniel, "O'Malley Clears Up Plan to Aid Minors with Cash from TV," *The Sporting News*, December 7, 1955, 4; "O'Malley Proposal Would Enable Minors to Share in TV Receipts," *New York Times*, November 29, 1955, 35.
20. John Drebinger, "Majors Continue Bonus Rule and Reject Players' Demands," *New York Times*, December 7, 1955, 52; Edgar Munzel, "Widen Commissioner's Power, Frick Urges," *The Sporting News*, December 14, 1955, 11.
21. Dan Daniel "Player Salaries Heading for Peak of $50,000,000," *The Sporting News*, January 11, 1956, 2.
22. Carl Lundquist, "'Save Minors' Fund of

$500,000 by Major Committee," *The Sporting News*, August 8, 1956, 4; "Major Loops Act to Succor Minors," *New York Times*, August 3, 1956, 13.

23. Carl Lundquist, "Opening-Day Cut to 28 Players by Majors Planned," *The Sporting News*, September 26, 1956, 4.

24. John Drebinger, "Major League Owners Lift All Restrictions on Signing of College Players," *New York Times*, December 12, 1956, 67.

25. J. G. Taylor Spink, "Fund of $500,000 Okayed by Majors for Aid to Minors," *The Sporting News*, October 17, 1956, 27.

26. Carl Lundquist, "Committee of Six Chosen to Supervise Expenditures," *The Sporting News*, November 7, 1956, 5.

27. "DeWitt in New Post," *New York Times*, December 4, 1956, 65; "Bill DeWitt Hopes Minors' Aid Project Can Be Extended Over Several Years," *The Sporting News*, December 19, 1956, 6.

28. John Drebinger, "Owners Lift All Restrictions on Signing of College Players," *The Sporting News*, December 12, 1956, 67; Edgar Munzel, "Majors Bury College Rule, Coaches Howl," *The Sporting News*, December 19, 1956, 5–6.

29. Munzel, "Majors Bury College Rule," 6.

30. Bill Paddock, "Some College Rule Needed, Says Frick; 'Up to Schools Now,'" *The Sporting News*, January 2, 1957, 20.

31. John C. Hoffman, "Frick and Wilson Exchange Dusters Over College Issue," *The Sporting News*, February 6, 1957, 8.

32. *Organized Professional Team Sports: Hearings Before the Antitrust Subcommittee of the Committee on the Judiciary, House of Representatives*, 85th Cong. 1826–1850 (1957) (testimony of Leslie M. O'Connor, President, Pacific Coast League).

33. Jack Walsh, "Anti-Trust Bills Tossed at O.B.," *The Sporting News*, March 6, 1957, 1, 4.

34. "Celler Calls Frick Baseball Dictator," *New York Times*, March 12, 1957, 41; "Frick Defended by Keating, Blasted by Celler," *The Sporting News*, March 20, 1957, 16.

35. Paul A. Rickart, "DeOrsey Goes to Bat for O.B. Overhaul—Draws Only Dusters," *The Sporting News*, March 20, 1957, 16.

36. "Baseball Names a Defense Group," *New York Times*, March 23, 1957, 22; "Game's Leaders Map Course Toward Pending Legislation," *The Sporting News*, March 27, 1957, 25.

37. Frederick G. Lieb, "Game Tightens Belt in Preparation for Legislative Attack," *The Sporting News*, April 3, 1957, 11.

38. Jack Walsh, "Hearings Reveal Red Ink Pools in Majors," *The Sporting News*, June 26, 1957, 13.

39. *Organized Professional Team Sports: Hearings Before the Antitrust Subcommittee of the Committee on the Judiciary, House of Representatives*, 85th Cong. 91 (1957) (testimony of Ford C. Frick, Commissioner of Baseball).

40. J. Gordon Hylton, "Why Baseball's Antitrust Exemption Survives," *Marquette Sports Law Journal* 9 (1999), 401.

41. Virgil Cory, "Coast Bolts Door Against Major Invasion," *The Sporting News*, September 10, 1947, 1, 4.

42. John Drebinger, "Rejection Is Seen for Elevation Bid," *New York Times*, December 11, 1947, 51.

43. Dan Daniel, "Majors Reject Coast Bid for Big Time Rating," *The Sporting News*, December 17, 1947, 5.

44. "Majors for Coast—Frick," *The Sporting News*, April 7, 1948, 24.

45. "Frick Hosts Coast Party and Is Guest at Another," *The Sporting News*, March 31, 1948, 29.

46. "Shocked by Ouster," *The Sporting News*, December 27, 1950, 6.

47. Dan Daniel, "Frick Outlines Plan to Build Up New Majors," *The Sporting News*, November 21, 1951.

48. John Drebinger, "Majors' Recall Rule Stands; Player Limit Is Kept at 25," *New York Times*, December 10, 1951, 47.

49. "Starr and Laws See Major Status for PCL by 1957," *The Sporting News*, December 12, 1951, 26.

50. John B. Old, "Game's Head Sees Coast's Rise as Unit," *The Sporting News*, April 2, 1952, 13.

51. Andrew Goldblatt, *The Giants and the Dodgers: Four Cities, Two Teams, One Rivalry* (Jefferson, NC: McFarland, 2003), 135–140.

52. "Frick Predicts Major League Ball in West but Warns Against Haste," *New York Times*, November 21, 1952, 30.

53. "Big Leagues Vying for Coast Entries," *New York Times*, July 19, 1953, S3.

54. J. G. Taylor Spink, "Webb Sees K.C. as Major League Entry," *The Sporting News*, July 22, 1953, 1–2.

55. Dan Daniel, "Brooklyn and Not Browns Sought by L.A.—O'Malley," *The Sporting News*, September 2, 1953, 6.

56. "Frick Puts Gag on Talk of Major Shifts," *The Sporting News*, May 12, 1954, 9.

57. "'No Park, No Franchise,' Frick Tells Los Angeles," *The Sporting News*, August 18, 1954, 11.

58. "Frick Tells 'Frisco It Needs Big Park to Get Major Ball," *The Sporting News*, October 13, 1954, 6.

59. "Stadium Bond Issue Adopted," *New York Times*, November 4, 1954, 44; Dan Daniel, "National League to Discuss Plans to Invade Coast," *The Sporting News*, November 17, 1954, 2.

60. Dan Daniel, "Plans for Expansion Placed on Shelf at New York Sessions," *The Sporting News*, February 9, 1955, 21; Joe King, "Enough Players to Go Around," *The Sporting News*, February 9, 1955, 21.

61. Carl Lundquist, "Giants Vision 'Dream Park' in Manhattan," *The Sporting News*, April 11, 1956, 22.

62. Roscoe McGowen, "All-Weather Dome Would Put Brooks in Seventh Heaven," *The Sporting News*, December 7, 1955, 8.

63. John B. Old, "O'Malley Peeks at Possible Site for Park in L.A.," *The Sporting News*, 15.

64. David Plaut, *Chasing October: The Dodgers-Giants Pennant Race of 1962* (South Bend, IN: Diamond Communications, 1994), 20.
65. Rube Samuelsen, "L.A. Officials Seek Light on Dodger Plans," *The Sporting News*, March 6, 1957, 14, 16.
66. Roscoe McGowen, "Coast Group Confers With O'Malley in Bid to Move Dodgers to Los Angeles," *New York Times*, March 7, 1957, 49.
67. "'Three Major Leagues in Frick's Crystal Ball," *New York Times*, May 8, 1957, 62; Jack Gallagher, "Frick Foresees 'Three Majors in My Lifetime,'" *The Sporting News*, May 15, 1957, 34.
68. "San Francisco Mayor Consults Here With Giants and Dodgers," *New York Times*, May 11, 1957, 16; Rube Samuelsen, "O'Malley Kept Busy Looking, Listening on His Visit to Coast," *The Sporting News*, May 15, 1957, 8.
69. "Coast Mayor Hints at Shift of Giants, Brooks in 1958," *New York Times*, May 12, 1957, S1.
70. Joe King, "Frick Calls for 'Expansion Instead of Shifts,'" *The Sporting News*, May 22, 1957, 5.
71. Michael Strauss, "Frick Sidetracks Three Redlegs After Avalanche of Ohio Votes," *The Sporting News*, June 29, 1957, 27.
72. "Redleg Fans Rail Against Frick for Vetoing 3 of Their All-Stars," *New York Times*, June 30, 1957, S2.
73. Bob Husted, "The Case of Mr. Frick," *Cincinnati Enquirer*, June 30, 1957; Oscar Ruhl, "Cincy Fans See Red After Ump Frick Calls Out Three," *The Sporting News*, July 10, 1957, 15.
74. J. G. Taylor Spink, "Frick Favors Player Vote for All-Stars," *The Sporting News*, August 7, 1957, 1, 4.
75. Munzel, "Majors Re-Elect Frick, Extend Minors' Pact," 6.
76. Joe King, "Yankees Seeking Bar on Any A.L. Club in Brooklyn," *The Sporting News*, July 31, 1957, 9; "Yankees Assert Sole Rights Here," *New York Times*, July 26, 1957, 15.
77. Bill Becker, "Giants Will Shift to San Francisco for 1958 Season," *New York Times*, August 20, 1957, 1, 30.
78. "Decision Greeted Calmly on Coast," *New York Times*, August 20, 1957, 30.
79. "Frick Boosts Third Major," *The Sporting News*, August 28, 1957, 12.
80. "Quotes," *The Sporting News*, August 28, 1957, 16.
81. Edgar Munzel, "Bargaining Over New York Territory Looms," *The Sporting News*, October 9, 1957, 9.
82. Emanuel Perlmutter, "Dodgers Accept Los Angeles Bid to Move to Coast," *New York Times*, October 9, 1957, 1, 37.

Chapter 13

1. Edgar Munzel, "Majors Re-Elect Frick, Extend Minors' Pact," *The Sporting News*, July 17, 1957, 5–6.
2. Dan Daniel, "'Game Facing Its Most Critical Period'—Frick," *The Sporting News*, July 17, 1957, 5.
3. "Short Meeting, Long Term for Frick," *The Sporting News*, July 17, 1957, 12.
4. Roger Kahn, "Baseball's Reluctant Czar," *Esquire*, July 1958, 35–37.
5. Ed McAuley, "NFL's Bell Acts in Tradition of Judge Landis," *The Sporting News*, August 21, 1957, 12.
6. Dan Daniel, "New Huddles Fail to Solve Realignment," *The Sporting News*, November 20, 1957, 21; Roscoe McGowen, "Frick Hopes Minor Realignment Can Be Achieved Without Draft," *New York Times*, November 13, 1957, 45.
7. John Drebinger, "Meetings at End, Disputes Remain," *New York Times*, December 8, 1957, S1–2; Edgar Munzel, "Bankrolls Now Only Limit on Bonus Bids," *The Sporting News*, December 18, 1957, 11–12.
8. John Drebinger "Minors Call on Congress to Reopen Inquiry on Baseball," *New York Times*, December 6, 1957, 40; Edgar Munzel, "Shag Hurls Sunday TV Fight in Majors' Teeth," *The Sporting News*, December 11, 1957, 5.
9. "Frick Supports Minors in Fight Over Sunday TV," *The Sporting News*, December 11, 1957, 5; Drebinger, "Minors Call on Congress," 40.
10. Jack Walsh, "Celler, Keating Give 'Sympathy,' Promise Help to Minors on TV," *The Sporting News*, January 22, 1958, 11; "Congress Action to Aid Minors in TV Fight Is Held Unlikely," *New York Times*, January 15, 1958, 35.
11. "Minor Leaguers Fail to Win Aid," *New York Times*, January 16, 1958, 37; "Congress Action to Aid Minors," 35.
12. Drebinger, "Meetings at End," S2; Munzel, "Bankrolls Now Only Limit," 11.
13. John Drebinger, "Baseball Committee Clears Way for Second Team in New York," *New York Times*, January 4, 1958, 11; Joe King, "Los Angeles Tabbed as Two-Team City," *The Sporting News*, January 15, 1958, 1–2.
14. Dan Daniel, "Frick 'Delighted' by Proposals on Territory Rights," *The Sporting News*, January 15, 1958, 2.
15. "Baseball Leaders Act to Speed Return of National League to This City," *New York Times*, April 29, 1958, 36.
16. Roscoe McGowen, "Majors Put Off Changes in Rule on 2-Club Cities," *New York Times*, January 26, 1958, S1–2; Harold Rosenthal, "Door Left Ajar for N.L. Return to New York," *The Sporting News*, February 5, 1958, 13.
17. Dan Daniel, "Frick Proposes Minimum Park HR Distances," *The Sporting News*, May 14, 1958, 27; John Rendel, "Frick Asks 325-Foot Minimum at Foul Lines in New Ballparks," *New York Times*, May 6, 1958, 45.
18. Dan Daniel, "Frick Favors Two 12-Team Major Loops," *The Sporting News*, January 15, 1958, 6.
19. Al Hirshberg, "Ford Frick Says: Super-Stadium," *This Week*, May 4, 1958, 8–9, 34.
20. Roscoe McGowen, "Managers, Players and

Coaches to Pick Baseball All-Star Teams," *New York Times*, January 31, 1958, 15.

21. Ray Gillespie, "Fans Back Frick's Ruling on Players' All-Star Picks," *The Sporting News*, February 12, 1958, 11.

22. "Frick All-Star Selection Plan Won't Succeed, Gabe's Belief," *The Sporting News*, February 12, 1958, 11.

23. Dan Daniel, "Player Voting on All-Stars to Start June 22," *The Sporting News*, June 4, 1958, 23.

24. Roscoe McGowen, "Only 2 Yanks to Start as All-Stars," *New York Times*, June 28, 1958, 11; Ed Rumill, "Fans Merit Chance to Cast Ballots for All-Stars, Says Lane," *The Sporting News*, July 2, 1958, 6.

25. Joe Reichler, "Players Ask Voice on Field Standards," *The Sporting News*, February 19, 1958, 1–2.

26. Jack Walsh, "4 Player Delegates Support Keating in Fight on Sports Bill," *The Sporting News*, March 19, 1958, 4; "Players Divided on Congress Bill," March 13, 1958, 34.

27. Jerry Holtzman, "Players Reverse Stand, Now Fight Celler Measure," *The Sporting News*, March 26, 1958, 1.

28. "Players Extend Lewis Contract," *New York Times*, March 31, 1958, 32.

29. Lionel S. Sobel, *Professional Sports and the Law* (New York: Meilen Press, 1977) 38–41; Jack Walsh, "Celler Bill Sent to House Floor but Dissenters Offer Substitute," *The Sporting News*, June 25, 1958, 14.

30. Jack Walsh, "Senate Speeds Sports Bill—Stars Called to Hearing," *The Sporting News*, July 9, 1958, 15.

31. Organized Professional Team Sports: Hearings Before the Subcommittee on Antitrust and Monopoly of the Committee on the Judiciary, United States Senate, 85th Cong. 158 (1958) (testimony of Ford C. Frick, Commissioner of Baseball, accompanied by Paul A. Porter, of Arnold, Fortas & Porter, Washington, D.C.).

32. Jack Walsh, "Sport Bill Goes Too Far, Says Celler in Lashing Lobbying," *The Sporting News*, August 6, 1958, 25.

33. Sobel, *Professional Sports and the Law*, 41.

34. Dave Brady, "Game's Brass Backs Trust-Exemption Bill," *The Sporting News*, May 17, 1961, 7; "Senate Gets Bill to Govern Sports," *New York Times*, May 12, 1961, 36.

35. Sobel, *Professional Sports and the Law*, 49.

36. "Major Plaster of $50 Fine to Halt Beanball Seen as Trial Balloon," *The Sporting News*, June 18, 1958, 10.

37. Frederick G. Lieb, "N.L. Weighing Expansion to Ten Teams," *The Sporting News*, July 16, 1958, 1–2.

38. Dan Daniel, "Frick Questioned on Shifts to West and Nat Situation," *The Sporting News*, July 30, 1958, 8.

39. Dan Daniel, "Frick Favors 10, Later 12 Clubs in Major Loops," *The Sporting News*, September 3, 1958, 25; "Frick Denies' Majors' Expansion Will Be Asked by Him," *New York Times*, September 4, 1958, 25.

40. Edgar Munzel, "Leagues to Hold at Eight Clubs, Will Try to Rebuild from Within," *The Sporting News*, September 17, 1958, 7–8; Edgar Munzel, "Majors Vote Earliest Opening in Years," *The Sporting News*, September 17, 1958, 7; "Majors Favor Return to Bonus Rule as Spending Curb," *New York Times*, September 10, 1958, 44.

41. Arthur Daley, "Was This Trip Necessary?" *New York Times*, September 12, 1958, 29; "Time Not Ripe for Major Expansion," *The Sporting News*, September 17, 1958, 12.

42. Dan Daniel, "No Swoops, Swipes for Dan," *The Sporting News*, September 24, 1958, 2.

43. "Magnates Run Into Trick Play Off Diamond," *The Sporting News*, September 24, 1958, 12.

44. Roscoe McGowen, "Frick Undergoes Appendectomy and Will Miss Series Contests," *New York Times*, September 24, 1958, 31; "Frick Reported Improved, Will Miss Series Opener," *The Sporting News*, October 1, 1958, 23.

45. Dan Daniel, "Frick Adopts New Policy Twist in Disclosing Series Plasters," *The Sporting News*, October 22, 1958, 1, 4; "Duren to Pay Fine with 'Big Smile,'" *New York Times*, October 15, 1958, 55.

46. Roscoe McGowen, "Baseball Stars Fly to Venezuela," *New York Times*, November 7, 1958, 31; "Big Leaguers, Led by Frick, in Venezuela," *The Sporting News*, November 12, 1958, 18.

47. Dan Daniel, "Clinics' Venezuelan Success May Bring Future Latin Trips," *The Sporting News*, November 26, 1958, 35.

48. Ruben Rodriguez, "League Resumes Action After Halt in Castro Revolt," *The Sporting News*, January 14, 1959, 20.

49. "Players in Cuba Can be Recalled," *New York Times*, January 3, 1959, 13; Rodriguez, "League Resumes Action," 20.

50. John Drebinger, "Majors Ease Restrictions on Winter League Employment in Caribbean Area," *New York Times*, February 1, 1959, S2; Joe King, "Majors Loosen Latin-Ball Clamp," *The Sporting News*, February 11, 1959, 1–2.

51. Bob Seaman, "Pan-American Play Hailed by Fanfares at Texas Launching," *The Sporting News*, May 20, 1959, 35; "U.S. Clubs Delayed by Red Tape," *The Sporting News*, May 20, 1959, 35.

52. Dan Daniel, "Frick Declares Cuba Off Limits to U.S. Players," *The Sporting News*, September 7, 1960, 1, 6.

53. Dan Daniel, "Cuban Crisis Aired at Top-Trio Huddle Arranged by Frick," *The Sporting News*, January 11, 1961, 6; John Drebinger, "Baseball Fears Action by Castro to Prevent Cubans From Playing in U.S.," *New York Times*, January 5, 1961, 36.

54. Dan Daniel, "Demand for 20 Per Cent Divvy Stuns Owners," *The Sporting News*, December 10, 1958, 5–6; John Drebinger, "Majors Reject Players' Request for 20 Per Cent of Club's Gross Receipts," *New York Times*, December 5, 1958, 42; Hy Hurwitz, "Ire Aroused, Yawkey Talks of Withdrawal," *The Sporting News*, December 10, 1958, 5.

55. Frederick G. Lieb, "Attorney Lewis Out as Player Counsel," *The Sporting News*, April 1, 1959, 4; "Lewis Dismissed as Baseball Players' Lawyer," *New York Times*, March 25, 1959, 29.
56. Lieb, "Attorney Lewis Out as Player Counsel," 4.
57. Marvin Miller, *A Whole Different Ballgame* (New York: Birch Lane Press, 1991), 6.
58. Robert Frederick Burk, *Much More Than a Game: Players, Owners, and American Baseball Since 1921* (Chapel Hill: University of North Carolina Press, 2001), 5–7.
59. Oscar Kahan, "Peace Dove Hovers Over Cordial Confab of Players, Magnates," *The Sporting News*, December 16, 1959, 2, 6.
60. Daniel, "Demand for 20 Per Cent Divvy Stuns Owners," 6; Drebinger, "Majors Reject Players' Request," 42.
61. Ed Prell, "Week-Apart Starts, Interloop Trading Okayed by Majors," *The Sporting News*, July 22, 1959, 6; "Majors Approve Fall Trade Rule," *The Sporting News*, July 11, 1959, 13.
62. Oscar Kahan, "Scribes Strong for Inter-Loop Deals," *The Sporting News*, December 23, 1959, 1–2. Much of the issue was devoted to quotes from all three groups praising the rule.
63. Ernest Mehl, "'Wide Survey to Aid Game'—Johnson," *The Sporting News*, December 17, 1958, 1–2.
64. Oscar Kahan and Clifford Kachline, "Frick Helps Save Minors' Realignment," *The Sporting News*, December 10, 1958, 7.
65. "Pass Without Pitching Is Illegal, Says Frick," *New York Times*, January 17, 1959, 15; "Texas Votes to Waive Pitches in Issuing Intentional Walks," *The Sporting News*, January 21, 1959, 23.
66. Harold Rosenthal, "Frick Bans Rule Tinkering Gimmicks," *The Sporting News*, February 4, 1959, 1–2.
67. John Drebinger, "Harridge Quits as American League Head; Cronin Looms Successor," *New York Times*, December 4, 1958, 55; Oscar Kahan, "Problems Facing Majors Call for Younger Leader—Harridge," *The Sporting News*, December 10, 1958, 5.
68. Joe King, "Cronin to Put 'Dash and Color' Into A.L.," *The Sporting News*, February 11, 1959, 9; Roscoe McGowen, "Cronin Receives 7-Year Contract," *New York Times*, February 1, 1959, S1–2.
69. Hy Hurwitz, "New Headquarters of A.L. Officially Opened by Cronin," *The Sporting News*, March 11, 1959, 4.
70. "Frick Says Trust Laws Barred TV and Radio Curbs for Minors," *New York Times*, February 11, 1959, 52; "Frick on Stand Three Hours at Trial of Lawrence's Suit," *The Sporting News*, February 18, 1959, 2.
71. Red Foley, "Frick Wins Dismissal in Lawrence TV Suit," *The Sporting News*, February 25, 1959, 7; Edward Razal, "Damages Denied in Baseball Suit," *New York Times*, February 14, 1959, 16.
72. Roscoe McGowen, "Majors Weighing 2d All-Star Game," *New York Times*, May 2, 1959, 17; "Executive Council Approves Playing Two All-Star Games," *The Sporting News*, May 6, 1959, 6.
73. Dan Daniel, "Two All-Star Games Seen as Certain by '60," *The Sporting News*, May 13, 1959, 1–2.
74. "Don't Overwork the Golden Goose," *The Sporting News*, May 27, 1959, 10.
75. Louis Effrat, "Frick Attacks 'Sledge-Hammer' Tactics of City's Bid for New Major Club," *New York Times*, November 14, 1958, 32.
76. Dan Daniel, "Lonesome Commissioner Boils Over Outlaw Idea," *The Sporting News*, November 26, 1958, 5.
77. Harry Grayson, "Baseball Bungling Invites 'Outlaws,'" November 18, 1958.
78. John Drebinger, "City Preparing 'Concrete' Offer to Frick on a Third League," *New York Times*, November 15, 1958, 14.
79. Earl Flora, "Conditions for New Circuit Listed at Top-Level Huddle," *The Sporting News*, May 27, 1959, 11, 18.
80. Dan Daniel, "Frick's Leadership Shown in Mapping Majors' Expansion," *The Sporting News*, June 3, 1959, 17.
81. Arthur Daley, "Trojan Horse," *New York Times*, May 26, 1959, 39.

Chapter 14

1. Dan Daniel, "Second All-Star Game to Gross 500 Gees," *The Sporting News*, June 17, 1959, 5.
2. Louis Effrat, "Big Leagues to Play a Second 1959 All-Star Aug. 3," *New York Times*, June 9, 1959, 46.
3. C. C. Johnson Spink, "Many Players Were Uncertain of Purpose of All-Star Repeat," *The Sporting News*, June 17, 1959, 5; "Paul Richards: 'I'm Gonna Ask for Two Xmases a Year,'" *The Sporting News*, June 17, 1959, 5.
4. Les Biederman, "Bitter Controversy Likely Over Fate of 2nd All-Star Game," *The Sporting News*, August 12, 1959, 4.
5. John Drebinger, "Kuenn Will Ask Players to Vote to Restore Old All-Star Set-Up," *New York Times*, July 15, 1960, 27.
6. Joe King, "Two All-Star Tilts Okayed for '61," *The Sporting News*, August 3, 1960, 1.
7. Joe King, "Big Hassle Brewing on All-Star 'Cutback,'" *The Sporting News*, August 10, 1960, 9.
8. Bill Paddock, "Red Sox to Host Second All-Star Game Next Year," *The Sporting News*, October 26, 1960, 8.
9. Dan Daniel, "Player Reps Nix Switch to One Game," *The Sporting News*, August 9, 1961, 1, 20; "Players Vote for Continuation of 2 All-Star Games a Season," *New York Times*, August 2, 1961, 20.
10. "Two All-Star Contests in '62 Recommended by Committee," *The Sporting News*, October 11, 1961, 16.

11. Dan Daniel, "Two Star Games Backed at Huddle of Players' Reps," *The Sporting News*, December 6, 1961, 31.
12. John Drebinger, "New 'Bonus Rule' Voted by Majors," *New York Times*, December 3, 1961, S1, S6; Clifford Kachline, "Owners May Kayo All-Star Encore After 1962," *The Sporting News*, December 13, 1962, 5–6.
13. Dan Daniel, "Exec Council Nixes Second All-Star Game," *The Sporting News*, October 13, 1962, 6.
14. Dan Daniel, "Owners and Player Reps Agree to Kayo Second Star Game," *The Sporting News*, December 8, 1962, 20; "Major Leagues Agree to Drop Second All-Star Game," *New York Times*, November 30, 1962, 37.
15. Roscoe McGowen, "Shea Declines Kefauver Offer of Bill to Aid 3d Major League," *New York Times*, July 2, 1959, 28; Joe King, "Asserts Celler, Kefauver Back 3rd Big League," *The Sporting News*, July 8, 1959, 24.
16. "Nixon Favors Third League, Even Suggesting Some Cities," *The Sporting News*, July 15, 1959, 6.
17. Dan Daniel, "3rd Loop Faces 'Name' Player Hurdle," *The Sporting News*, July 1, 1959, 1–2.
18. Frederick G. Lieb, "Federal's 'Third Major' War Proved Costly," *The Sporting News*, July 1, 1959, 5.
19. "Cronin Fears Another Major Would Wreck Minor Leagues," *The Sporting News*, July 1, 1959, 10.
20. "Formidable Problems for Third Major," *The Sporting News*, July 1, 1959, 12.
21. Burton Hawkins, "Talk of Third Major League Called Politics," *The Sporting News*, July 1, 1959, 12.
22. Dick Young, "Talent No Problem; 'It Will Come From the World'—Rickey," *The Sporting News*, July 1, 1959, 10.
23. "Frick Sets Aug. 18 as Date for Confab on Third Loop," *The Sporting News*, July 22, 1959, 7; "Baseball Parley Set," *New York Times*, July 18, 1959, 10.
24. Howard M. Tuckner, "Third Major League Is Formed in Baseball," *New York Times*, July 28, 1959, 1, 30: Dan Daniel, "Third Leaguers Putting Majors on Spot," *The Sporting News*, August 5, 1959.
25. John Drebinger, "Hold Everything," *New York Times*, July 28, 1959, 30.
26. Organized Professional Team Sports: Hearings Before the Subcommittee on Antitrust and Monopoly of the Committee on the Judiciary, United States Senate, 86th Cong. 74–75 (1959) (statement of Ford Frick, Commissioner of Baseball).
27. Dave Brady, "Richards Suggests 'Free Agents Draft' at Senate Hearings," *The Sporting News*, August 5, 1959, 17, 22; "Frick Talks of Baseball Harmony," *New York Times*, July 30, 1959, 32.
28. Michael Shapiro, *Bottom of the Ninth: Branch Rickey, Casey Stengel, and the Daring Scheme to Save Baseball From Itself* (New York: Times Books, 2009), 122.

29. Dan Daniel, "Majors Flash Green Light to Third League," *The Sporting News*, August 26, 1959, 2.
30. Russell D. Buhite, *The Continental League: A Personal History* (Lincoln: University of Nebraska Press, 2014), 64–65.
31. Lionel S. Sobel, *Professional Sports and the Law* (New York: Law-Arts Press, 1977), 41–43, 48.
32. Dave Brady, "TV Officials Blast Game's Pleas for Minor Blackouts," *The Sporting News*, September 9, 1959, 25; "Frick Says Broadcasters Fight Measures to Curb Baseball TV," *New York Times*, September 3, 1959, 21.
33. Dave Brady, "Keating Blocks Bill Backed by Kefauver—Hearings Finished," *The Sporting News*, September 16, 1959, 14; "Frick Has Doubts on Third League," *New York Times*, September 5, 1959, 8; Sobel, *Professional Sports and the Law*, 43, 48.
34. "Cal and Frick Tangle Over Move," *The Sporting News*, October 14, 1959, 4; "Griffith Is Vague Regarding Shift," *New York Times*, October 14, 1959, 54.
35. Shirley Povich, "Nats' Pat Stand Calms Crisis in Capital," *The Sporting News*, October 28, 1959, 5–6; "Baseball Senators, Influenced by Poll, to Stay in Capital," *New York Times*, October 20, 1959, 51.
36. Dan Daniel, "A.L. Sets Goal—10-Club Loop for '61—Expansion Out for '60," *The Sporting News*, November 4, 1959, 7; "American League Presses Frick on Expansion; Interleague Plan Reported," *New York Times*, October 27, 1959, 44.
37. Buhite, *The Continental League*, 70–71; Shapiro, *Bottom of the Ninth*, 143–144.
38. Joe King, "Rickey Defies Roadblocks to Third League," *The Sporting News*, November 25, 1959, 2; "Third League Again Threatens to Be Outlaw Circuit if Needed," *New York Times*, November 17, 1959, 42.
39. John Drebinger "Frick Defends Majors," *New York Times*, November 18, 1959, 57; King, "Rickey Defies Roadblocks to Third League," 5.
40. John Drebinger, "National League Bars Expansion of Majors, Affirms Pledge to New Circuit," *New York Times*, December 8, 1959, 62; Oscar Kahan, "N.L. Blocks Junior Loop Expansion Plan," *The Sporting News*, December 16, 1959, 5.
41. "'Continental Has Door Open to Proceed,' Frick Declares," *The Sporting News*, December 16, 1959, 5.
42. Jack Walsh, "Keating Throws His Weight Behind Third-League Drive," *The Sporting News*, January 13, 1960, 9; "Third League Is Topic," *New York Times*, January 9, 1960, 16.
43. Jack Walsh, "'Don't Expect Dole,' Continental Warned in Sizeup by Frick," *The Sporting News*, January 20, 1960, 7; "Frick Predicts Rosy Future for New League," *New York Times*, January 12, 1960, 24.
44. Shapiro, *Bottom of the Ninth*, 159.
45. Dave Brady, "Blast by Frick Scorches Ears on Capitol Hill," *The Sporting News*, January 27, 1960, 6.

46. Joe King, "Frick, B.R. Open Summit Confabs," *The Sporting News*, February 10, 1960, 8.
47. Shapiro, *Bottom of the Ninth*, 42.
48. Buhite, *The Continental League*, 96–97; Shapiro, *Bottom of the Ninth*, 162.
49. Dan Daniel, "Majors Reap $4 Million Yearly in New Pact With Gillette, NBC," *The Sporting News*, March 2, 1960, 9; "Big Leagues Get New Video Pact," *New York Times*, February 25, 1960, 38.
50. Val Adams, "'Black Sox' Story for TV Canceled," *New York Times*, September 7, 1960, 83.
51. Gene Carney, *Burying the Black Sox* (Washington, DC: Potomac Books, 2006), 265–266; "Why Can't TV Let Well Enough Alone," *The Sporting News*, October 12, 1960, 10.
52. Val Adams, "Baseball Drama Taking New Form," *New York Times*, September 29, 1960, 70.
53. "The Witness (1960–1961)," *Internet Movie DataBase (imdb.com)*, October 9, 2015.
54. Lee Allen, *The American League Story* (New York: Hill & Wang, 1962), 100.
55. Joe Williams, "TV Black Sox Prove Sordid, Spurious Show," *New York World-Telegram*, January 28, 1961.
56. Eliot Asinof, *Bleeding Between the Lines* (New York: Holt, Rinehart and Winston, 1979), 12.
57. Dick Young, "Wally Moses' Tip: 'Throw Bat at Ball,'" *The Sporting News*, March 9, 1960, 23.
58. Dan Daniel, "Ford Frick Awaits Majors' Expansion, Then Retirement," *Pittsburgh Press*, August 27, 1960.
59. "Frick Nixes C.L. Player Pool Plan," *The Sporting News*, March 30, 1960, 6.
60. Jim Booker, "Frick to Discuss Talent-Pool Plans with C.L. Brass," *The Sporting News*, April 6, 1960, 2.
61. Neale Patrick, "W. Carolina Drops Continental Tie-Up," *The Sporting News*, April 27, 1960, 39.
62. Lee Lowenfish, *Branch Rickey* (Lincoln: University of Nebraska Press, 2007), 567.
63. Buhite, *The Continental League*, 115–116.
64. Neale Patrick, "Continental Clubs Set Up Pacts with Class D League," *The Sporting News*, May 11, 1960, 8.
65. "3d League Demands Help from Majors," *New York Times*, April 16, 1960, 13.
66. "Frick Says It's All Talk, No Action in New Circuit," *New York Times*, April 18, 1960, 38.
67. Bob Hunter, "Frick, Giles Roll Up Sleeves, Bark Back at Shea Ultimatum," *The Sporting News*, April 27, 1960, 14.
68. Arthur Daley, "Where from Here?," *New York Times*, April 29, 1960, 36; Dan Daniel, "N.Y. Gives C.L. Go-Ahead Signal," *The Sporting News*, May 4, 1960, 1–2.
69. "Death of Minors Feared by Frick," *New York Times*, May 6, 1960, 35.
70. Dan Daniel, "'If Game Operates Illegally, Put Us in Jail,' Fumes Frick," *The Sporting News*, May 11, 1960, 6; Bill Paddock, "Frick Blasts Bill Kefauver Claims Would Help C.L.," *The Sporting News*, May 11, 1960, 6, 12.
71. Organized Professional Team Sports: Hearings Before the Subcommittee on Antitrust and Monopoly of the Committee on the Judiciary, United States Senate, 86th Cong. 67, 68 (1960) (statement of Branch Rickey, President, Continental League); Shapiro, *Bottom of the Ninth*, 190.
72. Organized Professional Team Sports: Hearings Before the Subcommittee on Antitrust and Monopoly of the Committee on the Judiciary, United States Senate, 86th Cong. 39 (1960) (statement of William A. Shea, Chairman, Mayor's Baseball Committee of the City of New York).
73. Organized Professional Team Sports: Hearings Before the Subcommittee on Antitrust and Monopoly of the Committee on the Judiciary, United States Senate, 86th Cong. 91–134 (1960) (statement of Ford Frick, Commissioner of Baseball; accompanied by Louis Carroll, Counsel for the Commissioner; and Paul A. Porter, Counsel to the Commissioner).
74. Organized Professional Team Sports: Hearings Before the Subcommittee on Antitrust and Monopoly of the Committee on the Judiciary, United States Senate, 86th Cong. 46 (1960) (statement of Edwin Johnson, Denver, Colo.).
75. Dave Brady, "Frick Clears Sacks Testifying Against Kefauver Sport Bill," *The Sporting News*, May 25, 1960, 9, 12.
76. Dan Daniel, "Charges by Rickey Draw Quick Volley From Frick," *The Sporting News*, June 22, 1960, 15.
77. Sobel, *Professional Sports and the Law*, 43–48.
78. Ed Pollock, "Ford Frick Beams Over Senate Action," *Philadelphia Evening Bulletin*, June 29, 1960, 61.
79. Dave Brady, "C.L. Hopes Fade After Sports Bill's Failure in Senate," *The Sporting News*, July 6, 1960, 8; Gordon S. White Jr., "Rickey Says Setback in Senate Won't Halt Continental League," *New York Times*, June 30, 1960, 33.
80. George Metzger, "Frick's 'Flying Squad' Checks Park Gambling," *The Sporting News*, May 28, 1958, 28.
81. Frick, *Games, Asterisks, and People*, 218.
82. Watson Spoelstra, "Bye-Bye to Bangtails—Kaline 'Retires' as Race-Track Tycoon," *The Sporting News*, June 1, 1960, 17.
83. Hal Lebovitz, "Power Cleared of 'Jaking' Rap in Kaycee Game," *The Sporting News*, July 20, 1960, 8; "Action on Power Is Held Unlikely," *New York Times*, July 14, 1960, 30.
84. Jerry Holtzman, "Wrigley Field Gambling Raid Nets 20 Fans," *The Sporting News*, August 3, 1960, 28.
85. George Metzger, "Ex-Café Owner Found Guilty of Bribe Attempt," *The Sporting News*, August 10, 1960, 27.
86. "Loans by Gambler Reported to Frick," *New York Times*, August 14, 1960, S6.
87. Milton Richman, "Frick Urges Baseball to Keep Loyal Vigil Against Gambling," *Pittsburgh Press*, June 4, 1963.
88. C. C. Johnson Spink, "Does Game Have Double Standard," *The Sporting News*, June 8, 1963, 12.

89. Robert M. Lipsyte, "National League Decision Virtually Assures City of Second Baseball Team," July 19, 1960, 33; Ed Press, "Majors to Increase to Ten Each in '62," *The Sporting News*, July 20, 1960, 1–2.

90. John Drebinger, "Baseball Expands," *New York Times*, August 4, 1960, 19.

91. Jerry Holtzman, "Big Times Clearing Decks for Expansion," *The Sporting News*, August 10, 1960, 3–4.

92. Dan Daniel, "Topping Gains New Backers in Coast Pitch," *The Sporting News*, August 24, 1960, 1–2.

93. Louis Effrat, "National League Admits New York, Houston for 1962," *New York Times*, October 18, 1960, 1, 49; Ed Prell, "Senior Circuit Grabs New York and Houston," *The Sporting News*, October 26, 1960, 2.

94. Paddock, "Red Sox to Host Second All-Star Game," 8.

95. Mark Armour, *Joe Cronin: A Life in Baseball* (Lincoln: University of Nebraska Press, 2010), 266–267.

96. John Drebinger, "American League, in '61, to Add Minneapolis and Los Angeles," *New York Times*, October 27, 1, 46; Joe King, "A.L. Speeds Expansion—Ten Clubs in '61," *The Sporting News*, November 2, 1960, 3.

97. Oliver E. Kuechle, "Judge Landis Must Be Spinning in His Grave," *Milwaukee Journal*, October 28, 1960.

98. Dan Daniel, "Frick 'Disturbed' by A.L. Decision to Expand for '61," *The Sporting News*, November 2, 1960, 4; John Drebinger, "Problems Ahead, Cronin Is Warned," *New York Times*, October 28, 1960, 34.

99. John Drebinger, "Obstacles Face Expansion in 1961," *New York Times*, October 29, 1960, 21.

100. Joe King, "'No More Expansion Surprises,' Says Frick," *The Sporting News*, November 9, 1960, 1, 4; Joseph M. Sheehan, "Frick Gets Pledge at Meeting Here," *New York Times*, November 2, 1960, 46.

101. "Frick Rules A.L. Rosters Frozen Until After Draft," *The Sporting News*, November 16, 1960, 4.

102. "Draft for Mets, Colts Begins Today," *New York Times*, October 10, 1961, 50; "Draft Over—N.L. Clubs Start Calling Up Top Kids," *The Sporting News*, October 18, 1961, 6.

103. Dan Daniel, "Dove of Peace Coos Over Expansion Turmoil," *The Sporting News*, November 23, 1960, 11, 40; Louis Effrat, "Expansion Move Faces Misgivings," *New York Times*, November 16, 1960, 52.

104. Bob Hunter, "Frick Fires Expansion Warning in L.A.," *The Sporting News*, November 16, 1960, 1, 4.

105. Arthur Daley, "Momentous Meeting," *New York Times*, November 16, 1960, 52; Dan Daniel, "Frick Sets Up Barrier to A.L. Expansion Plan," *The Sporting News*, November 23, 1960, 11, 40.

106. John Drebinger, "Dodgers Oppose Intrusion in 1961," *New York Times*, November 22, 1960, 43.

107. Dan Daniel, "Fans Want Something New, Get it in 9-Club Majors, Inter-Loop Play," *The Sporting News*, November 30, 1960, 1–2; John Drebinger, "9-Team Circuits Included in Plan," *New York Times*, November 23, 1960, 32.

108. Edward Prell, "American League Hurls Defi at Frick on Expansion Program," *Chicago Tribune*, November 17, 1960, sec. 6, 1; John Drebinger, "Bergen, Williams Fail in Their Bids," *New York Times*, November 18, 1960, 36.

109. Dan Daniel, "Green Light Reported for A.L. Leap to Coast," *The Sporting News*, December 7, 1960, 1, 6; John Drebinger, "Giles and Cronin to Present Views," *New York Times*, November 30, 1960, 49; Joseph M. Sheehan, "Expansion Talks to Resume Today," *New York Times*, December 1, 1960, 48.

110. John Drebinger, "Peace Offer Due in Majors Today," *New York Times*, December 7, 1960, 60.

111. Dan Daniel, "Expansion Accord Hailed as Guidepost," *The Sporting News*, December 14, 1960, 1–2, 8. John Drebinger, "Vote Unanimous on Ten-Club Plan," *New York Times*, December 8, 1960, 48.

112. Arthur Daley, "How to Lose Gracefully," *New York Times*, December 9, 1960, 43.

113. Dan Daniel, "Expansion Peace Bears Galbreath Stamp," *The Sporting News*, December 21, 1960, 6.

114. Dan Daniel, "Mail Vote Clears Way for Houston, N.Y. Farm Clubs," *The Sporting News*, January 25, 1961, 4; John Drebinger, "Giles and Cronin See Frick Today," *New York Times*, January 4, 1961, 37.

Chapter 15

1. Frank Hoffmann, *Baseball and American Culture: Across the Diamond* (Philadelphia: Haworth Press, 2003).

2. Wendell Smith, "Spring Training Woes," *Chicago's American*, January 23, 1961.

3. Jack E. Davis, "Baseball's Reluctant Challenge: Desegregating Major League Spring Training Sites, 1961–1964," *Journal of Sport History* 19, no. 2 (Summer, 1992): 144–162.

4. "Game's Shining Record on Racial Issue," *The Sporting News*, February 22, 1961, 10; Dan Daniel, "All Players 'Segregated' in Old-Time Camps," *The Sporting News*, February 22, 1961, 10.

5. Oliver Kuechle, "Ford Frick Does Baseball Another Disservice," *Milwaukee Journal*, March 5, 1961.

6. Davis, "Baseball's Reluctant Challenge," 159.

7. Fred Lieb, "Florida Airs Housing Plan for Negroes," *The Sporting News*, May 3, 1961, 27.

8. Daniel, "Player Reps Nix Switch to One Game," 1, 20; "Players Vote for Continuation of 2 All-Star Games a Season," 20.

9. Dave Brady, "'No Trace of Color Line in Pro Loops'—Frick's Testimony," *The Sporting News*, July 27, 1963, 6.
10. William C. Kashatus, *September Swoon: Richie Allen, the '64 Phillies, and Racial Integration* (University Park, PA: Penn State University Press, 2004), 43–44.
11. "Superb Testimony by Frick," *The Sporting News*, August 3, 1963, 14.
12. John Drebinger, "Baseball and Integration," *New York Times*, July 30, 1963, 21.
13. John Drebinger, "The Little Rock Story," *New York Times*, August 23, 1963, 13.
14. Hy Hurwitz, "Showers and Slingers Finish Neck and Neck," *The Sporting News*, August 9, 1961, 6–8.
15. Ford Frick II, personal interview, Denver, CO, September 21, 2015.
16. Ford Frick II, telephone interview, November 18, 2015; Kelly (Frick) Richards, telephone interview, November 21, 2015.
17. *Telecasting of Professional Sports Contests: Hearings Before a Subcommittee on the Judiciary*, United States Senate, 87th Congress (statement of Ford Frick, Commissioner of Baseball); Dave Brady, "Frick, with Eye to Future, Backs Celler's TV Bill," *The Sporting News*, September 6, 1961, 17.
18. Sobel, *Professional Sports and the Law*, 583–585.
19. Oscar Kahan, "Bigwigs Rap Runner-Up Tag Tacked on Game," *The Sporting News*, January 31, 1962, 1, 6.
20. "Frick Quotes Gate Growth as Proof of Game's Health," *The Sporting News*, April 20, 1963, 4.
21. Edward Prell, "Frick Sings Tune Called Long Green," *Chicago Tribune*, July 9, 1963.
22. Joe King, "Frick Tackles Minors' New Setup," *The Sporting News*, April 25, 1962, 3, 6.
23. Til Ferdenzi, "Frick Unfrocks 'Old Prof' Over Plug for Brew," *The Sporting News*, May 2, 1962, 29; "Frick Strikes Out Casey at the Bunt; Kathy Now Batting," *New York Times*, April 25, 1962, 43.
24. Lowell Reidenbaugh, "'A Day I Will Always Remember,'" *The Sporting News*, October 12, 1963, 19, 22.
25. Mark Armour, *Joe Cronin: A Life in Baseball* (Lincoln: University of Nebraska Press, 2010), 275.
26. Hy Hurwitz, "Cronin Tosses Spitball Debate to Rules Group," *The Sporting News*, June 14, 1961, 1–2.
27. Dan Daniel, "Frick Sees Spitter as Slab Aid," *The Sporting News*, November 15, 1961, 9; William Miller, "Frick Endorses Use of Spitball," *New York Times*, November 7, 1961, 43.
28. John Drebinger, "Baseball Rules Committee Votes, 8 to 1, to Retain Ban on Spitball Pitches," *New York Times*, November 27, 1961, 40; Clifford Kachline, "Rules Makers Take Toehold on Spitter, Beat it Down, 8–1," *The Sporting News*, December 6, 1961, 8.
29. "Proposal for Wider Plate Nixed by Rules Committee," *The Sporting News*, December 6, 1961, 8.
30. "Segar Succeeds Gallagher as Head of Rules Group," *The Sporting News*, October 27, 1962, 4.
31. "Segar Well Grounded on Rules," *The Sporting News*, November 10, 1962, 12.
32. Bob Joyce, "Hurlers Hail New Strike Zone, Expanded by '10 to 12 Inches,'" *The Sporting News*, February 9, 1963, 4.
33. "More Whiffs, Fewer Walks and Speedier Games: Story of '63," *The Sporting News*, October 26, 1963, 8.
34. Clifford Kachline, "Pitch to Shake Up Minors' Structure Hits Roadblock," *The Sporting News*, December 6, 1961, 7.
35. Edgar Munzel, "Majors Guarantee to Back 100 Minor League Clubs," *The Sporting News*, June 2, 1962, 13.
36. Edgar Munzel, "Majors Appear Ready to Absorb Trautman Office," *The Sporting News*, June 2, 1962, 13.
37. "Putting Minors on Solid Footing," *The Sporting News*, June 2, 1962, 12.
38. "Only Five Scribes on Hand to Cover Meeting of Moguls," *The Sporting News*, June 2, 1962, 13.
39. Clifford Kachline, "Overhaul of Minors Flops; Farm Chiefs Try to Mend Flaws," *The Sporting News*, October 6, 1962, 24.
40. Clifford Kachline, "Majors Pick Up $10 Million Tab in Minors," *The Sporting News*, December 15, 1962, 5; Oscar Kahan, "Frick Ties Up Loose Ends in Minor Leagues," *The Sporting News*, December 15, 1962, 8.
41. Frederick G. Lieb, "Trautman Was Tower of Strength for Minors," *The Sporting News*, July 6, 1963, 13.
42. Cy Kritzer, "Int Chiefs Cool to Frick's 12-Club Plan," *The Sporting News*, October 12, 1963, 8.
43. Clifford Kachline, "PCL Expands to 12 Clubs—Int Cut to Eight," *The Sporting News*, December 14, 1963, 7–8; "Circuit's Range Now 4,500 Miles," *New York Times*, December 3, 1963, 71.
44. Paul Zimmerman, "Forecast by Frick—24 Big-Time Clubs, Three Minor Loops," *The Sporting News*, April 5, 1961, 8.
45. Hy Hurwitz, "Frick Forecasts Major Growth to 12-Club Leagues," *The Sporting News*, May 24, 1961, 25.
46. Dan Daniel, "'12-Club Loops Require 2 Years Planning'—Frick," *The Sporting News*, June 23, 1962, 6.
47. Clifford Kachline, "Frick Calls for Expansion Blueprint," *The Sporting News*, December 21, 1963, 1–2.
48. "Giants' Victory in '51 Attributed to Spy," *New York Times*, March 23, 1962, 40.
49. Dan Daniel, "Daniel Traces Signal-Swiping History to '76," *The Sporting News*, April 4, 1962, 15–16.
50. Louis Effrat, "Special Lens for Baseball TV Shuttered by Frick's Request," *New York Times*,

July 14, 1959, 33; Dick Young, "Horace 'Will Get a Broom,'" *The Sporting News*, July 29, 1959, 12.
51. Dan Daniel, "Frick Probes 'Binocular' Charges," *The Sporting News*, July 14, 1962, 1, 8.
52. Bill Veeck with Ed Linn, *Veeck—As in Wreck: The Autobiography of Bill Veeck* (Chicago: University of Chicago Press, 1962), 240–242.
53. Ibid., 250.
54. Arthur Daley, "The Literary Bulldozer," *New York Times*, August 19, 1962, 148.
55. Bob Burnes, "Author Veeck Spares None as Neck-Wringer," *The Sporting News*, June 16, 1962, 12.
56. Chester L. Smith, "Critics Causing Major Leagues to See 'Ghosts,'" *Pittsburgh Press*, July 19, 1962.
57. John E. Peterson, *The Kansas City Athletics: A Baseball History, 1954–1967* (Jefferson, NC: McFarland, 2003), 123; Dan Daniel, "Hooray! No More A's–Yanks Trades," *The Sporting News*, January 4, 1961, 9.
58. Peterson, *The Kansas City Athletics*, 148–153; "Frick Apologizes to Mehl for 'Poison Pen' Award," *The Sporting News*, August 30, 1961, 5.
59. Dave Brady, "'Courts Would Back A.L., Not Finley'—Frick," *The Sporting News*, February 15, 1964, 1, 4.
60. Peterson, *The Kansas City Athletics*, 194–195; "Half 'Porch' Held Better Than None," *New York Times*, April 14, 1964, 42; Dick Mackey, "A.L. Snoozes While Yanks Win, Finley Claims," *The Sporting News*, April 25, 1964, 5.
61. Jerome Holtzman, "Frankie's Shift Report Triggers Finley Explosion," *The Sporting News*, April 17, 1965, 34.
62. Frederick G. Lieb, "Inter-Loop Schedule Among Two Proposals Sent to Major Execs," *The Sporting News*, July 21, 1962, 2; Joseph Sheehan, "A Shorter Season Asked by Players," *New York Times*, July 10, 1962, 36.
63. Clifford Kachline, "Lowdown on Frick Pitch for Inter-Loop Play," *The Sporting News*, September 15, 1962, 2.
64. John Drebinger, "Frick Opposes Interleague Baseball Schedules," *New York Times*, February 19, 1963, 16.
65. "Frick Rules Wills Has 1 Game 'Left,'" *San Francisco Examiner*, September 21, 1962, 60.
66. Arthur Daley, "Banditry Without Asterisks," *New York Times*, October 1, 1962, 42; "Frick Puts 154-Game Limit on Wills' Record Theft Bid," *The Sporting News*, September 29, 1962, 7.
67. Steven Travers, *A Tale of Three Cities: The 1962 Baseball Season in New York, Los Angeles, and San Francisco* (Washington, D.C.: Potomac Books, 2009).
68. David Plaut, *Chasing October: The Dodgers-Giants Pennant Race of 1962* (South Bend, IN: Diamond Communications, 1994), 163–164.
69. Dan Daniel, "Frick Reveals Plans for Baseball Clinics South of the Border," *The Sporting News*, July 21, 1962, 10.
70. Dan Daniel, "Planned Latin Trip Canceled by State Dept.," *The Sporting News*, October 13, 1962, 4.

71. Watson Spoelstra, "Bengals Leave for Orient Without Frick and Cronin," *The Sporting News*, October 27, 1962, 15.
72. "Frick Okays Hawaii Games, Waives Rule on Exhibitions," *The Sporting News*, October 27, 1962, 15.
73. Dick Young, "Young Looks Back to Highlights as Series Scribe," *The Sporting News*, October 21, 1972, 13.
74. Armour, *Joe Cronin*, 274–275.
75. Ferd Borsch, "'No Plans to Retire—Yet,' Asserts Frick," *The Sporting News*, November 3, 1962, 19.
76. Clifford Kachline, "Will Dick Nixon Be Next Commissioner," *The Sporting News*, December 15, 1962, 1–2.
77. Dan Daniel, "Frick Quashes Story He Plans to Retire Soon," *The Sporting News*, August 17, 1963, 14.
78. "Frick, Back at Desk, Holds Huddle on Reshaping Minors," *The Sporting News*, September 8, 1962, 4.
79. Dick Young, "Card, Phil Purchases Cooking," *The Sporting News*, September 8, 1962, 12.
80. Tom Kelly, "Sentiment's the Thing," *St. Petersburg Evening Independent*, September 6, 1962, 10-A.
81. Fred Lieb, "New Name for Park at St. Pete Would Honor Hug and Old Case," *The Sporting News*, January 26, 1963, 11.
82. Joe King, "Frick Set to Toss Super-Sales Pitch," *The Sporting News*, April 13, 1963, 1, 4.
83. Oscar Kahan, "New Booklet Pinpoints Values of Following Diamond Career," *The Sporting News*, May 25, 1963, 2.
84. Oscar Kahan, "Frick Opposes Plan to Award Trophies on TV," *The Sporting News*, July 6, 1963, 21.
85. Hal Lebovitz, "Writers Reject Plan for TV Award Show," *The Sporting News*, July 20, 1963, 20.
86. Oscar Kahan, "Giles Ends Balk Ruckus; Revises 'Stop' Regulation," *The Sporting News*, May 4, 1963, 27.
87. "Braves Get a Lesson on Balks: He Who Hesitates Saves $100," *New York Times*, May 7, 1963, 49.
88. Joe King, "Umps Instructed to Slow Down on Strict Balk Calls," *The Sporting News*, May 18, 1963, 1, 6; Gordon S. White Jr., "Frick Restores a Uniform Code," *New York Times*, May 8, 1963, 46.
89. Bill Paddock, "Committee Poll Drops 'Second' From Balk Rule," *The Sporting News*, May 25, 1963, 7; "One-Second Clause on Balk Deleted Officially by Majors," *New York Times*, May 15, 1963, 64.
90. Tommy Devine, "Rah-Rah Mentors Bar Scouts, Except as Cash Customers," *The Sporting News*, May 14, 1958, 20.
91. Watson Spoelstra, "Majors, College Coaches Huddle," *The Sporting News*, August 20, 1958, 1–2.
92. William R. Conklin, "A Curb on Signing of Players by Majors Is Coaches' Aim," *New York Times*, January 6, 1960.

93. Clifford Kachline, "Minors Veto Proposals for Bigger Handouts," *The Sporting News*, December 7, 1960, 11, 16; Clifford Kachline, "A.L. Blocks Farm Plan for New Clubs," *The Sporting News*, December 14, 1960, 2.
94. Abe Chanin, "Coaches Hail O.B. Pact as Campus Game Hypo," *The Sporting News*, January 18, 1961, 1, 6.
95. Oscar Kahan, "Big Time May Add New Restriction on Signing Collegians," *The Sporting News*, May 25, 1963, 35.
96. Oscar Kahan, "Amended Rule on Inking Collegians Gets O.B.'s Okay," *The Sporting News*, August 10, 1963, 22.
97. Oscar Kahan, "Summer Loops for Collegians Urged," *The Sporting News*, December 22, 1962, 1–2.
98. Oscar Kahan, "Frick's Efforts Open Up Road for College Summer Circuit," *The Sporting News*, June 22, 1963, 2.
99. William N. Wallace, "Majors Subsidize College Nines with N.C.A.A.'s Cooperation," *New York Times*, January 8, 1964, 29.
100. Oscar Kahan, "Majors Set Up $75,000 Fund for College Ball," *The Sporting News*, December 19, 1964, 7.
101. Oscar Kahan, "Tub Thumpers Beat Drums to Give Star Game Back to Fans," *The Sporting News*, December 14, 1963, 2; "Players to Ask Frick to Let Fans Name All-Star Teams," *The Sporting News*, December 14, 1963, 2.
102. Arno Goethel, "Computer Proposed in All-Star Balloting," *The Sporting News*, February 1, 1964, 22.
103. "Proposal to Let Fans Pick All-Star Teams Is Rejected," *New York Times*, May 8, 1964, 22.
104. "Return of All-Star Vote to Fans to be Studied," *New York Times*, December 3, 1964, 64.
105. Bowie Kuhn, *Hardball: The Education of a Baseball Commissioner* (New York: Times Books, 1987), 52–53.
106. Dave Brady, "Rich Clubs Agree to Divvy Video Pot," *The Sporting News*, February 8, 1964, 1, 4.
107. "Problems Delay TV-Spectacular Plans," *The Sporting News*, June 6, 1964, 13.
108. Walker and Bellamy, *Center Field Shot*, 114.
109. Leonard Koppett, "Majors Finally Catch Up to 60's During Chicago Summer Talks," *New York Times*, August 12, 1964, 24.
110. "Major League Owners Urge More Authority for Commissioner of Baseball," *New York Times*, November 7, 1964, 21.

Chapter 16

1. C. C. Johnson Spink, "Braves' Shift Needs Only Okay by N.L.," *The Sporting News*, July 11, 1964, 1.
2. Joseph Durso, "Braves Ready to Transfer Franchise from Milwaukee to Atlanta Next Year," *New York Times*, July 3, 1964, 15.
3. "Frick Annoyed: Says Brave Situation Is Matter for N.L.," *The Sporting News*, July 25, 1964, 8.
4. Bob Wolf, "Frick Insists His Hands Are Tied," *Milwaukee Journal*, July 9, 1964.
5. Leonard Koppett, "Baseball's Going Marxian (Groucho)," *New York Times*, January 8, 1969, 55; Bob Wolf, "Frick Should Have Said 'No' to Braves' Shift, Asserts Gabe," *The Sporting News*, January 18, 1969, 36.
6. Bob Wolf, "Milwaukee Solon Wants TV Pool, Expansion; Frick Vetoes Ideas," *The Sporting News*, August 1, 1964, 11.
7. "Frick Asks Chance for Local Group," *Milwaukee Journal*, October 7, 1964.
8. "Braves Lose Plea for Federal Court," *New York Times*, November 7, 1964, 23.
9. Bob Wolf, "'Unpack,' N.L. Tells Itchy-Footed Braves," *The Sporting News*, November 21, 1964; "League Refuses to Allow Braves to Move Till '66," *New York Times*, November 8, 1964, S1.
10. "Expansion Will Come, Says Frick, But Not for a While," *The Sporting News*, June 5, 1965, 6.
11. Ralph Ray, "Bombers' Sale Stirs Bees' Nest of Boos," *The Sporting News*, August 29, 1964, 1–2, 6.
12. "A.L. Affirms Yankee Sale; Government Inquiry Likely," *The Sporting News*, September 19, 1964, 9.
13. Letter from Paul A. Porter to Ford Frick, October 26, 1964, Baseball Hall of Fame Archives.
14. Lester Smith, "All A.L. Owners Asked to Reveal Holdings in CBS," *The Sporting News*, December 5, 1964, 26; Doug Brown, "Owners Allow Iglehart to Keep CBS Holdings," *The Sporting News*, April 10, 1965, 18.
15. Memo of September 9, 1964, Ford C. Frick Papers, National Baseball Hall of Fame and Museum, Cooperstown, NY.
16. Professional Sports Antitrust Bill—1965: Hearings Before the Subcommittee on Antitrust and Monopoly of the Committee on the Judiciary, United States Senate, 89th Cong. 38–76 (1965) (statement of Ford Frick, Commissioner of Baseball; accompanied by Paul Porter and John T. Hayes, Counsel; L.F. Carroll, Counsel for the National League and the Commissioner's Office; Joseph Cronin, President, American League; and John E. Fetzer, Owner, Detroit Tigers, and Chairman, Joint American-National League Radio-Television Committee).
17. Dave Brady, "Senate Hearing Aids Support for CBS," *The Sporting News*, March 6, 1965, 1–2; Leonard Koppett, "Frick Testifies on Stock Policy at Senate Study of Yanks' Sale," *New York Times*, February 20, 1965, 18; Harold Rosenthal, "Justice Department Drops Inquiry," *The Sporting News*, March 6, 1965, 4.
18. Stuart Banner, *The Baseball Trust: A History of Baseball's Antitrust Exemption* (New York: Oxford University Press, 2013), 146.
19. "Frick Makes it Official; Will Retire Next Year," *New York Times*, August 6, 1964; "Frick Makes It Official, Won't Seek Re-Election," *The Sporting News*, August 15, 1964, 12.

20. Leonard Koppett, "Frick to Stay On for 1965 Series," *New York Times*, August 11, 1964.
21. Ford Frick, Speech to Owners, Phoenix, November 5, 1964, Baseball Hall of Fame Archives.
22. Russell Schneider, "The Judge Would Have Been Proud of Frick," *The Sporting News*, November 21, 1964, 5.
23. Melvin Durslag, "The Right Speech—Too Late," *Los Angeles Herald Examiner*, November 8, 1964.
24. Leonard Koppett, "Baseball's Open Secret," *New York Times*, November 6, 1964, 43.
25. C. C. Johnson Spink, "Club Owners Act—Game Moves Forward," *The Sporting News*, November 21, 1964, 5–6; "Major League Owners Urge More Authority for Commissioner of Baseball," 21.
26. Joseph Durso, "Big Leagues Vote Free-Agent Draft, Restoration of Commissioner's Power," *New York Times*, December 4, 1964, 48; Clifford Kachline, "Club Owners Vote Absolute Power to Baseball's Boss," *The Sporting News*, December 19, 1964, 6.
27. Carl Lundquist, "Topps Honors Rookie Stars at Annual Awards Luncheon," *The Sporting News*, November 7, 1964, 21.
28. Joseph Durso, "Frick, in Last Year, Warns Big Leagues," *New York Times*, January 3, 1965, S1.
29. Tommy Holmes, "Frick Defends Tenure as Baseball's Boss," *Houston Post*, July 13, 1965, sec. 4, 2.
30. C. C. Johnson Spink, "Owners Cut Commissioner List to 16 Names," *The Sporting News*, August 7, 1965, 5.
31. Jim McCulley, "Sports Serenade," *New York Daily News*, January 22, 1965, C26.
32. Dan Daniel, "Majors Hint Move Toward Free-Agent Draft," *The Sporting News*, July 5, 1961, 5–6.
33. Oscar Kahan, "Big Timers See 40 Per Cent Cut in Bonus Spree," *The Sporting News*, December 13, 1961, 5–6; Drebinger, "New 'Bonus Rule' Voted by Majors," S1, S6.
34. Dan Daniel, "'Bonus Rule Proving Effective,' Frick Declares," *The Sporting News*, May 16, 1962, 12.
35. "Stop-Gap Methods Won't Save Minors" *The Sporting News*, December 15, 1952, 12.
36. Clifford Kachline, "'Socialism Threatens Game'—O'Malley," *The Sporting News*, December 22, 1962, 1–2.
37. Clifford Kachline, "Free-Agent Draft in Works; Brass Gives 'Go-Ahead,'" *The Sporting News*, January 25, 1964, 4.
38. Hy Hurwitz, "Frick Checking on Free-Agent Draft," *The Sporting News*, March 28, 1964, 4.
39. Barney Kremenko, "Free-Agent Draft by Spring of '65—That's Frick's Goal," *The Sporting News*, April 4, 1964, 10.
40. Oscar Kahan, "NCAA Seeking Ban on Pro-Sport Draft of College Students," *The Sporting News*, July 18, 1964, 12.
41. Jerome Holtzman, "Majors Split on Free-Agent Draft, Table Plan," *The Sporting News*, August 22, 1964.
42. C. C. Johnson Spink, "G.M.s Meet Issues Head-On and Urge Club Owners to Act," *The Sporting News*, November 14, 1964, 8.
43. Spink, "Club Owners Act—Game Moves Forward," 5; "Major League Owners Urge More Authority," 21.
44. Joseph Durso, "Baseball's Minors Follow Pro Football Pattern in Backing Free-Agent Draft," *New York Times*, December 3, 1964, 64.
45. Clifford Kachline, "Frick Lauds 'Great Progress Program,'" *The Sporting News*, December 19, 1964, 1–2; Durso, "Big Leagues Vote Free-Agent Draft," 48.
46. Clifford Kachline, "Free-Agent Draft Launched Without a Hitch," *The Sporting News*, June 19, 1965, 7.
47. Clifford Kachline, "Selectors Stub Toe on Names; Ruling by Frick," *The Sporting News*, June 26, 1965, 16.
48. Clifford Kachline, "Coaches' Proposal Would Hurt Game's Recruiting Methods" *The Sporting News*, July 31, 1965.
49. Clifford Kachline, "Quit Nabbing Pro Greenies, 2 Execs Urge," *The Sporting News*, July 17, 1965, 8.
50. Leonard Koppett, "Majors Oppose Sports-Bill Rider, Vote to End First-Year Rule in '65," *The Sporting News*, August 7, 1965, 5.
51. Lee Kavetski, "Frick, Nippon Czar Work Out Treaty on Exchanging Players," *The Sporting News*, November 10, 1962, 14.
52. Ford Frick, Letter "To All Clubs," February 16, 1965, Baseball Hall of Fame archives.
53. "Frick Severs Relations With Japanese Baseball," *New York Times*, February 19, 1965, 40; "Frick Suspends Americo-Japanese Relations Over Murakami Dispute," *The Sporting News*, February 27, 1965, 24.
54. "Murakami Has 'No Intention' of Playing Baseball in U.S.," *New York Times*, February 23, 1965.
55. Ford Frick, Letter "To All Clubs."
56. "Murakami Case Threatening Buc Japan Tour, Says Frick," *The Sporting News*, March 13, 1965, 7.
57. Robert Trumbull, "Giants Portrayed as Bad Yanks as Murakami Case Stirs Japan," *New York Times*, March 28, 1965, S2.
58. "Pitcher from Japan Returning to Giants for the '65 Season," *New York Times*, March 17, 1965, 58.
59. "Giants Make a New Pitch to Get Hurler Murakami," *The Sporting News*, May 8, 1965, 20.
60. Hal Lebovitz, "Action, Plenty of it, at a Game in Mexico; Fans Attend to That," *The Sporting News*, March 27, 1985, 9; "Frick, Cronin Honored," *The Sporting News*, March 27, 1985, 30.
61. "Japanese Ignore Terms of Agreement," *The Sporting News*, June 26, 1965, 14; "Pirates Lose Japan Trip," *New York Times*, June 15, 1965, 51.
62. Dick Young, "Hungry 'Have-Nots' Eyeing TV Melon," *The Sporting News*, September 7, 1963, 1–2.

63. "Giles Discourages Pool of TV Money," *New York Times*, July 19, 1964, S19.
64. Carl Lundquist, "Majors Unwrap Video Xmas Gift, $12 Million Package for '65–66," *The Sporting News*, December 26, 1964, 17, 26.
65. James R. Walker and Robert V. Bellamy Jr., *Center Field Shot: A History of Baseball on Television* (Lincoln: University of Nebraska Press, 2008), 114–116.
66. Ed Wilks, "'Don't Give Video Fan Too Much'—Frick," *The Sporting News*, May 1, 1965, 1, 26.
67. Dave Brady, "Leo Steals Show With Signal Swiping on TV," *The Sporting News*, May 22, 1965, 2.
68. "TV Cameras Don't Belong in Dugouts," *The Sporting News*, May 22, 1965, 14.
69. Bob Burnes, "Writers Protest to Frick Over TV Dugout Cameras," *The Sporting News*, July 24, 1965, 34.
70. Arthur Daley, "In Search of a Commissioner," *New York Times*, October 19, 1965, 54; Bob Hunter, "Writers Toss Party as Tribute to Frick," *The Sporting News*, October 23, 1965, 27.
71. "Dedication," *1965 World Series Official Souvenir Program*, 1.
72. Joseph Durso, "Baseball Club Owners Reduce List of Candidates for Commissioner to Ten," *New York Times*, October 20, 1965, 54; Edgar Munzel, "Five-Man Board to Serve Under Baseball's Boss," *The Sporting News*, October 30, 1965, 8, 16.
73. Joseph Durso, "Club Owners Create 'Cabinet' of 5 Deputies to Aid Baseball Commissioner," *New York Times*, October 21, 1965, 62; "7 Still in Race for Post of Commissioner," *The Sporting News*, November 6, 1965, 6.
74. Bob Wolf, "'Milwaukee Rates a Place in Expansion Plan'—Frick," *The Sporting News*, November 27, 1965, 11; "Frick Supports Shift of Braves," *New York Times*, November 13, 1965, 21.
75. Dick Young, "Frick Seen as Martyr Blocking Collusion Rap," *The Sporting News*, November 27, 1965, 14.
76. Bob Wolf, "Lawyers Slap Muzzle on Frick in Wisconsin's Antitrust Quiz," *The Sporting News*, December 11, 1965.
77. "No Plan to Give Milwaukee Franchise, Frick Testifies," *The Sporting News*, January 1, 1966, 10.
78. Ralph Ray, "Another Sherman's Heat Felt in Atlanta," *The Sporting News*, April 30, 1966, 5–6.
79. "The Fan Has a Stake in the Game," *The Sporting News*, April 30, 1966, 14.
80. Maury Allen, *All Roads Lead to October: George Steinbrenner's 25-Year Reign Over the New York Yankees* (New York: St. Martin's, 2000) 144.
81. Jim Enright, "Eckert, Baseball's New Boss, Has Standout Military Record," *The Sporting News*, November 27, 1965, 13; "Out of the Blue: William Dole Eckert," *New York Times*, November 18, 1965, 63.
82. Dick Young, "Sinister Plot?," *The Sporting News*, January 18, 1969, 14.
83. John Helyar, *Lords of the Realm: The Real History of Baseball* (New York: Villard, 1994), 78.
84. "Gen. Eckert, Former Commissioner, Dies at 62," *The Sporting News*, May 1, 1971, 26.
85. "New Commissioner Considers Reducing Five-Man 'Cabinet,'" *New York Times*, November 20, 1965, 41.
86. Leonard Koppett, "Frick Steps Down as Baseball Head," *New York Times*, December 4, 1965, 23.
87. Clifford Kachline, "Only Top Execs Participated in Frick Farewell," *The Sporting News*, December 18, 1965, 6.

Chapter 17

1. Joe Trimble, "All the Trimmings" (undated clip, Baseball Hall of Fame Archives, Cooperstown, NY).
2. "Majors Okay Ford Frick Awards for Rookie Picks," *The Sporting News*, January 1, 1966, 27.
3. Stan Isle, "Frick 'Thanks' Move St. Louis Hot Stove Fete," *The Sporting News*, February 12, 1966, 13.
4. Joseph Durso, "Stengel Elected to Hall of Fame in Surprise Balloting," *New York Times*, March 9, 1966, 31; Barney Kremenko, "'An Amazing Thing!' Says Casey of Shrine Election," *The Sporting News*, March 19, 1966, 4.
5. "Ol' Case Seen in Moment of Greatest Glory," *The Sporting News*, January 7, 1967, 28.
6. "Shrine Heroes Introduced; Frisch New Veteran Voter," *The Sporting News*, August 6, 1966, 5.
7. "Frick to Aid 1976 Olympic Bid," *New York Times*, June 24, 1966, 40.
8. Ethan Trex, "No Thanks: Why Denver Turned Down the 1976 Olympics," Mental Floss website, February 3, 2014 (published 2010). http://mentalfloss.com/article/31291/no-thanks-why-denver-turned-down-1976-olympics.
9. "City Hires Frick as Consultant," *New York Times*, March 1, 1967, 53; Stan Isle, "Sports Capsules," *The Sporting News*, March 18, 1967, 2.
10. "Frick and Barr Elected to Ruth's Hall of Fame," *The Sporting News*, December 28, 1968, 26.
11. "Caught on the Fly," *The Sporting News*, November 8, 1969, 47.
12. Oscar Kahan, "Baseball Groping for New Direction," *The Sporting News*, December 21, 1968, 25; Leonard Koppett, "Victim of Circumstance: Eckert, Chosen as Compromise, Leaves Post Made Powerless by Owners," *New York Times*, December 7, 1968, 66.
13. Leonard Koppett, "Baseball Owners Meet in Chicago Today to Pick a Commissioner," *New York Times*, December 20, 1968, 35.
14. Jack Lang, "Frick, Combs and Haines New Hall of Famers," *The Sporting News*, February 14, 1970, 29; "Frick, Combs and Haines Selected for Baseball Hall of Fame by Old-Timers," *New York Times*, February 2, 1970, 41.

15. "Insiders Say," *The Sporting News*, February 21, 1970, 4.
16. "Happy Takes a Swing at Frick's Credentials," *The Sporting News*, March 7, 1970, 28.
17. Terry Housholder, "Ford Frick Dies at 83," *Ligonier Advance-Leader*, April 11, 1978, 1–2.
18. Ford Frick to Harold and Virginia Frick, June 28, 1970, Baseball Hall of Fame Archives, Cooperstown, NY.
19. Neil Amdur, "Old Baseball Feats Recalled at Hall of Fame Induction," *New York Times*, July 28, 1970, 51.
20. "Hall of Fame Induction Ceremonies, Cooperstown, New York, July 27, 1970" (transcript), Baseball Hall of Fame Archives, Cooperstown, New York.
21. Edgar Munzel, "Frick Aims Shrine Message at Youth of U.S.," *The Sporting News*, August 8, 1970, 5.
22. Bob Sudyk, "Too Bad They Can't Bend Rules for Satchel," *The Sporting News*, December 19, 1964, 40.
23. Dick Young, "Baseball's Undirty Old Man," *New York Daily News*, April 5, 1973.
24. Bill James, *Whatever Happened to the Hall of Fame? Baseball, Cooperstown, and the Politics of Glory* (New York: Fireside Books, 1995), 186–187.
25. Bowie Kuhn, *Hardball: The Education of a Baseball Commssioner* (New York: Times Books, 1987), 110–111.
26. "Ex-Commissioner Frick Injured in Fall at Home," *The Sporting News*, December 4, 1971, 40.
27. Jerome Holtzman, "Jerome Holtzman," *The Sporting News*, February 26, 1972, 30.
28. Bob Broeg, "Traynor Sparkles as Pinch-Hitting Speaker," *The Sporting News*, March 18, 1972, 30.
29. Carl Lundquist, "Weak or Strong? Kuhn's Role Aired," *The Sporting News*, May 27, 1972, 33.
30. Bob Broeg, "Spink Award Coveted by Writers," *The Sporting News*, December 10, 1977, 56.
31. Bob Broeg, "Daniel, Lieb and Stockton Win Spink Award," *The Sporting News*, December 9, 1972, 41.
32. Ford Frick, *Games, Asterisks, and People* (New York: Crown Publishers, 1973), 208.
33. Kelly (Frick) Richards (granddaughter), personal interview, November 23, 2015.
34. David Rohde, "Frank Slocum, 71, an Executive in Baseball and a Writer for TV," *New York Times*, May 19, 1997, B9.
35. Bob Broeg, "The Pleasant Prose of a Pleasant Poet," *The Sporting News*, March 24, 1973, 34.
36. Joe Pollock, "Frick Looks Down Memory Lane," *The Sporting News*, June 9, 1973, 13.
37. Red Smith, "Myths and Truths About a Favorite American Pastime," *New York Times*, May 20, 1973.
38. Young, "Baseball's Undirty Old Man."
39. Jerome Holtzman, "Bouton's Bid Fails," *The Sporting News*, February 26, 1972, 30.
40. Many of the insights of this manuscript were presented in a paper co-authored by John Lofflin, Professor of Journalism at Park University in St. Louis. The paper was titled "Ford Frick's *Big Leaguer*: A Commissioner's (Complicated) Love Letter to His Sport," and was presented to the 2014 Cooperstown Symposium on Baseball and American Culture at the Baseball Hall of Fame. I am indebted to Prof. Lofflin for his insights on baseball literature.
41. Jerome Holtzman, *No Cheering in the Press Box* (New York: Holt, Rinehart and Winston, 1973), 198–214.
42. Jerome Holtzman, "Frick Proud of His Role in Birth of Hall of Fame," *The Sporting News*, February 19, 1977, 35.
43. Kelly (Frick) Richards (granddaughter), personal interview, November 23, 2015.
44. Ford Frick II (grandson), personal interview, Denver, CO, September 21, 2015.
45. Gerald Eskenazi, "Ford Frick, Former Head of Baseball, Is Dead at 83," *New York Times*, April 10, 1978, B2.
46. Red Smith, "Ford Frick: He Wasn't a House Dick," *New York Times*, April 11, 1978, 48.
47. Joe Marcin, "Mel Allen, Red Barber Share Frick Award," *The Sporting News*, August 5, 1978, 19; "Allen and Barber Named as Frick Award Winners," *New York Times*, July 23, 1978, S7.

Bibliography

Books

Alexander, Charles C. *Breaking the Slump: Baseball in the Depression Era*. New York: Columbia University Press, 2002.

Allen, Lee. *The American League Story*. New York: Hill & Wang, 1962.

Allen, Maury. *All Roads Lead to October: George Steinbrenner's 25-Year Reign Over the New York Yankees*. New York: St. Martin's Press, 2000.

_____. *Roger Maris: A Man for All Seasons*. New York: Donald I. Fine, Inc, 1986.

Armour, Mark. *Joe Cronin: A Life in Baseball*. Lincoln: University of Nebraska Press, 2010.

Asinof, Eliot. *Bleeding Between the Lines*. New York: Holt, Rinehart and Winston, 1979.

Banner, Stuart. *The Baseball Trust: A History of Baseball's Antitrust Exemption*. New York: Oxford University Press, 2013.

Bavasi, Buzzie, with John Strege. *Off the Record*. Chicago: Contemporary, 1987.

Berrett, Jesse. "Diamonds for Sale: Promoting Baseball During the Great Depression." In *Baseball History 4: An Annual of Original Baseball Research*, ed. Peter Levine (Westport, CT: Meckler, 1991), 51–61.

Boxerman, Burton A., and Benita W. Boxerman. *Jews and Baseball*. Vol. 1, *Entering the American Mainstream, 1871–1948*. Jefferson, NC: McFarland, 2007.

Brown, Warren. *Win, Lose, or Draw*. New York: Van Rees Press, 1947.

Buhite, Russell D. *The Continental League: A Personal History*. Lincoln: University of Nebraska Press, 2014.

Burk, Robert Frederick. *Much More Than a Game: Players, Owners, and American Baseball Since 1921*. Chapel Hill: University of North Carolina Press, 2001.

Carney, Gene. *Burying the Black Sox*. Washington, D.C.: Potomac, 2006.

Chandler, Happy, with Vance Trimble. *Heroes, Plain Folks, and Skunks*. Chicago, IL: Bonus Books, 1989.

Clavin, Tom, and Danny Peary. *Roger Maris: Baseball's Reluctant Hero*. New York: Touchstone, 2010.

Creamer, Robert W. *Babe: The Legend Comes to Life*. New York: Simon & Schuster, 1974.

Feldmann, Doug. *September Streak: The 1935 Chicago Cubs Chase the Pennant*. Jefferson, NC: McFarland, 2003.

Frick, Ford. *Games, Asterisks, and People: Memoirs of a Lucky Fan*. New York: Crown, 1973.

_____. *Sports Memories That Are Sports Records*. New York: Richfield Oil, 1931.

Gallup, George H. *The Gallup Poll: Public Opinion, 1935–1971*. New York: Random House, 1972.

Ginsburg, Daniel E. *The Fix Is In: A History of Baseball Gambling and Game Fixing Scandals*. Jefferson, NC: McFarland, 1995.

Goldblatt, Andrew. *The Giants and the Dodgers: Four Cities, Two Teams, One Rivalry*. Jefferson, NC: McFarland, 2003.

Goldstein, Richard. *Spartan Seasons*. New York, NY: Macmillan, 1980.

Halberstam, David. *October 1964*. New York: Fawcett Columbine, 1995.

Helyar, John. *Lords of the Realm: The Real History of Baseball*. New York: Villard, 1994.

Hoffmann, Frank. *Baseball and American Culture: Across the Diamond*. Philadelphia: Haworth, 2003.

Holtzman, Jerome. *The Commissioners: Baseball's Midlife Crisis*. New York: Total Sports, 1998.

_____. *No Cheering in the Press Box*. New York: Holt, Rinehart and Winston, 1973.

Holway, John B. *Voices from the Great Black Baseball Leagues*. Revised Edition. Mineola, NY: Courier Dover, 2012.

James, Bill. *Whatever Happened to the Hall of Fame? Baseball, Cooperstown, and the Price of Glory*. New York: Fireside, 1994.

Jordan, David M. *Occasional Glory: The History of the Philadelphia Phillies*. Jefferson, NC: McFarland, 2012.

Kashatus, William C. *September Swoon: Richie Allen, the '64 Phillies, and Racial Integration*. University Park: Penn State University Press, 2004.

Klein, Alan M. *Baseball on the Border: A Tale of Two Laredos*. Princeton, NJ: Princeton University Press, 1997.

Koppett, Leonard. *Koppett's Concise History of Major League Baseball*. New York: Carroll & Graf, 1998.
Kuhn, Bowie. *Hardball: The Education of a Baseball Commissioner*. New York: Times Books, 1987.
Lamb, Chris. *Conspiracy of Silence: Sportswriters and the Long Campaign to Desegregate Baseball*. Lincoln: University of Nebraska Press, 2012.
Lieb, Fred. *Baseball as I Have Known It*. New York: Coward, McCann, & Geoghegan, 1977.
Lowenfish, Lee. *Branch Rickey*. Lincoln: University of Nebraska Press, 2007.
Mantle, Mickey, and Herb Gluck. *The Mick*. New York: Doubleday, 1985.
Marshall, William. *Baseball's Pivotal Era: 1945–1951*. Lexington: University Press of Kentucky, 1999.
Mead, William B. *Even the Browns: Baseball During World War II*. Chicago: Contemporary, 1978.
Miller, Marvin. *A Whole Different Ballgame*. New York: Birch Lane Press, 1991.
Moffi, Larry. *The Conscience of the Game: Baseball's Commissioners from Landis to Selig*. Lincoln: University of Nebraska Press, 2006.
Montville, Leigh. *The Big Bam: The Life and Times of Babe Ruth*. New York: Doubleday, 2006.
Oakley, Ronald. *Baseball's Last Golden Age, 1946–1960*. Jefferson, NC: McFarland, 1994.
Peterson, John E. *The Kansas City Athletics: A Baseball History, 1954–1967*. Jefferson, NC: McFarland, 2003.
Peterson, Robert. *Only the Ball Was White: A History of Legendary Black Players and All-Black Professional Teams*. Englewood Cliffs, NJ: Prentice-Hall, 1970.
Pietrusza, David. *Judge and Jury: The Life and Times of Judge Kenesaw Mountain Landis*. South Bend, IN: Diamond Communications, 1998.
_____. *Lights On! The Wild Century-Long Saga of Night Baseball*. Lanham, MD: Scarecrow, 1997.
Plaut, David. *Chasing October: The Dodgers-Giants Pennant Race of 1962*. South Bend, IN: Diamond Communications, 1994.
Robinson, Jackie. *Baseball Has Done It*. Edited by Charles Dexter. Philadelphia: J.B. Lippincott, 1964.
Rosenfeld, Harvey. *Roger Maris: A Title to Fame*. Fargo, ND: Prairie House, 1991.
_____. *Still a Legend: The Story of Roger Maris*. Lincoln, NE: iUniverse, 1991.
Schiavone, Michael. *Sports and Labor in the United States*. Albany: State University of New York Press, 2015.
Shapiro, Michael. *Bottom of the Ninth: Branch Rickey, Casey Stengel, and the Daring Scheme to Save Baseball from Itself*. New York: Times Books, 2009.
Skipper, John C. *A Biographical Dictionary of the Baseball Hall of Fame*. Jefferson, NC: McFarland, 2000.
Smith, Ken. *Baseball's Hall of Fame*. New York: Grosset & Dunlap, 1966.
Sobel, Lionel S. *Professional Sports and the Law*. New York: Law-Arts Press, 1977.
Stewart, Wayne. *Babe Ruth: A Biography*. Westport, CT: Greenwood, 2006.
Sullivan, Dean A., ed. *Late Innings: A Documentary History of Baseball, 1945–1972*. Lincoln: University of Nebraska Press, 2002.
_____, ed. *Middle Innings: A Documentary History of Baseball, 1900–1948*. Lincoln: University of Nebraska Press, 1998.
Surdam, David George. *Wins, Losses, and Empty Seats: How Baseball Outlasted the Great Depression*. Lincoln: University of Nebraska Press, 2011.
Travers, Steven. *A Tale of Three Cities: The 1962 Baseball Season in New York, Los Angeles, and San Francisco*. Washington, D.C.: Potomac, 2009.
Turner, Frederick. *When the Boys Came Back*. New York: Henry Holt, 1996.
Tygiel, Jules. *Baseball's Great Experiment: Jackie Robinson and His Legacy*. New York: Oxford University Press, 1997.
Vail, James F. *The Road to Cooperstown: A Critical History of Baseball's Hall of Fame Selection Process*. Jefferson, NC: McFarland, 2001.
Veeck, Bill, with Ed Linn. *Veeck—As in Wreck: The Autobiography of Bill Veeck*. Chicago: University of Chicago Press, 1962.
Vlasich, James A. "Alexander Cleland and the Origin of the Baseball Hall of Fame." In *Cooperstown Symposium on Baseball and the American Culture* (1989), ed. by Alvin L. Hall (Westport, CT: Meckler, 1991), 1–17.
_____. *A Legend for the Legendary: The Origin of the Baseball Hall of Fame*. Bowling Green, OH: Bowling Green State University Press, 1990.
Walker, James R., and Robert Bellamy, Jr. *Center Field Shot: A History of Baseball on Television*. Lincoln: University of Nebraska Press, 2008.
Walsh, Christy. *Adios to Ghosts*. Self-published, 1937.
Ward, Geoffrey C., and Ken Burns. *Baseball: An Illustrated History*. New York: Alfred A. Knopf, 1994.
Warfield, Don. *The Roaring Redhead*. South Bend, IN: Diamond Communications, 1987.
White, G. Edward. *Creating the National Pastime: Baseball Transforms Itself, 1903–1953*. Princeton, NJ: Princeton University Press, 1996.
Wilbert, Warren N. *Baseball's Iconic 1–0 Games*. Lanham, MD: Scarecrow, 2013.
Woodward, Stanley. *Sports Page*. New York: Greenwood, 1968.
Zimbalist, Andrew. *In the Best Interests of Baseball? The Revolutionary Reign of Bud Selig*. Hoboken, NJ: John Wiley & Sons, 2006.

Articles

"Airplane Views of Pueblo Flood." *El Paso County Democrat*. June 10, 1921, 5.

American Society of Newspaper Editors (ASNE). *Problems of Journalism.* vol. 5 (Washington, D.C.: ASNE, 1927), 99.
_____. *Problems of Journalism.* vol. 7 (Washington, D.C.: ASNE, 1929), 26.
Anderson, William B. "Crafting the National Pastime's Image: The History of Major League Baseball Public Relations." *Journalism & Mass Communication Monographs* 5, no. 1 (Spring 2003): 22–23.
_____. "Major League Baseball Under Investigation: How the Industry Used Public Relations to Promote Its Past to Save Its Present," *Public Relations Review* 30, no. 4 (November 2004): 439–445.
_____. "The 1939 Major League Baseball Centennial Celebration: How Steve Hannagan & Associates Helped Tie Business to Americana." *Public Relations Review* 27, no. 3 (Autumn 2001): 353–366.
Balinger, Edward F. "Dodger Players Riot as Bucks Win, 9–5." *Pittsburgh Post-Gazette,* May 28, 1943.
Barra, Allen "The Myth of Maris' Asterisk." Salon.com, October 3, 2001. Accessed December 11, 2013.
Bernstein, Anita. "Question Autonomy, with an Asterisk." *Emory Law Journal* 54 (2005): 239–260.
Bingham, Walter. "Assault on the Record." *Sports Illustrated,* July 31, 1961, 8–11.
Bohn, Michael K. "Knute Rockne's Untimely Death: An Early Airline Crash 80 Years Ago." McClatchy Tribune Information Services, March 31, 2011.
Boyle, Robert H. "Perfect Man for the Job," *Sports Illustrated.* April 9, 1962.
Briley, Ron. "Baseball and the Cold War: An Examination of Values," *OAH Magazine of History* 2, no. 1 (Summer 1986): 15–18.
Carvalho, John, and John Lofflin. "Ford Frick's *Big Leaguer*: A Commissioner's (Complicated) Love Letter to His Sport." Paper presented to the Cooperstown Symposium on Baseball and American Culture, Baseball Hall of Fame, Cooperstown, NY, May 2014.
Carvalho, John, and Loren Hawkins. "We Know the Name; Do They Know the Game? 'Celebrity' Articles About the 1924 and 1932 World Series." *Journal of Sports Media* 1, no. 1 (Spring 2006): 73–89.
Chacar, Aya S., and William Hesterly. "Innovations and Value Creation in Major League Baseball, 1860–2000." *Business History* 46, no. 3 (July 2004): 407–438.
Christofferson, Nancy. "Frederick Cowing: Businessman, Stockbroker, and Mason." http://www.huerfanojournal.com/node/4182. Retrieved November 27, 2013.
Coates, Dennis, and Brad R. Humphreys. "Do Economists Reach a Conclusion on Subsidies for Sports Franchises, Stadiums, and Mega-Events?" Working Paper Series, Paper No. 08–18, International Association of Sports Economists, August 2008, 2.
Considine, Bob. "More Money Than Friends." *New York Journal-American,* May 22, 1955.
Corum, Bill. "Baseball Does Itself Proud." *New York Journal-American,* September 21, 1951.
Daniel, Daniel M. "Frick Faces Varied Problems." *New York World-Telegram and Sun,* September 22, 1951.
_____. "Frick, New National League President, Received First Big Break." *New York Telegram,* November 15, 1934.
_____. "The Wise Leadership of Ford Frick." *Baseball Magazine,* April 1949, 373–375.
Davis, Jack E. "Baseball's Reluctant Challenge: Desegregating Major League Spring Training Sites, 1961–1964." *Journal of Sport History* 19, no. 2 (Summer, 1992): 144–162.
De Bonis, J. Nicholas, Robert S. Kahan, J. David Pincus, Edgar P. Trotter, and Stephen C. Wood. "The Baseball Commissioner's Public Communication Role: A Test of Leadership." *Cooperstown Symposium on Baseball and the American Culture,* ed. Alvin Hall (Westport, CT: Meckler, 1990), 187–211.
"'Dimout' Hits Night Baseball on East Coast." *Pittsburgh Post-Gazette,* April 30, 1942.
Durslag, Melvin. "The Right Speech—Too Late." *Los Angeles Herald Examiner,* November 8, 1964.
Eskenazi, David, and Steve Rudman. "Wayback Machine: Rajah, Rivera, '51 Rainiers." Sportspress Northwest (website), http://sportspressnw.com/2128720/2012/wayback-machine-rajah-rivera-51-rainiers. Posted March 27, 2012.
"Flashback: In 1960, Allentown Nearly Had Pro Baseball's First Woman Umpire." *Allentown Morning Call,* August 23, 2010.
Follansbee, Robert, and E.E. Jones. "The Flood of June, 1921, in the Arkansas River, at Pueblo, Colorado." *Proceedings of the American Society of Civil Engineers* 47, no. 10 (December 1921): 769–774.
"Ford Frick Warns Frisch to Keep Dizzy Dean Quiet After Lifting Suspension." *Reading Eagle,* June 5, 1937.
"Frick Asks Chance for Local Group." *Milwaukee Journal,* October 7, 1964.
"Frick Rules Wills Has 1 Game 'Left.'" *San Francisco Examiner,* September 21, 1962, 60.
"Frick Started Climb to New Post as Local Sports Scribe." *Colorado Springs Gazette,* September 21, 1951, 14.
Frick, Ford. "Baseball Has Its Musical Angles." *Music Journal* 14, no. 6 (July–August 1956): 11–12, 32.
_____. "Baseball Will Find You!" *All-America Sports Magazine,* June 1935.
_____. "Cowboys Never Threaten and C.C. Uses Second and Third String Men Registering Year's Record Win." *Colorado Springs Telegraph,* February 26, 1922.
_____. "Dedication." *1965 World Series Official Souvenir Program,* 1.
_____. "'Gangway! I'm Coming Through!'" *Red Blooded Stories,* January 1929, 57–66.

_____. "'Mail-Order' Morse: A Story of Hearts and Diamonds." *Liberty,* April 21, 1928, 33.
_____. "Radio Editorial, WOR and Wins—1932," Collection of Kelly (Frick) Richards.
_____. "Telegraph Reporter Sees Death and Ruin from an Airplane." *Colorado Springs Evening Telegraph,* 1.
_____. "They've Got to Be Right." *Saturday Evening Post,* January 26, 1935.
_____. "Who Will Win the National League Pennant?" *Liberty,* April 20, 1935.
Gendzel, Glen. "Competitive Boosterism: How Milwaukee Lost the Braves." *Business History Review* 69, no. 4 (1995): 530–566.
Giestchier, Steven "Slugging and Snubbing: Hugh Casey, Ernest Hemingway, and Jackie Robinson—A Baseball Mystery." *NINE: A Journal of Baseball History and Culture* 21, no. 1 (Fall 2012): 12–46.
Graham, Frank. "Big League Owners Hired a Newspaperman." *New York Journal-American,* September 24, 1951.
_____. "They Wound Up with One, However." *New York Journal-American,* September 24, 1951.
Harmon, Pat. "Frick Restores English Language." *Cincinnati Post,* May 3, 1956.
Hill, John Paul. "Commissioner A.B. 'Happy' Chandler and the Integration of Baseball: A Reassessment." *NINE: A Journal of Baseball History and Culture* 19, no. 1 (Fall 2010): 28–51.
Hirshberg, Al. "Ford Frick Says: Super-Stadium." *This Week,* May 4, 1958, 8–9, 34.
Holland, Gerald. "Baseball and Ballyhoo." *American Mercury.* May 1937, 82–83.
Holmes, Tommy. "Dashing First Baseman, Quarter Mile Runner, Teacher and Writer." *Brooklyn Eagle,* November 9, 1934.
_____. "Frick Defends Tenure as Baseball's Boss." *Houston Post,* July 13, 1965.
_____. "New Baseball President Becomes Successor to John A. Heydler." *Brooklyn Eagle,* November 8, 1934.
Housholder, Terry. "Ford Frick Dies at 83." *Ligonier Advance-Leader,* April 11, 1978, 1.
"How Aeroplane Made Trip to Pueblo Flood." *Colorado Springs Evening Telegraph,* June 4, 1921, 1.
Hylton, J. Gordon. "Why Baseball's Antitrust Exemption Still Survives." *Marquette Sports Law Review* 9, no. 2 (Spring 1998): 391–402.
Jordan, David M., Larry M. Gerlach, and John P. Rossi. "A Baseball Myth Exploded: The Truth About Bill Veeck and the '43 Phillies." *National Pastime: A Review of Baseball History* 18 (November 1998): 3–13.
Kahn, Roger. "Baseball's Reluctant Czar." *Esquire.* July 1958, 35–37.
Kelly, Tom. "Sentiment's the Thing." *St. Petersburg Evening Independent,* September 6, 1962.
King, Joe. "Nl History Hints Frick Will Be Tough Czar." *New York World-Telegram,* September 22, 1951.
Kuechle, Oliver E. "Ford Frick Takes the Bull—By the Tail." *Milwaukee Journal,* June 10, 1963.
_____. "Judge Landis Must Be Spinning in His Grave." *Milwaukee Journal,* October 28, 1960.
Macy, Guy E. "The Pueblo Flood of 1921." *Colorado Magazine,* November 1940, 201–211.
Mann, Jimmy. "150-Pound Scrapper" ("Mann on the Move" column). *St. Petersburg Times.* May 6, 1964, 37.
McLaughlin, Tom. "Looking Them Over." *Colorado Springs Gazette-Telegraph* [1951?].
"Obituary: Dr. Frederick Frick, a Research Scientist, 75." *Boston Herald,* September 14, 1992.
Pollock, Ed. "Baseball Lost a Point When Frick Barred Attorney." *Philadelphia Bulletin,* December 9, 1953.
_____. "Ford Frick Beams Over Senate Action." *Philadelphia Evening Bulletin,* June 29, 1960.
Price, Jim. "Bouchee Dies at 79." *Spokesman-Review,* January 25, 2013.
Rennie, Rud. "Ford Frick—President." *Baseball Magazine,* January 1935.
Richman, Milton. "Frick Urges Baseball to Keep Loyal Vigil Against Gambling." *Pittsburgh Press,* June 4, 1963.
Ridgway, Arthur O., R.G. Hosea, and George G. Anderson. "Papers and Discussions: The Flood of June, 1921, in the Arkansas River, at Pueblo, Colorado." *Proceedings of the American Society of Civil Engineers* 47, no. 9 (November 1921): 535–560.
Rosenthal, Harold. "Frick Says Commissioner's Job Means Change in Way of Life." *New York Herald Tribune,* September 23, 1951.
Rubin, Louis. "Babe Ruth's Ghost." *Sewanee Review* 101, no. 2 (Spring 1993): 240–248.
Ruth, Babe. "'I Feel Great, and Ready to Go,' Declares Ruth." *The New York Evening Journal,* March 23, 1933, 23.
_____. "Keep an Eye on the A's Outfield." *New York Evening Journal,* March 29, 1933, p. 23.
Sainsbury, Ed. "Young Comiskey Turned Tide by Insisting Magnates Make Selection." *New York World-Telegram and Sun,* September 21, 1951.
Smith, Chester L. "Critics Causing Major Leagues to See 'Ghosts.'" *Pittsburgh Press,* July 19, 1962.
Smith, Red. "He Will Make Mistakes." *New York Herald Tribune,* September 22, 1951.
Smith, Wendell. "General Public Must Be Changed." *Pittsburgh Courier,* February 25, 1939, 1, 16.
_____. "Spring Training Woes." *Chicago's American,* January 23, 1961.
Summers, Danny. "Baseballs, Kangaroos, and Ford Frick." *Pikes Peak Courier,* February 5, 2014. http://pikespeakcourier.net/stories/Baseball-kangaroos-and-Ford-Frick,144481. Accessed June 13, 2014.
"Telegraph Gives World First News, and Plane Photos of Pueblo Flood." *Colorado Springs Evening Telegraph,* June 6, 1921, 6.
Trex, Ethan. "No Thanks: Why Denver Turned Down the 1976 Olympics." Mental Floss website, February 3, 2014 (published 2010). http://mentalfloss.com/article/31291/no-thanks-why-denver-turned-down-1976-olympics.
Williams, Joe. "Ford Frick's Excellent Pick as

Game's Boss." *New York World-Telegram and Sun,* September 22, 1951.
_____. "TV Black Sox Prove Sordid, Spurious Show." *New York World-Telegram,* January 28, 1961.
Wolf, Bob. "Frick Insists His Hands Are Tied." *Milwaukee Journal,* July 9, 1964.
_____. "He's Boss." *Milwaukee Journal,* January 15, 1956.
Woodward, Stanley. "National League Averts Strike of Cardinals Against Robinson's Presence in Baseball." *New York Herald Tribune,* May 9, 1947.
_____. "Views of Baseball." *New York Herald Tribune,* May 10, 1947.
Young, Dick. "Baseball's Undirty Old Man." *New York Daily News,* April 5, 1973.

Newspapers

New York Evening Journal, 1924–1933
New York Times, 1934–1978
Sporting News, 1934–1978

Interviews and Correspondence

Frick, Ford C., II. Interview with author. Denver, CO, September 21, 2015.
_____. Telephone interview with author. November 18, 2015.
Lepird, Mary Jane. Interview with author. Brimfield, IN, August 8, 2012.
O'Connell, Jack. Email to author. January 18, 2014.
Richards, Kelly (Frick). Telephone interview with author. November 23, 2015.

Manuscript Collections

Ford C. Frick Papers. National Baseball Hall of Fame and Museum, Cooperstown, NY.
Frick Letters and Manuscripts. Private Collection of Kelly [Frick] Richards.
Minutes of the National League Annual Meeting, December 11–12, 1934. National Baseball Hall of Fame, and Museum, Cooperstown, NY.
Minutes of the National League Reconvened Annual and Schedule Meeting, February 9, 1943. National Baseball Hall of Fame and Museum, Cooperstown. NY,
Minutes of the National League Special Meeting, January 18, 1935. National Baseball Hall of Fame and Museum, Cooperstown, NY.

Government Documents

Broadcasting, and Televising Baseball Games: Hearings Before a Subcommittee of the Committee on Interstate and Foreign Commerce, United States Senate, 83rd Cong., 1st Session (1953). Statement of Ford C. Frick, Commissioner of Baseball.
Organized Baseball: Hearings Before the Subcommittee on Study of Monopoly Power of the Committee on the Judiciary, 82nd Cong. (1951).
Organized Professional Team Sports: Hearings Before the Subcommittee on Antitrust and Monopoly of the Committee on the Judiciary, United States Senate, 85th Cong., 2nd Sess. (1958).
Organized Professional Team Sports: Hearings Before the Subcommittee on Antitrust and Monopoly of the Committee on the Judiciary, United States Senate, 86th Cong., 1st Sess. (1959).
Organized Professional Team Sports: Hearings Before the Subcommittee on Antitrust and Monopoly of the Committee on the Judiciary, United States Senate, 86th Cong., 2nd Sess. (1960).
Professional Sports Antitrust Bill—1965: Hearings Before the Subcommittee on Antitrust and Monopoly of the Committee on the Judiciary, United States Senate, 89th Cong, 1st Sess. (1965).
Subjecting Professional Baseball Clubs to the Antitrust Laws: Hearings Before a Subcommittee of the Committee on the Judiciary, United States Senate, 83rd Cong., 2nd Sess. (1954).
Telecasting of Professional Sports Contests: Hearing Before the Antitrust Subcommittee of the Committee of the Judiciary, House of Representatives, 87th Cong., 1st Sess. (1961).

Index

Aaron, Hank 194, 231
Adams, Charles 63, 65
Addie, Bob 51
Allen, Ethan (filmmaker) 78
Allen, Ethan (Yale baseball coach) 187
Allen, Mel 177, 178, 238, 271
Allen, Richie 231
Alston, Walter 162
Anderson, William B. 145
Arledge, Roone 258
Asinof, Eliot 220, 269
Autry, Gene 229

Baer, Bugs 132
Barber, Red 178, 271
Barr, George 71–72
Barrow, Ed 90, 101, 105
Baseball Writers' Association of America 12, 17–18, 19, 45, 60, 75, 116, 181, 194
Bavasi, Buzzie 86, 136, 243, 256
Bell, Bert 198
Bellamy, Robert 166–167
Benson, Ted 117
Berra, Yogi 78
Big Leaguer 269
Bingham, Walter 14–15
Bonds, Barry 19, 22, 23, 75
Bouchee, Ed 155
Boudreau, Lou 265
Bradley, Alva 104, 137
Brandt, Dr. William 59
Branham, William 57, 76
Breadon, Sam 73, 92, 97, 102, 104, 111–112, 121, 123–126, 130
Brimfield, Indiana 26–29
Brisbane, Arthur 36–37, 38, 44
Broeg, Bob 268
Bronxville, New York 38–39, 59, 147–148, 263, 268
Broun, Heywood 39, 269
Brown, Warren 44
Butler, Dick 209
Byers, Walter 254–255
Byrnes, James 100

Cain, Cullen 54–55
Cannon, Raymond 208
Cannon, Robert 208, 214, 231, 246

Cape Cod Summer League 246
Carpenter, Robert, Jr. 96, 139, 160, 262
Carpenter, Robert, Sr. 96
Carroll, John 223
Carroll, Lou 112
Castro, Fidel 206
Celler, Rep. Emanuel 143–144, 188–190, 199, 202–203, 215–216
Chadwick, Henry 74, 77
Chandler, Happy 103, 105–107, 128–129, 133–134, 142–143, 145, 149, 154, 158, 173–174, 189–190, 265; integration 120–121, 126
Chapman, Ben 126, 127
Christopher, George 193
Cicotte, Eddie 220
Clark, Stephen 74–76
Cleland, Alexander 74–76
Cobb, Ty 14, 16, 19, 45, 75, 142, 144, 232, 241
Cohan, George M. 52
Colorado College 31, 35
Colorado Springs Gazette 31
Colorado Springs Telegraph 31, 33–35
Comiskey, Charles II 147
Continental League 215–218, 221–223, 225–226
Corum, Bill 140, 148
Cox, William 94–97; banned from baseball for betting 96–97
Cronin, Joe 97, 178, 214, 215, 226–229, 235, 240, 242–243, 244, 262; elected American League president 209; Roger Maris home run record 18
Crosby, Bing 65
Crosley, Powel 57, 65, 201
Crystal, Billy 22

Daley, Arthur 14, 102, 123, 125, 134, 140, 184, 204, 212, 239
Daniel, Dan 12, 17, 18, 19, 39, 46, 58, 59, 101, 113, 122, 140, 148, 171, 204, 210, 211–212, 215, 230, 267, 270
Dean, Daffy 59
Dean, Dizzy 59 71–73, 119, 258
Dean, Patricia 71
DeOrsey, C. Leo 188
DePauw University 29, 50
DeWitt, Bill 139, 187, 223
Dirksen, Everett 159

Doubleday, Abner 74
Drebinger, John 63, 101, 103, 231, 270
Dudley, Charles 31, 35
Dunne, Finley Peter 50
Duren, Ryne 205
Durocher, Leo 78–79, 84, 112, 132, 135, 177, 259
Dyer, Eddie 112, 125

Eastman, Joseph 92–93
Eckert, William "Spike" 248, 260–261, 262, 264
Effrat, Louis 109
Eisenhower, Dwight 146, 206
Eisenhower, Milton 146, 177
El Paso Club 35
Engle, Eleanor 153
ethics, journalism 39–42

Farley, James A. 103, 104, 106, 146
Farnsworth, Bill 38, 39
Feller, Bob 182, 184, 198
Fetzer, John 247, 251
Finley, Charles 239–240
Ford, Whitey 232
Frick, Christian 25, 26
(Frick) Couts, Clara 26, 28, 130
Frick, Eleanor (Cowing) 30–31, 59, 136, 152, 169, 204, 206, 210, 257
Frick, Emma (Prickett) 25–27
Frick, Ford: amateur draft 253–256; anti-integration uprising 123–126; birth and childhood 26–28; in Colorado Springs 31–37; commissioner search of 1945 101–107; and curling 80, 132; Dizzy Dean suspension 71–73; gambling 161–162, 223–224; ghostwriting for Babe Ruth and others 42–43, 44–48, 129; literary efforts 50–51; memoirs 13, 19, 28, 38, 41, 42, 49, 53, 61, 73, 110, 117, 119, 124–125, 133, 223, 267, 267–268; and player fights 79, 112; and player safety 82–84; promoting the spitball 178–179, 235; radio career 51–54, 57; reporting of the Pueblo flood 33–35; second All-Star game 210, 213–214; and umpires 68–70; in Walsenburg, Colorado 29–30; West Coast franchise relocation 189–196
Frick, Ford II (grandson) 30, 36, 50, 232, 259, 270
Frick, Frederick 29, 31, 50, 86–88, 259
Frick, Gertrude 26–27
Frick, Harold 265
Frick, Jacob 25–28, 130
(Frick) Richards, Kelly 31, 50, 88, 232, 268, 270
Friend, Bob 214
Frisch, Frankie 72–73, 97, 107, 232
Fuchs, Judge Emil 56; and dog racing at Braves Field 62–63
Fuller, Buckminster 192
Furlong, Bill 204

Gaffney, James 62
Galbreath, John 173, 211, 224
Galvin, Maureen 153

Garagiola, Joe 159
Gardella, Danny 110, 133, 143
Gehrig, Lou 42, 45
Gerlach, Larry 118
Giamatti, A. Bartlett 22, 97
Giles, Bill 246
Giles, Warren 17, 93, 102, 105–106, 143, 150, 162, 173, 179, 183, 190, 203, 214, 226–229, 244, 263; 1951 commissioner election 146–148
Goldman, Harry 65
Graham, Frank 38
Graves, Abner 74
Greenberg, Hank 173
Griffith, Calvin 188, 204, 217, 226, 228, 235, 258
Griffith, Clark 86, 90, 92, 103, 104, 105, 110, 140, 179

Haines, Jesse 265
Halberstam, David 17
Hannagan, Steve 76, 141
Hannegan, Robert 105–106
Harridge, Will 62, 66, 76, 86, 92–93, 94, 97, 99, 100, 102, 104, 108, 110, 114, 120, 129, 138, 143, 160, 178, 179, 209
Harris, Bucky 96
Hart, Philip 203
Hearst, William Randolph 36, 38, 41, 44
Heydler, John 54, 56–57, 60, 74, 76, 142
Hillings, Rep. Patrick J. 144, 188
Hofheinz, Judge Roy 249
Holland, Gerald 61
Holmes, Tommy 253
Holtzman, Jerome 27, 28, 29, 48, 121, 270
Hoover, J. Edgar 103, 104
Hope, Bob 59
Hornsby, Rogers 45, 142
Huggins, Miller 42–43, 48, 243
Hurwitz, Hy 15
Husted, Bob 194
Hyland, Dr. Robert 124

Johnson, Arnold 176
Johnson, Ban 57, 77
Johnson, Sen. Edwin 158–159; Continental League participation 215, 222; criticism of television 166–167
Johnson, Lyndon 206
Johnson, Walter 16, 19, 75
Jordan, David 118
Jurges, Bill 67, 79

Kahn, Roger 197–198
Kaline, Al 15, 213, 223
Keating, Kenneth 199, 202–203, 206, 217, 222
Kefauver, Estes 215–217, 219, 221–223
Kelly, Gene 177–178
Kelly, Jack 89, 95
Kennedy, John 207
Kerr, Paul 77, 266
Kieran, John 39, 57, 60, 67, 68, 73, 74
Kiner, Ralph 151, 163
King, Joe 13, 234
Kling, Johnny 28

Index 315

Koppett, Leonard 17, 20, 119, 252, 264
Korean War 84, 153
Kostelanetz, Andre 54
Kuechle, Oliver 21, 226
Kuenn, Harvey 213
Kuhn, Bowie 246, 265, 266–267, 270

Lacy, Sam 123
LaGuardia, Fiorello 91
Lamb, Chris 116
Landis, Judge Kenesaw Mountain 49, 51, 52, 60, 61, 76, 86, 88, 89, 92–93, 97, 98–99, 138, 198, 251; death 100, 105; integration 119–120; and major-minor league agreement 80–82, 85
Lane, Frank 165, 204, 240
Lardner, Ring 39, 40, 269
Latham, Arlie 142
Lausche, Frank 105–106, 142, 146–147
Lavagetto, Harry "Cookie" 67
Lawrence, Frank 168, 210
LeBetard, Dan 75
Leonard, Buck 120
Lepird, Mary Jane 26–27
Levy, Dr. Leon 119
Lewis, J. Norman 162–164, 171–172, 174, 175, 184, 207–208
Lieb, Fred 36, 39, 40, 267, 270
Linkletter, Art 177
Little League World Series 134–135, 234
Lopat, Eddie 162

MacArthur, Douglas 146
MacPhail, Larry 64, 65–67, 70, 74, 82, 83, 84, 103, 121–123
MacPhail, Lee 243, 245
Magerkurth, George 89, 107
Mainichi (newspaper chain in Japan) 169
Major League Players Association 175
Mann, Arthur 116
Mansfield, Jayne 177
Mantle, Mickey 11–16, 20–21, 213
Marion, Marty 115
Maris, Roger 11–23, 176
Martin, Whitney 152
Mathews, Ed 15, 152–153
Mathewson, Christy 14, 20, 75
Mays, Charles 33–34
Mays, Willie 194
McGeehan, W.O. 39, 40
McGowen, Roscoe 116, 164
McGranery, James P. 168
McGrath, J. Howard 161
McGraw, John 55, 77
McGwire, Mark 16, 22, 23, 75
McHale, John 200
McNamee, Graham 51, 52
Medwick, Joe 82
Mehl, Ernie 240
Mercer, Sid 77
Meyer, Russ 135–136
Miller, Marvin 208
Moffatt, Donald 22–23
Moran, Charlie 73
Murakami, Masanori 256–257

Murphy, Robert 112–113
Musial, Stan 15, 17, 78, 83, 97, 194, 203, 235

New York *American* 42, 44
New York *Journal* 42, 43–44, 48, 52, 53, 77
night baseball 65–67, 88–91, 98, 128, 137–138, 151
Nixon, Richard 215, 243
Nugent, Gerry 89, 94–95, 118, 119

O'Connor, Leslie 99, 100, 102, 104, 187–188
O'Donnell, Maj. Gen. Emmett (Rosie) 146
O'Dwyer, Paul 132
Old Timers Committee 76–77
Olmo, Luis 110
O'Malley, Walter 11, 140, 180, 186, 191–195, 201, 227–228, 254
Owen, Mickey 83, 111, 113

Pacific Coast League 144–145, 152, 187, 189–190, 198, 200
Paige, Janis 177–178
Paige, Satchel 266
Parker, Dan 40
Parres, Murray 72
Pasquel, Bernardo 109–111
Pasquel, Jorge 109–111
Paul, Gabe 201, 248
Perini, Lou 139, 159–160, 225
Perry, Charles 118
Pietrusza, David 119
Pollock, Ed 95, 172
Porter, Paul 203, 250
Poulson, Norris 193
Povich, Shirley 14, 270
Power, Vic 224
Pueblo flood of 1921 32–34, 39
Pulitzer, Joseph 41

Quigley, Ernest 71
Quinn, Bob 65
Quinn, John 224
Quinn, William 242

Ramsdell, Sayre 94
Reardon, "Beans" (umpire) 69, 107–108
Reese, Pee Wee 78, 179
Reichler, Joe 18
Rennie, Rud 124
Reynolds, Allie 163
Rice, Grantland 39, 40, 151
Richards, Paul 213
Rickenbacker, Eddie 44, 59
Rickey, Branch 57, 83, 84, 97, 105, 120–122, 127, 132, 168; Continental League presidency 216, 217–219, 221–223, 225
Rivera, Jim 154–155
Rizzuto, Phil 238
Roberts, Robin 181, 208
Robeson, Paul 119
Robinson, Humberto 224
Robinson, Jackie 115, 120–128, 263
Rockne, Knute 45
Rocky Mountain News (Denver, Colorado) 31
Roe, Preacher 179

Index

Rogers, Hyde 36
Roller, Judge Elmer 260
Roosevelt, Franklin 66, 88–89, 102, 104–105
Rose, Pete 16, 19, 97
Rosenfeld, Harvey 17
Rosenthal, Harold 124
Rosenthal, Ken 21
Rossi, John 118
Roth, Mark 50
Rozelle, Pete 232–234
Runyon, Damon 36, 39, 40
Ruppert, Jacob 64
Ruth, Babe 12, 19, 27–28, 42, 44–50, 63–64, 75, 128–130
Ruth, Claire 16, 22
Ryan, Nolan 16, 19

Saigh, Fred 137–139, 157–158
Sears, "Ziggy" 69
Segar, Charlie 148, 164, 205, 232, 235
Shapiro, Michael 149
Shaughnessy, Frank 157, 167, 237
Shaw, Dr. Lloyd 31
Shea, Bill 210, 215, 217–218, 221–222, 225
Shecter, Leonard 23
Sing Sing Prison 52–53
61* 22–23
Slocum, Bill 39, 45, 132
Slocum, Frank 45, 173, 246, 268
Smith, Red 89, 95, 148, 171, 172, 268, 270
Smith, Wendell 116–117, 230
Sosa, Sammy 16, 22, 75
Sotos, Mary 268
Spalding (sporting goods company) 12, 93–94
Spink, John 54
Stanky, Eddie 162
Stann, Francis 14
Stark, Dolly 69
Stengel, Casey 60, 234–235, 243, 263–264
Stephen Fitzgerald Co. 179
Stephens, Verne 111
Stevens, Julia (Ruth's stepdaughter) 16
Stoneham, Charles 65, 66
Stoneham, Horace 88, 91, 132, 192–195, 257
Sullivan, Billy 152
Susskind, David 220

Tebbetts, Birdie 238
Terry, Bill 79

Thomson, Bobby 238
Toolson, George: and Supreme Court ruling 170–171, 188, 250
Topping, Dan 195, 225
Traband, Harvey 57
Trautman, George 76, 153, 182, 188, 237
Traynor, Pie 46
Truman, Pres. Harry 129, 142, 146, 161
Tygiel, Julius 118, 122, 126

Uchimura, Yushi 256–258

Valentine, Lewis 90
Veeck, Bill 17, 118–119, 160, 165, 213, 238–239
Veterans Committee 77–78, 263, 264–265
Vincent, Fay 22

Wagner, Robert 209
Walker, Dixie 97, 114
Walker, James 166–167
Walker, Jimmy 98
Walker, Rube 162
Walsh, Christy 44–45, 47, 48
Webb, Del 139, 191–192, 224, 228
Weiss, George 127, 157
Wells, Willie 119
White, Bill 231
Williams, Joe 148–149, 185, 220
Williams, Ted 203
Wills, Maury 241–242
Wilson, Kenneth L. "Tug" 187
Winchell, Paul 178
Wolf, Bob 47
Woodward, Stanley 123–126
WOR radio station 48, 52
Wright, George 61, 77
Wrigley, Philip 94, 104, 121, 152, 157, 193
Wrigley, William 70

Yawkey, Tom 62, 112, 121, 163, 193, 207, 213
Yomiuri (newspaper chain in Japan) 169, 257–258
Young, Cy 181
Young, Dick 13, 14, 20, 23, 124, 195, 220–221, 238, 244, 260, 261, 266, 269

Zimbalist, Andrew 73, 121–122

www.ingramcontent.com/pod-product-compliance
Ingram Content Group UK Ltd.
Pitfield, Milton Keynes, MK11 3LW, UK
UKHW041924140426
5217IPUK00014B/297